Contents

This book is dedicated to my family:

Vlasta A. Benson
Robert M. Benson
Patricia A. Benson
Haley S. Benson
Susan Sabisch Benson

Acknowledgments

I would like to thank Rudy Shur of Square One Publishers for his enthusiasm and confidence in this project. Without him, this book would not have seen the light of day. I would also like to thank Carol A. Rosenberg for her editing skill in organizing, simplifying, and producing a much better book. My heartfelt thanks also go to friends who have helped in my experiments—especially Shelley Goetz and Mary Jo Riley.

Preface

I have studied and tested the I Ching and I Ching-related knowledge for more than thirty years. However, I am highly critical of almost all popular I Ching books available today. My successes using the I Ching, and the dismal state of this area of knowledge, have compelled me to produce this book. In these pages, I provide users of the I Ching with three new things.

I designed this I Ching to be highly understandable as well as accurate. The two basic approaches to editing an I Ching book are either to give a *literal translation* of the text or to give an *interpretive translation* of the text. However, recent research leads to the conclusion that *no translation* can accurately represent what the I Ching truly is. *None* of the I Ching books currently on the market shows how the I Ching is actually a comprehensive philosophical statement about how our lives undergo change. Perhaps even worse, none are an effective *practical guide* to using the I Ching. I wrote this book to say what hasn't been said before. I wanted this book to open new doors—to be a breakthrough book for novice users, but to also be filled with critical insights for experienced users.

I reveal how the I Ching is a *system of ideas;* not just a random collection of oracular visions by ancient wise men. In this I Ching, the text is based on using the I Ching's internal conceptual framework in combination with meanings from the most accurate, historical translations in English. Thus, the many inadequacies that exist in the traditional text are corrected here by relying on what the original structure of ideas says should be in the text. Through this methodology, the I Ching now begins to make sense.

Finally, I also reveal advanced, nontraditional ways of using the I Ching oracle. I have done a great deal of testing and experimentation, and there are many ways you can use the I Ching. Few books explore these methods, and none give the wide range included here. They can enrich your use of the I Ching.

I believe this is the first book in our modern era that attempts to integrate our modern concepts of thinking and experimenting with the wisdom of the ancient Chinese. I believe that this integration has produced an I Ching that is remarkably usable, understandable, and meaningful to the modern user. My intention was to provide a complete resource for the novice user rather than an academic study for serious students. While I have generally achieved this, I have also tried to include powerful insights to those who thirst for more knowledge.

There is still more knowledge available about the I Ching—and related systems—that goes beyond the scope of this book. For example, there are more advanced systems of prediction, such as calendar-based methods, that tie into the I Ching. If you wish to explore these further you can do so through my website at http://www.newagequest.com/iching.

—Robert G. Benson

Introduction

The I Ching (pronounced *ee-jing*) is one of the oldest written documents. It is called a "book of divination," or fortunetelling, but it is also an expression of ideas that became incorporated into the important philosophies of Taoism and Confucianism in ancient China. The I Ching has been fundamental to Chinese culture for more than two thousand years, and now its influence is spreading into the Western world.

Some of the I Ching's concepts, for instance *yin* and *yang,* are comparatively well known in the West. According to this idea, all things in the universe can be classified by their nature into one of two complementary qualities. Female is yin and male is yang; winter is yin and summer is yang; home is yin and workplace is yang, and so on. The I Ching incorporates other principles, particularly with regard to the nature of change, which you will come to understand as you read this book.

The I Ching text is divided into sixty-four major sections, each of which describes an important concept. Each of these sections also has a corresponding unique six-line figure called a *hexagram.* When you "consult the oracle" to determine what prediction applies to your question, you are generating hexagrams to look up in the book.

Chapter 1 explains how to use the I Ching. That is, both how to create your own predictions, and how to use this book. Chapter 2 provides an overview of the history of the I Ching. It has a surprisingly complex past, and knowing this will enrich your use of it. Chapter 3 explores the theory behind the I Ching. What are its guiding principles? What do the different hexagram lines mean? These and other questions are addressed.

The I Ching text follows the three introductory chapters. Each major section of the text has a general meaning described below the hexagram title, and following

1

that, subparts contain specific meanings for variations within the general concept. In this book, all the subparts are clearly numbered to keep things neatly in place, and cross-references to other hexagrams are shown so internal conceptual links can be seen.

The I Ching is an amazingly valuable tool when used properly. This book gives you the tools you will need to use it successfully. The I Ching will give you a new way to understand your life, as well as give you new perspectives on life in general.

1

METHODS
How to Use the I Ching

You do not need to perform any special rituals to consult the I Ching, although the oldest method of consulting the I Ching was conducted in a ritualistic manner. The original method (using yarrow stalks) selected the hexagrams—which provide the answer to your query—in a slow, line-by-line process. Today, however, there is a variety of methods you can use. Some speed up the line-by-line selection process. Others allow you to select a complete hexagram in one or two steps for multiple prediction methods. There are also ways of structuring your query to bring out a number of related answers rather than just a single one. All of these methods work well and with equal validity when performed correctly and with the proper tools. In this chapter, you'll learn about the many different methods and the necessary tools for consulting the I Ching. First, though, you need to understand what a hexagram is and how it relates to the prediction the oracle obtains.

UNDERSTANDING THE HEXAGRAMS

All the inquiry methods for consulting the I Ching oracle are designed to find a six-line figure known as a *hexagram*. There are sixty-four hexagrams described in the I Ching text. The hexagram that the oracle selects is a symbolic representation of the situation into which you are inquiring. (The methods for choosing a hexagram will be discussed later in this chapter.) After the oracle has selected a hexagram, that hexagram's text should be consulted and interpreted in light of your individual situation. (This will also be discussed later in this chapter.)

The Lines of the Hexagram

When the oracle is giving you a hexagram in a line-by-line divination process, you will need to record each line on a piece of paper until the hexagram is complete. There are two types of lines you can get in a hexagram—*yin* and *yang*—and two types of each. The four different yin and yang lines are traditionally represented graphically as shown in Figure 1.1 below. Alternatively, the lines can also be represented by the numbers 0 and 1. You will need to know how to write down the lines as you generate them, and you can use either the graphic or the number format.

young yang: 1 ⎯⎯⎯⎯   young yin: 0 ⎯ ⎯

old yang: <u>1</u> ⎯⊖⎯   old yin: <u>0</u> ⎯✕⎯

Figure 1.1. The representations of yin and yang lines.

The old lines represent a condition of maximum attainment or excess. Like a pendulum about to return from the end of its swing, that line will later become a young line of the *opposite* type. Thus, an old yang becomes a young yin, and an old yin becomes a young yang. These are called "changing" or "moving" lines, and will be discussed in more detail below.

The six lines that make up the hexagram are generated sequentially from the bottom up. The bottom three lines and the top three lines form a pair of three-line figures called *trigrams.* There are only eight possible trigrams, and they are used as a quick way to find the hexagram in Tables 1.1 and 1.2 provided on page 6 . Exactly how this is done will be explained further below. Figure 1.2 below is a graphic representation of this explanation.

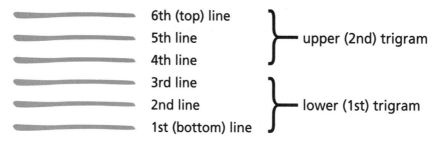

Figure 1.2. The sequence of the six hexagram lines with upper and lower trigrams.

For example, the hexagram you might have obtained consulting the oracle, with both young and old lines, could look like Figure 1.3 below.

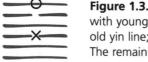

Figure 1.3. Example of graphic hexagram with young and old lines. The 3rd line is an old yin line; the 6th line is an old yang line. The remaining lines are young lines.

Alternatively, in a somewhat more modern manner, the above hexagram could be represented with numbers, in left to right order, as shown in Figure 1.4 below.

$$110 \quad 101$$

Figure 1.4. Same hexagram with young and old lines represented by numbers.

Finding the Hexagram Number

Once the six lines of the hexagram have been recorded, it is then possible to determine which hexagram has been produced. To do this, only the yin or yang identity of the line is needed; the "age" of the line does not matter at this point.

Traditionally, a matrix using the eight trigrams is used to determine the hexagram number. Turn to Table 1.1, "Traditional Hexagram Lookup," on page 6. This table shows all eight trigrams in both the lower and upper positions in the hexagram. (Note that in this book, the trigrams are also represented in the more modern style by the letter codes A through H.) Now, look at Figure 1.3 on page 4. Identify the two trigrams (ignoring for now the "age" of the line) and find where they intersect in the table. If you've done this correctly, you should see the number 38.

Now, turn to Table 1.2, "Alternative Hexagram Lookup," on page 6. This does the same job as Table 1.1, but in a slightly different way. Look at the hexagram example using the line numbers in Figure 1.4 above. (Note, however, you can also use the graphic representation of the lines.) Using step one in the table, identify the two trigrams. Then, using step two, find the trigram pair showing the hexagram number. Again, you should see number 38. Remember, the numbers are read from left to right, so the first three numbers represent the lower trigram and the second three numbers represent the upper trigram. Likewise, the first letter code represents the lower trigram and the second letter code represents the upper trigram.

There are certain advantages to the alternative tables. The trigram letter codes are generally less confusing than the line patterns, and can provide a way to double-check your finding even when the graphic representation is used. (Note also, these letter codes are used throughout this book to refer to the trigrams.) The main advantage, however, is when you become so proficient that you've memorized the letter codes of all eight trigrams, you can immediately move to step two. Using this small table is easier, faster, and less error-prone than the matrix in Table 1.1. For your convenience, these tables are repeated on pages 325 and 326.

Using the Changing Lines

After the hexagram number has been found, then the changing lines (the "old" yin and yang lines), *if any,* can be considered. These are important, because they tell

Table 1.1. Traditional Hexagram Lookup

UPPER / LOWER	A ☰	B ☷	C ☶	D ☷	E ☷	F ☰	G ☷	H ☰
A ☰	1	34	5	26	11	9	14	43
B ☷	25	51	3	27	24	42	21	17
C ☶	6	40	29	4	7	59	64	47
D ☷	33	62	39	52	15	53	56	31
E ☷	12	16	8	23	2	20	35	45
F ☰	44	32	48	18	46	57	50	28
G ☷	13	55	63	22	36	37	30	49
H ☰	10	54	60	41	19	61	38	58

Table 1.2. Alternative Hexagram Lookups

STEP 1: Identify the trigram letters by number or graphic representation.

STEP 2: Use the pair of trigram letters to identify the hexagram number. The left letter is the lower (first) trigram.

000	☷	E
001	☳	D
010	☵	C
011	☴	F
100	☶	B
101	☲	G
110	☱	H
111	☰	A

A		B		C		D	
AA	1	BA	25	CA	6	DA	33
AB	34	BB	51	CB	40	DB	62
AC	5	BC	3	CC	29	DC	39
AD	26	BD	27	CD	4	DD	52
AE	11	BE	24	CE	7	DE	15
AF	9	BF	42	CF	59	DF	53
AG	14	BG	21	CG	64	DG	56
AH	43	BH	17	CH	47	DH	31
E		**F**		**G**		**H**	
EA	12	FA	44	GA	13	HA	10
EB	16	FB	32	GB	55	HB	54
EC	8	FC	48	GC	63	HC	60
ED	23	FD	18	GD	22	HD	41
EE	2	FE	46	GE	36	HE	19
EF	20	FF	57	GF	37	HF	61
EG	35	FG	50	GG	30	HG	38
EH	45	FH	28	GH	49	HH	58

us how to determine the prediction. In I Ching usage, there are three possibilities: *no* changing lines; *one* changing line; or *multiple* changing lines. In Figure 1.3 on page 4, there is an old yin in line three, and an old yang in line six. Therefore, "multiple changing lines" occur in this example.

No changing lines. This is a more fixed situation than that produced by the other two possibilities. The text describing the hexagram as a whole is the prediction. For example, the prediction for Hexagram 1 (see page 59) says, "He is acting fiercely, and this is beneficial." There is supplementary information provided about the meaning of the hexagram to help you better understand the prediction's various meanings and possible applications.

One changing line. This is a more dynamic, more specific situation than no changing lines. In the I Ching, there is a prediction written for each changing line in each hexagram. For example, Hexagram 1 line 1 (shown as 1.1 on page 59) says, "To resist being overcome, he hides his actions and talents. Safety now lies in remaining hidden." Again, there is supplementary information given below this text to help you better understand its various meanings and possible applications.

Multiple changing lines. This is also a more dynamic situation than no changing lines. However, in this case, the I Ching does not have a prediction written for each possibility—this would not be feasible due to the large number required. So, when multiple changing lines occur in a hexagram, the general meaning of *two* hexagrams is consulted to produce the prediction. The first is the original hexagram. The second is the hexagram that is produced by all the old lines completing their evolution into their opposites and retaining the unchanging young lines. Using the earlier example of Hexagram 38 containing two changing lines: "110 101" changes to "111 100," which is Hexagram 34. Graphically, it appears this way:

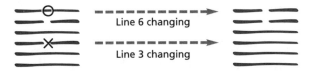

Line 6 changing

Line 3 changing

Figure 1.5. Hexagram 38 with old lines 3 and 6 changing creates Hexagram 34.

In the case of multiple changing lines, the general meaning of both hexagrams 38 and 34 should be consulted. Some I Ching books say that the original hexagram indicates the present situation, and the hexagram it changes into indicates the future. However, a better explanation is that one changing line and multiple changing lines represent the same kind of process of change that is occurring, and differ only in how explicitly the answer is given.

In the cases of no changing lines and one changing line, you can simply look up the hexagram meaning in the text, and the basic idea is right there in front of you. In the case of multiple changing lines, however, the meaning must be developed from combining the individual meanings of both the original and second hexagrams together in an evolutionary fashion. To do this successfully, it is necessary to have a good understanding of the nature of change and the meanings in the I Ching. One easy way to approach this is to write down the original hexagram's title as seen in the text, write down a linking word (such as *then, but, while,* or *becoming*), and then write down the second hexagram's title. This gives the basic flow of ideas. Now they can be fleshed out with more detail as you think about their various meanings and how they might apply to your situation.

This is the basic idea behind consulting the I Ching. However, before you can look up your answer, you need to know how to ask your question. There are a variety of ways in which the oracle can be consulted, and understanding these will give you even more options in using it.

PLANNING YOUR INQUIRY

Two basic issues need to be resolved before you can consult the I Ching: how your question should be framed and how the inquiry should be structured.

Framing the Question

It is best to use the I Ching to inquire into complex or murky situations that involve you personally. The proper use of the oracle is to use it as a guide to help you choose your best courses of action. Of course, you will still need to "do the hard work" in life. You *cannot* use the oracle to tell you if a specific outcome will *definitely* occur—it just does not work that way. It can tell you if a specific outcome is *possible* for you or *impossible.* When the I Ching works well, it will broaden your understanding, and you may be amazed by what it reveals. However, when you are not yet ready to accept what it is telling you, you will simply be confused.

When you ask the oracle a question, you are using the *ad hoc* inquiry process. (See the inset "Other I Ching Prediction Methods" on page 11 for a brief discussion of other inquiry methods.) *Ad hoc* inquiries reveal the *current situation* and its *natural evolutionary tendency.* It is *not* a deterministic predictor of future events, so it will fail if you try to use it as a crutch. For example, the oracle can provide highly consistent answers that you strongly desire if the situation allows that as a real possibility for you. However, if (or when) the external situation changes so that your desired outcome is no longer possible, then suddenly the oracle will now give you the *new, correct, but undesired answer.* This situation, to say the least, can be very disconcerting. How, then, should you best use the oracle to avoid deceiving yourself?

Before you begin an inquiry, you should properly prepare yourself. It is best to calm yourself and think deeply and dispassionately about your situation. Be aware of your doubts, fears, desires, and needs, but do not let them overwhelm you or cloud your judgment. If it truly is worth your time and effort to consult the oracle, make sure that you are focused on what is truly at the heart of your inquiry. Not doing this can lead to rash judgments about what the oracle is really saying. Misunderstanding the oracle is very easy to do if your emotions are strong.

The oracle does not provide simple "yes" or "no" answers to an inquiry. Rather, it paints a descriptive picture of the situation you asked about using its inventory of answers. It is then up to you to see how the response applies to your situation. It is not possible to play word games with the oracle. Neither is it fruitful to ask insignificant questions, because at best you will get insignificant answers. Therefore, your question should be about an important situation you want revealed. However, to make the most sense of it, it needs to be something about which you are familiar. This is why personal life questions work best. Questions can be very personal or impersonal, but the less personal they are the more difficult the answers will tend to be to interpret. If you are unclear about an answer, try asking additional questions from different perspectives.

Questions can be entirely about others, about you as well as others, or focused entirely on you. They can be oriented to concrete, physical matters or to emotional, spiritual, or intellectual ones. Remember, however, the oracle's answers to questions about more concrete and realistic issues are often easier to understand. Ultimately, you are the limiting factor in understanding the I Ching.

Your question can be broad or it can be quite specific. Either/or questions may not be easy to interpret, and should generally not be asked, although they can be. Questions can be oriented to the past as easily as to the present. Events too far in the future aren't good topics. When events in the future turn out as predicted, it is because they evolved along the path of natural evolution—sometimes with your assistance and sometimes without.

After you have formulated your question, it is always a good idea to write it down, along with the date and time, and the response. It is best to keep a notebook of your questions and answers. This way, you will be able to study past responses and improve your understanding of how the oracle works, as well as improve your understanding of your own situation over time.

Structuring the Inquiry

Your inquiry can be conducted a number of different ways. The traditional approach used just one way, but there are alternatives that will display the answer in a variety of structures.

When doing a simple *ad hoc* inquiry, consulting the oracle multiple times for each question will usually provide you with a better perspective on the situation. This is what the ancient Chinese did. Sometimes this is the only way to gain a good understanding of the situation, and relying on a single response can more easily lead to misinterpretation. Thus, obtaining two or three responses to your question in one session is generally better, but is not required. If you do many oracle readings on the same question in the same session, you will notice that there will be a point when the significance of the answers drops off. Thus, to gain a good understanding of a complex, long-standing issue in your life, consult the oracle several times for each question, but spread out your sessions over a long period—even months apart. Now, what other options do you have for structuring your inquiry?

For a basic answer to your inquiry, use a single hexagram display. Remember, though, better responses are usually provided when the inquiry is repeated to produce several hexagrams as your answer. For instructions on generating a single hexagram, refer to "Basic Hexagram Selection Methods," below. Later in this chapter, you'll learn what type of responses you will likely get from *ad hoc* oracle inquiries. (See "Results of *Ad Hoc* Oracle Inquiries" on page 18.)

To see your answer as a *multi-step evolutionary process,* or as a *conceptual map,* use a method that gives you *multiple hexagrams* for your answer. You can do this either to see the evolution of the situation through a sequence of steps, or for answers displayed as specific elements in a map of concepts (based on the idea of Tarot card spreads). For instructions on generating these types of predictions, refer to "Multiple *Ad Hoc* Oracle Prediction Methods" on page 15. Note that when you use these multiple prediction methods, you are still making *ad hoc* oracle inquiries.

BASIC HEXAGRAM SELECTION METHODS

The basic methods build hexagrams line by line. Therefore, six separate steps are necessary to make one hexagram. To generate additional hexagrams, the entire process must be repeated for each hexagram. There is only one traditional method still in wide use, and that is the *three coins method.* The other traditional method—the *yarrow stalk method*—declined after the three coins method came into common usage almost 2,000 years ago. (The history of the oracle is discussed further in Chapter 2.) However, there are some good alternatives to these methods, which are not commonly known. These are described in "Alternatives to the Traditional Hexagram Selection Methods" on page 12.

The Original Oracle: The Yarrow Stalk Method

The *yarrow stalk method* uses fifty pieces of yarrow stalk in a complex and slow process to select each line. It also requires careful attention to detail to be performed successfully. Statistically, the odds of getting the different types of lines are not equal in this method. While it is true that the odds are equal of getting a yin or a yang line, the odds are one in every sixteen times of getting an old yin, and three in sixteen times of getting an old yang. There is no theoretical justification for this skewed pattern because yin and yang are equal forces, and so must always be represented in the same proportions. Therefore, due to this and to the other disadvantages noted above, this method is *not* recommended, and consequently will not be described here. Note, however, that those who want to try using this system can do so by using the Bead Bag Method (described under "Alternatives to the Traditional Hexagram Selection Methods" on page 12), but with the following variation: one old yin, seven young yin, three old yang, and five young yang.

Other I Ching Prediction Methods

In the following chapters, you will learn that the Chinese developed other ways of accessing the I Ching's knowledge of how change occurs in life. The most important of these is the calendar-based oracle, referred to in this book as the *I Ching Lifechart*. This method, which uses birth date and time, links the I Ching text to a method of generating time-specific predictions. It gives validity to the I Ching's text as a general description of the patterns of change that occur in life, and complements what we can discover from the *ad hoc* oracle because it can show what changes will be occurring, and when they will be occurring. When both methods are used together, they can provide better information than either can separately.

Another prediction system (which has a number of variants within it, including use of date and time) is *Plum Blossom Numerology*. This system is also inherently related to the I Ching. Both of these prediction methods were developed by the famous Chinese scholar Shao Yung, who will be discussed in later chapters.

Because of their complexity, these prediction methods are primarily of interest to more advanced I Ching users, and go beyond the scope of this book. However, if you are interested in learning more about them, visit http://www.newagequest.com/iching. This website provides an effective variant of *Plum Blossom Numerology* that is rather easy to use. It also provides information about how to obtain an *I Ching Lifechart* kit.

The Common Oracle: The Three Coins Method

The *three coins method* simply involves shaking three identical coins in cupped hands, dropping them to the ground, and noting how they land, heads or tails. The first toss is for the first line (the bottom of the hexagram), and further tosses determine each subsequent line in order up the hexagram. The four line types are determined as Table 1.3 shows.

Table 1.3. Three Coins Method Line Types

EACH COIN TOSS	LINE DESCRIPTION	LINE AS GRAPHIC	LINE AS NUMBER
if 3 heads	old yang (a "9 line")	——O——	<u>1</u>
if 1 head	young yang (a "7 line")	————	1
if 1 tail	young yin (an "8 line")	—— ——	0
if 3 tails	old yin (a "6 line")	——X——	<u>0</u>

This table shows the possibilities of each three-coin toss. The "line description" gives the description of the line type. (The number 6 or 9 shown in parentheses is the traditional numeric value of that type of line that was determined through use of the yarrow stalk oracle. This number is often still used to refer to the line. Old yang is always 9, old yin is always 6, young yang is always 7, and young yin is always 8. Since the I Ching describes only changing lines, only the "yin 6" and "yang 9" lines have hexagram text.) The "line as graphic" column shows the traditional graphic representation of the line type in the hexagram. The "line as number" column indicates the line type represented as a 0 or 1.

ALTERNATIVES TO THE TRADITIONAL HEXAGRAM SELECTION METHODS

There are a few alternatives to the traditional methods discussed above. These include the Bead Bag Method, the Beads-on-a-String Method, and the Pinwheel Spinner. They do require some initial preparation, but if they are kept in good condition, they can be used again and again.

The Bead Bag Method

This method is one of the easiest to set up and use. A small pouch or container is used to hold small, nearly identical objects such as beads, buttons, or shells. Each object should be visually marked or colored in one of four ways as Table 1.4 below shows. To create each line of the hexagram, the user simply reaches into the bag, mixes the contents around, and—without knowing the type of bead being touched—removes one. The line type is recorded, and then the bead is replaced. This is repeated until all six lines have been determined.

Table 1.4 shows how the bag should be set up. The markings listed below are only suggestions since you can choose your own pattern based on the types of beads at hand. However, a system like this has the advantage of being easy to decode—light colors are yang, and dark colors are yin, and stripes indicate a changing line.

Table 1.4. Bead Bag Method Setup

CONTENTS OF BAG	LINE DESCRIPTION	LINE AS GRAPHIC	LINE AS NUMBER
1 light bead, striped	old yang (a "9 line")	——O——	1
3 light beads, solid	young yang (a "7 line")	————	1
3 dark beads, solid	young yin (an "8 line")	—— ——	0
1 dark bead, striped	old yin (a "6 line")	——X——	0

Remember, select only *one* bead each time to determine the type of line before putting it back with the others!

The Beads-on-a-String Method

This is a simple variation on the Bead Bag Method. Rather than having the beads loose, where they might get lost, place the beads on a strong string, alternating them and pushing them firmly together. Now, to select a line type, spin the string around (lying the string on a flat surface works well) and, without looking, grasp one. Record the line type, then repeat the process for each new line. You can also make longer strings: sixteen beads would require twice as many of each kind of bead; twenty-four beads would require three times as many. For longer strings, the beads should alternate in the same sequence for optimal randomization.

The Pinwheel Spinner

Another simple device that can be used to construct a hexagram line by line is a *pinwheel spinner*. To construct a pinwheel spinner, you will need a circular piece of cardboard a few inches in diameter; a spindle, such as a needle or a pushpin; a cardboard arrow; a small metal washer; and a small eraser from the end of a pencil.

Mark the cardboard circle, as shown in Figure 1.6 on page 14, into eight *equal* pie shapes, marking them yin and yang alternating around the circle. Mark *one* of each type as its changing line. (You can also label each segment with a letter, from A through H, so that the wheel can select trigrams. See "Trigram Selection Methods" below.) Assemble the pinwheel by (1) pushing the circular cardboard, centered and face up, onto the pin; (2) placing the metal washer on the pin; (3) pushing the arrow, centered, onto the pin; and (4) pushing the eraser on the top of the pin.

Top view of disc and pointer.

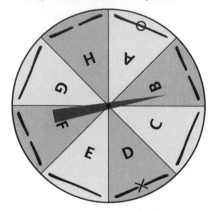

Side view showing spinner construction.

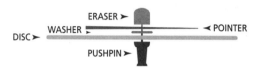

Figure 1.6. How to set up the Pinwheel Spinner.

To use the Pinwheel Spinner, rapidly spin the arrow (or the base, if that is easier) while firmly holding the spindle. When it stops, the arrow will be pointing to one of the four different line types. Record the line. Spin the device once for each of the six lines in the hexagram. This device works well as long as the circle is divided equally, the arrow points clearly to one segment or another, and the device can spin easily. For its ease of use and versatility, this is the method I recommend above all the others, although it has the most complex setup of these alternative methods.

MORE EFFICIENT HEXAGRAM SELECTION METHODS

The traditional methods build individual hexagrams line by line. However, there are other ways to select hexagrams. In fact, there are two basic approaches: One is to select the two trigrams that form the hexagram, and the other is to select the hexagram directly. A notable disadvantage of these methods, however, is that a separate step is required to generate a changing line when it is required, or desired. (The easiest way to obtain a changing line number with these methods is by additionally rolling a six-sided gaming die as each hexagram is selected. The number appearing on the die is the changing line.)

Trigram Selection Methods

Since a hexagram is made up of two trigrams, one lower trigram and one upper trigram can be selected in two steps. One method is to use the Pinwheel Spinner or the Beads-on-a-String methods on page 13, by marking the eight trigram letters either on the segments of the pinwheel or on the beads. Another simple but effective method is to label eight chopsticks (or something similar) with a trigram letter, and randomly select one chopstick at a time. Perhaps the major disadvantage of these methods is that the pair of trigrams needs to be converted into the hexagram number, which requires an additional lookup step.

Hexagram Selection Methods

There are three hexagram selection methods that are relatively easy to make and use. One is the Beads-on-a-String method on page 13, except instead of putting eight large beads on the string, you put on sixty-four smaller ones, each labeled with a different hexagram number.

The second is to use I Ching cards, which can sometimes be found in stores. Each card represents one hexagram. You can also make your own cards by using a heavy marker to write each hexagram number on the face of sixty-four cards—which is about a deck and a half of normal playing cards, omitting the face cards.

A third possibility is to use sixty-four chopsticks (or something similar), each labeled with a hexagram number. Keeping them together as a set is easier if you keep them in a container (such as a shoe box).

If you make your own device, be sure to additionally identify orientation for the numbers 6, 9, 19, and 61—for example, by underlining—to avoid confusion when the number is viewed upside down. Also, be sure that the digits can always be distinguished from one another, as people may sometimes confuse 1 and 7, or even 4 and 9.

To find a hexagram, randomly select one item—bead, card, or chopstick—from the collection. You can add changing lines by tossing a six-sided gaming die as an adjunct step as each hexagram is selected. The number on the die is the changing line. If a moving line is added, it is only for selecting a more specific prediction, and second hexagrams will not be produced.

MULTIPLE AD HOC ORACLE PREDICTION METHODS

It was mentioned above that *multiple* answers could be obtained for even a simple question to provide enhanced insight. This section shows how that idea can be used to produce sets of answers. The methods that follow should be used only by those who have become competent at the more basic method of selecting one or a few hexagrams for an answer to an inquiry. One good reason for this is that this section presents you with many more options, not only in terms of what you can get, but also the means you can use to get it. A multiple answer oracle reading is made up of a series of hexagrams that are placed in a *sequential list* or on a *conceptual map.*

A *conceptual map* is a visual representation of a series of ideas, rather like a Tarot card spread. That is, different places on the paper (or tabletop if cards are being used) will hold different kinds of information. For example, one position could reflect the immediate past, the one next to it could reflect the present, and the one next to that could reflect the immediate future. (This map is shown on page 17 in Figure 1.7.) There are many others possibilities.

As the name suggests, a *sequential list* is a list of hexagrams in order. However, there are two basic forms of this: the Six-Step List and the Flexible List. Both of these are also described below.

There are many ways to generate the hexagrams for these maps and lists. It is possible to simply use the basic, line-by-line hexagram selection methods. However, if you needed six or seven hexagrams, it would require almost fifty separate steps (such as coin tosses) with a line-by-line method. Therefore, you may want to use a more efficient way to select hexagrams.

With multiple prediction methods, you can choose whether or not to incorporate changing lines. These methods do not directly incorporate changing lines in the same step in which the hexagram is produced. However, as mentioned above, you can add changing line values by tossing a six-sided gaming die as an adjunct step as each hexagram is selected. Remember, if a moving line is added, it is only for selecting a more specific prediction, and second hexagrams will not be produced.

Conceptual Maps

In *Moving With Change,* Rowena Pattee describes several I Ching card spreads that are based on Tarot spreads. However, note that instead of using real cards, a *virtual* version of this idea can be used. That is, you can use other methods to generate the hexagrams and write them on a paper form of the conceptual map. You don't need to spread physical cards out in front of you. Following are some examples of conceptual maps. You also can create your own based on your own needs.

The Past-Present-Future Map

Look at Figure 1.7 on page 17. The "past" card indicates what has happened in the recent past. The "present" card indicates the current situation. The "future" card indicates the trend into the near future. This idea can easily be extended to use more cards. If seven cards are used, for example, a single center card can represent the present, and the others (an equal number on each side) would be past and near future. If nine cards are used, for example, they should be grouped equally among past, present, and near future.

Figure 1.7. The Past-Present-Future Map.

The Magic Seven Map

Look at Figure 1.8 below. Card 1 indicates what has happened in the past; Card 2 indicates the current situation; Card 3 shows possibilities for the future. Card 4 tells you how you can improve the current situation; Card 5 shows how the current situation is affecting your environment at home, at work, or in social situations; Card 6 reveals any forces that oppose your desires; and Card 7 represents the possible outcome by taking into account all of the factors.

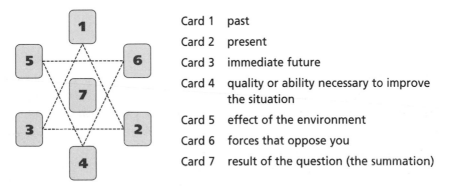

Card 1   past

Card 2   present

Card 3   immediate future

Card 4   quality or ability necessary to improve the situation

Card 5   effect of the environment

Card 6   forces that oppose you

Card 7   result of the question (the summation)

Figure 1.8. The Magic Seven Map.

The Key Card Map

In this map, shown in Figure 1.9 below, a key card (or concept) is specifically selected to represent the subject of the inquiry, and it is removed from the deck. This card serves as the focal point of the reading. The cards above it (the number can be selected by you) represent influences going into the situation. The cards below it (again you select the number) represent its outcomes.

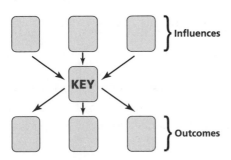

Figure 1.9. The Key Card Map. In this example, only three cards are used above and below to represent the influences and outcomes, but you can use as many cards as you like.

Hexagram Lists

Hexagram lists are similar to the conceptual maps in that they display hexagrams in a conceptual scheme. However, instead of it being a pictorial display, it is simply a list.

The Six-Step List

To prepare the Six-Step List, first focus on your question, and then randomly select *six (and only six) hexagrams* in a row using a method that produces only hexagram numbers (that is, with *no* changing lines). Then, to each of the selected hexagrams assign—*in sequence*—the line numbers one through six. Thus, the first hexagram selected is assigned line number one, the second is given line number two, and so on.

In this display, the first three lines show the early aspects of the situation, and the last three lines show the latter aspects. The first line indicates the beginning, and the sixth line indicates the end. The idea behind this display is that your life is continually evolving through separately identifiable steps using the patterns of change revealed in the I Ching—which describes an evolutionary process. By obtaining six random hexagrams without line numbers, you are automatically fleshing out the evolutionary process in your inquiry. This type of display is highly beneficial for viewing an entire situation as it changes over time.

The Flexible List

The Six-Step List is very rigid in its structure and how it works. In contrast, the Flexible List is entirely adaptable. To illustrate the Flexible List, look at the description of the card definitions below the Magic Seven Map on page 17. Now, imagine that instead of placing seven cards into this pattern on a tabletop, that you're just listing hexagrams on a piece of paper adjacent to those definitions. This illustrates the idea that you can create any *list of concepts* that you want to explore on paper, and then generate the hexagrams for them (including line numbers or not, as you choose).

RESULTS OF *AD HOC* ORACLE INQUIRIES

Answers to *ad hoc* oracle inquiries provide insight into circumstances at the time of the inquiry. The items below explain the results you can expect from *ad hoc* oracle inquiries in more detail.

1. Answers about a situation can be simple, direct, clear, and entirely appropriate, but often need to be interpreted in light of the situation. Therefore, it is best to think deeply about each answer, and see how it reflects the different aspects of the situation.

2. Answers can predict the future successfully when the events that follow are the natural evolution of the situation, but situations are not guaranteed to follow this path because the *ad hoc* oracle is accurately revealing only the past and present.

3. In some situations, answers may seem only tangential, being neither affirmative nor negative to the essential inquiry. Such responses can be correct statements about the situation, but the effect of the answer is to indicate the matter is still not yet clear enough to describe in terms of the question. Obtaining additional hexagrams, or inquiring from a different perspective, will tend to improve understanding.

4. Answers about a situation can remain consistent for weeks, months, and even for years when that situation is stable. That is, nothing about that situation has changed.

5. Answers can remain the same through repeated inquiries over days, weeks, or even months before the pattern suddenly collapses into a different answer altogether, where it thereafter remains stable. This occurs when (a) initially there is a strong connection between this answer and the inquirer's desires or fears, and (b) external factors that initially allowed the *possibility* of this result have suddenly changed.

6. Too many inquiries focused on one question in too short a period can produce an overabundance of answers, giving progressively less significant information until, eventually, chaos.

7. Inquiring into a topic with no meaning for the inquirer can produce insignificant or even chastising results.

8. Answers cannot be fixed with assurance to specific time periods. A different method of I Ching consultation must be used for time-specific predictions. (See the inset "Other I Ching Prediction Methods" on page 11.)

CONCLUSION

This chapter explained the basic methods behind the use of the I Ching. All of the methods detailed in this book are examples of the *ad hoc* oracle. In using this type of oracle, however, you should be sensitive to its strengths and weaknesses as described in this chapter. If you intend to be only a casual I Ching user, you may simply begin using it now without reading further. The I Ching text in this book is designed to be as straightforward and understandable as possible. There are also a few notes at the beginning on page 57 to help explain its format, and to help with interpreting answers.

There is far more to the I Ching, however. There is a rich historical and theoretical background going back thousands of years. By reading Chapters 2 and 3, you will gain a stronger understanding of the I Ching.

2

HISTORY
How the I Ching Came to Be

I t is not easy for us to fully understand the origins of the I Ching. Its birth is believed to have occurred more than 3,000 years ago in China, roughly around 1100–1200 B.C.E. However, as with any historical record from that long ago, the data is open to some doubt. Parts of it appear to be even older. Therefore, researchers have also greatly depended on archeological studies of early China to understand the history of the I Ching. In this chapter, we will explore these origins, as best as we can understand them now. You will learn that the I Ching commonly sold in bookstores today is *not* the original I Ching. You will also learn that the I Ching itself has been an integral part of Chinese culture and intellectual thought throughout its evolution.

A LIVING MYSTERY OF THE ANCIENT PAST

The I Ching was not originally a "book" as we view it, but rather a set of oracles that were conveyed as much through oral tradition as by primitive written symbols placed in columns on strips of bamboo. Similar to the other ancient classics *The Illiad* and *Gilgamesh,* the I Ching has survived in large part because it was a set of stories, many about real events, designed to be remembered through its literary, poetical style. The rhyming technique was used skillfully by ancient people to help preserve literary works before writing became the primary means of preservation. The hexagram symbols used in the I Ching were important as a conceptual map, and helped serve as a memory aid to the meaning of the oracles.

However, the I Ching commonly available in bookstores today is not the original I Ching. Archaeological discoveries made in the last hundred years, in addition to a more studied and careful analysis of China's ancient history, have led to the realization that the traditional text (originating from the Han period about 2,000 years ago), known as the *Classic of Change,* or I Ching, is not the original text, which was known as the *Chou I.*[1] There have been many changes made to the original meanings—from bad transcriptions to language changes to lost meanings of textual references and even to very early versions of the text "vanishing" for reasons unknown. To make matters worse, the I Ching was deliberately altered during the Han Dynasty for political reasons. Thus, the I Ching on bookshelves today—even if translated accurately from the existing written Chinese text—bears both striking and subtle differences from the original system of ideas. (For more on this, see the inset "Problems with the Traditional I Ching Text" on page 23.)

The Chinese of 3,000 years ago viewed the world around them through fundamentally different concepts and tools of understanding from ours. Therefore, even when we study the I Ching, we cannot comprehend how it was intended to be understood without knowledge of the distant past. Lack of this knowledge results in fundamental errors in interpretation and understanding not only for ordinary users, but also for many I Ching translators. This version of the I Ching minimizes these problems by heavy reliance on the oldest historically accurate versions of the text, as well as basing this version on the underlying interconnected structure of the hexagrams and lines. We will now take a deeper look and see how the I Ching evolved over time.

AN OVERVIEW OF THE DEVELOPMENT OF THE I CHING

Understanding the history of the I Ching is an important first step in understanding this ancient text. However, trying to get to the truth is not easy. One way of helping to unravel the story is to separate the I Ching's early development into three threads—China's dynastic history, the evolution of Chinese oracles, and the development of the I Ching text. These threads ran largely parallel in time. Subsequent development of the I Ching largely occurred in two later periods: the Neo-Confucian period and twentieth-century exploration by Western researchers. The discussions below provide you with the basic, important facts. (For quick reference, see the inset "The Early Historical Timeline" on page 26, which interweaves China's history with the development of the I Ching.)

The Dynastic History of Ancient China

China's first dynasty, the Hsia Dynasty, began around 2200 B.C.E. Although their stone-age tools were primitive, this dynasty is believed to have instituted large-scale public works to control the flow and distribution of water and to provide for the

Problems With the Traditional J Ching Text

Some of the problems in the I Ching text began with the very creation of the original text itself. Others crept in before the text was "standardized" into the traditional text we see now. Thus, many of the problems have not been easy to root out. However, the following are the most significant types of problems with some examples of each.

Problems With Translation

To illustrate the difficulty in translating the I Ching, consider the general meaning of Hexagram 1, which is made up of only four Chinese characters, known as ideograms. In their I Ching book, Kerson and Rosemary Huang note that a modern literal translation of these four symbols would read something like "Great well-being furthering perseverance," but based on their historical and linguistic analysis, they translate the text to mean "Sign of the Great Sacrifice. Auspicious omen."[2] Based on his historical and linguistic analysis, researcher Greg Whincup translates it more lyrically to mean, "Strong action will be supremely blessed. It is favorable to keep on."[3] The noted Russian sinologist I. K. Shchutskii, who was one of the first to attempt historical analysis of the I Ching early in the twentieth century, translated this into Russian (which is here rendered into English) as "Great accomplishment; steadiness is favorable."[4] In the well-known, more traditional version by Richard Wilhelm as translated by Cary F. Baynes (hereafter referenced as Wilhelm/Baynes), the meaning is given as "The Creative works sublime success, furthering through perseverance."[5] As you can see, even so simple a hexagram text as this one cannot be clearly understood by us today without ambiguity and debate.

Problems Due to Obsolete Language

The Chinese language has undergone changes that make it very difficult for even today's readers of Chinese to understand the intended meanings of many ancient texts. For example, the ideogram in Hexagram 1, which is translated today as "chastity," "loyalty," or "perseverance," really meant "divination" to the ancient authors of the I Ching text.[6] Since the word "perseverance" occurs throughout most I Ching translations today, it is clear that a significant misinterpretation could be occurring.

Problems Due to the Written Chinese Language

The I Ching text is written in *ideograms*, symbols that directly identify an idea or an object, rather than symbols that directly represent the sounds of speech as the written English language does. The text was extremely terse, so no concepts are explained at length, and there are no punctuation symbols. Therefore, it is unclear where the flow of ideas should pause or stop. Consequently, the text presents itself rather like a "stream of consciousness" to the reader, and thus is open to a lot of interpretation. Moreover, written Chinese doesn't differentiate between genders or even tenses, nor does an ideogram change form as it changes function. There are no parts of speech, such as nouns, verbs, adjectives, and adverbs. Instead, the function of an ideogram is indicated by its position relative to other ideograms.[7] Due to these problems, it is difficult for a translator to understand what was originally meant.

Problems Due to Lost Knowledge

In the original text, many historical events are cited as examples and illustrations, but are not fully explained. In the tradition of folk history, the examples would evoke the memory of the incident, which would then provide the full background and meaning. Unfortunately, the connection between the text and many of these events had been lost by the time the I Ching became the book we know today. For example, one phrase in the I Ching turns out to have actually been the title of a Chou prince, which had been quickly forgotten and subsequently misinterpreted for 3,000 years.[8] Also, with the passage of time, true understanding of many of the symbols in Taoism—particularly with reference to the I Ching—were no longer properly understood even among most philosophers.[9] Thus, it is not surprising that misinterpretations and differences from the original meanings are normal in the I Ching texts available today.

Problems Due to Transcription Errors

Modern analysts have concluded that there also appear to have been errors in transcription when the written text was created, so the commonly used texts now incorporate the wrong words at times, thus causing some significant and fundamental errors. Notable examples include hexagrams 33 and 36. In Hexagram 33, the traditional text gives us the word "retreat," although modern analysis indicates it is more likely to be "piglet." Similarly, in Hexagram 36 the traditional text reads "light is wounded"—clearly a nearly unintelligible phrase—which now is better understood to be "bright pheasant."[10] There are other examples where the earliest versions of the text (which are fragmentary) sometimes contain a small number of different symbols—some with the same sounds but different meanings—from the commonly used texts.[11] Thus, once again, we see meanings other than the ones originally intended have crept into the text.

Problems Due to Confucian Reinterpretations

The Confucian reinterpretation of the I Ching, which is explained on pages 28 and 30, added a whole new theoretical structure that has further complicated attempts to understand the original material. For example, the text of Hexagram 1—translated above as "Great Well-being Furthering Perseverance"—was interpreted by Confucians to have special meaning. They declared Hexagram 1 to be a list of the "Four Virtues of the I Ching," and these "virtues" were given a great deal of emphasis in their philosophical interpretation of the text.[12] However, the original text was meant to describe events around the person making an inquiry of the oracle. It was not intended to be a code of ethics as the Confucians tried to make it.

Problems Due to Worldview Changes

There are significant social and psychological differences between the society to which the I Ching text spoke when it was created and the world to which it speaks now. The ancient Chinese view of hierarchical society, relations of superiors and inferiors, and how to promote and manage conflict is often not appropriate to our more egalitarian and legalistic society. Thus, modern readers could easily incorrectly infer meanings somewhat different from what was originally intended, even when the issue of proper translation is moot.

Problems of Too Much Confusion

Finally, just stepping back and observing the text objectively, it appears that it is not much of an exaggeration to say that the hexagram texts now commonly in use are perhaps one-quarter reasonably understandable, one-quarter largely unintelligible, and the remaining half varying between. This confused text is why most users find it difficult to consistently obtain a clear answer. Yet, there seems to be enough truth coming through to encourage many users to continue using the I Ching.

common defense. Their territory covered the northern plains and the Chinese heartland, but not the full extent of the land we know today as China.

In approximately 1783 B.C.E., the Shang overthrew the Hsia's corrupt king Jie and took control. Shang was a Bronze-Age culture. They easily defeated the Hsia with their superior metal weapons and horse-drawn chariots. They dotted the land with a series of fortified villages and kept tight control over their more advanced technology to maintain military dominance. The Shang territory was divided among a number of vassal states. There was a continual shift of power among them, at times reflected in armed conflict. Most historians believe that the Shang played the vassal states against one another to keep them weak and divided. However, fate would have it otherwise: the vassal state of Chou rose in prominence and became the Shang's appointed "Guardians of the West."

The Early Historical Timeline

Due to the lack of good historical evidence, there is a great deal of uncertainty about the oldest dates, even though dates are often specified in Chinese historical records. The abbreviation *c.,* for *circa,* means "about." B.C.E. and C.E. stand for *before the Common Era* and *Common Era.*

Date uncertain.	Use of bone and tortoise shell oracles begins.
2200 B.C.E. (Stone Age)	Hsia Dynasty begins.
1783 B.C.E. (Bronze Age)	Shang Dynasty begins.
c. mid-2nd millennium B.C.E.	Use of yarrow-stalk oracle begins.
1122 B.C.E.	Chou Dynasty begins; *Chou I* completed.
c. 1000 B.C.E.	Western Chou period begins.
771 B.C.E.	Eastern Chou "Spring and Autumn" period begins; first widespread versions of I Ching in a commonly shared text.
c. 600–500 B.C.E.	Early Taoist philosophical sources; life of Lao-Tzu.
551–479 B.C.E.	Confucius' life; I Ching interest developed close to the end of his life.
500 B.C.E. (Iron Age)	Eastern Chou "Warring States" period begins; Confucian philosophy applied to I Ching.
221–206 B.C.E.	Ch'in Dynasty; destruction of most books.
206 B.C.E.–220 C.E.	Han Dynasty; official version of I Ching based on Confucian philosophy promulgated.
618–906 C.E.	T'ang Dynasty; printing process enables wider I Ching readership.
960–1279 C.E.	Northern Sung Dynasty; Neo-Confucian Revival studies Chinese roots.
1011–1077 C.E.	Shao Yung's life and work; predestination studies based on Taoism and I Ching.
1130–1200 C.E.	Chu Hsi's life and work; very popular standardized I Ching created.

Then, in approximately 1122 B.C.E., the Chou overthrew the Shang. The Shang Dynasty had by then become corrupt and engaged in extensive barbaric ritualistic practices. Recent excavations have found hundreds of ritually killed victims in Shang royal tombs.

Three great Chou leaders brought their dynasty to power. The first was King Wen. Technically, he was not a king, but received the title twenty years after his death when the Chou came to power. He was responsible for giving Chou a secure position in the western half of the Shang kingdom. He was renowned for his wisdom and was able to take the critical step of establishing peaceful ties and a leadership role with other vassal states. He also formulated the strategy for Shang's eventual defeat.

According to history, King Wen was heavily involved in developing the system of symbols and hexagram text used in the *Chou I* ("Changes of Chou"), which eventually became the I Ching. It was, however, common in ancient China for those who developed something new to attribute it to a venerated leader. Therefore, it is possible that several people—not just one wise king—contributed to the I Ching's early development.

Using his father's strategy, King Wen's son Wu overthrew the Shang Dynasty and established Chou as the dominant power in northern China. A few years later, King Wu died and the Duke of Chou, his brother, became Regent. Despite a rebellion by others in the royal family with some of the Shang nobility, the Chou Dynasty became firmly established and, indeed, was at the height of its power during the regency. Reportedly, the duke also contributed greatly to the I Ching by creating the meanings for the 384 hexagram lines.

By about 1100 B.C.E., the political struggle behind the rise of Chou was over. References in the I Ching's text to commonly known events of this and earlier periods, and the absence of any mention of later events, leads to the conclusion that the Chou I text was completed about ten years after the conquest of Shang.[13]

Chou's power lasted throughout what is known as the Western Chou period, until 771 B.C.E. Sometime between 1000 B.C.E. and the end of this period is most likely when early written versions of the I Ching began spreading across the country. The Eastern Chou period (771 B.C.E. to 221 B.C.E.) began with the moving of the Chou capital to the east. Rather than being the large power it once was, Chou had become just a medium-sized state among other larger and smaller ones. When they could not maintain order through either military power or moral authority, war began to break out among the states. This period is known as the Warring States period, and lasted from about 500 to 221 B.C.E., which is when the Eastern Chou period ended.

It was during this deeply troubled period of great social and political change that China was blessed with its most outstanding philosophers—Confucius, Lao-Tzu, Mencius, and others. It is perhaps because there was so much discord and confusion that philosophy itself was seeded with the need to expand its horizons. This was the period when Confucius, near the end of his life, reportedly discovered the I Ching and began to study it. He left a strong following, and for the next few hundred years, Confucian interpretations of and supplementations to the I Ching text became the major force in its evolution.

The Warring States period ended when the ruler of the Ch'in state conquered all of China and established the first true countrywide government and its shortest dynasty. The Ch'in Dynasty held power for only fifteen years, from 221 to 206 B.C.E. The founding emperor placed an iron-yoke of control on his countrymen. As part of his program, he systematically destroyed "unnecessary" literature and books throughout the country. The I Ching survived this destruction because it was considered necessary. The Ch'in emperor also did some good for China: in addition to a number of other improvements, he created the first Great Wall, and standardized weights and measures and the writing system. The original Ch'in emperor survived only about ten years. His son took his place, but had few supporters and many enemies. Within about five years Liu Bang overthrew him and established the Han Dynasty.

The Han Dynasty lasted from 206 B.C.E. to 220 C.E. The Hans were greatly attracted to the values of Confucianism, which emphasized obedience and obligation, so they made it the official state religion. Thus, after almost 1,000 years of existence, the I Ching, now with its Confucian influence, began its long history as part of official Chinese philosophy and government. However, as Confucian values and philosophy were emphasized, this accelerated the loss of the original ancient oracular meanings in the I Ching.

The dynasties to follow also realized that the strong Confucian emphasis on duty and obedience furthered their aims of stability and continuity in the country. Study of the *Five Classics,* which included the I Ching, became an important part of the countrywide civil service examinations. These were the first civil service examinations in the world open to members of different social classes. This allowed virtually anyone with ability and education to achieve a position of status and financial success through service to the state. The I Ching remained a part of these exams until the modern era, when Western ideas and scientific concepts became important in China.

In some significant ways, the development of the I Ching text paralleled the political history of China. As China was coming together as a nation, and as its culture matured, so was the I Ching text progressing through a process of refinement and standardized distribution.

The Development of the I Ching Text

In ancient China, we know of three divination texts—the Lien Shan, the Gui Gang, and the Chou I (the oldest name for the I Ching). Today, virtually nothing is known about the Lien Shan and the Gui Gang, since their use died out so long ago. There is some evidence that the Lien Shan and the Gui Gang might have used hexagrams with a somewhat different organization from the I Ching, or perhaps they weren't as well defined. However, the evidence is too incomplete to draw any firm conclusions. The I Ching simply survived whereas the others did not.

As a whole, the I Ching is a collection of stories that serve as illustrations of principles. Although these stories appear to describe the different kinds of challenges an individual faces in life, most of the text was written about the events surrounding the founding of the Chou Dynasty.[14]

Keep in mind that 3,000 years ago in China, common knowledge was passed from one person to another via the spoken word. The rudiments of symbolic representation—what we call written language—were only then being created, and they were restricted to relatively few people. The language was neither standardized nor universal. For example, the Shangs' written language differed in many ways from the Chous' written language.

Although the creation of the trigrams, hexagrams, titles, and text have been attributed to famous historical figures of the Chou Dynasty, it is likely that many people were involved in creating and verbally passing down the ideas and stories in the I Ching. Even though the facts of how the I Ching text was created are not known, its close association with the Chou Dynasty seems clear and implies that most of the written text emerged from the Chou court.

Analysis of the text also indicates that it is composed of three distinct layers. I. K. Shchutskii determined that each layer was written during a different period because of the distinct styles of language used in each layer.[15] The oldest layer is simply the name of each hexagram. The second layer is the later addition of explanatory statements to more fully describe the meanings of the hexagrams. Finally, the last layer was the meanings of the hexagram lines.

Fortunetelling was considered a vital government function, and diviners (the priests who consulted the oracle) were important court officials, since they were associated with religion and forms of ancestor worship. The transmission of knowledge, however, was still largely verbal. The text tried to compensate for the shortcomings of the written language. The way the I Ching is structured, its terse, often rhyming statements served as much as memory aids to recollecting historical events as they were explanations of relationships, trends, or characteristics.

Unfortunately, since the full story and meaning of the events referred to in the text had to be conveyed through these early ages by verbal recitation, over time many of the stories lost their historical connections and, thus, their deeper meanings. At the same time, the symbolic meaning of the text became better preserved through the improvement and expansion of the written Chinese language. This resulted in a degradation of the original meanings while the text itself was becoming better preserved.

The philosophy expressed in the I Ching shared common roots with Taoism, and it was becoming increasingly prominent in Chinese culture in the first millennium before the Common Era. For example, the concepts of *yin* and *yang, Tao,* and the nature of change were becoming widely known. (These concepts are discussed in Chapter 3.) However, the I Ching is not referenced in the works of the early Taoists Lao-Tzu or Chuang-tzu, so its direct influence on early Taoist works is unclear.[16]

It is not known exactly how the I Ching was transmitted and preserved after its creation in the Chou court prior to its becoming a circulating written document. Perhaps it was transmitted through a professional class of fortunetellers and priests. In any event, by about 500 B.C.E., its written text was in circulation.[17] A history authored by Chuo Chuan, dating from about the time of Confucius (551–479 B.C.E.), cites earlier historical references to the I Ching in events that occurred in the years 644 B.C.E., 574 B.C.E., and 563 B.C.E. Since the text given does not match the current I Ching text, this clearly shows there have been textual changes from earlier versions.[18] Shchutskii also cites sixteen written instances of I Ching use between 671 B.C.E. and 487 B.C.E. These references show that the I Ching had a prominent role in court politics in different states, so its use was spreading.[19]

As mentioned earlier, Confucian scholars were responsible for radically transforming the book by interpreting its symbols and stories in light of Confucius' philosophical principles. They also contributed important additional explanatory text and essays known as the Ten Wings, which were appended to the text. The I Ching—interpreted according to Confucian social and personal ideals—became widespread throughout China during the Han Dynasty, and was no longer reserved just for the Court or intellectuals.

Most of the I Ching texts used today can be traced back to versions dating from around the seventh or eighth century—after the text had been around for more than 1,500 years in various forms. Another version that gained some prominence is by Wang Bi from the third century. Research into the older origins of the text has uncovered one version dating from the second century B.C.E., and some even older fragments have been found. Although in many places identical, there are other places where significant differences exist between the oldest known text fragments and today's accepted text.

The original text is primarily rooted in a political power struggle. It thus reflects a practical way of approaching situations or problems. The Confucian interpretation shifted the text's emphasis away from a pragmatic oracle and toward a philosophical worldview. However, there clearly is a strong relationship between the ideas expressed in both versions, and our understanding and use of the oracle is enriched by knowing this.

The Evolution of Chinese Oracles

The true story about the origins of the Chinese oracles lies buried in the distant past. Interestingly, the most ancient forms of fortunetelling used large bones (such as the shoulder blades of oxen) or, preferably, large tortoise shells. The diviners would carefully prepare a bone or tortoise shell for divination by carving depressions on the back sides, thinning the material. Sometimes they would scratch symbols into the surface to indicate the query, and sometimes the date. They would then apply a red-hot poker to the surface of the bone or shell, causing it to crack. The diviners would then interpret the pattern of cracks as an answer and oftentimes would carve the answer into the shell or bone. The Chinese believed their deceased ancestors were responsible for the oracle's answers. This spiritual aspect sanctified the practice of fortunetelling for the Chinese.

This elaborate fortunetelling process was undertaken and repeated so often that there are now many tens of thousands of tortoise shell and bone artifacts. For hundreds of years, the Shang performed a fortunetelling for every week, as well as separate ones for significant questions. The tortoise shell archives show us that the official diviners at the Shang court had the responsibility of predicting the weather, determining omens for important state matters, and providing answers to important personal questions for the kings, such as prospects for hunting expeditions, battles, and marriages. The diviners would sometimes record the results of an event along with the prediction. It seems that they were trying to refine their art by keeping track of and studying their successes and failures.

However, divination was not limited to the nobility. There is archeological evidence that commoners relied on numerology—the study of numbers and their relationship to life events—for divination. Even during the Shang period, there is evidence on bones and tortoise shells of numbers being used in the divination process. These numbers, in fact, often appear to be in some sort of hexagram pattern. There are also representations of yin and yang lines in the archeological record as well.[20] The use of numbers and yin and yang lines in early oracular methods was transferred to the yarrow-stalk method of divination, which was used with the I Ching.

Yarrow (also known as milfoil) is a woody-stemmed plant, which was found widely in China. Pieces of stalk over a foot long were cut and dried for use in the divination process. They were easy to get, inexpensive, and reasonably durable. In use, the stalks were manipulated in a complex, ritualistic, dividing-and-counting scheme to produce a number to indicate what type of line it was.[21] Six repetitions of this procedure would be done to produce the six lines of the hexagram.

The earliest record of yarrow-stalk divination dates from about 1250 B.C.E., during the Shang Dynasty. However, there is no evidence that the Shang had used the yarrow-stalk oracle. Exactly how the yarrow-stalk oracle began is unclear, but there are some clues. For one thing, it seems to have been a deliberate rejection of Shang divination methods. A more important clue lies in the strong interest of the ancient Chinese—and Taoist philosophy—in the relationship of the integer numbers. (Integers are all the positive whole numbers, negative whole numbers, and zero.) Magic squares were constructed to demonstrate various characteristics of the low integers. (See the inset "What Is a Magic Square" on page 33.)

Numerology was thought to be a key to the oracle. Numbers were understood to be fundamental expressions of the universe. In the Taoist understanding of the world, which was coming into being as the high mark of Chinese intellectualism (although it wouldn't be called Taoism for centuries), the primary numbers held great significance and helped in understanding everything in existence. Thus, numbers generated by chance through yarrow-stalk manipulation had basic qualitative meanings that helped define the I Ching oracle. (This is discussed in a little more detail in Chapter 3.)

After Chou conquered Shang, the yarrow-stalk method gradually became established as the predominant form of divination. The bone and tortoise shell methods were still used by the court, especially for more important inquiries, but their use gradually died out. The yarrow-stalk method had several natural advantages over the bones and tortoise shells: it needed no elaborate preparation, cost virtually nothing, and was quicker to perform. Indeed, the term "I" in *I Ching* itself can also mean "easy" as well as "change," and this could be an important meaning behind its name, as it was the "easy oracle."

Almost a thousand years later, after the I Ching attained widespread status within Chinese society, further research into its meaning continued. During the Han Dynasty, there was extensive scholarly research into the philosophical aspects of the I Ching as understood through Confucianism. This research focused on the philosophy expressed in the text, not on the oracle's predictive powers. There was, however, a change in the oracle-consulting process during the Han period. They found that tossing three coins and recording the result could represent one line of a hexagram. Thus, six quick and easy coin tosses became the method most often used for consulting the I Ching oracle, although the more ritually oriented

What Is a Magic Square?

A magic square demonstrates how integer numbers can balance each other in different ways. Sum up the numbers by column, row, or diagonal in the magic square below—and you'll see that they all total fifteen! In fact, you can sum them up eight different ways here and they are all the same! The Chinese constructed far more complex magic squares for various purposes, including use in astrological systems. This was a particularly important one, and it was called *Lo Shu.*

4	9	2
3	5	7
8	1	6

process of the yarrow stalks continued for a long time for divinations of more importance.

In the 2,000 years since the three coins method came into use, the process of consulting the I Ching oracle has largely remained the same for most users. There have been alternative ways of consulting the oracle, but these have never gained widespread use. However, different types of prediction systems were created by extending the numerological connections associated with the I Ching's conceptual model. This reached its culmination with the work of Shao Yung.

The Neo-Confucians and Shao Yung

During the Northern Sung Dynasty, about 960–1279 C.E., there was a resurgence of nationalistic awareness, and Confucianism was reinvigorated by a philosophical movement we term *Neo-Confucianism,* and the Chinese call *learning of the Tao.* In part, this was a reaction to the strong influence of Buddhism in the country, which had come from India several centuries before. The Chinese had been fascinated with the I Ching for nearly 2,000 years, so it was still studied. However, it was not as significant a cultural element as it had been. The Neo-Confucians were primarily involved in advancing the philosophical aspects of Taoism and Confucianism rather than in the development of prediction systems and the study of numerology.

One significant exception was the great Neo-Confucian scholar Shao Yung (also known as Shao K'ang-chieh). He was a brilliant and reclusive scholar who was involved in philosophy in general, but he was also deeply involved with the issue of prediction as an aspect of the fundamental structure of the universe. He did not follow the traditional path in I Ching study. He was a model-builder more like the greatest philosophers of the West than were his Chinese brothers. Using Taoist numerological and cosmological principles coupled with the I Ching, he built a descriptive system that describes how everything in the entire world is related. As you might imagine, it was quite complex and sophisticated.[22] His world model also incorporates predestination—that is, the ability to view reality from any point in time. He classified things and events, and then by applying evolutionary principles, he could place them into the predictable sequence of time.

Shao Yung was far ahead of his time in his philosophical concerns and knowledge. He also reached back into the past to delve into some of the rich, virtually unknown sources of ancient esoteric knowledge. He incorporated knowledge from a far wider spectrum than did all his contemporaries, and he anticipated many of the philosophic concerns that would arise in the coming centuries. Even with more conventional wisdom, he often used it in unconventional ways. Consequently, many of his contemporaries said that they just simply did not understand him.[23]

Some of Shao Yung's ideas on the I Ching gained widespread use, although most did not. He was deeply interested in the Taoist cosmological heritage and its models, and linked them to the I Ching through astrology, numerology, predestination, and geomancy (*feng shui*). Shao came near the middle of the Neo-Confucian period. While his work undoubtedly incorporated some of the work of earlier Taoists, it was the culmination of this avenue of research. He gained a widespread reputation as an accurate seer, and a number of his prediction systems have been studied and used ever since. They have not become popular, however, due to their complexity and difficulty in use. (For more on his other prediction systems, see the inset "Shao Yung's Prediction Systems" on page 35.)

Some of Shao's most important ideas subsequently influenced mainstream Chinese thinking on the I Ching. Other developments of his, such as his system of calendar-based predictions based on a person's birth data (referred to here as *I Ching Lifecharts*), have been largely ignored. His pictorial arrangement of the hexagrams based on their line sequence became quite popular. When the great Western mathematician Gottfried Wilhelm Leibniz first saw Shou's pictorial arrangements—which were designed more than 500 years before his own "original" work—he instantly recognized that they were a binary arrangement of the numbers zero through sixty-three.

About one hundred years after Shao Yung another Neo-Confucian philosopher, Chu Hsi, had an even greater impact on the common use of the I Ching, although his work was not as advanced as Shao Yung's. He integrated Taoist, Confucian, and Buddhist concepts and appended them as notes to the text of the I Ching to help increase its usability for people in general. He succeeded in greatly increasing the I Ching's popularity, and it became the commonly used format for centuries thereafter. Today, with the I Ching in the West, there are now other interpretations and influences being brought to it.

The I Ching in the West: New Explorations and Explanations

Widespread interest in the I Ching in the West is comparatively recent. Those Westerners who studied it at the turn of the twentieth century—and earlier—were true pioneers. Their legacy, like that of the Chinese themselves, is a mixed blessing. Those responsible for popularizing the text in the Western world—Legge (in English), Wilhelm (in German), and Wilhelm/Baynes (in English)—made the work widely accessible while attempting to communicate what was then the current state of the work in Chinese. With the benefit of historical and archaeological investigations into ancient China, in the twenty-first century we know that the I Ching now popularly in print is not the same as the most ancient versions. This awareness has led to a small but significant effort to attempt to rediscover what the original I Ching was trying to communicate. The books of Greg Whincup and Kerson and Rosemary Huang are particularly noteworthy in this area. This has been a slow process, but it has produced some significant results. In turn, these form an important basis for this book.

In the West, there has also been a veritable explosion of diverse books about the I Ching written from many different viewpoints. However, rather than digging into ancient source materials for understanding, authors too often have been

Shao Yung's Prediction Systems

Shao Yung developed an I Ching *ad hoc* oracle that is based on numerology called *I Ching Mei Hwa Shu* (or *Plum Blossom Numerology*). This system includes some variants that use date and time as an element; some other variants work only with trigrams. His most comprehensive, and perhaps most accurate, calendar-based predestination system is titled *Ho Lo Li Shu* (which translated means *Ho Map Lo Map Rational Number*, but in this book it is referred to as *I Ching Lifecharts*). This has an extremely complex calculation process using birth date and time data. This system is also based on principles derived from Figures 3.4, 3.5, and 3.6 on pages 52 and 53 in Chapter 3, as well as on a number of other principles. It is remarkably effective.[24]

Shao is also reputed to have developed two other systems. One of these, *T'ieh Pan Shen Shu* (or *Iron Plate Divine Number*), was originally a secret system, so even though there are some printed versions of this available (currently only in Chinese), it is not certain that this system reflects Shao's work. The other system is *Chiu Kung Ming Li* (or *Nine Star Astrology*), which uses a complex system of evolving magic squares. This system has a relationship to *feng shui*—the practice of harmonizing spiritual forces with the structure in which they reside.

merely retranslating the already corrupted text, or applying whatever new or different thematic principles they want to express. Since this approach can't accurately reveal the processes of change that are embodied in the I Ching hexagrams, these books often end up not being as effective as the I Ching hexagrams really are at heart.

One important addition in explaining the I Ching was made by the great psychologist Carl Jung. He developed his own hypothesis of why the oracle worked, and termed this "synchronicity." His idea became widely popular in the West, although there are some serious difficulties with it.

While interest in the I Ching has been growing steadily in the West in the twentieth century, its interest in the East had been declining until recently. The lowest point in the I Ching's usage in China probably occurred shortly after the establishment of the Communist Chinese state in the middle of the twentieth century with its quest for Westernism, modernism, and the rejection of "nonscientific" thought. Still, the use and study of the I Ching was never completely eliminated. Today, the I Ching is experiencing a revival primarily due to the search for cultural roots among the Chinese, especially those outside of Mainland China.

CONCLUSION

Interest in the I Ching is now becoming worldwide, and incorporates influences from both the West and the East. There is no universal consensus at this time, however, on what the I Ching *really* says. As you have learned, over the ages there has been extensive research into the I Ching and development of related systems, some of which actually incorporate the I Ching text even though they use different types of prediction methods.

The I Ching has had a long and complex history. That it has survived would seem to be due to its ability to, in some fashion, satisfy the needs of its users. In large part, this probably is because of what it says, or in other words, the philosophy that is embedded within it. In the next chapter, we will explore this philosophical viewpoint in more detail.

3

THEORY
Understanding the I Ching

When people talk about the I Ching, they are usually talking about two different things—although they may not know it. The first is the *patterns of change* revealed in the I Ching text, which shows how events in life can change into different events. This means that the changes in our lives are not wholly chaotic, but rather seem to follow defined patterns. The second is how *predictions are generated.* Both of these are commonly, yet incorrectly, combined. They are distinctly different, and thus require separate discussions. This chapter examines the theoretical basis of the patterns of change as well as the methods by which the oracle is consulted.

UNDERSTANDING THE PATTERNS OF CHANGE

Although the ancient roots of the I Ching also nourished Taoism, the I Ching as a written document doesn't seem to have had any significant influence on Taoism until after the well-known Taoists Lao-Tzu and Chuang-tzu.[1] The following discussion of principles explains Taoism as it relates to the I Ching and how change occurs as revealed by the I Ching. Taoism as a philosophy is also involved with a number of other concepts (for example, virtue was a major interest) that are not covered in this book.

The two early classic Chinese philosophical works, *Tao Te Ching* and *I Ching,* are complementary in an interesting way. While the *Tao Te Ching* is a broad philosophical statement of Taoist concepts, the I Ching is more akin to a manual for putting Taoist principles into practice. Both works were developed many hundreds of years apart, and they were not planned to fit together like this. Nevertheless, by exploring the nature of the Tao, we can come to understand the essence of the patterns of change used in the I Ching. (For understanding the Tao through personal experience, see the inset "Experiencing the Tao" on page 40.)

Understanding the Tao is not easy. It is a highly abstract concept, and the word itself has many meanings. It can refer to an individual's unique path through life. It can also refer to the path itself, the rules on the path, the principle behind the path, or even personal inspiration and enlightenment in a specific time, place, or situation.[2]

Although the Tao is often referred to as an objective methodology—that is, a method for viewing life realistically and living it well—the Tao has a highly subjective quality to it. Regarding this, the scientist Johnson Yan says, "Its scope is much wider, sounding the depths of an ultimate reality beyond the reach of intellect. Unlike science, the *Tao* does not strive to be objective, quantitative, or precise." He then goes on to quote Han Yi, a Chinese philosopher from the T'ang Dynasty of about 1,500 years ago, who said, "People talk about their own *Tao,* which may not be my *Tao.*"[3] Clearly, the Tao cannot be simply or easily understood. Nevertheless, there *are* some underlying principles behind the operation of the Tao. In the spirit of Taoism, however, these would never be written out like steps in a recipe as they are below, but doing this will give a clearer view of these principles.

First Principle: The Tao Is a Dynamic Process

The universe as a whole is called *T'ai-chi.* It is the absolute, the all encompassing, the "everything in existence." This complex reality is represented in Figure 3.1 below, which you have likely seen before. Chances are, up to this point you have known this figure only as the yin/yang symbol. (More about yin and yang below.)

Figure 3.1. T'ai-chi.
The Universe as a whole;
everything in existence.

Since *T'ai-chi* is such a broad concept, other concepts were defined to refer to different aspects of it. The *Tao,* one of these concepts, represents the process and methods of how the universe expresses itself through action and over time. However, the ancients understood that the names given to *T'ai-chi* and *Tao* were just labels that cannot fully describe what they attempted to name. For instance, Shao Yung thought that the Tao wasn't a real thing, but rather a term for the interaction of the forces of yin and yang.[4]

Second Principle: "Factual Knowledge" Does Not Bring True Understanding

The *Tao,* and *T'ai-chi* as well, are inherently not understandable to the intellect. As a subjective thing, the Tao can be felt and, therefore, understood—but only as part of the human experience. Parts of it may, of course, be understood intellectually through the acquisition of factual knowledge, but they are not the Tao in its entirety or even truly in reality, and thus do not accurately express the Tao. In fact, as will be noted later, using the I Ching is a part of the process of coming to know *your* Tao through *your* experience in reality. (See the inset "Experiencing the Tao" on page 40.)

Third Principle: Yin and Yang Are the Forces of Change

The forces behind change are known as *yin* and *yang.* These are not forces in opposition; rather, these are forces that complement each other, and interact in different ways to produce a range of varied results. With *true opposites,* one force would undo what the other does. With these *complementary opposites,* however, both forces together create a new reality.

In this sense, knowing that yin and yang are also representations for male and female qualities is highly beneficial. For example, male and female qualities combine in many different ways to create our complex social environments—expressed in love, family, work, culture, and so on. This illustrates that yin and yang work together quite well in reality. This example also illustrates another important quality: Neither force can be wholly separate or independent of the other. Together, the forces create the wholeness of *T'ai-chi,* which they separately cannot. As one grows greater in intensity, the situation becomes unstable, and the impetus for the other force to grow in intensity increases. Thus, there is an inherent dynamic with the forces of yin and yang mixing in a continuous, inevitable process.

These principles are illustrated in Figure 3.1 on page 38. One color represents yin, and the other represents yang, and each flows into the other. The tiny drop of one color inside the greatest concentration of the other represents how intensity naturally breeds the birth of the opposite. These concepts were seen as not only applying to the realm of human relationships, but also to the realm of the physical world.[6] The forces of weather and the seasons are good natural examples of this.

Fourth Principle: Change Flows Through a Pattern of Possibilities

There is a constant ebb and flow among the various types of change that *yin* and *yang* bring about. No state is constant or steady for more than a brief moment in time. It is when one force is at its peak that the impetus to change becomes greatest. I am not

Experiencing the Tao

How can you *truly experience* the Tao? To begin with, this experience is more akin to an awareness that one arrives at through the unconsciousness of meditation. You cannot understand the Tao by *thinking*. You *become aware of the Tao*—without thought—using your body and your subconscious awareness of your life. You do this by ignoring your philosophical, religious, and political thoughts. Stop asking *what should be* and *what you think is.* Your whole intellectual process must be put to sleep. Only what you experience without thought is a full realization of reality. Do not think or analyze, rather just *be,* centering yourself wholly on the present. If you do this, you will eventually become aware of *what actually is.* Do not give your awareness names or judge it, for that interferes with *experiencing* it. Doing this, your path—*your Tao*—becomes part of you.[5]

When you act in accord with the understanding that you have gained from letting go of your thoughts, you will seem to instinctively follow the path of least resistance. If you do stray from this path, consciously trying to put yourself back on it will not find it. Yet, when you are ready, you will slip back onto the path without effort or thought. If you are striving for a goal but the time is not ripe, you cannot force it to come. Instead, when it is the proper time, the necessary things will happen easily. Thus, the Tao is elusive.

You experience the Tao as cycles, ever waxing and waning, which form your path. What you leave behind will come again. What you gain you will later lose. Something of what you lack can always be found within you. You feel a kinship with the world around you, and you know that nothing is entirely separate from you. You perceive the world as One Thing, knowing that the cycles of *yin* and *yang* are its pulse and that you are but one speck in its reality. Experiencing this, you are at the heart of the Tao.

Intellectually, you cannot help but be aware of these ideas, but this awareness is not *knowledge of the Tao.* The Tao is not a *thing.* It is *the necessary;* it is the empty center into which everything flows. You cannot point to it; you cannot *comprehend* it. You

talking about the direction of change as though it were a simple either/or choice like a railroad line that goes one way or the other. Rather, using the compass as an analogy, I am talking about the full circular range of all the compass directions.

Since the sixty-four hexagrams of the I Ching represent the universe of all the possible types of situations, they are all spaced around this imaginary compass rim. Each hexagram has, directly opposite it on this compass, the position of its complementary hexagram. When one hexagram changes into another, it is thus shown on this compass by a movement into another direction.

can only *experience* it. It is always present and ever changing, hidden behind the face of your daily life. Time and time again, we brush against it and do not know it. Thus, the Tao is subtle.

The processes of your *becoming* and *unbecoming* are all part of the Tao. There is no right or wrong in the Tao. There are only gradations of easy/hard, quick/slow, strong/weak, clear/confused, and other dualistic aspects. Your awareness of your Tao is uncertain but ultimately cannot be lost. Your cares are distractions from your experience of your Tao, as are your aspirations and fears. All are equal before it; all are influences you feel that ultimately do not truly matter. Your struggles define your life, within you and without, but they do not surmount the Tao. You are child of the Tao, and yet an inconstant orphan from it. Your potential is never greater than your Tao.

The Tao is both the most real and the most illusory of anything we can know in this life. It is both our salvation and what condemns us to spend our lives searching. The Tao is effortless, and we toil with the burdens of life. In some views it can be likened, in part, to fate and, in others, to God's guiding hand. It is neither, and it is both. It is the heart of the Working of Everything. Your Tao is the "magic touch" in your life.

One of the secrets of the I Ching is that it reveals something of the Tao to those who close their eyes to the clamor of the world and listen with their whole being. Using it, you can come closer to the essence of your Tao. Be careful though: your use of the I Ching will provide you only with a representation of your Tao—not its reality. Because it is not truly your Tao, it can mislead you if you listen with your desires or fears rather than with your whole essence. The I Ching, however, may be as close as we can come on this plane of existence to objectively seeing the Tao at work. Most important, if used correctly, it is the best means by which your essence can be refreshed by touching the Tao.

As you can see, the Tao is very deep. To come to know it, you must experience it through a different mode of awareness. Viewing the I Ching's answers can provide you with an alternate awareness of the essence of your life. This is a good way to begin experiencing the Tao. However, meditation on your life is the only way to truly attain this experience.

It is the ebb and flow of yin and yang qualities in different aspects of the situation that determine which new direction will be taken. This can be seen structurally in I Ching hexagrams by *changing lines,* sometimes called *moving lines.* They point to a different direction—that is, to another hexagram—in the inquirer's situation. (Refer to page 4 in Chapter 1 for a discussion of how changing lines are generated when the oracle is consulted.) Which specific hexagram a changing line is linked to is determined by the overall structure of the I Ching. Figure 3.2 on page 42 illustrates something of what this looks like from the perspective of a single hexagram.

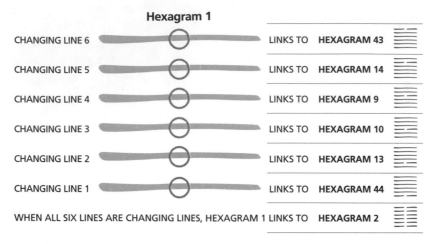

Figure 3.2. The hexagrams that result from each changing line of Hexagram 1, as well as all lines changing to Hexagram 2.

Figure 3.2 above shows that each of the changing lines in Hexagram 1 is linked to one other hexagram. Also, when all lines change to their opposites, it makes a link to Hexagram 2, the complementary hexagram. Note, however, this figure does not show the outcomes of multiple lines changing in different positions. In Hexagram 2, all lines changing links back to Hexagram 1. This situation can also be shown from the perspective of all the hexagrams. Figure 3.3 on page 43 shows the same linkages as Figure 3.2, but from the perspective of all sixty-four hexagrams.

The solid circle represents Hexagram 1. The heavy-lined circle represents the complementary Hexagram 2, with the thick connecting link indicating *all lines changing*. The six thin links radiating from Hexagram 1 represent the individual changing lines linking to, and deriving meanings from, six other hexagrams. Note, however, this diagram cannot show that Hexagram 1 can link to *any* of the unlinked hexagrams with the right combination of changing lines. For example, if two, three, four, or five changing lines occur in various line positions, Hexagram 1 will change into other hexagrams accordingly.

Fifth Principle: Change Is Predictable

The ancient Chinese realized that change was predictable in that it always *progresses through certain stages.* Indeed, this is one of the most important concepts in the I Ching. All life goes through a process of birth, growth, maturity, and death. Reality is always an expression of the process of coming into being, growing, declining, and passing out of existence—*in sequence.* The six lines of the hexagrams represent different statements of these processes applied to different life situations. How

Figure 3.3. The changing line linkages of Hexagram 1 from the perspective of all sixty-four hexagrams.

this is used in the I Ching text is discussed in more detail in "The Hexagram Lines" on page 48. In the West, we have a different perspective, and apply probability theory to try to understand change. For a perspective on how probability can give us insights into predictability in the I Ching, see the inset "The Probabilities of Change in the I Ching" on page 44.

All of these ideas of how change and evolution occur are based on the idea that how the universe behaves is replicated through the I Ching's system of hexagrams. There is an underlying structure that defines how the hexagrams are built and function. This will be discussed in the next section.

BUILDING THE I CHING'S HEXAGRAMS

To understand how the I Ching hexagrams are constructed, we must begin with the universe, already referred to as *T'ai chi*. The two primary qualities within *T'ai chi* have been previously identified as *yin* and *yang*. Yin and yang are also called the "two modes of action." *Yang* is the quality of action, maleness, light, heaven, and so on. *Yin* is the quality of receptivity, femaleness, darkness, earth, and so on. In the hexagrams, yin and yang are expressed by diagrammatic symbols as follows:

yang ⸺ *yin* ⸺ ⸺

As mentioned in Chapter 1, there are young and old versions of both line types. They also traditionally have numeric values assigned to them. (These values—6, 7, 8, and 9—are listed in Table 1.3 under the Three Coins Method on page 12.) In the I Ching, text is given *only* for the changing lines, but in defining the conceptual structure of the hexagrams, these changing lines aren't a factor.

Rather, the hexagram structure is built upon the principle that replicating a line

The Probabilities of Change in the J Ching

Statistical analysis can be applied to the I Ching's map of concepts to determine how often different kinds of situations will occur. In any of the basic methods for consulting the oracle described in Chapter 1, the probability of getting any of the sixty-four hexagrams is equally likely. However, this is not true for the changing lines within the hexagram. The following probabilities were calculated based on the Three Coins Method.

1 line changing	six possibilities	35.06% chance
2 lines changing	fifteen possibilities	29.66% chance
no lines changing	one possibility	17.80% chance
3, 4, and 5 lines changing	forty-one possibilities	17.45% chance
all lines changing	one possibility	00.03% chance
Totals	sixty-four possibilities	100.00%

Thus, there is a distinct bias toward different kinds of change that is built into the I Ching. This bias indicates which kinds of change will tend to occur more often (that is, in a general sense without regard to any specific situation). Thus, simply reading the text of the lines in a hexagram gives strong insights into the kinds of common results occurring in that hexagram's situation. Perhaps the ancient Chinese understood the importance of one changing line, since they felt the need to create text for each occurrence.

(that is, adding another level to the figure) automatically halves the characteristics to be described there. For example, take "water" as a concept and divide it into two concepts, and you then have "flowing water" and "frozen water" as the two new categories. This idea underlies how the entire I Ching is built, because working from the ground up, everything can be incorporated this way.

The two modes interact dynamically to create the four cycles of existence (previously mentioned in the Fifth Principle on page 42). These four cycles are called the "four images," and are represented by yang + yang as *greater yang,* yang + yin as *lesser yang,* yin + yang as *lesser yin,* and yin + yin as *greater yin.* These have also been used to represent a variety of fourfold actions, such as the four phases of the moon, the four compass directions, and the four seasons. Shao Yung thought the fourfold basis of change was a critical element in understanding evolution both in how things changed shape as well as how numerology reflected reality.[7]

The images then interact with the modes, adding a third line, and create the eight *trigrams.* The trigrams define basic categories of objects. When the trigrams interact with one another, they create the hexagrams, which are able to represent everything in the world—what the ancients called the "ten thousand things." Trigrams and hexagrams are more fully discussed below.

The Trigrams

There are only eight trigrams. Each trigram has a name and various unique attributes. However, there is some debate about what these attributes actually should be. A number of attributes are shown below, but there are many others not listed here, including materials, shapes, colors, numbers, elements, sounds, animals, Chinese astrology, parts of the body, illnesses, places, types of buildings, rooms, times of day, months, seasons, compass directions, weather, foods, tastes, plants, and so on. In fact, everything in the world should have a trigram to represent it.

The ancient Chinese used the trigrams to help define the meaning of each hexagram through symbolic interpretation too complex to easily explain here. The trigrams have also been used instead of hexagrams in other prediction systems related to the I Ching. Trigrams thus have an important relationship to the I Ching, but they need to be used carefully because they can be very easily misused. Some of their more important characteristics are shown below.

Trigram A
111 in number format

name:	Ch'ien (sounds like "chien")
phenomenon:	heaven
family member:	father
other person:	ruler, older man
characteristics:	strong, brave, active, solid, decisive, vital, powerful
abstraction:	creation, strong continued action

(Refer to Hexagram 1 on page 59 for the clearest expression of this trigram.)

Trigram B
100 in number format

name:	Chen (sounds like "jen")
phenomenon:	thunder
family member:	eldest son
person:	mature man
characteristics:	active, excited, diligent, threatening, angry, nervous, successful, musical, shocking, flying
abstraction:	movement, shock, initially strong but fading

(Refer to Hexagram 51 on page 265 for the clearest expression of this trigram.)

Trigram C

010 in number format

name:	K'an (sounds like "khan")
phenomenon:	water, clouds, rain
family member:	middle son
other person:	young man, adventurer, thief
characteristics:	dangerous, cunning, deceitful, aimless, clever, busy, depressed, sad, disturbed
abstraction:	gradually sinking, surrounded by pitfalls

(Refer to Hexagram 29 on page 175 for the clearest expression of this trigram.)

Trigram D

001 in number format

name:	Ken (sounds like "ghen")
phenomenon:	mountains
family member:	youngest son
other person:	teenager, bachelor, unemployed
characteristics:	independent, slow, indecisive, secretive, stagnant, quiet, stubborn, tough, contradictory
abstraction:	immobile, weak and stopped

(Refer to Hexagram 52 on page 270 for the clearest expression of this trigram.)

Trigram E

000 in number format

name:	K'un (sounds like "coon")
phenomenon:	earth
family member:	mother
other person:	queen, farmer, peasant, wife, servant, the masses
characteristics:	devoted, soft, flexible, weak, calm, empty, passive, cowardly, sickly
abstraction:	receptive, powerless

(Refer to Hexagram 2 on page 63 for the clearest expression of this trigram.)

Trigram F

011 in number format

name:	Sun (sounds like "soon")
phenomenon:	wind
family member:	eldest daughter

other person: middle-aged woman, widow, recluse
characteristics: yielding, gentle, weak, indecisive, fragrant, neat, obedient, excitable, restless
abstraction: gentle, penetrating, uniting with
(Refer to Hexagram 57 on page 290 for the clearest expression of this trigram.)

Trigram G
101 in number format

name: Li (sounds like "lee")
phenomenon: fire, sun
family member·   middle daughter
other person: middle-aged woman, intellectual, student
characteristics: light-giving, hot, agitated, enlightened, beautiful, dedicated
abstraction: reflecting brilliance, surrounded by glory
(Refer to Hexagram 30 on page 179 for the clearest expression of this trigram.)

Trigram H
110 in number format

name: Tui (sounds like "dway")
phenomenon: lake, cloud
family member: youngest daughter
other person: young girl, concubine, maid, servant, witch
characteristics: happy, smiling, laughing, harmonious, soft, gossipy, slanderous, broken, quarrelsome, critical
abstraction: joyous, free
(Refer to Hexagram 58 on page 294 for the clearest expression of this trigram.)

The Hexagrams

The wisdom of the I Ching as a pattern of changes is expressed through the hexagrams, not through the trigrams. As a student of the I Ching, this is where your energy and thought should be devoted initially. Each hexagram has a theme or central idea. Note that the meanings of the hexagrams are not consistently related to any trigram meaning, with the exception of the eight "doubled-trigram" hexagrams. In doubled-trigram hexagrams, both upper and lower trigrams are identical and are, therefore, the purest expression of that trigram's meaning in the hexagrams.

In the other hexagrams, there are diverse meanings for each trigram in the hexagram in which it falls; there is no simple, direct relationship, so it is not easy to describe. This is because different meanings can be attributed to the trigrams in different contexts. Therefore, you must be careful in trying to apply trigram meanings to hexagrams, such as the Chinese often did. In general, it is best *not* to apply the meaning of trigrams to specific hexagrams. There are other things, such as the hexagram lines, that are far more important to understanding the prediction.

The Hexagram Lines

The sixty-four hexagrams form only the "first level" of predictions that the I Ching gives. When the oracle produces a "changing line" in a hexagram, the prediction now gets additional meaning from a second hexagram. It is said at this point that the original hexagram is "evolving into" a second hexagram. Thus, in addition to the sixty-four basic meanings of hexagrams, the I Ching text contains an additional written meaning for each of the six lines in the hexagrams. This process defines a "second level" in the I Ching of 384 possible meanings.

Three factors are involved in how the meanings of the hexagram's six lines are determined. First, what is the meaning of the *original hexagram*? Second, what is the meaning of the *second hexagram*? And third, what is the meaning of the *line position in the hexagram*? To explain this latter factor, you need to know that each of the six line positions in the hexagram has its own meaning as an aspect of change. Taken as a whole, the six different lines convey the story of how the theme of each hexagram evolves over time. The first line represents the beginning of the theme. Each line above it represents an additional increment in time, which requires an increment of change. The top line represents the culmination of that theme. In any specific line, all three factors combine to produce the underlying meaning of the situation that the I Ching text is trying to convey.

When you read the text, you should always be very careful in taking its literal judgments to heart—that is, if it says that situation is good or bad—for several reasons: For one thing, *every* situation has both good and bad elements mixed in it. Be very aware of this and do not exaggerate the consequence. For another, depending on your specific situation, the reason something is good or bad might differ somewhat from what is assumed in the text. You might actually want a "bad" thing that is mentioned! Finally, the insights into the factual situation are what is truly important. The good or bad judgment is intended only as a guide to help you evaluate your course of action; it is usually not nearly as important as the other part.

There is one other special situation that should be noted—the case of *all lines changing*. While this occurs only rarely, it is important in the conceptual framework of the I Ching. All lines changing produces the *complementary opposite* to a hexagram. Showing this meaning for each hexagram (which the traditional text does only for hexagrams 1 and 2) helps in understanding the meanings of both of them.

The following are the general meanings of the different line positions in the hexagrams:

1st (bottom) line. This line usually represents the individual beginning something. He enters the lower trigram having low social position and little power or experience. Beginning is usually not in and of itself a very beneficial or very dangerous situation, although new beginnings can be favorable when appropriate. Other images implicit in this line are weakness, tentativeness, half-heartedness, and youth.

Parts of the body associated with this line are the feet and ankles, and the chin and mouth. This line also represents the peasantry or people as a mass. Sexually, it indicates potential that cannot yet be attained. This line thus also represents a foundation, but note that a foundation by itself is of little value and will not survive without other things to protect it.

2nd line. This line usually represents the individual obtaining a first position or goal in his endeavors. Now the benefits or dangers inherent in the situation are clear and the individual may have experienced and overcome them to some extent. However, usually this is a good and secure position. Other images implicit in this line are gaining confidence or strength, and the vigor of young adulthood.

Parts of the body associated with this line are the calves and knees, and the cheeks and lips on the face. This line also represents people as skilled workers, technicians, and scientists. Sexually, it indicates an adolescent sexual orientation. This line thus also represents strong supports upon which greater endeavors can be built.

3rd line. This line usually represents the place of the most difficulty or danger in the hexagram since it is the last line of the lower trigram and faces a gap or gulf in the transition to the upper trigram. The individual is now about to reach out and cross into the higher trigram, and this attempt could be a difficult or dangerous endeavor. Beginning such a transition is seen as the most vulnerable point for the individual. Other images implicit in this line are becoming a mature adult, the presence of external stress, and goals now becoming obstacles.

Parts of the body associated with this line are the thighs and the nose. This line also represents people as bureaucrats, politicians, and functionaries. Sexually, it indicates sexual adventuring and insecurity. This line thus also represents ideas and dreams struggling against reality.

4th line. This line usually represents the individual having completed the transition into a more elevated situation, but the position is not yet a fully mature or strong one. For example, the individual may have been awarded a high position by his leader; however, he still may be somewhat weak and dependent upon him.

Other images implicit in this line are success in setting new directions, overcoming significant difficulties, attaining new goals, being rewarded with responsibility, and reaching a position of leadership.

Parts of the body associated with this line are the abdomen and the ears. This line also represents people as consultants, administrators, or advisors to high officials. Sexually, it indicates partnership, marriage, and pregnancy. This line thus also represents assurance, competence, and creativity in the world.

5th line. This line usually represents the controlling position in the ideal hexagram, although many hexagrams have other controlling lines (the second line being the next most common). For example, the individual may have now risen to a position of true power and prestige, or have gained the maximum that he can from the direction this hexagram is going. This is generally the position of greatest intensity of the meaning of the hexagram. Other images implicit in this line are reaching full maturity, being in a position of the greatest authority, or having the greatest benefit.

Parts of the body associated with this line are the torso (chest and back), and the eyes. This line also represents people as high officials, leading officers of companies, presidents, and famous leaders of causes. Sexually, it indicates the peak of both male sexual dominance and female sexual nurturing. This line thus also represents the main support of a group, cause, or thing.

6th (top) line. This line usually represents the transition into another, different state. For example, this might be a conflict with the leader (since he has now risen above the leader in the fifth line), or the effect of excess, which can lead to a new beginning. So, transition is once again eminent. This transition is preparatory to the major change represented by the case of all lines changing. Thus, images of conflict, rejection, and reaction, or those of excess and culmination are common.

Parts of the body associated with this line are the neck, head, and forehead. This line also represents people as sages or retired leaders who still exercise moral leadership. Sexually, it indicates retiring from active sexual participation. This line thus also represents farsightedness and involvement in activities of a higher order.

All lines changing. This rare situation represents the change to the complementary hexagram. Refer to Figures 3.2 and 3.3 on pages 42 and 43 to see this concept expressed diagrammatically. Refer to Hexagrams in Number Order on page 327 for a list of all the complementary hexagrams. They also give a feel for how all the changing lines are conceptually linked to other hexagrams, so the entire structure of the I Ching forms an interwoven fabric of ideas, rather like a piece of chain mail, with all the circles interlocked.

Individual parts of the body do not relate to this, since the entire body is referred to. As to people, this represents a rebirth, so it could mean a child, a totally reformed person who has renounced his past, or the next life after death. All lines changing represents the qualities of the situation having changed into their *complementary opposite* values. For example, in Hexagram 1 (which means acting fiercely), it represents strong action going with the flow, so it feels effortless. In Hexagram 2 (which means going with the flow), it represents gaining the power and ability to act strongly without struggling to attain it.

Although this idealized progression through the lines generally holds true, each hexagram is unique, and so each situation has been individually evaluated. This was done by determining how the line fits into the meaning of the hexagram—both thematically and structurally. Does that type of line (*yin* or *yang*) work effectively in that place in the hexagram? What about the relationship with the trigrams? Clearly, these are complex considerations and require thoughtful judgment. In addition, the original I Ching text preceded the development of much of this thinking by Confucians, and for that reason the original meanings deserve greater emphasis rather than those later annotations.

BEYOND THE BASICS

The structure of the trigrams and hexagrams are only some of the conceptual models that are related to the I Ching. Some of the earliest models the ancient Chinese developed were numerological. The most ancient numeric map is the *Ho T'u* (shown in Figure 3.4 below). Look closely and you will see it is like a primitive magic square since it has certain balancing properties. Later, a true magic square called the *Lo Shu* was constructed (this is the one used in "What is a Magic Square?" on page 33). The ancient Chinese derived a number of important numerical properties from these diagrams. For example, in Figure 3.4, by defining the odd numbers as yang (they called them *heavenly numbers*) and the even numbers as yin (called *earthly numbers*), they determined that the sum of heavenly numbers is 25, and the sum of earthly numbers is 30. Through incorporating the two modes of action (doubling these numbers), they determined there were 50 heavenly cycles and 60 earthy cycles. While further discussion goes beyond the scope of this book, this became an important component in other prediction models. This illustrates how these concepts—which derive from the foundation of the I Ching—were built by the Chinese into ever more complex models.

The ancient Chinese also created two "compass arrangements" of the trigrams to illustrate their relationship to the fundamental concepts of *season, direction,* and *number* (see Figure 3.5 on page 52). (If these are a little confusing at first, note

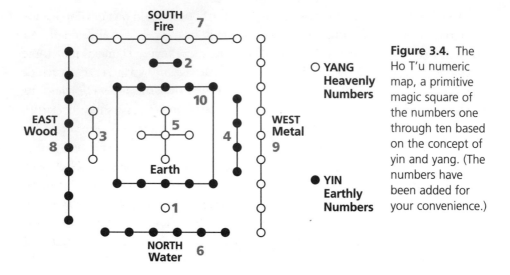

Figure 3.4. The Ho T'u numeric map, a primitive magic square of the numbers one through ten based on the concept of yin and yang. (The numbers have been added for your convenience.)

that in Chinese compasses North is placed at the bottom.) The Earlier Heaven compass arrangement, on the left, has its trigrams positioned according to ancient Chinese principles of evolutionary change. Notice also the trigrams make a magic square here, since all the axes balance (by summing to 111). The Later Heaven compass arrangement, on the right, superimposes a later arrangement of trigrams onto the *Lo Shu* (the magic square shown on page 33), and thereby gives different numerical values to the trigrams. This arrangement represents the trigrams' application to matters in the human realm, and so these trigram numbers are critical in many different esoteric Chinese systems, which are also related to the I Ching.[8]

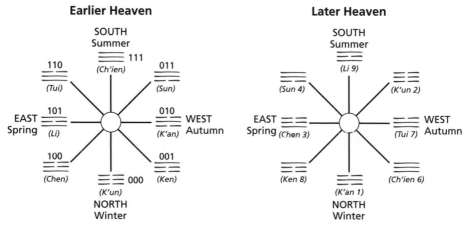

Figure 3.5. The relationship of the trigrams to the concepts of season, direction, and number as shown by ancient Chinese compass arrangements based on magic squares.

Later during the Neo-Confucian period, Shao Yung created another way of organizing the yin-yang principle and understanding how it relates to the hexagrams. This is shown in the *Hsien T'ien* (see Figure 3.6 below). (The column at the left has been added for clarification.) The 0 level is the Supreme Ultimate, which was a Neo-Confucian designation for *T'ai-chi.* Level 1 shows the emergence of yin and yang from it. Level 2 gives a further illustration of how yin and yang properties emerge and are expressed. Level 3 contains the trigrams (indicated here by the letter codes A through H). Levels 4 and 5 represent intermediate states that occur in the nature of things. At the top, level 6, are the sixty-four hexagrams. The hexagrams are not in random order. In fact, Shao Young used this order of the hexagrams (which is given in Hexagrams in Line Order on page 330) to construct his famous sequential list of hexagrams, as represented by the combination of the numbers 0 and 1. This order is referred to mathematically as a "binary sequence." He also arranged this as a circle, showing that the evolution could cycle indefinitely. He understood this sequence of hexagrams to be an actual description of the evolution of events through time, and he incorporated this into the *I Ching Lifechart.* (See the inset "Shao's Perspectives on I Ching Prediction" on page 54.)

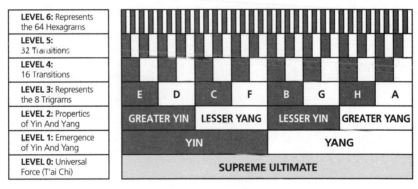

Figure 3.6. The Hsien T'ien. This diagram shows how the sixty-four hexagrams emerge from the Supreme Ultimate.

These ancient analytical models are representative of the kinds of products that came out of centuries of thought and investigation by many talented minds. Briefly discussing them as I have here does not convey their depth or richness. These models are critical to more sophisticated usage of the I Ching, the *I Ching Lifechart, feng shui,* and other related systems. Fortunately, however, to use the I Ching it is not necessary to master any of these, because the I Ching text itself expresses predictions comparatively easily. In this text, the underlying organizing principles have been clearly emphasized, so that the problems you face as a user are mostly of application of predictions, rather than their derivation from the ancient original text.

Shao's Perspectives on J Ching Prediction

Shao Yung's chief goal was to show people how to view the world to see the truth, that is, as though they were impartial, observant, wise men. He was very concerned with our normal inability to truthfully perceive things in the world around us. Shao insisted that the "stages [of change]" and "categories," which he used to describe the world, are *real*, and not just subjective perceptions or artificial constructs. He believed that the I Ching was a critical document because it was structured the same way as reality. Shao also emphasized the importance of learning as being essential for understanding destiny and for perfecting one's character. Use of the I Ching, thus, is an important part of learning about ourselves, the world around us, and our destinies.

Clearly, Shao makes big claims, but should we really take them seriously? In fact, how effective was he in his predictions? While it is hard to know the truth, there are many amazing stories preserved in Chinese folklore and literature of Shao's predictions, even of predicted events occurring after his death. Also, the noted Chinese philosopher Ch'eng I, who did not approve of Shao's numerological systems or worldview, quite

THE ORACLE'S ACCESS TO THE HIDDEN PATTERNS IN LIFE

In contrast to the voluminous writing on the Tao and the I Ching over the millennia, there has been very little written about theories underpinning how the predictions are obtained. That is, why does the *specific methodology* that the oracle uses *work*? In Chapter 2, it was noted that the ancient Chinese believed the oracle's answers came from ancestors who were trying to help guide them. As ancestor worship gradually declined, this became somewhat more generalized to mean simply "heaven" providing guidance to those on earth who were seeking it. This idea has apparently not changed much in China over the last 2,000 years.

Johnson Yan, a biological scientist and student of the I Ching, notes that Han Yi in the T'ang Dynasty made the comment that, "The *I* is strange but regular and lawful." Yan goes on to indicate that it likely means that the I Ching is able to produce "order out of chaos."[9] Yan further compares the Tao to science, calling it "informative, systematic, deductive and predictive." Yet, paradoxically, he also says that it is the ultimate principle of change and incorporates chance. He says the ability of the Tao to predict the future depends on its ability to take chance and randomness into account. This ability to change, he says, is the "most peculiar aspect of the Tao."[10]

clearly affirmed that Shao was able to predict people's life spans.[11] Based upon our strong emphasis on proof, his being able to predict things such as this would be considered a remarkable feat, and serve as strong substantiation for his theories.

His calculation systems (such as *Plum Blossom Numerology* and *I Ching Lifecharts*) have special significance for us today because of our heavy emphasis on empirical research. The best of his systems are testable, although they are computationally complex. Unfortunately, there do not appear to have been any serious empirical studies of them. However, informal investigation indicates that some of them truly seem to work. Thus, there seems to be real support for his ideas about hidden patterns in life, even though this concept is usually not taken seriously in our world today.

In retrospect, looking at Shao's work, we are struck by some of its parallels to modern science. Shao insisted that the foundation of the world was based on fundamental organizing principles, and in particular, on numeric structures. He used mathematics and classifying principles to create an objective calculation process. He believed an empirical perspective on the world would further our attainment of human values. Although he lived a thousand years ago, what he was saying fundamentally makes sense in our time.

The questions these ideas raise are formidable. How can the oracle be *systematic, deductive,* and *predictive,* as well as *changing and incorporate chance*? Aren't these two sets of qualities contradictory? How can predictions be both "predestined"—based on the external tables of numbers that Shao's method uses, for example—and yet be capable of incorporating change in some dynamic, random way? There is no simple answer to this, and I know of no ancient Chinese answers to this question.

You have learned that the I Ching can be used in two very different ways to generate predictions. One is the traditional *ad hoc* inquiry method using yarrow stalks, coins, or other random-chance generators, which are those methods described in Chapter 1. The other is through more advanced systems such as the I Ching Lifecharts, based on Shao Yung's work. However, regardless of the system used, the I Ching text is a statement of how things evolve in the world through *the patterns of change.* This is a road map of how one situation evolves into another. It does not matter if you enter the map from one edge or the other; the terrain is still on the map. Figure 3.7 on page 56 illustrates the two different types of prediction systems—*ad hoc* and lifecharts—and how they relate to the I Ching's text.

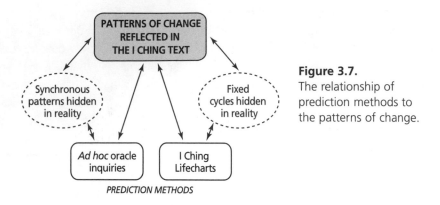

Figure 3.7.
The relationship of
prediction methods to
the patterns of change.

CONCLUSION

This chapter discussed the I Ching as it related to the Tao. Also, it has explored the connection between the Tao and the patterns of change. We've looked at the structure of the trigrams and hexagrams and have gone beyond the basics to look at the development of other prediction systems, which opens a new perspective on the I Ching.

Having the ability to obtain both time-specific *and* accurate patterns tells us one important thing: the patterns of change described in the text of the I Ching are fundamentally valid as they apply to human life. In a broad way, this also confirms the reality of the Tao and the numerical basis of reality.

I CHING

THE HEXAGRAMS
With Interpretive Text

Before you begin to explore this version of the I Ching text, it's helpful to understand how the text is laid out. Although the numbers of the hexagrams are always the same in I Ching books, hexagram titles may vary from one translation to another. The titles given in this text are designed to express the general meaning of the hexagrams as succinctly as possible. In addition to listing the common traditional titles, the titles given by Greg Whincup and by Kerson and Rosemary Huang are sometimes noted. Their recent historical translations of the I Ching more accurately convey the original meanings. When other titles do not reasonably convey the meaning of the hexagram, they are described here as being "misleading."

Below each hexagram number and title, a note is made of the trigrams and lines that make up the hexagram. In this book, alphabetic codes (A through H) are used to represent the eight trigrams, and the numbers 0 and 1 are used to represent the yin and yang lines that compose the hexagram. (See page 5 for an explanation of how to use these to find a hexagram number; also refer to the hexagram lookup tables on pages 325 and 326.) Following that, the complementary hexagram number and its general meaning are given. The complementary hexagram represents the "complementary opposite" meaning of the hexagram. It is created by changing yin lines to yang lines, and vice versa. (Refer to page 5 for a full discussion of changing lines, and to Hexagrams in Number Order on page 327 for a list of all the hexagrams.)

As you learned previously, eight of the hexagrams are created by doubling each of the eight trigrams. When a hexagram is made up of doubled trigrams, special note is made immediately following the general meaning of the hexagram. For a discussion on doubled trigrams, see page 47.

Following a full description of the hexagram's meaning, the meaning of each line is conveyed. The hexagram and changing line numbers are shown at the left of the page in the format 11.1, which indicates that the hexagram is number 11, and the changing line is number 1. The situation of all lines changing is shown by 11.all. Adjacent to the hexagram and line number, you will see either *Yang 9* or *Yin 6.* These labels indicate which type of changing line (Yin 6 or Yang 9) occurs in that position. (The numerical values are kept here for reasons of historical accuracy, and you need not concern yourself with them in using the I Ching text.) The "derives from" reference further to the right indicates the connection between that line and the hexagram that helps give the line its symbolic meaning. See page 48 for more on how the meanings of the lines are derived. For an overview of how all the hexagrams interconnect through the changing lines, see Hexagram Interconnections on page 332.

Please note that although masculine pronouns (he, his, and him) are used throughout the text, they represent people of either sex in all situations. This was done to avoid awkward phrasing within sentences. Similarly, the leader mentioned in the text can be a supervisor, a partner, a spouse, a moral or religious authority, or someone you look up to. When leadership is mentioned, it doesn't necessarily indicate a formal arrangement; it can be an organizing and uniting influence that allows people to get along, accomplish goals, and share rewards. Submission is the opposite of leadership. It reflects people accepting their roles and assisting their leaders.

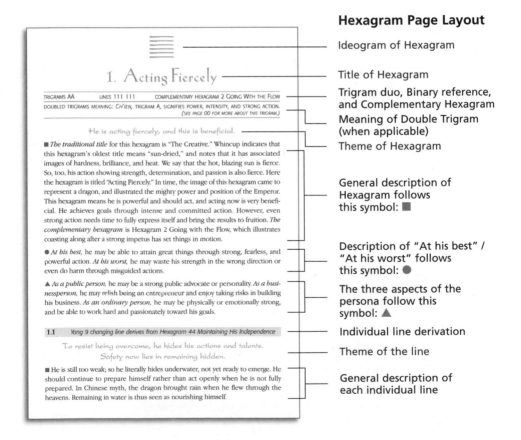

Hexagram Page Layout

Ideogram of Hexagram

Title of Hexagram

Trigram duo, Binary reference, and Complementary Hexagram

Meaning of Double Trigram (when applicable)

Theme of Hexagram

General description of Hexagram follows this symbol: ■

Description of "At his best" / "At his worst" follows this symbol: ●

The three aspects of the persona follow this symbol: ▲

Individual line derivation

Theme of the line

General description of each individual line

1. Acting Fiercely

TRIGRAMS AA   LINES 111 111   COMPLEMENTARY HEXAGRAM 2 GOING WITH THE FLOW

DOUBLED TRIGRAMS MEANING: *CH'IEN,* TRIGRAM A, SIGNIFIES POWER, INTENSITY, AND STRONG ACTION.
(SEE PAGE 45 FOR MORE ABOUT THIS TRIGRAM.)

He is acting fiercely, and this is beneficial.

■ *The traditional title* for this hexagram is "The Creative." Whincup indicates that this hexagram's oldest title means "sun-dried," and notes that it has associated images of hardness, brilliance, and heat. We say that the hot, blazing sun is fierce. So, too, his action showing strength, determination, and passion is also fierce. Here the hexagram is titled "Acting Fiercely." In time, the image of this hexagram came to represent a dragon, and illustrated the mighty power and position of the Emperor. This hexagram means he is powerful and should act, and acting now is very beneficial. He achieves goals through intense and committed action. However, even strong action needs time to fully express itself and bring the results to fruition. *The complementary hexagram* is Hexagram 2 Going with the Flow, which illustrates coasting along after a strong impetus has set things in motion.

● *At his best,* he may be able to attain great things through strong, fearless, and powerful action. *At his worst,* he may waste his strength in the wrong direction or even do harm through misguided actions.

▲ *As a public person,* he may be a strong public advocate or personality. *As a businessperson,* he may relish being an entrepreneur and enjoy taking risks in building his business. *As an ordinary person,* he may be physically or emotionally strong, and be able to work hard and passionately toward his goals.

| 1.1 | Yang 9 changing line derives from Hexagram 44 Maintaining His Independence |

To resist being overcome, he hides his actions and talents.
Safety now lies in remaining hidden.

■ He is still too weak; so he literally hides underwater, not yet ready to emerge. He should continue to prepare himself rather than act openly when he is not fully prepared. In Chinese myth, the dragon brought rain when he flew through the heavens. Remaining in water is thus seen as nourishing himself.

● *At his best,* he may be a scholar or recluse who has subtle or hidden effects, or he may be a strong person preparing himself. He will not desire power or fame, and he will enjoy a quiet life. *At his worst,* he may be a recluse living poorly. He struggles, but cannot easily develop his own inner power and so suffers accordingly.

▲ *As a public person,* he may expect to remain behind the scenes or be a little-used resource. *As a businessperson,* he may find that his preparations are not yet complete. *As an ordinary person,* he could experience a period of inactivity, but if he does not prepare himself, he could experience many troubles later.

1.2	*Yang 9 changing line derives from Hexagram 13 Serving on a Team*

He seeks to join those who can help him progress.

■ He appears publicly, ready to use his talents, but he should first find those from whom he can gain valuable information. Finding good helpers now is important.

● *At his best,* he may rise greatly in life and gain fame and wealth due to his talents and the assistance of others. *At his worst,* he may succeed, but to a lesser extent.

▲ *As a public person,* he may find someone from whom he learns key information, which he can use to great effect. *As a businessperson,* he may develop a successful partnership. *As an ordinary person,* he may expect profits due to an association with another or a marriage with someone who complements him.

1.3	*Yang 9 changing line derives from Hexagram 10 Taking Risky Action*

He acts carefully and is alert to danger.
Thus, his risky actions cause him no harm.

■ He actively works toward his goals, yet he is watchful and prepared for danger from unexpected quarters. With this attitude, he can develop his goals and no harm will come to him.

● *At his best,* he may rise as much by his sense of caution as well as by his accomplishments. He is able to take difficult problems and handle them easily. *At his worst,* he may be inconsistent or lazy, and could succeed as much by luck as by his own efforts. He may also be too self-centered to notice how his actions may harm others.

▲ *As a public person,* he may find himself very involved in something and be concerned about his reputation because of it, but nothing really harmful comes of it. *As a businessperson,* he may experience much activity but fear too little profit, or fear conflicts from competitors or disloyal employees. *As an ordinary person,* he may be very busy, and have continual worries that disturb his rest.

1.4 *Yang 9 changing line derives from Hexagram 9 Restraining Himself*

His attempt to progress results in some success,
but because he restrains himself he gains only a place of safety.

■ He is successful in his striving to some degree; however, he found only safety. So, it is only a limited degree of improvement.

● *At his best,* he may be recognized for his courage and other attributes. He may not become famous, but he will be respected and enjoy a good position. *At his worst,* he may find himself limited by his fear; he may not respect his abilities, and so only attempt easy things. This brings him only modest attainments and some unhappiness.

▲ *As a public person,* he may seek advancement, but it may become a dead end. *As a businessperson,* he may develop an enterprise that succeeds and becomes a stable niche business. *As an ordinary person,* he may find the period generally good, or he may get a stable and secure job.

1.5 *Yang 9 changing line derives from Hexagram 14 Relying on His Allies*

He gains through his allies. Working with them and with others
better than himself, he can attain greater things than he could alone.

■ Now is the time for him to seek out allies or even a great leader. While his own accomplishments can be significant, working with powerful allies (especially someone greater than himself) gives him an important opportunity to grow profoundly and to achieve even greater things. The greater his communal effort, the more effective his results will be.

● *At his best,* he may attain a high office or become a widely respected leader. Wealth may not be a concern, yet he will have plenty of money and enjoy a good life. *At his worst,* he may often interact with important leaders, and feel small by comparison. He may desire even greater fame and fortune, yet not learn the lessons he needs to attain his goal. He may, however, still enjoy a bountiful life.

▲ *As a public person,* he may reach a high position and learn how to preserve his position from other officials. *As a businessperson,* he may gain good profits, and learn important business tips from very shrewd businessmen. *As an ordinary person,* he may enjoy a very positive period, and may be helped by his superior or through his mate, or develop a good relationship with someone who instructs him.

1.6   *Yang 9 changing line derives from Hexagram 43 Escaping Harm*

He has gone too far in his actions and regrets it.
Now he can avoid more harm only by changing his course of action.

■ He has pushed himself beyond a safe or desirable limit and experiences regret. He may have isolated himself, or perhaps he got in trouble by not following good advice, or perhaps he now realizes that he can never fully attain his goals. Understanding his limitations in his present situation brings him regret. Changing his actions will allow him to escape greater harm later.

● *At his best,* he may learn from his error, and his regrets will make him sensitive to how to improve in the future. This could bring him some benefit and balance his regret. *At his worst,* he may be lost in his isolation or arrogance. This could bring him unhappiness and grief.

▲ *As a public person,* he may face demotion due to a bad decision or retirement. *As a businessperson,* through his own greed, he may find himself trapped in a business deal which is turning sour. *As an ordinary person,* he may expect ongoing problems due to a bad decision, or it could also be the time for a major change.

1.ALL   *All lines changing derives from Hexagram 2 Going with the Flow*

He is one of a group of leaders, none of whom is supreme.
With such collective strength, he progresses just by going with the flow.

■ In the traditional text, the image here is of a band of dragons, none of which is superior to the others. Thus, he is part of a team of powerful equals. Such a team can be extraordinarily effective. (This illustrates the first half of the complementary pairing of hexagrams. Here the transition is from Hexagram 1 Acting Fiercely to Hexagram 2 Going with the Flow; see Hexagram 2 for the second half.)

● *At his best,* he may be part of a group that changes the world in a positive way. He will thus enjoy success and happiness. *At his worst,* he is one of a group that cannot resolve questions of leadership or means to their goals among themselves, and, as a result, too much of their energy and time is wasted on internal squabbles. Thus, their practical result is far less than it should be. While this is unfortunate, he will still gain desirable results.

▲ *As a public person,* he may be part of a powerful governing committee. *As a businessperson,* he may be a business leader who is easily able to work with others, or one of a group of partners. *As an ordinary person,* he may be in a group or clique, or volunteer in a community or service organization.

2. Going With the Flow

TRIGRAMS EE	LINES 000 000	COMPLEMENTARY HEXAGRAM 1 ACTING FIERCELY

DOUBLED TRIGRAMS MEANING: *K'UN*, TRIGRAM E, SIGNIFIES CALM, PASSIVENESS, OBEDIENCE, AND ACCEPTANCE.
(SEE PAGE 46 FOR MORE ABOUT THIS TRIGRAM.)

He is going with the flow of events, and being receptive is beneficial.
If he struggles, he will lose his way. Yet, by being receptive he will
eventually regain it. If he pushes others, he will lose friends;
however, if he looks within, he will gain new ones.
Receptivity in all its forms brings some benefit.

■ *The traditional title* for this hexagram is "The Receptive." The meaning of this hexagram is based on one of the most ancient images in the traditional text, that of water flowing over the land, following the terrain. Most commentators today title this "Receptiveness" or "Responsiveness." Here it is titled "Going with the Flow" in line with its earliest and most essential image. Later images of this hexagram related it to the earth (which is the meaning of the trigram in this doubled-trigram hexagram) but kept the essential meaning the same. Gently flowing water is responsive to what directs it to the highest degree. What could better symbolize receptivity to the Tao? Although a responsive stance might seem weak or negative, it is, in fact, powerfully positive. Receptivity to the Tao brings enlightened self-interest, which is essential for happiness as well as for success. He progresses by preparing and positioning himself, then having things come to him without struggling for them. *The complementary hexagram* is Hexagram 1 Acting Fiercely, which illustrates that going with the flow ultimately can even incorporate acting strongly, which is the culmination of enlightened self-interest.

● *At his best,* he may understand the tendencies in the world around him, and by his subtle "non-action," he prepares himself and benefits. *At his worst,* he may be blind and weak, a victim of things outside his understanding.

▲ *As a public person,* he may ride a wave of public opinion, relying on polls and his party for support. *As a businessperson,* he may be in the right place at the right time with his business. *As an ordinary person,* he may find it easier to go along with external events than to try to manipulate them to get what he wants.

He is beginning a relationship but knows it cannot progress now.
He will have to wait until later.

■ In the traditional text, he is treading on frost, and knows that deeper snows will lie ahead. He needs to learn when to halt and what other decisions are proper to a time of resistance to progress. Progress can only come later.

● *At his best,* he may be careful and prepare well for decline and stoppage so that later he can advance easily again. *At his worst,* he may scheme and manipulate others to try to get what he wants now.

▲ *As a public person,* he may feel misrepresented or misunderstood. *As a businessperson,* he may encounter resistance through increasing regulations, growing competition, or other deterioration in the market. *As an ordinary person,* he may find that he is overwhelmed by growing personal problems; however, these problems are not as significant to a young person as they are to an older one.

He is dutiful and proper in how he leads others.
Although he is not strong, matters are generally beneficial for him.

■ In the traditional text, he is "straight and square." His imperfections are likely due to competing demands and limited abilities. Although he is a very good subordinate, he is not as effective as a real leader might be. In this situation, however, even he can gain some benefit.

● *At his best,* he may rise to a high position, faithfully doing whatever works, and gain fame and an easy life in this way. *At his worst,* he may be stubborn and rigidly honest, perhaps offending others around him, yet hc will still enjoy a modest life through his integrity.

▲ *As a public person,* he may advance under the tutelage of a great leader. *As a businessperson,* he may achieve recognition as a very honorable businessman and enjoy both profits and a good reputation. *As an ordinary person,* he may benefit slightly by doing the right things, such as being a good worker, dutiful mate, or good citizen.

2.3   *Yin 6 changing line derives from Hexagram 15 Acting with Propriety*

In a difficult situation, he acts properly. This does him no harm, although immediate benefits do not come. Ultimately, success comes from acting with humility, patience, and propriety.

■ He serves in a role in which his talents and abilities are hidden. He likely feels limited by difficulties and problems. He will find success only by doing the right thing consistently.

● *At his best,* he may be valued after he has shown he can contribute. *At his worst,* he may attain only modest recognition and benefits from long-lived loyalty.

▲ *As a public person,* he may work for a long time behind the scenes for an important goal, and ultimately gain public recognition from his contribution. *As a businessperson,* he may find that he is working hard to prepare his enterprise for eventual success. *As an ordinary person,* he may not gain what he hoped at the time, but his leader (or mate) will eventually bring benefits to him.

2.4   *Yin 6 changing line derives from Hexagram 16 Standstill*

He is at a standstill and does not use his talents, so he will neither gain nor lose. He knows he must wait longer before he can progress.

■ His talents remain unused and his potential remains unfilled. Thus, he is at a standstill and cannot advance. In time, this will change.

● *At his best,* he may be in a restricted position, attain some limited success, but ultimately have little effect. *At his worst,* he may be a lackadaisical or cowardly person and gain only very modest attainments, but he will not really suffer from his situation.

▲ *As a public person,* he may believe that he should not risk anything. *As a businessperson,* he may decide to wait for better times before acting. *As an ordinary person,* he may experience a stagnant period with few opportunities or rewards, or find himself in a closed-in situation.

2.5   *Yin 6 changing line derives from Hexagram 8 Entering an Alliance*

He is entering an alliance, and with this gains a favorable situation.

■ Whincup notes that it has been suggested that this line, which traditionally is read as "yellow skirt," actually should be read as "jade pendants." Jade pendants were used in ancient times to indicate a high official. Usually the highest position that can be attained going with the flow is that of advisor or minister.

● *At his best,* he may achieve high status, be respected by many people, and be blessed with a very fortunate life himself. *At his worst,* he may not achieve great things, but he will be comfortable and respected.

▲ *As a public person,* he may attain a powerful yet secure position. *As a businessperson,* he may profit greatly with little risk or without gaining enemies. *As an ordinary person,* he may enjoy a very good period, gain a fine home or job, or get beautiful clothing or jewelry.

2.6   *Yin 6 changing line derives from Hexagram 23 Being in a Collapsing Situation*

He is in a collapsing situation and fighting a struggle that perhaps no one can win.

■ He is no longer docile and receptive, but is struggling mightily in a difficult, collapsing situation. He sweats from effort, or even bleeds from his wounds. The result is in doubt.

● *At his best,* he may have attained a responsible position that he now feels forces him into a struggle he does not wish but must pursue. *At his worst,* his arrogance or conceit may have blinded him and brought this conflict about when it could have been avoided.

▲ *As a public person,* he may be involved in a struggle with another official or a policy. *As a businessperson,* he may find business competition intense and damaging, or be very active in internal competition in his company. *As an ordinary person,* he may expect a difficult and eventful period, especially conflicts with a coworker, family member, or friend.

2.ALL   *All lines changing derives from Hexagram 1 Acting Fiercely*

By going with the flow, he will gain power naturally.

■ Here he expresses perfect harmony with the Tao. He will not struggle, and yet he will attain power. Once he has power, he will then be able to act, exercising his power fiercely. (This illustrates the completion of the first complementary pairing of hexagrams, whereby the meaning of Hexagram 2 is transformed back into Hexagram 1 when all its lines become their opposites.)

● *At his best,* he may possess perfect clarity of mind and so can sense outside motivating forces and respond to them minimally but accurately. With such grace and ease, he will enjoy great benefit regardless of what he does. *At his worst,* he may be still, not as a result of internal clarity but from stress. His doubts and fears will inhibit his perceptions and actions, and thus he will not gain as much, nor will he enjoy his life as much.

▲ *As a public person,* he may be sought by those who want his approval. *As a businessperson,* he may truly understand his market and be happy it is moving in his direction. *As an ordinary person,* he may enjoy a period of rest and relaxation, recover strongly from past ills, or have some bounty come to him without effort.

3. Gathering Support

TRIGRAMS BC   LINES 100 010   COMPLEMENTARY HEXAGRAM 50 GOVERNING MATTERS

It is beneficial for him to gain supporters rather than pursue his goals by himself. It is even better to find those who will act for him.

■ *The traditional title* for this hexagram is "Difficulty at the Beginning," although this is somewhat misleading. Here the title "Gathering Support" is used. This signifies that before he can begin his advance, he must prepare himself properly. Finding those who will support him is essential, and he should not act before this has been done. If he can find those who will act along with him, or even in his stead, he will be even stronger and more effective. *The complementary hexagram* is Hexagram 50 Governing Matters, which illustrates how support is used after it has been gathered.

● *At his best,* he may understand what he needs to succeed and be able to reach out to others for those qualities. *At his worst,* he may feel his weaknesses so much he tries to gain emotional support from others rather than addressing his other more important needs.

▲ *As a public person,* he may have the ability to make public appeals for volunteers or causes. *As a businessperson,* he may know how to select assistants for business projects. *As an ordinary person,* he may gather others and work toward shared goals, or know how to obtain assistance to help him with his needs.

3.1   *Yang 9 changing line derives from Hexagram 8 Entering an Alliance*

At the start he has serious doubts, so he strengthens his position by gaining allies before proceeding.

■ He is hesitant and has grave doubts. In the very beginning, this may be beneficial prudence. To eliminate his concerns, he should correct weaknesses and find others who will guide and assist him. A proper beginning is an important first step, and through these actions, he will have done all he can to assure success.

● *At his best,* he may turn his doubts into highly effective corrective actions and beneficial relationships, and thereby be highly successful later. *At his worst,* he may be filled with suspicion, doubt, and indecision, and struggle to compensate but not be very successful.

▲ *As a public person,* he may decide that it is essential for him to build alliances now as a hedge to potential problems. *As a businessperson,* he may succeed by looking for and finding critical people who can help him or inside information. *As an ordinary person,* he may feel very uncertain and need to rely on friends and family to compensate.

3.2   *Yin 6 changing line derives from Hexagram 60 Having Limited Resources*

He has gathered his forces, but he still cannot progress.
An important alliance he seeks is refused because of his limited
resources. This alliance could come about after more preparation.

■ He believes himself properly prepared; yet, his progress is halted before he has accomplished his goal. The leader he intended to join (or the woman he intended to marry) has refused to accept him. Although seriously disappointing, it is only a temporary setback, since he can eventually progress with more preparation.

● *At his best,* he may have some relationship troubles in this period but deals with them calmly and appropriately, so in his later life he can gain happiness and success through these same relationships. *At his worst,* he may act badly when confronted with rejection and cause irreparable harm to them, but from this he may eventually learn how to deal with relationships and then gain benefits from new ones.

▲ *As a public person,* he may carefully and unhurriedly build his reputation or program, knowing that ideas take time to bear fruit. *As a businessperson,* he may enter into a period of stagnation or of partnerships that fall through. *As an ordinary person,* he may desire a marriage with someone who initially rejects him, have a pregnancy or childbirth delayed, or be involved in a lengthy litigation before it is resolved in his favor.

3.3   *Yin 6 changing line derives from Hexagram 63 Beginning a New Task*

His attempt to gather support halts. Continuing would make
matters worse because of his lack of experience or ability.

■ In the traditional text, he is likened to a hunter pursuing game into a forest without assistance from a forest guide. He does not know what lies ahead, and pressing ahead alone would bring him only trouble.

● *At his best,* he may be able to temper his enthusiasm and energy with the wisdom of knowing when to hold back. Although he may be disappointed, he avoids more serious misfortune. *At his worst,* he may not be able to stop from recklessly pursuing his goals when warning signs appear, and thus continually suffers from his mistakes.

▲ *As a public person,* he may be accused of corruption or seeking influence improperly, or have troubles due to lack of preparing necessary alliances. *As a businessperson,* he may suffer losses due to inadequate information or lack of properly skilled staff. *As an ordinary person,* he may break the law and be caught and punished, or generally get into trouble due to inadequate preparation.

3.4   *Yin 6 changing line derives from Hexagram 17 Hunting*

His hunt for support succeeds in finding a sincere alliance.
Now his forces are ready, and this is a favorable time to advance.

■ Now it is favorable for his desired marriage to proceed. His forces are ready, waiting, and this time he will succeed. The doubts at the beginning clear, and positive action results in good fortune.

● *At his best,* he may have properly prepared himself and waited until the time for alliance was right, and now the alliance comes to fruition fully reflecting the needs and desires of all parties. *At his worst,* he may gain an alliance, but it may have been somewhat forced, or in some other way not be as auspicious or beneficial as he expects it to be.

▲ *As a public person,* he may find his promotion comes through his allies. *As a businessperson,* he may expect a merger or joint activities to be highly profitable. *As an ordinary person,* he may enter a good period financially through his friends' help, or he may get married.

3.5   *Yang 9 changing line derives from Hexagram 24 Beginning a Relationship*

He is hoarding his resources at the beginning of a relationship.
For a weak person, this conserves strength; for a strong person,
it shows lack of commitment.

■ He is hoarding his resources to keep his power intact. For a person with few resources, this is the proper course of action. However, for a person who has already amassed wealth or power, this is not the proper course of action, because his resources should be invested in the new relationship to show his commitment.

● *At his best,* he may be weak, but he will effectively continue to build his strength, and will be respected by others for his prudence and modesty. *At his worst,* he may be seen as overly ambitious or greedy, and will be neither respected by others nor happy with what he has.

▲ *As a public person,* he may be in a state of decline by being largely inactive. *As a businessperson,* he may conserve too much to gain good profits. *As an ordinary person,* he may find that saving is beneficial now, or if he was seriously ill, he is now recuperating.

3.6   *Yin 6 changing line derives from Hexagram 42 Gaining Benefits*

His alliance stands ready, yet he still experiences unhappiness
and misfortune. He cannot gain benefits in the way he tried.

■ He did not make good use of his forces, or he tried to use them the wrong way. To gain benefits, he must look in a new direction or try something different.

● *At his best,* he may temporarily lose connections he needs, and he will suffer some losses. *At his worst,* he may suffer very serious losses of friends and family, and he could become disabled.

▲ *As a public person,* he may experience slander or misrepresentations, which leads to loss of allies or demotion. *As a businessperson,* he may experience lies, collapse of his partnerships, or financial losses. *As an ordinary person,* he may make mistakes and suffer rejection or losses due to them.

3.ALL   *All lines changing derives from Hexagram 50 Governing Matters*

The support he needs has been gathered,
and he can begin to govern matters successfully.

■ He has gathered all the support he needs, and now he finds that major advances can be easily and correctly handled. When everything is done right, continuing progress seems so easy.

● *At his best,* he will find that major progress comes very easily because he can rely on those he has gathered around him. *At his worst,* he may be able to launch major endeavors, but success still takes a great deal of struggle.

▲ *As a public person,* he may have gained wide respect and a valuable reputation, which helps him achieve major goals. *As a businessperson,* he may have developed business relationships, which now all work to his profit. *As an ordinary person,* he may have won a wide circle of friends who are willing to assist him when he calls on them.

4. Acting Impetuously

TRIGRAMS CD   LINES 010 001   COMPLEMENTARY HEXAGRAM 49 BEING REVOLUTIONARY

He is acting impetuously. When he has doubts
he should seek the advice of someone wiser,
although he may not be able to benefit from the answer.
It is better for him not to act at all, rather than to act wrongly.

■ *The traditional title* for this hexagram is "Youthful Folly," although this is some-what misleading. As Whincup notes, the literal meaning of the title has a number of different meanings, including a growing shoot, darkness, blindness, ignorance, to cover, and to receive. All of these reflect different aspects of the meaning of the hexagram. "Acting Impetuously" is chosen here as the title to represent the process of youthful growth, which in most of the lines is likened to a growing plant seedling. The general meaning of this hexagram is that an enthusiastic youth tends to seek quick and easy answers, and thus is unable to slow down and more fully grasp life's subtleties to act wisely. In this latter case, he should remain as he is and not forge ahead into trouble for which he is not ready. The "someone wiser" referred to in the traditional text is the oracle, but clearly, the concept has broader application. *The complementary hexagram* is Hexagram 49 Being Revolutionary, which illustrates how youthful and impetuous ideas can mature and become pow-erful forces that radically change the world.

● *At his best,* he may be youthfully enthusiastic rather than foolhardy. *At his worst,* he may have poor judgment coupled with ambition and a compulsion to act.

▲ *As a public person,* he may be appealing and enthusiastic but prone to rushing to judgment. *As a businessperson,* he may be a neophyte or serving as an intern. *As an ordinary person,* he may be seeking good information, or a youth with poor judgment and unrealized potential.

4.1	*Yin 6 changing line derives from Hexagram 41 Declining Influence*

Because being impetuous reduces his ability, he should try to be
careful and restrained, otherwise he is likely to get into trouble.

■ His immaturity and enthusiasm lessens his ability to deal properly with matters. Without restraint he would get into trouble, so being restrained by outside influences at this time is best for him. He needs to tone down his expectations.

● *At his best,* he may have wisdom and morality taught to him by those he would be pleased to learn from. *At his worst,* he may be petulant or childish and resent the restrictions he feels even though they keep him safe.

▲ *As a public person,* he may be given a powerless role (perhaps dealing with information), or be overshadowed by a powerful elder statesman. *As a businessperson,* he may enter a new field and need to lean on the advice and experience of experts. *As an ordinary person,* he may experience disputes with family and friends, or even suffer imprisonment.

4.2   *Yang 9 changing line derives from Hexagram 23 Being in a Collapsing Situation*

Being bold is an advantage after his situation collapses.
He should now find a partner, establish his own household,
and build toward the future.

■ Youthful enthusiasm has its place. He should now advance and seek out a mate or partner, and establish his own household or enterprise. He should seek to build his position when he is able to, and in this way will benefit in the future.

● *At his best,* he may have true understanding and succeed in creating a good home or partnership. *At his worst,* he may understand what he should do but find that it is not so easy to get what he strives for.

▲ *As a public person,* he may find a stable position and establish good ties with a superior. *As a businessperson,* he may establish his own business or prepare for one. *As an ordinary person,* he may marry or have children, or find a new, prosperous job.

4.3   *Yin 6 changing line derives from Hexagram 18 Nursing an Illness*

He should nurse his problems to deal properly with his situation.
He should not be impetuous or seek shortcuts.

■ In the traditional text, he does not choose the woman before him for marriage, since he understands that this relationship is not right for him. He does not seek a quick gain of riches to solve his problems. These may be difficult decisions, but they are the right ones for him. He knows he will have to deal with his problems another way.

● *At his best,* he may be a perceptive and capable person, find his way himself, and be happy with the results. *At his worst,* he may unhappily choose the right course of action and suffer through a difficult period.

▲ *As a public person,* he may shy away from an alliance with a great leader or cause, and possibly even suffer from this decision. *As a businessperson,* he may withdraw from a proposed partnership or seek to remain independent. *As an ordinary person,* he may not marry or join a leader he'd hoped, or he may become involved in a financial or legal dispute and seek appropriate counsel.

4.4   *Yin 6 changing line derives from Hexagram 64 Continuing a Task*

He overreaches his abilities and is overwhelmed by difficulties because of being impetuous. Continuing effort will be required to deal with his problems.

■ He strove to do too much with his limited abilities, and so he has been overwhelmed. He will need to continue to deal with the results of this situation in the future.

● *At his best,* he may grow a great deal as he deals effectively with the problems he has caused. *At his worst,* he may struggle seemingly hopelessly to resolve the problems.

▲ *As a public person,* he may have promised more than he can deliver. *As a businessperson,* he may find that others are taking advantage of him, or his enterprises are not making a profit. *As an ordinary person,* he may experience a difficult period with financial, friendship, and other losses that require continual effort on his part to keep under control.

4.5   *Yin 6 changing line derives from Hexagram 59 Things Are Swept Clear*

Things are swept clear for him, and he gains benefits despite being impetuous.

■ He is in the right place at the right time, and benefits greatly. This is largely because he is aware of his limitations, he can learn from others and gain their assistance, and most important of all, he now understands what path he should take. Indeed, someone might have even cleared his path for him. His good fortune opens the way for him.

● *At his best,* he may have great gains in his life, learn important lessons that will benefit him in the future, and be happy. *At his worst,* he may gain some benefits in the short term, but not learn things that will serve him well in the future.

▲ *As a public person,* he may suddenly be promoted to a better position because of those he associates with, or gain prominence due to unexpected events outside his control. *As a businessperson,* he may find success comes almost accidentally, or he profits from shortages or disasters. *As an ordinary person,* he may be close to a boss or family member, and may find benefits coming from that relationship which dramatically improve his life, or may find that learning greatly benefits him.

4.6   *Yang 9 changing line derives from Hexagram 7 Serving as an Officer*

He is being taught a lesson: he needs to work with others
in serving a greater good rather than be impetuous
or pursue selfish goals.

■ He is having a serious restraint imposed on him, which will educate and mature him, and make him more valuable to society. He needs to learn to work with other individuals, deal effectively with organizations, more fully assume group values and goals, and generally be less selfish.

● *At his best,* he may learn cooperation, respect, and discipline, and find a responsible position in a powerful organization. *At his worst,* he may be punished for his independent or antisocial actions, and he may never learn to accept and work within socially accepted ideals.

▲ *As a public person,* he may be demoted for too much independence. *As a businessperson,* he may learn that his product did not succeed because he didn't pay proper attention to market needs, or he may be punished for engaging in unethical practices. *As an ordinary person,* he may experience problems caused by others, or suffer from poor communication skills, a lack of commitment or too much egoism, or he could join the military.

4.ALL   *All lines changing derives from Hexagram 49 Being Revolutionary*

Youthful ideas and strong actions when undertaken properly
can succeed in radically changing the world.

■ Youthfulness brings vitality as well as fresh perspectives and hope into the world. Revolutions are usually based on the young for this very reason. Here his youthful ideas and strong actions do succeed and help change the world.

● *At his best,* he may embody the best ideas and sentiments of the coming generation, and his actions in bringing those into fruition in the world will benefit those around him as well as himself. *At his worst,* he may be blinded to the benefits of the status quo and may be intolerant of other viewpoints. He could bring much unhappiness into the world and into his life.

▲ *As a public person,* he may help resolve important problems with revolutionary approaches, or he may create a large following for himself and greatly gain in power. *As a businessperson,* he may gain profits from radically new products or processes, or through communications products oriented to new markets or causes. *As an ordinary person,* he may be committed to radical ideas or social causes, or succeed in making his own way through life using new social or economic principles.

5. Acting Prematurely

TRIGRAMS AC   LINES 111 010   COMPLEMENTARY HEXAGRAM 35 ADVANCING DUE TO FAVOR

He is acting prematurely, so he would benefit
by having a capable ally to help him with difficult tasks.

■ *The traditional title* of this hexagram is "Waiting," although this is somewhat misleading. Whincup indicates that the more likely meaning is getting wet, which in ancient times was written the same way. The story of the lines portrays the task of fording a stream before the high water level goes down. Remember that in ancient times there were no bridges, so this could be a difficult or even dangerous task. In fording the stream prematurely, he would benefit from having an ally, especially one more experienced and capable, to assist him. Here "Acting Prematurely" is used as the title to convey the essence of these ideas. *The complementary hexagram* is Hexagram 35 Advancing Due to Favor, which illustrates how acting too soon on his behalf becomes waiting for others' support to complete his efforts to advance himself.

● *At his best,* he may find a capable friend to guide him in actions that succeed in benefiting him. *At his worst,* he may take actions that bring him some trouble because of things he didn't understand or anticipate.

▲ *As a public person,* he may launch a campaign without obtaining all the information he needs from his allies or the public. *As a businessperson,* he may prefer taking swift action to taking more time to be sure of taking the right action. *As an ordinary person,* he may feel a desire to act and need assistance to do so well.

5.1	*Yang 9 changing line derives from Hexagram 48 Being Renewed*

He has acted prematurely, so there are difficulties; however,
he can be easily renewed and recover from them.

■ In the traditional text, he is so far out in the countryside that advancing from that position poses immediate problems. However, being there makes it easy for him to fulfill his fundamental needs and prosper as a result. In general, difficulties at the beginning can be easily recovered from.

● *At his best,* he may quickly recognize the situation, temporarily put aside his goal, and be content with what he has. *At his worst,* he may push ahead regardless of the difficulties, struggle, and not be rewarded for his efforts.

▲ *As a public person,* he may recognize dangers in a new policy and persuade others to support the status quo. *As a businessperson,* he may explore a new business; recognizing that it yields insufficient profits, he returns to his old one. *As an ordinary person,* he may find continual minor problems or accidents, or some major problems coming from a recent major life change.

5.2   *Yang 9 changing line derives from Hexagram 63 Beginning a New Task*

He succeeds in beginning a new task,
although his premature action may bring some difficulties.

■ He succeeds in beginning a new task, but the problems he encounters may take some time and effort to overcome. Others may also criticize him, but this does not truly harm him. Eventually, with continued effort, he can succeed, but still others may not properly respect him or his effort.

● *At his best,* he may work hard to accomplish an important goal, as well as resolve difficulties with others, to finally leave a good reputation. *At his worst,* he may trick others for his own profit, or his reputation may be damaged by his personal qualities.

▲ *As a public person,* he may lead a large undertaking and have to deal with much criticism along the way. *As a businessperson,* he may find his success is offset by the opposition he faces from his business associates or his poor reputation in the marketplace. *As an ordinary person,* he may have problems if he is too fixated on his goal or doesn't work with those around him, or he may become involved in a lawsuit.

5.3   *Yang 9 changing line derives from Hexagram 60 Having Limited Resources*

Others can prey on him, and because he has not yet been able
to gain enough resources to protect himself, matters will deteriorate.

■ The traditional text says he is now standing in the mud beside the river. Being in the mud illustrates deterioration and vulnerability. While he is trapped in the mud, raiders come and rob him. He may have made himself vulnerable at a bad time, or he may simply have not been able to accumulate enough resources for his security when he needs it.

● *At his best,* while he may have tried to be prudent, he could still find himself harmed by the actions of others. *At his worst,* he may have caused terrible damage and losses by his recklessness or incompetence.

▲ *As a public person,* he may try to deal with a serious situation and find that opponents attack him. *As a businessperson,* he may find himself overextended and unable to recover without serious losses. *As an ordinary person,* he may be robbed, or find he has been tricked into a crooked investment, or have a relationship deteriorate into deceit and victimization.

5.4   *Yin 6 changing line derives from Hexagram 43 Escaping Harm*

He flees too soon from what he saw as harm
and goes into potentially greater danger.

■ The traditional text shows him being driven from his refuge, a cave. When he emerges, he is bloodied. While he has suffered some minor harm, now he has even less protection, and greater danger lies ahead.

● *At his best,* he may flee to another place of security and not suffer greater harm. *At his worst,* he may begin a long period of wandering; lose hope, faith, and security; and suffer serious financial and physical harm.

▲ *As a public person,* he may hold fast to his position until he is forced out by public opinion. *As a businessperson,* he may need to change the base of his operations or his product line, and thereby potentially lose his business. *As an ordinary person,* he may be forced to leave his home, job, or marriage, or he could suffer physical injury.

5.5   *Yang 9 changing line derives from Hexagram 9 Restraining Himself*

He is easily distracted from completing his goal by premature
success. To truly succeed, he must keep on his course.

■ Here the traditional text says he is celebrating by binging on wine and food. Some success has come, but true success still eludes him. In order to truly succeed, he must persevere in his efforts and not halt halfway.

● *At his best,* he may reapply himself to his cause after his momentary distraction and not harm the ultimate attainment of his aims. *At his worst,* he may be completely derailed by celebrations and egoism, and because of this, he ultimately fails in his goals.

▲ *As a public person,* he may be promoted or honored by his associates as a means to distract him from his course. *As a businessperson,* he may allow early successes to deter him from continuing to develop the market or his product. *As an ordinary person,* he may fall prey to an opportunist, marry a little too young, or become too easily distracted.

5.6   *Yin 6 changing line derives from Hexagram 11 Easily Progressing*

Potential allies come to him prematurely.
If he wins their assistance, he will be easily able to progress.

■ The traditional text says he is visited by three guests unexpectedly, so he is not ready for them. If he deals with them properly, they will help him achieve his goals. This has traditionally been interpreted as showing them suitable honor, although more realistically it probably means to gain their friendship and support.

● *At his best,* he may be able to seize the moment and win important friends who will help him achieve his goals. *At his worst,* he will benefit to a limited extent from natural allies, and his own efforts will not help him materially.

▲ *As a public person,* he may have unexpected emissaries approach him regarding an alliance. *As a businessperson,* he may find others are proposing to be his business partners, or want to contribute skills or ideas. *As an ordinary person,* he may find that his finances may unexpectedly improve, or that he has unexpected guests or friends.

5.ALL   *All lines changing derives from Hexagram 35 Advancing Due to Favor*

He looks now to advance through the favors and efforts of others.

■ This shows he is looking for older and wiser leaders to take him (a capable younger person) under their wings. The older leaders recognize his ability and potential despite the errors of his premature attempts to advance by himself. Now, his advance through the efforts of those with power and authority is highly auspicious. It means that he will not make grave mistakes and suffer from their consequences. Others with higher positions and greater wealth can directly benefit him as well as provide the wisdom of their experience. He thus can gain in several ways.

● *At his best,* he may gain a great man as a mentor, and benefit from his teaching, his friendship, and new professional opportunities. *At his worst,* he may manipulate his appeal in a personalistic way, instead of growing as much as he could professionally.

▲ *As a public person,* he may craft his public image to gather support and enhance his position. *As a businessperson,* he may be dependent on other business associates to keep his enterprise solvent. *As an ordinary person,* he may gain assistance through elders who appreciate him, through members of the opposite sex who are attracted to him, or through friends who are charmed by him.

6. Having a Complaint

TRIGRAMS CA   LINES 010 111   COMPLEMENTARY HEXAGRAM 36 SERVING AS AN ASSISTANT

He has a complaint against his leader, so his service is now halfhearted and cautious. Halting this conflict halfway is beneficial, but forcing it to an end is not. He should seek to speak with his leader; he should not break away on his own.

■ *The traditional title* of this hexagram is "Conflict." Whincup titles it "Grievance," and notes that it refers to legal proceedings, and the Huangs title it "Court." Here "Having a Complaint" is used because the conflict is actually a problem that he has with his leader. In a situation where he has a complaint with his leader, his abilities and allegiance are impaired. The situation must eventually be resolved. He can either try to force his demands, or honestly negotiate and compromise with the leader. The latter course is better, since it is not yet time for him to go out on his own. *The complementary hexagram* is Hexagram 36 Serving as an Assistant, which illustrates how those who serve as assistants to those greater than themselves should have no causes for complaint with their leaders if their services are to be effective.

● *At his best,* he may know he is justified in his complaints and honestly seek to rectify problems he is experiencing. *At his worst,* he may be angry at slights and disappointments, which clouds his judgment and impairs his performance, and may experience a strong desire to break away on his own.

▲ *As a public person,* he may make a public issue of wrongs done to him to gain wider support. *As a businessperson,* he may deal with his complaints through effective consultations and by looking at the facts and figures. *As an ordinary person,* he may deal with personality conflicts, attainment of personal goals, and learning how to work together.

6.1   *Yin 6 changing line derives from Hexagram 10 Taking Risky Action*

Criticizing his leader now is taking a risky action.
However, even though ill words may be spoken of him,
in the end they will do him no harm.

■ He raises a complaint with his leader, and doing so is not without its dangers. He also may be criticized in turn for doing this. However, he will not be harmed by raising his issues, and some benefit may come from his actions.

● *At his best,* he may be intelligent and loyal, so his complaint is respected for what it truly represents. *At his worst,* he may be petty and egotistical, and thus driven into a poor course of action that will not benefit him.

▲ *As a public person,* he may arouse a flurry of negative publicity. *As a businessperson,* he may raise serious business issues that would benefit the company if resolved. *As an ordinary person,* he may suffer defamation or lawsuits, go through a divorce, or become ill.

6.2   *Yang 9 changing line derives from Hexagram 12 Being Blocked*

His complaint to his leader is blocked, so he backs down.

■ After he has brought a complaint to his leader, it is rejected, and, therefore, he backs down. He is now blocked in his relationship with his leader, so he could even go further and withdraw for a time on a retreat.

● *At his best,* he may be strong in character, and realize that he should wait and let time heal the rift with his leader. *At his worst,* he may be angry and hostile over this rejection, and withdraw to nurse his resentments.

▲ *As a public person,* he may return to his supporters or activity base after his appeal fails. *As a businessperson,* he may return to a more conservative attitude or program. *As an ordinary person,* he may have problems at work that are not resolved in his favor, lose lawsuits, or become separated from his mate.

6.3   *Yin 6 changing line derives from Hexagram 44 Maintaining His Independence*

Because he has a complaint with his leader, he maintains
his independence and lives off his own resources.
This could be dangerous, but he comes to no harm.
Depending on another now would not be beneficial.

■ He possesses some independent means, and he uses these to support himself. He does not need riches or a grand style; what he has is enough. Being dependent on someone now wouldn't allow him the freedom he needs.

● *At his best,* he may have enough to enjoy a good life, and also be pleased that he can stand up for what he believes. *At his worst,* he may find it difficult to survive, and he may have to balance many competing demands.

▲ *As a public person,* he may find it best to maintain his independence using his present resources rather than making use of opportunities proffered by others. *As a businessperson,* he may choose not to enter into a proposed partnership or not to modify his business enterprise on the representations of others. *As an ordinary person,* he may establish his own career or household, or withdraw from the demands of an overbearing friend.

| 6.4 | *Yang 9 changing line derives from Hexagram 59 Things Are Swept Clear* |

His complaint to his leader is rejected, but it helped
sweep matters clear between them. He can now
accept some things he could not before.

■ Although his complaint was not resolved in the manner he desired, airing it did accomplish some good. He can now better accept his situation.

● *At his best,* he may come to appreciate various benefits coming from his leader that compensate for the complaints he still has. *At his worst,* he may feel his complaints remain a serious problem, so the exchange shows him that he will need to change his situation.

▲ *As a public person,* he may receive a setback in pubic opinion or in the confidence of his superiors, which returns him to more conventional and successful approaches. *As a businessperson,* he may decide to continue his enterprise despite some setbacks from those who might have assisted it. *As an ordinary person,* he may find that his problems with his superior or mate have not been resolved, yet he decides to put up with them.

| 6.5 | *Yang 9 changing line derives from Hexagram 64 Continuing a Task* |

His complaint to his leader has been accepted.
Continuing good fortune comes from this.

■ He is successful in getting a positive response to his complaint. Not only does this bring immediate benefit, but more important, it also opens up an ongoing dialog with his leader from which future benefits are likely to come.

● *At his best,* he may become very effective at working through others, and become widely respected because he uses his influence to benefit good causes. *At his worst,* he may enjoy some limited benefits coming through his rapport with his leader.

▲ *As a public person,* he may obtain public honors because of his forward thinking actions, and be able to use this for further public good. *As a businessperson,* he may win a dispute that promises future revenues. *As an ordinary person,* he may be very persuasive in winning the respect, cooperation, and benefits he desires from a superior or mate.

6.6 Yang 9 changing line derives from Hexagram 47 Advancing by Hard Work

He has worked hard for his leader, but now he sees that some of the promises made to him were lies.

■ Promises from his leader regarding his complaints ultimately are measured by concrete responses. Without those, the promises of his leader will be shown to have been lies.

● *At his best,* he may have recognized from the beginning the possibility that he was being manipulated and lied to, and thus prepared himself for this eventuality. *At his worst,* he may suffer in many ways, including emotionally and financially, from his betrayed trust.

▲ *As a public person,* he may be demoted or retired, or have his reputation or accomplishments distorted or buried by secret enemies in high places. *As a businessperson,* he may have his business greatly harmed by misrepresentations of partners. *As an ordinary person,* he may be lied to by those especially important to him who he trusted.

6.ALL All lines changing derives from Hexagram 36 Serving as an Assistant

Having his complaints honestly redressed by his leader allows him to recommit himself, and to serve and assist his leader better.

■ Having his true needs expressed and resolved is highly beneficial, and serves both him and his leader. This is especially powerful because it allows them to work closely, and more effectively, together toward the same goal.

● *At his best,* he may gain much from his leader, and he will enjoy personal as well as professional benefits. *At his worst,* he may know that while to some extent his needs have been addressed, they will drive him to leave his leader in the future.

▲ *As a public person,* he may reaffirm an alliance with powerful leaders, putting aside his earlier doubts. *As a businessperson,* he may have a favorable decision restore lost business prospects. *As an ordinary person,* he may have a mate fix a significant problem that restores their relationship, or a persistent health issue could be resolved.

7. Serving as an Officer

TRIGRAMS CE   LINES 010 000   COMPLEMENTARY HEXAGRAM 13 SERVING ON A TEAM

He is serving as an officer.
If he is capable, strong, and committed, he may progress.

■ *The traditional title* of this hexagram is "An Army," which is somewhat misleading. The title used here is "Serving as an Officer," which is derived from the leadership roles and actions indicated in the lines. Officers are concerned with marshalling, conserving, and using organizational resources. Being an officer also requires strong character, and significant rewards for good performance are given. Being an officer means being dutiful, enjoying some measure of power, and having the respect and obedience of others. *The complementary hexagram* is Hexagram 13 Serving on a Team, which illustrates that effective leadership ultimately is a role in a team effort.

● *At his best,* he may be capable of creative leadership and by disposition happy to lead others. *At his worst,* he may rely on rules for guidance rather than understanding, status rather than earned respect, and express the attitude that he is better than those he leads.

▲ *As a public person,* he may gain recognition for his successes. *As a businessperson,* he may succeed in obtaining the solutions needed for his programs and endeavors. *As an ordinary person,* he may be relied on for his abilities to deal with whatever comes up as well as for his ability to help organize others when needed.

7.1   *Yin 6 changing line derives from Hexagram 19 Leading Others*

He begins as an officer and finds it easy to benefit.
He is guided by rules and is supported by others.

■ His beginning position is that of an officer. Beginning officers are regulated by their superiors, supported by their assistants, and obeyed by their subordinates. Thus, he will have guidelines and support that guarantee some success for him even at the beginning.

● *At his best,* he may work and study hard, learn valuable life lessons from superiors and subordinates, and build a record of success that will support his future career. *At his worst,* he may rely on his position for his present success, look to the support of others for his advancement, and enjoy his privileges rather than develop his capabilities and skills.

▲ *As a public person,* he may receive an important appointment that opens up a new area of responsibility or activity. *As a businessperson,* he may have joined an enterprise in a high position and he succeeds. *As an ordinary person,* he may go into a new area of life as a leader, or he may be respected as a community leader.

| 7.2 | *Yang 9 changing line derives from Hexagram 2 Going with the Flow* |

He is trusted with a responsible position, and finds that
matters progress easily for him. He may even be
singled out for special recognition.

■ He is put in a responsible position, but finds it is no burden at all. From his perspective, matters just seem to work themselves out. His superiors, however, view his success as notable and reward him through special recognitions or awards.

● *At his best,* he may be given a high position from which he does much good and profits substantially. *At his worst,* he may be given honors for doing things that do not benefit those who need help.

▲ *As a public person,* he may be given a respected but easy position perhaps as a reward for past service or as a prelude to retirement. *As a businessperson,* he may serve as a consultant to a strong and stable company, or serve as a figurehead of a prominent organization. *As an ordinary person,* he may experience a very good period with respect and financial rewards.

| 7.3 | *Yin 6 changing line derives from Hexagram 46 Promoting Himself* |

He overly promotes his abilities, makes mistakes,
and fails in his position. Those around him also suffer.

■ He put his self-promotion ahead of his responsibilities to assure the safety of his followers and the success of his mission. As a consequence, he has damaged his ability to lead, and harmed those around him who relied on him.

● *At his best,* he may learn from his mistakes, but there is very little he can do now to compensate for the damage he has caused. *At his worst,* he may mainly regret that his failures and mistakes have harmed his career, and not care about the consequences of his rash or immature actions.

▲ *As a public person,* he may be demoted for a major error in judgment, or suffer the approbation of his public for a position he has taken. *As a businessperson,* he may suffer the failure of a promotional venture, or go through a bankruptcy. *As an ordinary person,* he may suffer from unrealistic attitudes such as behavioral delusions or unrealistic expectations about inheritances, and harm those nearest and dearest to him.

7.4   *Yin 6 changing line derives from Hexagram 40 Getting Free*

He seeks a safe retreat. Freeing himself from
problem situations is, at times, the wisest course.

■ A cautious withdrawal from conflict or problems can be the proper course of action, even if it is not seen so by others at the time. Deliberate withdrawal based on wisdom and not cowardice is a desirable ability, and could show his maturity and fortitude. This is a necessary quality for a leader, and it could be essential to the survival of his followers and his mission.

● *At his best,* he may understand when to fall back and protect himself and his organization, and when to unrelentingly press ahead for success. *At his worst,* he may be overly concerned with his personal position, and retreat to protect it even when his mission could be achieved with more fortitude.

▲ *As a public person,* he may pull out of the public eye or back down on important issues. *As a businessperson,* he may pull back from riskier investments. *As an ordinary person,* he may obtain a new home, journey to a safer place, or retrench his life or career.

7.5   *Yin 6 changing line derives from Hexagram 29 Being Trapped*

He has reached the high position he aimed for,
but now feels trapped in his situation. He should talk with others
to avoid making mistakes, and he should assign those
with ability to do difficult tasks for him.

■ He has succeeded in reaching a notable position in his organization, but now he discovers it isn't the way he thought it would be. Problems appear different now that he is responsible for dealing with them. Possible solutions also appear different from what he expected, and he is still dependent on others for his success. In order for him to succeed, he will need to talk to his staff. He can learn much from them, and he will need to know who are the able assistants he can rely on to get difficult tasks done.

● *At his best,* he may awaken to the realities of his situation, and realize that he needs his staff working with him to be successful in his role. *At his worst,* he may abuse his position and not fully gain the trust and cooperation of his staff, and thereby experience failures and feel even more trapped in his position.

▲ *As a public person,* he may be assigned an important position, or be put into a difficult leadership spot. *As a businessperson,* he may gain significant advancement in his organization, or take over another company. *As an ordinary person,* he may get what he desired and discover that he is even more dependent on those around him than he expected and, therefore, should admit to them how much he needs them.

7.6   *Yin 6 changing line derives from Hexagram 4 Acting Impetuously*

He impetuously wants to establish a household or organization
that will endure. The grander and more unrealistic
the scheme is, the more likely it is to fail.

■ Up to this point, he has succeeded in his efforts, but now he envisions something greater and grander than himself. He envisions leaving something for his posterity, or possibly even for history. To some extent this may be possible, at least for a time, but the bigger and grander his vision, the more difficult and more unlikely it is to succeed. The more modest his goals, the more likely they are to be achieved.

● *At his best,* he may leave something of value to his posterity and be treasured for it. *At his worst,* he may not understand the actual consequences of his legacy, and those who come after will resent what he has done to them.

▲ *As a public person,* he may strive to create an enduring political alliance, or establish a political entity. *As a businessperson,* he may develop a family business in the hopes that it will endure through time. *As an ordinary person,* he may obtain an inheritance that he hopes to pass on to his children, begin a family, or start a new home.

7.ALL   *All lines changing derives from Hexagram 13 Serving on a Team*

A true leader in the end is serving with his followers.
In truly joining their team, he overcomes his
own limitations and gains their strengths.

■ Leadership ultimately is about a leader furthering his followers. Too often, leaders are those who have skills in organization and manipulation, and lose sight of what is important to their followers. Thus, leaders who transcend the consequences of their leadership and become true vehicles for their people can gain great things in the world as well as become spiritually enriched.

● *At his best,* he may become wise and respected, and happily nurture the development of his people through time. *At his worst,* he may become a fanatical adherent of a partisan viewpoint, which ultimately works against the interests of the people he had hoped to further.

▲ *As a public person,* he may become a powerful voice for his people publicly. *As a businessperson,* he may become a consumer advocate and work to correct ills that he sees in the business world. *As an ordinary person,* he may gain a new perspective on his family and other close relationships, and learn to be gentler and work with them more closely to further their happiness as well as his own.

8. Entering an Alliance

TRIGRAMS EC	LINES 000 010	COMPLEMENTARY HEXAGRAM 14 RELYING ON HIS ALLIES

Entering an alliance is beneficial, but it is even more beneficial to have allies before trouble begins.

■ *The traditional titles* for this hexagram include "Holding Together" and "Union." Whincup uses "Alliance," and notes this word literally includes the meanings of side-by-side, get close to, assist, and enter into an alliance. The Huangs use "Support." The title used here is "Entering an Alliance," which comes from the meaning conveyed via the hexagram that anyone can be made stronger through an alliance. Thus, its connotations include partnership, marriage, and alliance with someone stronger. Such alliances are especially beneficial when trouble threatens, but waiting too long before establishing these alliances is not beneficial. The traditional text here again implies that the ancient diviners repeatedly probed the same situation, trusting that subsequent responses would provide additional useful information. *The complementary hexagram* is Hexagram 14 Relying on His Allies, which illustrates that when alliances are used they grow stronger as well as provide benefits to the partners.

● *At his best,* he may easily be able to build the relationships and alliances he will need later in life. *At his worst,* he may not have the support he needs and may have to struggle to find allies when he is already hard pressed.

▲ *As a public person,* he may be able to clarify issues and gather supporters for causes. *As a businessperson,* he may build productive connections targeted for tangible results. *As an ordinary person,* he may make friends, join causes, and build communities with shared values.

8.1	*Yin 6 changing line derives from Hexagram 3 Gathering Support*

He seeks the support of an alliance,
and gaining strong allies protects him from harm.

■ He understands that having strong allies benefits him. Thus, he reaches out to those he wishes to enlist and persuades them. Having gained the alliance he sought, his position is strengthened, and his allies protect him from problems.

● *At his best,* he may attract others who, regardless of their ranks or positions, value him and are truly committed to him. *At his worst,* he may gain the cooperation of others, but not be able to forge an unbreakable bond with them.

▲ *As a public person,* he may understand the needs of others and create alliances based on being able to meet those. *As a businessperson,* he may be able to create business cooperatives, or associations of different types of companies, gaining profit for all. *As an ordinary person,* he may join with a friend or associate and bring profits or other benefits to both their lives, or he may get married.

8.2   *Yin 6 changing line derives from Hexagram 29 Being Trapped*

He is trapped into a stronger alliance with those already close, and he benefits.

■ He already has some ties to others, but now he is forced into an even stronger alliance by events outside his control. He doesn't have any choice in this, although he strongly benefits.

● *At his best,* he may see the necessity as well as the reward of this strengthened alliance, and thus truly benefit from it. *At his worst,* he may see only the necessity of this change and therefore feel trapped in the alliance.

▲ *As a public person,* he may need to retrench his position by reaffirming his alliances. *As a businessperson,* he may need to develop a partnership with business associates. *As an ordinary person,* he may be forced to marry, or find himself drawn into close relations with a neighbor or work associate.

8.3   *Yin 6 changing line derives from Hexagram 39 Bumbling by Himself*

He bumbles by having an improper alliance, and some misfortune may come from this.

■ The alliance he has is seriously flawed in some important ways. It is an improper alliance: illegal, immoral, unethical, or worthless. Thus, this alliance, rather than strengthening him, may actually end up harming him.

● *At his best,* he may have entered this alliance for reasons that are meaningful to him, which do not help him as they should, but can still provide some other benefit. *At his worst,* he may have broken rules of law or morality and may reap a great deal of suffering without obtaining any lasting benefit.

▲ *As a public person,* he may suffer for a moral impropriety or secret deal exposed. *As a businessperson,* he may lose by a failed attempt to manipulate the market. *As an ordinary person,* he may become intimately involved with the wrong person, which may threaten his marriage or standing in the community.

8.4   *Yin 6 changing line derives from Hexagram 45 Serving a Leader*

He enters into an alliance with a powerful leader,
and this will benefit him over time.

■ He enters an alliance with a powerful leader, perhaps from outside his local circle. This new alliance greatly strengthens him, and will benefit him in the long term.

● *At his best,* he may find a leader who will give him the freedom and opportunity he needs to fully develop on his own, and yet be available when he is in need. *At his worst,* he may have given up a lot to gain the support of such a powerful leader, and this could greatly hinder him in the future.

▲ *As a public person,* he may enter into an alliance with another leader from outside his group. *As a businessperson,* he may find success in a foreign land or in a partnership in an unusual venture. *As an ordinary person,* he may easily obtain help from strangers or casual acquaintances.

8.5   *Yang 9 changing line derives from Hexagram 2 Going with the Flow*

His alliance goes with the flow. Inadequacies and errors are
accepted, so it is very strong and beneficial.

■ This line signifies that a truly strong alliance is based on both serious commitment and tolerance of faults. This alliance needs no gimmicks to strengthen it because it is based on the strong natural proclivities that bind its members together.

● *At his best,* he may have a true friend as an ally. *At his worst,* he may have an alliance that imposes no demands or duties on him.

▲ *As a public person,* he may go along with prevailing opinion rather than break with his allies to push radical views. *As a businessperson,* he may have strong working relationships with employees and associates. *As an ordinary person,* he may have a very forgiving spouse or very good friends.

8.6   *Yin 6 changing line derives from Hexagram 20 Preparing Himself*

His focus is now on himself, not on his alliances,
so they lose strength. Some misfortune could come from this.

■ He is now interested in other matters that are of concern primarily to him. Thus, he is not involved in maintaining his alliances and so their purpose weakens. Misfortune could easily result.

● *At his best,* he may develop skills that benefit and protect him in other ways. *At his worst,* he may lose perspective and endanger himself through his other interests.

▲ *As a public person,* he may lose touch with his principal allies and backers. *As a businessperson,* he may not pay attention to his business interests, or become overly involved in a new enterprise. *As an ordinary person,* he may be distracted from the most important things in his life by newfound interests, or he could prepare for a new venture or life style.

8.ALL *All lines changing derives from Hexagram 14 Relying on His Allies*

Using his alliances is the best way to maintain and strengthen them.

■ An alliance is a form of power, and power needs to be exercised to maintain it. Knowing this, he makes the effort to use his alliances to keep them strong.

● *At his best,* he may be respected for his strong and honorable nature as well as for the friends who support him. *At his worst,* he may treat alliances like tangible assets rather than the community of people they truly represent.

▲ *As a public person,* he may become an important power broker. *As a businessperson,* he may become heavily involved in business organizations and service groups. *As an ordinary person,* he may develop many friendships and contacts throughout his community, and he may become recognized as a valuable community leader.

9. Restraining Himself

TRIGRAMS AF   LINES 111 011   COMPLEMENTARY HEXAGRAM 16 STANDSTILL

He is restraining himself, so his potential remains unattained.

■ *The traditional title* for this hexagram is "Taming Power of the Small," although this is somewhat misleading. Here a more appropriate title, "Restraining Himself," is used. It signifies that because he is restraining himself he won't reach his potential. Some self-restraint is appropriate and beneficial when he knows his shortcomings because it prevents him from getting into trouble or unnecessarily wasting his resources. It can also give him the opportunity to build up his strength and prepare himself for the future when he will have a better opportunity to use it. However, too much self-restraint could be a hindrance to his future development. *The complementary hexagram* is Hexagram 16 Standstill, which illustrates how excessive self-restraint leads to stagnation and standstill.

● *At his best,* he may accept the need for his self-restraint and know when it is appropriate. *At his worst,* he may feel so weak that he is restraining himself too much, hindering his ability to attain his goals.

▲ *As a public person,* he may make ineffectual pronouncements or even take no action when he should. *As a businessperson,* he may find himself unable to take advantage of business opportunities due to his fears. *As an ordinary person,* he may find his life complicated by matters out of his control and the influences and actions of those around him.

9.1   *Yang 9 changing line derives from Hexagram 57 At His Leader's Mercy*

He is at his leader's mercy, so he graciously submits.
This cannot be faulted because there is some benefit in doing so.

■ He feels himself to be weak, so allying himself with someone who is strong and who offers protection and benefits is good judgment. The fact that his leader will exercise some degree of control over him, restraining him, is part of the price he must pay for the benefits he gets.

● *At his best,* he may happily submit to the restrictions under which he lives and works while he continues to develop his own resources. *At his worst,* he may resent the bargain he has made and squander his opportunity to quietly enhance himself.

▲ *As a public person,* he may gain entry to a leader's organization to further his career. *As a businessperson,* he may work for a company to gain information about its operations and products. *As an ordinary person,* he may seek refuge with a friend of a friend, join a paternalistic organization, or even get married.

9.2 *Yang 9 changing line derives from Hexagram 37 Serving in a Household*

He is restrained by household ties, yet some benefit comes from this.

■ His actions are restricted due to household obligations or persuasion by household members. These relations can be very strong and beneficial, so restraint here can be good.

● *At his best,* he may have good family relations and benefit from his ties with his family, if not now, then in the future. *At his worst,* he may suffer estrangement from his family, and restraint in this case could require him to rebuild family relations.

▲ *As a public person,* he may find there is a conflict between his duties and his family obligations. *As a businessperson,* he may need to make room for family in his business. *As an ordinary person,* he may bow to the wishes of family members, or suffer being restrained for his own good by family, or find that his career or stature are being limited by his family's origin or background.

9.3 *Yang 9 changing line derives from Hexagram 61 Having Limited Allegiance*

His connection to his leader is so weak it falls apart,
and everyone is angry about the result.

■ His connection to his leader is held by a mutual purpose or interest. The traditional text gives two examples of this: a carriage and axle hinge pin and a husband and wife. The traditional text depicts a connection so weakened that it has nothing holding it together. Without the allegiance of his associates, he is not able to maintain his part of the connection. Furthermore, due to the strong feelings of anger, rebuilding the connection would take time and effort.

● *At his best,* he may cool down and contribute to rebuilding his association. *At his worst,* he may stubbornly make reconciliation and correction impossible, which contributes to continuing weakness.

▲ *As a public person,* he may lose his position or his influence in an alliance. *As a businessperson,* he may have serious losses in a market, or with a partnership that splits up. *As an ordinary person,* he may suffer serious marital problems, possibly even divorce, severe health problems, or have professional problems with coworkers.

9.4   *Yin 6 changing line derives from Hexagram 1 Acting Fiercely*

> By strong action, he proves his faithfulness and allegiance.
> Concerns about his self-restraint fade away.

■ At last he has a chance to redeem himself in others' (especially his leader's) eyes. His strong action not only brings him some recognition, but also helps him feel better about himself.

● *At his best,* he may have benefited much emotionally as well as in terms of wealth and status. *At his worst,* he may view this as only a temporary respite from his accustomed role, and he may not be able to continue to strengthen his position.

▲ *As a public person,* he may win a good position because of his salesmanship. *As a businessperson,* he may redeem his value to the organization. *As an ordinary person,* he may find doing the right thing will mitigate a problem, or demonstrating his commitment to family or friends can now bring him benefits.

9.5   *Yang 9 changing line derives from Hexagram 26 External Restraint*

> He completely submits to others' guidance,
> and from this good fortune comes to him.

■ Here he fully accepts restraint, and even goes beyond that to offering complete submission. Although the traditional text uses the word "neighbor" rather than "leader," the relationship implied is between a follower and a superior to whom he is particularly close or submissively allied. His leader recognizes his value and rewards him appropriately. Note also that part of this reward can be seen as proximity to greatness or as ready access to the leader.

● *At his best,* he may obtain riches and high status through his leader due to his strong ties, honorable service and deep respect. *At his worst,* he may be slavishly subservient to his leader, and be kept on a tight leash for his material needs.

▲ *As a public person,* he may be unswervingly committed to a policy or party that benefits him. *As a businessperson,* he may attain riches through his relationship to a very important person, or attain fame as commercial spokesperson. *As an ordinary person,* he may obtain help from his mate, his family, or his superior, and thus have his needs met.

He restrains himself too much to take the action he needs.
He remains uncommitted, and is confused by threats.
By doing nothing, he cannot progress.

■ His self-restraint is revealed as a deep character flaw. He is confounded by threats
and confused, and thus he vacillates and delays. He cannot act, but if he is to succeed, he must force himself to act. Acting, however, is fraught with danger, too. His
fear of acting wrongly leads him to not act at all, and this is just as bad.

● *At his best,* he may begin to address the problems within himself. *At his worst,* he
may be blind to the true root of his problems, and be held powerless by his own
demons.

▲ *As a public person,* he may be seen to not know what to do, and consequently
suffers deteriorating public support. *As a businessperson,* he may not be able to
oppose threats from competitors or creditors. *As an ordinary person,* he may suffer from mental problems or face bankruptcy.

He has finally reached the lowest point, and he gives up hope
of progress. His self-restraint turns into complete standstill.

■ The principle of action is essential for progress. Without it, stagnation results.
Giving up on his hope for advancement, he gives up being able to act at all. Thus,
he arrives at complete standstill.

● *At his best,* he may withdraw into himself and yet recuperate, rebuilding his spirit and rethinking his plans. *At his worst,* he may be hopelessly mired in defeat and
dejection.

▲ *As a public person,* he may be seen to be completely ineffectual or uncaring. *As
a businessperson,* he may give up entirely competing in the market. *As an ordinary
person,* he may withdraw completely into himself, or live as simply and minimally as
possible.

10. Taking Risky Action

TRIGRAMS HA   LINES 110 111   COMPLEMENTARY HEXAGRAM 15 ACTING WITH PROPRIETY

He is taking risky action, but he is not harmed.

■ *The traditional titles* of this hexagram are "Treading" or "Conduct," which are somewhat misleading. The ideogram used in the title literally means shoe, and the story given in the traditional text is about stepping on a tiger's tail. Normally an act such as this would be quite dangerous, but he is not harmed now. The title used here is "Taking Risky Action," since it better conveys the meaning of the hexagram. *The complementary hexagram* is Hexagram 15 Acting with Propriety, which illustrates how taking risky actions should give way to taking actions that are appropriate and safe to be effective.

● *At his best,* he may understand what he needs, and the limits to which he can act safely. *At his worst,* he may take risky actions that he may later regret even though they may do him no immediate harm.

▲ *As a public person,* he may be a bold advocate for unpopular or lesser-known viewpoints. *As a businessperson,* he may attempt untried business practices or products. *As an ordinary person,* he may be fearless in his personal life, be capable of facing difficult situations that demand unusual solutions, or be very lucky in what others see as foolhardy actions.

10.1   *Yang 9 changing line derives from Hexagram 6 Having a Complaint*

He raises a complaint, but he is not harmed by doing so.

■ The action he takes is of the least risky kind: he raises a complaint with his leader. This does not harm him.

● *At his best,* he may persuasively discuss his complaint and receive some positive response that benefits him. *At his worst,* he may be ignored or even be pushed aside, but he is not harmed in any real way.

▲ *As a public person,* he may use publicity to stir interest in a problem or issue, and find that it has little effect. *As a businessperson,* he may try to get justice in a court or hearing, but has his complaint denied. *As an ordinary person,* he may protest to government, employer, or family, and find little justice but no real harm.

10.2   *Yang 9 changing line derives from Hexagram 25 Having No Expectations*

He has no real expectations from his risky action. Anything he gets will please him, and even if he gets nothing, it will not harm him.

■ He is in a position where his flexibility and lack of expectation are very beneficial. Perhaps he took a wild gamble. If he does not succeed, it will not harm him, so anything he gets is a benefit.

● *At his best,* he may be supremely confident in himself, and his dependence and vulnerability is minimal, and from this he can face even failure with equanimity. *At his worst,* he may need what he strives for, and even though he might have no expectations of getting it, he could still need it.

▲ *As a public person,* he may not have a feeling for how the public will react to his actions, but he still believes he will keep his position. *As a businessperson,* he may release a test product. *As an ordinary person,* he may tend to have a mellow temperament that complements his striving.

10.3   *Yin 6 changing line derives from Hexagram 1 Acting Fiercely*

He acts strongly, and possibly unwisely, by disregarding the limitations of the situation. Therefore, it is easy for him to be harmed.

■ He does not pay proper attention to his limitations, or he does not understand the realities of the situation. Even worse, he does not do things halfway: he acts very strongly, so strong responses are likely. Harm is easy to encounter in such a risky situation.

● *At his best,* he may have a strong character that strives to do right, but may not easily understand his role in life or his limitations, and so experiences problems too often. *At his worst,* he may not accept the realities around him and consequently live immersed in fantasies of his own strength and ability, thereby causing harm to those near him.

▲ *As a public person,* he may be demoted or penalized because of improper actions. *As a businessperson,* he may lose profits as well as stature through very poor business decisions. *As an ordinary person,* he may bring disaster to himself or to his family, he may be imprisoned, or suffer because of negligence.

10.4　*Yang 9 changing line derives from Hexagram 61 Having Limited Allegiance*

His risky action causes a situation more difficult or dangerous
than he anticipated. At first, he does not know what to do,
but by getting help, it can end well.

■ He learns he has overstepped his abilities, and this makes him upset and perhaps even afraid. However, he finds that by getting the support of someone with the right abilities, he can surmount the difficulty.

● *At his best,* he may be able to win an ally who gladly helps him. *At his worst,* he may find someone who can help him, but it takes a great deal to persuade that person to help.

▲ *As a public person,* he may find his reputation is at stake, and he must reach out and gain an ally who he might not otherwise seek. *As a businessperson,* he may need to hire consultants and experts to resolve his business problems. *As an ordinary person,* he may need to look outside of himself and gain new allies to succeed.

10.5　*Yang 9 changing line derives from Hexagram 38 Looking for a Leader*

He is looking for a leader while he takes risky action.
It is dangerous to continue like this.

■ He is not focused on his current situation. Because of this, it is easy for him to make serious errors, and impossible for him to properly compensate when things start to go wrong. This could be a very dangerous situation.

● *At his best,* he may allow current details to escape his notice due to his focus on more fundamental, perhaps spiritual, matters. *At his worst,* he may be either greedy for new goals or too distracted by life's pleasures to pay attention to what he should.

▲ *As a public person,* he may be attempting to win new allies while his old allies desert him and his matters deteriorate. *As a businessperson,* he may not pay attention to his cash flow or other aspects critical to his business. *As an ordinary person,* he may not properly prepare himself for his desired career, not understand the desires of his romantic interest, or not look where he is going and physically hurt himself.

10.6　*Yang 9 changing line derives from Hexagram 58 Sharing Himself*

He shares his goals and plans with others as he takes risky action.
With their cooperation he can succeed.

■ Sharing with others allows him to make them his confederates and companions in his endeavor. This enhances his effective power, and makes success easier and greater than if he had not enlisted them. This line also mentions consulting oracles or the heavenly powers for enhancing success; however, a more general meaning might include researching the appropriate information for success.

● *At his best,* he may be wise enough to understand a leader needs allies and associates, and he will choose companions who will greatly benefit him in the future. *At his worst,* he may succeed, but not gain strong adherents.

▲ *As a public person,* he may marshal public opinion to assist in achieving his plans. *As a businessperson,* he may persuade others to go along with his business ideas and form new partnerships. *As an ordinary person,* he may make friends easily, or have the ability to reach others in his time of need.

10.ALL   *All lines changing derives from Hexagram 15 Acting With Propriety*

He advances by acting with propriety, and taking small
and discrete steps. This minimizes his risky actions,
and yet still allows him to progress toward his goals.

■ He has learned that progress need not always be fierce and violent; rather, progress can also be achieved through small movements, hidden activities, and persuading others in their actions.

● *At his best,* he may become gifted at understanding the subtleties around him, and he can gain his ends without fierce battles or harming others. *At his worst,* he may become a deceitful manipulator who acts without regard for others' needs as he struggles for his goals.

▲ *As a public person,* he may become an expert at behind-the-scenes politics. *As a businessperson,* he may be able to read market changes before they become apparent to most. *As an ordinary person,* he may be well appreciated by friends and family for how considerate he is of them as well as how effective he is.

11. Easily Progressing

TRIGRAMS AE	LINES 111 000	COMPLEMENTARY HEXAGRAM 12 BEING BLOCKED

He is easily progressing because he faces
little or no strong opposition.

■ *The traditional title* of this hexagram is given widely differing interpretations. The Huangs use "Peace," although Whincup notes that most Chinese commentators use descriptions such as "Getting Through," "Successful," and "Smooth and Auspicious." Whincup chose "Flowing" because of its associations with water. Here it is titled "Easily Progressing" because it is closer to the hexagram's real meaning. It signifies he is able to advance easily because he is not opposed by someone stronger. *The complementary hexagram* is Hexagram 12 Being Blocked, which illustrates how easy progress must eventually end when it runs into competing interests from someone stronger.

● *At his best,* he may concentrate his efforts on doing things right because he doesn't face serious opposition. *At his worst,* he may become lackadaisical because everything seems to go so easily and smoothly for him.

▲ *As a public person,* he may easily achieve prominence or become a popular spokesperson. *As a businessperson,* he may find business success comes easily. *As an ordinary person,* he may be able to satisfy his needs easily, be generally well liked, or succeed in his goals.

11.1   *Yang 9 changing line derives from Hexagram 46 Promoting Himself*

He is in a low position and striving to promote himself.
This is beneficial.

■ The traditional text uses the example of ground-hugging grass. From such a low position almost anything is a step up, and with little opposition an increase in status seems likely.

● *At his best,* he may have a realistic attitude about his position and abilities that allows him to market himself successfully. *At his worst,* he may simply be lucky in not having to face serious competition.

▲ *As a public person,* he may know how to appeal to the public positively. *As a businessperson,* he may begin a new "grassroots" business. *As an ordinary person,* he may begin preparing for a new job or court a mate.

11.2   *Yang 9 changing line derives from Hexagram 36 Serving as an Assistant*

In satisfying difficult demands on him, he strives to do his best.
He tries first one solution then another until he succeeds.
He earns his rewards.

■ He is serving as an assistant, but finds it is not as easy as he'd hoped. He tries to satisfy the demands of the situation. Although at first he may not succeed, eventually he will. He then truly appreciates the rewards he gets.

● *At his best,* he may be capable, patient, and not lose faith in his eventual success. *At his worst,* he may come to resent the lack of appreciation he suffers, even though eventually he will find some acceptance.

▲ *As a public person,* he may serve in a highly visible position in a very subordinate, subservient role. *As a businessperson,* he may work hard behind the scenes helping a superior with his business responsibility. *As an ordinary person,* he may deal with a difficult family member or supervisor at work.

11.3   *Yang 9 changing line derives from Hexagram 19 Leading Others*

Despite the resistance he is feeling now,
he needs to keep on his course until he does succeed.

■ Progress cannot always be smooth. Even when things are going easily, bottlenecks can slow the pace. Here he is feeling resistance to his progress. However, he needs to truly believe in himself and persevere in order to succeed.

● *At his best,* he may be strong in his faith and confident in his actions, and eventually his progress will resume. *At his worst,* he may be unclear, act somewhat erratically, and even doubt his eventual success.

▲ *As a public person,* he may be challenged publicly and need to keep a clear head, and act forthrightly and honorably before it is through. *As a businessperson,* he may need to keep developing and researching his business proposal. *As an ordinary person,* he may need to be outstanding in his job performance or need to act very properly with his mate to overcome a difficult period.

11.4 *Yin 6 changing line derives from Hexagram 34 Forcing Matters*

He forces progress by using those near him to support his efforts.
With their assistance, he succeeds easily.

■ He is able to enlist others to his cause. He can even overcome misfortunes with forceful actions. Progress in this way is easy now.

● *At his best,* he may have strong friendships that he can draw upon to help him succeed. *At his worst,* he may rely on manipulation of others to succeed.

▲ *As a public person,* he may lead a public campaign to achieve an important goal. *As a businessperson,* he may obtain a loan to help his business. *As an ordinary person,* he may experience many diverse troubles, and be dependent upon family and friends for assistance.

11.5 *Yin 6 changing line derives from Hexagram 5 Acting Prematurely*

He succeeds and is given many rewards.
However, his success was premature and it was too easy.

■ His success came so suddenly and easily. The traditional text says he is given a mate and other riches, so he has benefited greatly materially. While these material benefits are significant, he hasn't attained the depth of experience and personal strength that is the true wealth of character.

● *At his best,* he may understand the limits to his success, and enjoy and use his riches to the extent appropriate. *At his worst,* he may not understand the limits to his success, and this could cause him grief in the future.

▲ *As a public person,* he may suddenly rise to fame. *As a businessperson,* he may have a sudden business success that brings wealth. *As an ordinary person,* he may suddenly obtain a mate, or find that life suddenly became easy.

11.6 *Yin 6 changing line derives from Hexagram 26 External Restraint*

He now easily submits to restraint and little or no progress.
He can try to keep things in order, but he cannot gain
much from this, and might even suffer blame.

■ He cannot press ahead now, and he easily adapts to the restraints imposed on him. He can try to keep matters that are under his control in order. However, in this situation, he does not gain much and might even be blamed for matters outside his control.

● *At his best,* he may stoically accept this turn in his progress, and not take the negative aspects to heart. *At his worst,* he may let negative feelings overwhelm him and cloud his ability to deal effectively with the situation.

▲ *As a public person,* he may be ordered to a dead-end position by an enemy. *As a businessperson,* he may experience deterioration in his products or decline in his markets. *As an ordinary person,* he may have serious problems in work, family, or health.

11.ALL   *All lines changing derives from Hexagram 12 Being Blocked*

His time of easy progress has ended
now that he is blocked by others.

■ His progress was easy as long as he wasn't opposed. Now that he is opposed, he faces a serious blockage that will end his progress.

● *At his best,* he may resolve to rest, repair himself, and resume his efforts when times are more favorable. *At his worst,* he may not be able to forget his disappointments, and his resentments will weaken his judgment and poison his good will.

▲ *As a public person,* he may find his career is hamstrung by opponents. *As a businessperson,* he may find a vital market closed to him. *As an ordinary person,* he may experience many disappointments as well as the opposition of powerful people.

12. Being Blocked

TRIGRAMS EA   LINES 000 111   COMPLEMENTARY HEXAGRAM 11 EASILY PROGRESSING

His progress is blocked by someone much stronger than he is,
so he should not try to overcome the blockage.

■ *The traditional titles* for this hexagram include "Standstill" and "Stagnation," although these are somewhat misleading. Whincup uses "Blocked," and the Huangs use "Obstruction." Here the title "Being Blocked" is used. It signifies that he is facing such strong opposition that his progress is completely halted. Because of being so strongly blocked, he should not try to force anything, but rather wait for a better time to progress again. *The complementary hexagram* is Hexagram 11 Easily Progressing, which illustrates how those who are weaker will eventually find a time or place where those who are stronger will not hinder their attempts to advance.

● *At his best,* he may realize the nature of the blockage facing him and accept the wisdom of biding his time until he can progress again. *At his worst,* he may be forced into immobility and be poisoned by bitterness or anger.

▲ *As a public person,* he may be helpless to affect public opinion, or possibly may even be perceived as weak and ineffectual. *As a businessperson,* he may not be able to develop his business or product due to strong interference. *As an ordinary person,* he may feel helpless to achieve his goals due to the resistance of a family member, superior, or significant other.

12.1   *Yin 6 changing line derives from Hexagram 25 Having No Expectations*

He is in a low position and has no expectations of progress.
An adaptable attitude is advantageous even in a situation like this.

■ This line uses the same image of the ground-hugging grass that was used in Hexagram 11. Here he has weaker potential for progress. Yet, even here, in a time of stoppage, an attitude of adaptability, flexibility, and wide-open expectation can bring some benefit.

● *At his best,* he may look upon every situation with new eyes, experience every setback as an opportunity for growth, and rejoice in every unexpected benefit. *At his worst,* he may feel he has no opportunities, and lack a clear direction or desire to help guide him.

▲ *As a public person,* he may remain in a backwater position with little or no possibility for promotion. *As a businessperson,* he may find he has meager business or promotional prospects. *As an ordinary person,* he may find himself bothered by many minor problems, by troublesome people, or by feeling generally inhibited.

12.2 *Yin 6 changing line derives from Hexagram 6 Having a Complaint*

He has a complaint, but only those who are subservient
receive any benefit. He can achieve nothing directly by himself,
so he endures this.

■ His expectations of even modest progress in getting resolution to his complaint are denied. He sees that those who are servile to the powers that be do get some relief. However, if it is not possible for him to do this then he must endure.

● *At his best,* he may know his true worth and this will help sustain him. *At his worst,* he may not be able to easily face others of less worth benefiting before him, so he feels ashamed or even bitter.

▲ *As a public person,* he may not be able to gain what he needs from an opposition leader. *As a businessperson,* he may have defective products or processes needing correction, and he is unable to get this. *As an ordinary person,* he may have a difficult time with a boss, his mate, or a vendor, and he must bend over backward in order to get even the tiniest bit of help.

12.3 *Yin 6 changing line derives from Hexagram 33 Complying*

He is in such a completely blocked situation that all he can
do is comply. He endures this with deep unhappiness
and perhaps even some shame.

■ His situation is so restricted that he can do nothing to escape it. He must comply with the demands made of him. This makes him deeply unhappy, and perhaps he even feels shame.

● *At his best,* he may develop great fortitude through his sacrifices and suffering. *At his worst,* he may suffer serious depression and unhappiness and not feel he has gained anything of value.

▲ *As a public person,* he may find himself without power or prestige, existing solely on sufferance. *As a businessperson,* he may be fined and penalized, or squeezed by a cartel. *As an ordinary person,* he may be in jail or under a heavy court order, or he may find that he is existing under someone's heavy hand.

12.4   *Yang 9 changing line derives from Hexagram 20 Preparing Himself*

> He attempts to overcome blockage by seeking assistance,
> and he succeeds and gains benefits with their help.

■ He realizes that he cannot overcome the blockage by himself. However, he also knows that he must work on himself first, then approach someone else who might be able to help him. Ultimately he overcomes blockage through the help of someone else.

● *At his best,* he may improve himself, correct his own faults, and ultimately prove his value to those in positions of power. *At his worst,* he may become a true lackey and lose his own pride in himself.

▲ *As a public person,* he may redeem his career by becoming a public advocate of someone else's position, and he may later be accepted as that person's protégé. *As a businessperson,* he may change his business plans based on an improved awareness of the market, or by developing a new partner. *As an ordinary person,* he may turn to his mate or family, or other powerful friends for help.

12.5   *Yang 9 changing line derives from Hexagram 35 Advancing Due to Favor*

> He is blocked, and the blockage can only be overcome
> by the favor of someone powerful. In this situation,
> he must endure while he waits for relief.

■ He is in a difficult situation. All he can do himself is endure, and through this, he strengthens himself. He must find someone powerful who is willing to help him. In this way, he can escape harm. This could also mean that the person who is responsible for his dire situation relents.

● *At his best,* he may be in a difficult situation, but his character matures in grace and honesty, and he gains relief finally when his true nature is seen. *At his worst,* he may face danger that scorches him, and without assistance from others, he may become bitter and resentful.

▲ *As a public person,* he may be imprisoned or put on trial. *As a businessperson,* he may experience repeated failures of plans and suffer without assistance from a powerful sponsor. *As an ordinary person,* he may be very dependent on others, or experience career, finance, or other problems from which he cannot escape without help.

12.6   *Yang 9 changing line derives from Hexagram 45 Serving a Leader*

He finds a leader he can join.
He is very fortunate that he can progress again.

■ He has found a leader to join. This could be a person, a cause, or something larger and more important than he is to which he can devote his efforts. Now with outside help as well as with his own motivation he is able to progress again.

● *At his best,* he may join an important cause or serve a worthy personage, and from this gain a direction in his life that truly works for him. *At his worst,* he may come under the spell of a strong person who will use him rather than enrich him, and his gains turn out to be temporary.

▲ *As a public person,* he may be offered a position suitable to his abilities but under the direction of a strong leader. *As a businessperson,* he may begin to work for a large, important firm. *As an ordinary person,* he may find a wonderful mate who will light his life, join an important organization or cause, or discover the meaning of religion in his own life.

12.ALL   *All lines changing derives from Hexagram 11 Easily Progressing*

After the firm grip of blockage eases,
progress comes and flows easily through his life.

■ This blockage was like the winter of his life, freezing his energies and sapping his spirit. Now that it has ended, progress bursts forth. Like spring, it begins subtly, then rushes in everywhere. Soon he will take great strides and progress easily.

● *At his best,* he may become joyously active, attempting many different things and succeeding far more easily than he thought possible. *At his worst,* he may be overwhelmed by the possibilities, and thus only do what he feels most comfortable doing, and in succeeding in these, he gains satisfaction.

▲ *As a public person,* he may attract a large following of people who dote on his public campaigns. *As a businessperson,* he may become involved in a number of business ventures that are generally successful. *As an ordinary person,* he may enjoy better health, gain a new understanding of himself psychologically, which makes his life easier, or generally experience progress in his life and relationships.

13. Serving on a Team

TRIGRAMS GA   LINES 101 111   COMPLEMENTARY HEXAGRAM 7 SERVING AS AN OFFICER

He is serving on a team, and a team can bring benefits to them all.

■ *The traditional title* for this hexagram is "Fellowship with Men," although this is somewhat misleading. Whincup uses "With Others," and the Huangs use "Gathering." Here a more descriptive title, "Serving on a Team," is used. It signifies that he has joined himself with others and works with them in their joint endeavors. When everyone is on a team, working together toward a goal, the burden is shared, and everyone can contribute their different skills and perspectives. Everyone benefits by this. *The complementary hexagram* is Hexagram 7 Serving as an Officer, which illustrates how teams strive to find leaders (usually from among themselves) to help plan their goals and guide their activities.

● *At his best,* he may contribute and benefit greatly through his full and active participation on a team. *At his worst,* he may rely too much on his fellows and not contribute as much as he should, risking their criticism and reducing their success.

▲ *As a public person,* he may be a spokesperson or advocate for his team. *As a businessperson,* he may be part of a business team. *As an ordinary person,* he may engage in community sports; be involved in community, club, or church activities; or in other ways involve himself in cooperative and joint activities with those around him.

13.1   *Yang 9 changing line derives from Hexagram 33 Complying*

He complies with the requirements of the situation, and in this way,
his meeting others and joining a team goes smoothly.

■ Joining a group in the beginning often benefits from showing tractability and amiability. He understands this and complies with the requirements of the situation. Being in a group now is beneficial, and everyone will benefit.

● *At his best,* he may be involved with the formation of an important group, or have a strong position within a group. *At his worst,* he may not fully value how beneficial the group could be to him, and therefore not contribute as much as he could to it.

▲ *As a public person,* he may join an important committee or task force. *As a businessperson,* he may enter into important business alliances. *As an ordinary person,* he may establish important new relationships, take a journey, or establish a home in a new community.

| 13.2 | *Yin 6 changing line derives from Hexagram 1 Acting Fiercely* |

Acting too fiercely within his team gets him into trouble.

■ A group requires cooperative give and take. Here, however, he is acting too strongly, more like a boss than a team player. This causes a backlash and gets him into trouble with the others in the group.

● *At his best,* he may have ability, knowledge, and strength, which he wants to contribute to the group, but unfortunately, he does not yet have the wisdom or the personality to do it properly. *At his worst,* he may have a superior attitude toward the group or be contemptuous of it, and this may turn the group against him.

▲ *As a public person,* he may have taken liberties representing the group to others, or he may have tried to exalt his own position within it. *As a businessperson,* he may have alienated partners or competitors, and then suffered from reduced prospects or profits. *As an ordinary person,* he may experience many problems with those close to him at home or at work through his aggressive or unpopular behaviors.

| 13.3 | *Yang 9 changing line derives from Hexagram 25 Having No Expectations* |

He is concealing his true desires or goals,
or something unknown from his past. The harm that could
come from discovery could hurt him for a long time.

■ He has no expectations that the group would accept his true desires and goals, or some secret from his past or something else that is secret or hidden. He is afraid that if this were to become open knowledge, he would suffer for a long time, and this could be true.

● *At his best,* he may not suffer from hiding his "terrible secret," and in time, he may learn that others can accept him as he is. *At his worst,* he may become involved in shady or illegal activities, and his double-life could weigh uncomfortably on his heart and mind.

▲ *As a public person,* he may have a private life at odds with his public appearance. *As a businessperson,* he may be involved in business plots involving secret allies. *As an ordinary person,* he may have a belief system, outside interest, or sexual life that is so different from the beliefs around him that he conceals it.

13.4   *Yang 9 changing line derives from Hexagram 37 Serving in a Household*

He retreats to the safety of his household or closest supporters,
and there he feels secure.

■ He feels threatened, and so he looks to (or rejoins) the group that is closest to him. Typically, this is his family or those he considers to be like family. He now feels secure by getting close to them again, feeling their solidarity with him, and being offered assistance by them.

● *At his best,* he may turn to those he has shared much with in the past, so his retreat seems more like a joyous homecoming that nourishes them all. *At his worst,* he may impose himself on those he was closest to, and end up taking yet more from them again.

▲ *As a public person,* he may turn to his oldest or best constituents for support. *As a businessperson,* he may turn back to an old established product, market, partner, or lender. *As an ordinary person,* he may find comfort with favorite activities or with close friends.

13.5   *Yang 9 changing line derives from Hexagram 30 Gaining Enlightenment*

He gains enlightenment and realizes he does not need a team
for support. This brings him relief and recuperation.

■ A group can provide only so much support, and what it provides is inadequate. For example, groups are not capable of providing enlightenment (although they can try to facilitate it) because it is something that individuals must discover within themselves. Here he has finally taken that step and achieved enlightenment. With this inner strength, he no longer looks to the group to support him, and he can gain better perspective as well as relief and recuperation to help him on his further individual endeavors.

● *At his best,* he may blossom in emotional and spiritual ways, and thereby gain much happiness. *At his worst,* he may also succeed in being enlightened, but he may be more pragmatic in his awareness and his awards.

▲ *As a public person,* he may confront a major problem and gain much in stature because of how he solves it. *As a businessperson,* he may discover how to finesse a complex business problem. *As an ordinary person,* he may become devoted to a spiritual path, find freedom or get divorced, or find solace in a solitary activity.

13.6   *Yang 9 changing line derives from Hexagram 49 Being Revolutionary*

His team now dissolves itself because no one thinks it is
needed anymore. There is no regret over this.

■ Revolutionary change has come to his group. Indeed, the change is a sweeping dissolution of the group itself. All of the group's members feel strong and independent, and they have no regret over going their own ways.

● *At his best,* he may have learned a great deal from his association, may be realistic in his appraisals, and may be interested and anxious to break out on his own. *At his worst,* he may have unrealistic attitudes and beliefs, and thus be able to get into trouble too easily on his own.

▲ *As a public person,* he may have his group succeed in its stated objectives and thereupon dissolve. *As a businessperson,* he may have a partnership or alliance splinter apart from selfish interests. *As an ordinary person,* he may find that friends and associates of the past are drifting away, or that problems seem to resolve themselves if left alone for a time.

13.ALL   *All lines changing derives from Hexagram 7 Serving as an Officer*

He has emerged from a team. Now, by being strong in himself,
he can be an effective leader. This benefits him
as well as those around him.

■ His ability to lead others effectively comes from his experiences being with others in groups plus his own strengths and abilities. He now can make a valuable contribution by leading others, and he is pleased to do so. His leadership brings benefit to them as well as to himself.

● *At his best,* he may become an effective and popular leader. *At his worst,* he may have what is needed to gain leadership of a group, but not what is necessary to make himself truly honored and liked as a leader.

▲ *As a public person,* he may gain a high public office. *As a businessperson,* he may be able to rally other business people around him, perhaps forming a collective or association. *As an ordinary person,* he may retire from an organization or distinguish himself in the public's eye in some way.

14. Relying on His Allies

TRIGRAMS AG   LINES 111 101   COMPLEMENTARY HEXAGRAM 8 ENTERING AN ALLIANCE

He is relying on his allies to help him,
and it is very beneficial that he can do so.

■ *The traditional title* for this hexagram is "Possession in Great Measure," although this is somewhat misleading. The Huangs use "Great Harvest," while Whincup uses "Great Wealth." Here a more appropriate title, "Relying on His Allies," is used. Allies provide a major way of advancing his position as well as protecting what he has, and when used properly, can bring about significant accomplishments. Accumulating allies without using them does not provide great benefit, while relying on them to help him does. *The complementary hexagram* is Hexagram 8 Entering an Alliance, which illustrates how relying on his allies helps keep the alliance strong through the act of re-creating it.

● *At his best,* he may have powerful yet devoted allies willing to assist and support him. *At his worst,* he may be forced to rely on whatever friends and allies he has even though they may not be appropriate or adequate to his needs.

▲ *As a public person,* he may be able to link his cause to a greater one and obtain even wider support than just his closest allies and supporters. *As a businessperson,* he may count on his partners and associates to benefit him when he most needs it. *As an ordinary person,* he may have many friends, neighbors, and coworkers who are willing to assist him in times of troubles.

14.1   *Yang 9 changing line derives from Hexagram 50 Governing Matters*

In a time of weakness and vulnerability, he is alert to danger,
and he tries to control events as much as he can.
In this way, he survives a dangerous period.

■ By being alert to the dangers around him when he is weak and vulnerable, he is able to protect his position. He uses his allies and his other resources to help control the situation, and he is able to survive a dangerous or difficult situation.

● *At his best,* he may be sensitive to danger and opportunity, and his actions while protecting himself will later open up new possibilities for progress. *At his worst,* he may selfishly try to preserve his assets; in the process, he may gain some benefit that later will harm him.

▲ *As a public person,* he may skillfully exploit his friends and public opinion to protect his position. *As a businessperson,* he may perform his business activities very conservatively, or he may use techniques to spy on his opponents. *As an ordinary person,* he may be unusually sensitive to pitfalls around him and, by dint of luck and a commitment to firm principles, manage to avoid problems.

14.2   *Yang 9 changing line derives from Hexagram 30 Gaining Enlightenment*

> He becomes enlightened and is able to achieve prominence.
> Using his knowledge, allies, and position in a highly
> visible fashion is the right thing for him to do now.

■ Knowing what to with his allies is an important problem. Here, he has found the way through his enlightenment. Now can use his allies and his status in the community in a number of ways to reach out to others and achieve desirable goals.

● *At his best,* he may exercise very good judgment in using his resources and in reaching out to those in need, and he will benefit by gaining great respect and personal satisfaction. *At his worst,* he may flaunt his wealth and position believing that his good fortune will be a positive inspiration to others.

▲ *As a public person,* he may begin a major public campaign. *As a businessperson,* he may try to expand his business activities into new areas that also benefit the public. *As an ordinary person,* he may gain valuable possessions (perhaps a vehicle), make powerful friends, or learn important lessons through contemplation or study.

14.3   *Yang 9 changing line derives from Hexagram 38 Looking for a Leader*

> He looks outside himself to others in prominent positions.
> He realizes that his status should not be used to impress them,
> and he should not attempt to be something he is not.

■ Here the traditional text illustrates the common human tendency to reach beyond our own limitations and to try to be something we are not. Although he has gained some prominence, he is still basically an ordinary person, and he should realize this limit and not make a fool of himself by forgetting that. Thus, he should not inappropriately advance himself or try to hold a position of leadership for which he isn't qualified.

● *At his best,* he may come to understand his qualities and their limitations, and in this way, he can successfully deal with others who are also of high position but from other areas of society. *At his worst,* he may become enamored of his fantasies, try to make them reality, and could be shamed or insulted in doing so.

▲ *As a public person,* he may overrate his ability to appeal to other leaders in other areas of society. *As a businessperson,* he may not understand how different parts of society have different ways of thinking and feeling from his. *As an ordinary person,* he may find it difficult to impress his employer or a prospective mate, and it may be easy to get into trouble due to his lack of status in other areas.

14.4   *Yang 9 changing line derives from Hexagram 26 External Restraint*

He accepts the need for restraint, so he avoids displaying
his power. Doing this averts potential harm.

■ His friends and allies are such that he could easily flaunt them and thereby offend others or even make him a target. However, he avoids such inappropriate displays and actions. Thus, his discrimination and modesty avert harm.

● *At his best,* he may have a sense of propriety, which will stand him in good stead and help make others feel comfortable and friendly with him. *At his worst,* he may curb his excesses, but not win the benefits that true humbleness gives.

▲ *As a public person,* he may win both the trust of subordinates by displaying humanity and a lack of pomp, and the trust of superiors by a proper modesty. *As a business-person,* he may respect the bottom line and the benefits of reinvesting money, which could otherwise be wasted on nonproductive displays of wealth. *As an ordinary person,* he may be very fortunate in some of life's critical areas—for example, love, health, happiness, and truth—and he will be modest and sincere in dealing with these issues.

14.5   *Yin 6 changing line derives from Hexagram 1 Acting Fiercely*

He relies on his allies to act powerfully.
Benefits come to him from this.

■ He benefits by relying on his allies to act. Their powerful actions benefit him. In this situation, he cannot or should not act, yet this does not harm him; however, he may not be entirely pleased with his situation.

● *At his best,* he may have strong allies who gladly assist him for his benefit. *At his worst,* he may suffer from being vulnerable and dependent, and benefit only marginally from others' assistance.

▲ *As a public person,* he may be in the spotlight of publicity as he relies on others to deal with an uncomfortable event. *As a businessperson,* he may gain an important insight into his market or business environment as partners assist him. *As an ordinary person,* he may look to his friends for assistance when he needs help and cannot act himself.

14.6 *Yang 9 changing line derives from Hexagram 34 Forcing Matters*

Using his allies, he can force matters and succeed.
This is very fortunate.

■ Matters could hardly be going better for him. He has an understanding of the Tao, and he has resources to back up his goals with suitable actions. It is as though the Gods themselves are working for him.

● *At his best,* he may use whatever resources he has to best effect and without harming others as he succeeds. *At his worst,* he may succeed but with greater harm to those who oppose him, thus creating enemies to deal with in the future.

▲ *As a public person,* he may attain whatever goal he sets himself. *As a businessperson,* he may experience easy success. *As an ordinary person,* he may enjoy a good period and receive many substantial and diverse benefits from those around him, easy profits from his work, or great improvements in his outlook on life.

14.ALL *All lines changing derives from Hexagram 8 Entering an Alliance*

He is able to build strong alliances and connections to other people.
He realizes how important it is to do this.

■ Physical resources are only tools that people use; friendships and alliances are more powerful because they link people together to combine their ideas, energies, and resources. He realizes how important such connections are, so he is making alliances.

● *At his best,* he may be making alliances based on his feelings of true sympathy and cooperation, and not out of fear or desire for gain. *At his worst,* he may build alliances as a way to gain influence over others to increase his own position and power, rather than basing them on a natural coming together of similar souls and ideas.

▲ *As a public person,* he may take a lead in building a powerful alliance. *As a businessperson,* he may seek a cooperative arrangement for business purposes. *As an ordinary person,* he may especially reach out to others or become involved in charitable organizations.

15. Acting With Propriety

TRIGRAMS DE · LINES 001 000 · COMPLEMENTARY HEXAGRAM 10 TAKING RISKY ACTION

He is acting with propriety.
Even a strong leader can benefit from propriety.

■ *The traditional title* of this hexagram is "Modesty," but as the Huangs point out, modesty in terms of Chinese culture does not strictly represent humility or meekness. Rather, modesty essentially means proper social conduct. Thus, this hexagram is titled "Acting with Propriety" to better illustrate this concept. To the ancient Chinese this hexagram is the only one in which all the yin and yang lines are in positions wholly favorable to their natures, which gives an indication of the power of this symbol. *The complementary hexagram* is Hexagram 10 Taking Risky Action, which illustrates how at times taking risky action is necessary.

● *At his best,* he may know what is the proper thing to do and be committed to doing it. *At his worst,* he may know what is proper but for some reason have difficulties either wanting to do it or being able to do it.

▲ *As a public person,* he may benefit from being a powerful voice for what is the best thing to do. *As a businessperson,* he may skillfully help guide business matters to avoid problems and to provide stable growth. *As an ordinary person,* he may be able to make generally good life choices, and be viewed as a reliable friend and confidant by others because of his well-reasoned and sound opinions.

15.1 *Yin 6 changing line derives from Hexagram 36 Serving as an Assistant*

He is assisting others, and his small and correct actions
bring benefits to them all.

■ He has only a minor position in assisting others to achieve their goals. His actions should be small and correct to be favorable, however, his actions will benefit everyone.

● *At his best,* he may gain much from his positions as well as learn to act correctly. *At his worst,* he may not gain or learn as much, and he may merely be filling the role of servant.

▲ *As a public person,* he may serve in a small position on a committee or as an assistant to a great person. *As a businessperson,* he may serve as a broker, facilitating a commercial transaction. *As an ordinary person,* he may work as an assistant, devote himself to helping others, or try in small ways to improve the lives of those around him.

15.2   *Yin 6 changing line derives from Hexagram 46 Promoting Himself*

His propriety promotes him. He doesn't act rashly and is content with what he is offered, and so his position improves.

■ He is comfortable with his situation, and is not desirous of significant change. He is also pleased with what he receives. He always acts properly and so he is rewarded. Thus, he experiences both stability and some progress.

● *At his best,* he may be pleased and successful in his current situation, and his actions work to maintain the stability of his life and work. *At his worst,* he may not be entirely pleased with the limitations under which he works, and yet he is unable to see how to change matters for the better.

▲ *As a public person,* he may gain a public reputation for honesty and integrity, which strengthens his position. *As a businessperson,* he may work extensively with trade organizations or negotiating committees. *As an ordinary person,* he may be faced with much work, little praise, and little opportunity to better himself, or he may gain a reputation in his community for his moral strength.

15.3   *Yang 9 changing line derives from Hexagram 2 Going with the Flow*

It is proper for him to go with the flow of events. He may even be praised (perhaps undeservedly), which may be somewhat embarrassing; however, it causes him no real harm.

■ He does only what is easiest for him, acting with propriety and going with the flow of events. Doing so, however, results in succeeding and receiving praise. He knows that he did nothing special to gain this praise, and so he should continue to act with propriety in dealing with it.

● *At his best,* he may realize how lucky he was and why his praise should be dealt with modestly. *At his worst,* he may lose perspective on the true nature of his accomplishments and let his praises color his judgment concerning his abilities and potential.

▲ *As a public person,* he may gain prominence for dealing with a difficult problem.

As a businessperson, he may rescue a major portion of the business. *As an ordinary person,* he may face a number of difficulties and succeed in dealing with them all, and gain the appreciation of those around him.

15.4   *Yin 6 changing line derives from Hexagram 62 Independently Getting By*

He attains some power, although he is still weak,
so he needs to act with propriety to avoid problems.

■ He is in a position of some power, but he is either too weak or his position is seen as weak within his organization, so he must act with propriety in leading others. Forgetting his limitations or what is proper could easily lead to problems.

● *At his best,* he may well understand the requirements of the present situation, be able to do what is expected of him, and be able to craft a gradual plan of improvement for the future. *At his worst,* he may be weak by nature and only be able to maintain the status quo through dealing with others using propriety.

▲ *As a public person,* he may be promoted to a position heading a powerful bureaucracy. *As a businessperson,* he may gain ownership of a firm; yet, he may be considered an interloper. *As an ordinary person,* he may be promoted at work into a different area of the firm, or get married to a strong-willed mate.

15.5   *Yin 6 changing line derives from Hexagram 39 Bumbling by Himself*

He bumbles because of problems caused by those near him.
Now it is proper for him to act strongly.

■ He makes mistakes and experiences difficulties that are caused by those around or near him. In the extreme case, this could even be an attack upon him. He can use forceful measures in dealing with them, but this still needs to be done properly to succeed.

● *At his best,* he may have the insight to temper his power with propriety to achieve justice, which smoothes out the difficulties around him. *At his worst,* he may force his desires on others and thereby gain a temporary solution to his problems.

▲ *As a public person,* he may have a position that deals with troublesome clients, staff, or other contending officials. *As a businessperson,* he may have intense competition that hurts his business, or manage a contentious enterprise. *As an ordinary person,* he may have diverse problems (professional, legal, or marital), and find at times that losing his temper can do some good.

15.6   *Yin 6 changing line derives from Hexagram 52 Holding Back*

He holds back and relies on his reputation
to attract others to help him.

■ He is respected and widely known for his restraint and propriety. Thus, when he is threatened others come to his aid, and public opinion supports him and helps deal with his opposition. In this situation, he has little or no direct involvement in advancing his position at all.

● *At his best,* he has earned a place in the hearts of people who promote his position for him. *At his worst,* he may be respected and supported, but despite everything, his position may not be strong enough.

▲ *As a public person,* he may be an honored leader but too weak to fight his opponents. *As a businessperson,* he may have a concern for public issues, yet not be able to change company policies or products. *As an ordinary person,* he may need to gather the support of those around him to help resolve problems.

15.ALL   *All lines changing derives from Hexagram 10 Taking Risky Action*

He realizes now that he must take risky action to succeed.
He understands that if this is done properly,
he minimizes the harm that can come from it.

■ While propriety is often involved with respect for others, following proper procedures, and waiting for events to unfold, there is some point at which these approaches cannot be justified any longer. He has reached such a point, and he realizes that firm action, even risky action, is necessary now. However, even risky action can be taken properly to minimize the dangers.

● *At his best,* he may rise above conventional attitudes and fears, and by carefully defining his goal, having a strong commitment, and applying the proper approaches, he is able to take firm action and succeed. *At his worst,* he may lose control and act without sufficient forethought, and thereby risk some harm coming to him.

▲ *As a public person,* he may launch a publicity campaign to overcome political opponents. *As a businessperson,* he may participate in a power struggle in his business. *As an ordinary person,* he may take a firm stance in his family or community and attempt to swing opinion to support him.

16. Standstill

TRIGRAMS EB   LINES 000 100   COMPLEMENTARY HEXAGRAM 9 RESTRAINING HIMSELF

He is at a standstill, so sharing with others is helpful now.

■ *The traditional titles* of this hexagram are "Repose," "Enthusiasm," and "Broadcasting," among others. Whincup uses "Contentment," and the Huangs use "Weariness." All of these titles are misleading. Here it is titled "Standstill" to indicate both his inability to progress and his lack of motivation. Although he may be somewhat content, this is an illusory contentment because it is based more on a lack of motivating factors than anything else. Being with others and sharing with them allows him to mitigate the negative aspects of this situation somewhat. However, to truly move out of it, he must have both motivation and direction. *The complementary hexagram* is Hexagram 9 Restraining Himself, which is especially helpful in making the meaning of this hexagram clearer. It illustrates that standstill ends by realizing it is due in the first place to his own self-restraint.

● *At his best,* he may be at peace with himself and content in his life circumstances. *At his worst,* he may be numb emotionally, deaf to the voices of his dreams, and blind to the strivings of those close to him.

▲ *As a public person,* he may exemplify complacency and continually advocate patience. *As a businessperson,* he may be in a dead-end business or position and not be bothered by it. *As an ordinary person,* he may be worn out by age or accumulated stress, or have given up on hope for the future.

16.1   *Yin 6 changing line derives from Hexagram 51 At Fortune's Mercy*

Everyone can see he is at a standstill.
He thinks it is due to fortune's will, but this does not
ease his standstill or win the support of others.

■ He is at a standstill and believes that it is due to fortune's will rather than his own doing. He does not fight against it. His situation does not make him feel better or win the respect of those around him.

● *At his best,* he may have suffered some calamity or turn of fate that has halted him for the moment; with time, he will be able to understand his situation to help overcome it. *At his worst,* he may make his situation and feelings too well known, and thereby lose respect and compassion from those around him.

▲ *As a public person,* he may lose respect in public, or he may be jailed because of a stance he has taken. *As a businessperson,* he may suffer losses by not keeping business plans secret. *As an ordinary person,* he may suffer personal losses and offend those around him by his negative attitude.

16.2   *Yin 6 changing line derives from Hexagram 40 Getting Free*

He is able to break free from his standstill, but only for a while.

■ Here he has amassed enough power or resources to move out of standstill for a while, but he will need something more to get free of it for good.

● *At his best,* he may be energetic and optimistic; even though he might be disappointed when a slowdown or setback appears, he will be resolved to continue. *At his worst,* he may lapse back into a deeply negative state when a setback to his plans occurs.

▲ *As a public person,* he may experience a momentary wave of good news. *As a businessperson,* he may obtain good profits due to a short-term economic change. *As an ordinary person,* he may make unexpected gains and achieve special satisfaction, but soon his life will return to normal.

16.3   *Yin 6 changing line derives from Hexagram 62 Independently Getting By*

He is weak and independent, though getting by,
so he doesn't even understand he is at a standstill.
In time, however, he will come to understand this.

■ He cannot see or accept the whole truth about his position. Superficially, he thinks he is doing all right, but he is not. By not being able to see his problems, he is not able to take proper actions to rectify matters. Eventually when he does understand, then he will have cause for regret. His weakness is profound and affects his view of the world and his place in it.

● *At his best,* he may come to understand himself and his situation better, and grow in the process. *At his worst,* he may eventually be overwhelmed by regrets and uncertainties, and thus weaken himself further.

▲ *As a public person,* he may blindly follow policies, which he later regrets. *As a businessperson,* he may ignore warning signs because of his complacency with business as it is. *As an ordinary person,* he may simply not see what is happening around him in his life until it is too late, and then he would become very unhappy.

16.4   *Yang 9 changing line derives from Hexagram 2 Going with the Flow*

Matters will improve for him
when he goes along with a group of people.

■ He can overcome his standstill by using the power of a group of people to pull him along. Going with the flow of the energies of this group is not only easy, but also is the best thing he could do.

● *At his best,* he may better himself and come to find he has an important place with a special group of people. *At his worst,* he may simply ride their coattails until things get better for him.

▲ *As a public person,* he may become involved with a public campaign. *As a businessperson,* he may join other business people in a new endeavor. *As an ordinary person,* he may achieve notability among his friends and acquaintances, or he may marry.

16.5   *Yin 6 changing line derives from Hexagram 45 Serving a Leader*

He joins a leader hoping to progress, however, his standstill
continues. At least things do not get worse.

■ He has taken the step of attaching himself to a leader in the expectation that his situation will improve. However, perhaps due to the weakness of this leader, matters do not improve. But at least his situation does not deteriorate further.

● *At his best,* he may join a leader he respects and from whom he can learn. *At his worst,* he may be upset by conflicts and disappointments that continue to bedevil him.

▲ *As a public person,* he may join a major campaign and find that he does not gain in prominence or stature. *As a businessperson,* he may join a strong competitor and be disappointed that he does not prosper more. *As an ordinary person,* he may marry (or join a civic organization) hoping to improve his status, and he is disappointed with the results.

16.6   *Yin 6 changing line derives from Hexagram 35 Advancing Due to Favor*

He now advances due to someone's favor.
Thus, his standstill ends, but he is not truly pleased
because he was not responsible for it.

■ He is no longer at a standstill; someone has advanced him. While he did not like being at a standstill, he is even more displeased with how the end to his standstill has come about. This has had the effect of belittling him, or harming his perception of himself in some way, and thus is deeply unsettling.

● *At his best,* he may come to appreciate what others do for him, realize that the best way he can pay them back is by succeeding on his own, and thus grow out of his doubts. *At his worst,* he may remain deeply resentful of what others do for him, and this will continue to hinder him in his future endeavors.

▲ *As a public person,* he may be the beneficiary of a secret deal that gives him a prominent position. *As a businessperson,* he may be helped out of a business problem by a very successful ally. *As an ordinary person,* he may achieve publicity through slander or lawsuit, or be the recipient of someone's charity.

16.ALL *All lines changing derives from Hexagram 9 Restraining Himself*

Now he realizes the essence of his standstill came from restraining himself too much. Some self-restraint can be beneficial, but too much is debilitating.

■ In standstill, he is the true impediment to his progress. Through his excessive self-restraint, he was not able to see his options, marshal his abilities, or have faith in his success. Self-restraint can bring some good, but too much self-restraint brings standstill.

● *At his best,* he will have an insight into his life that will awaken his spirit and light his future direction. *At his worst,* he may struggle and begin to see that whatever happens, and despite his doubts and fears, he must keep trying in order to save his life.

▲ *As a public person,* he may find courage to take a public stance even though it leaves him vulnerable. *As a businessperson,* he may develop a prototype or proposal to advance his business. *As an ordinary person,* he may research courses to prepare for a new career, begin thinking seriously about finding a special person to share his life with, or gain important insights into his character through therapy.

17. Hunting

TRIGRAMS BH   LINES 100 110   COMPLEMENTARY HEXAGRAM 18 NURSING AN ILLNESS

He is hunting, and this can help him get what he needs.

■ *The traditional title* for this hexagram is "Following," although this is somewhat misleading. Here the hexagram is titled "Hunting." It signifies that things will not come to him unless he goes out after them. The purpose of hunting is to capture what is needed to sustain himself. Being committed to his hunt can ultimately bring him success. *The complementary hexagram* is Hexagram 18 Nursing an Illness, which illustrates that since external searches cannot always find what he needs, at times he must look within himself and nurse himself to get what he needs.

● *At his best,* he may know what he needs, actively search for it, and find it. *At his worst,* he may search for the wrong things, or search in such a way that it causes him more harm than good.

▲ *As a public person,* he may have a prominent role in an active public campaign. *As a businessperson,* he may be involved in searching for new opportunities or solutions. *As an ordinary person,* he may look outside of himself for specific things he needs.

17.1   *Yang 9 changing line derives from Hexagram 45 Serving a Leader*

He needs to find a new place for himself and join a new leader.

■ He may have lost his old position or for some reason realize he needs to find a new one. This is a difficult time for him, and he must now be especially persevering in maintaining what is essential to him. He must become involved in new endeavors, and once again prove his worth.

● *At his best,* he may come through this trying time with ease, demonstrating his worth by his skill and his emotional strength. *At his worst,* he may find it very difficult to begin, and need to rely on friends or family to help find a new place again.

▲ *As a public person,* he may suffer a demotion and have to look hard for a new position. *As a businessperson,* he may need to find a new location for his business.

As an ordinary person, he may suffer from loss of his job, home, or standing in the community, and have to begin again.

17.2   *Yin 6 changing line derives from Hexagram 58 Sharing Himself*

He makes only a small catch on his hunt, yet he shares it.
Sharing when he has only a little doesn't leave much for him,
so he will need to keep on hunting.

■ He succeeds in his hunt, but it is only a small prize, and there are great demands on it. He tries to share it, but this is not easy because it is so small. Thus, even though he has had some success, he will need to continue hunting.

● *At his best,* he may look upon sharing his prize as both a gift to others as well as an investment he is making in his future. *At his worst,* he may be resigned to the burdens he carries, and feel even more handicapped.

▲ *As a public person,* he may make a public show of disbursing wealth. *As a businessperson,* he may make some profits, yet find they cost more than they were worth. *As an ordinary person,* he may get married but not to the person he desired, or get a job or earn a profit that is disappointing.

17.3   *Yin 6 changing line derives from Hexagram 49 Being Revolutionary*

His hunt brought revolutionary change, and he gains much from it.
Yet, a radical change also comes with a small cost.
Since he has attained his goal, he should stop his hunt now.

■ He succeeds in his hunt. Perhaps this was through a revolutionary change or tactic, or perhaps the degree of success is such that it has brought a revolutionary change into his life. However, there is always a cost for revolutionary change; therefore, if this catch is sufficient for his needs, he should halt at this point.

● *At his best,* he may gain greatly and gratefully accept the cost that comes with his success. *At his worst,* he may find it hard to accept any disappointment, or find it hard not to be greedy and want to continue his hunt.

▲ *As a public person,* he may achieve a notable success through an unconventional tactic or alliance. *As a businessperson,* he may make gains although they cost more than he anticipated. *As an ordinary person,* he may obtain a promotion or advance that causes difficulties for his family and friends.

17.4   *Yang 9 changing line derives from Hexagram 3 Gathering Support*

By gathering support, he will be able to attain all his goals.
However, he should be careful because pushing his
hunt too far will eventually bring trouble.

■ His hunt succeeds because of his helpers and his allies. However, attempting too much, either by asking too much of his allies, gaining more of them than he needs, or gaining so much wealth that it causes dissension among his supporters will cause trouble. Knowing when to halt his hunt in a timely manner is important.

● *At his best,* he may know how much to ask his allies for assistance, and he will be graciously modest in his demands of their time and resources. *At his worst,* he may be so insistent for their assistance that he strains their ties with him, and even threatens his own gains.

▲ *As a public person,* he may try to gather a great coalition to assist him. *As a businessperson,* he may form a business coalition that could grow far beyond his control. *As an ordinary person,* he may enjoy the assistance of others, yet he should not involve them too much in his life or else there could be unanticipated consequences elsewhere.

17.5   *Yang 9 changing line derives from Hexagram 51 At Fortune's Mercy*

By a stroke of fate, his hunt is suddenly rewarded.

■ He is surprised to suddenly receive a reward or bounty in his hunt. This was completely unexpected and is a rich reward, so he takes great pleasure in this.

● *At his best,* he may be sincerely grateful for his bounty, and appropriate and modest in his use of it. *At his worst,* he may not treasure it or use it wisely, and thus waste a favorable turn of fortune.

▲ *As a public person,* he may be given an award or a position of honor. *As a businessperson,* he may be given a bonus or praise for his accomplishments. *As an ordinary person,* he may enjoy an extraordinarily beneficial period, possibly including marriage, promotion, or personal recognition.

17.6   *Yin 6 changing line derives from Hexagram 25 Having No Expectations*

Now he finds himself hunted. Although he does not know what
to expect, he will suffer somewhat from whatever comes.

■ Ultimately, he becomes the object of someone else's hunt. This means he could be a victim of his own success. He will accept whatever happens now, for he has had his successes, too. This represents a turning point for him, and he waits for the new direction to appear.

● *At his best,* he may sincerely accept the major changes in his life when they appear with little or no regret. *At his worst,* he may not be able to accept what he perceives as undeserved or cruel fate.

▲ *As a public person,* he may be required to provide support to someone else, or be placed in a figurehead position with little or no power. *As a businessperson,* he may find himself restricted by contractual obligations or be sought by competitors. *As an ordinary person,* he may find himself fleeing from the law, or be sought by certain people around him, or desired as a mate.

17.ALL   *All lines changing derives from Hexagram 18 Nursing an Illness*

He no longer needs to hunt for external things. Now he needs to take care of things within himself that need attention.

■ Previously, he was intensely focused outside of himself, engaged in the hunt for external things. Now he has come around to the point of needing to look within himself. He needs to devote time and attention to taking care of things within himself that need nurturing, rest, and repair.

● *At his best,* he may view this transition as a necessary and positive change as his life goes in a new direction. *At his worst,* he may view himself as weak or ill, and resent what he sees as sickness or failure.

▲ *As a public person,* he may write his memoirs, or turn his attention to issues of ethics and morality. *As a businessperson,* he may need to turn to what is really happening inside his business. *As an ordinary person,* he may need to devote time to his physical, emotional, or spiritual health.

18. Nursing an Illness

| TRIGRAMS FD | LINES 011 001 | COMPLEMENTARY HEXAGRAM 17 HUNTING |

He is nursing an illness;
it is beneficial to attend to it as soon as possible.

■ *The traditional titles* for this hexagram include "Work on What Has Been Spoiled" and "Decay," although these are somewhat misleading. The title specifically means poison or an illness caused by poisoning. Whincup notes that some commentators say it refers to a slightly different character that means "thing" or "business." Here the title "Nursing an Illness" is used. The word illness in this context can refer to a variety of problems that revolve around an individual's situation or condition, so the word illness when used below should be interpreted broadly. *The complementary hexagram* is Hexagram 17 Hunting, which illustrates how access to greater resources can be obtained by looking outside himself.

● *At his best,* he may understand the nature of his illness and know how to deal with it. *At his worst,* he may be upset or disturbed and not do what he should do to heal himself.

▲ *As a public person,* he may have a highly visible role dealing with health or moral issues. *As a businessperson,* he may understand what is wrong and know how to cure it. *As an ordinary person,* he may be dealing with an illness or other problem in his life that requires him to gradually turn things around by first changing himself.

18.1   *Yin 6 changing line derives from Hexagram 26 External Restraint*

By submitting to the constraints of his illness at the beginning,
he is able to overcome it more quickly.
Thus, it will not harm him as much as it could otherwise.

■ He promptly submits to the constraints that his situation imposes, and because of this, he is able to more quickly heal himself and attend to his problems. He thus minimizes the impact of the illness, and less harm comes from it.

● *At his best,* he may willingly accept that he will be limited and restrained, and he realizes that this is for the best in the long run. *At his worst,* he may not be able to accept such restraints, and in ignoring them, he runs the risk of more serious harm.

▲ *As a public person,* he may realize he has serious public relations problems that need to be overcome slowly. *As a businessperson,* he may need to correct deep-seated problems in his business before he can progress. *As an ordinary person,* he may need to attend to inherited problems, his illness or the illness of a parent, or even the death of a parent.

18.2   *Yang 9 changing line derives from Hexagram 52 Holding Back*

He is holding back from another's illness.
He should not get involved, although he feels drawn to it.

■ Someone else has a problem, and they need to deal with it themselves. However, for one reason or another, he finds himself pulled into their plight. It is really best if he does not get involved, but he may not be able to resist. The traditional text identifies this problem as his mother's illness.

● *At his best,* he may be compassionate or sensitive to others' needs, and his interest in helping them will not unduly burden him or them. *At his worst,* he may try to help others, but not be able to deal with the problems that come from doing so.

▲ *As a public person,* he may become improperly involved with establishing new policies as a temporary officeholder. *As a businessperson,* he may meddle in another's business. *As an ordinary person,* he may become involved with his parents' health, or become involved in a friend's affairs.

18.3   *Yang 9 changing line derives from Hexagram 4 Acting Impetuously*

He acts impetuously regarding his illness.
There may be some trouble coming from this, but no serious harm.

■ He is showing immaturity by acting without enough thought or maturity regarding his situation. As a consequence, he stirs things up and some trouble comes, but it is not enough to seriously harm him. The traditional text identifies this problem as his father's illness.

● *At his best,* he may have the strength and courage to do what must be done, but not enough wisdom to know exactly how to do it. *At his worst,* he may take excessive pleasure in his ability to do things, and not realize that he could cause even worse harm by his actions.

▲ *As a public person,* he may act too quickly, without sufficient evidence, or without proper authorization. *As a businessperson,* he may upset others with his revolutionary business practices, but it will not significantly affect his profits. *As an ordinary person,* he may feel himself beset by others' problems, bothered by many diverse difficulties and regrets, or concerned with immature outbursts or actions.

18.4   *Yin 6 changing line derives from Hexagram 50 Governing Matters*

He is so involved in dealing with other matters that he neglects his illness. Continuing in this will bring trouble.

■ He is very involved in pursuing other matters so he neglects his problems. Both ignoring a problem and not dealing with it adequately are ways to easily allow it to grow worse. He does not understand his limits or does not respect a weakness, and so he has a fundamental problem that will bring him trouble.

● *At his best,* he may be distracted by other concerns, or not yet understand the problem he is confronting, but eventually he will awaken to his proper course of action. *At his worst,* he may belittle the problem, or not truly understand it at all, and thereby suffer in the future.

▲ *As a public person,* he may be censured for things he should have done and didn't do. *As a businessperson,* he may be focused on gains today, rather than on correcting festering problems. *As an ordinary person,* he may neglect sustaining important relationships, his career rejuvenation, or his health.

18.5   *Yin 6 changing line derives from Hexagram 57 At His Leader's Mercy*

He submits to the power of his illness. Now he can deal with it properly, and perhaps even benefit.

■ At this point, he is fully feeling the effects of his problem, thus it likely has a more prominent place in his life. Now he can make a serious commitment to dealing with it, and do what is proper to resolve the problem.

● *At his best,* he may gain a deep insight into the nature of the problem, and devote enough effort and skill to it that he deals with it successfully. *At his worst,* he may try to do what is best, but find it isn't enough to fully resolve the problem.

▲ *As a public person,* he may ask to be placed in charge of a difficult situation and may earn praise for resolving it. *As a businessperson,* he may succeed in dealing with a long-standing problem, earn profits, and gain recognition. *As an ordinary person,* he may employ a new means to solve an old problem, may improve his position financially, have a child or get married, or give his child away in marriage.

18.6   *Yang 9 changing line derives from Hexagram 46 Promoting Himself*

Rather than attacking his illness directly,
he should strengthen and promote himself in other ways.

■ Unlike the earlier lines that focused on nursing his problems through ordinary means, this line advocates that he find a radically different path. He might now become involved in intellectual, moral, or spiritual matters. He is acting in a different way, and thereby attains a different kind of success.

● *At his best,* he may gain important insights that benefit him in new ways. *At his worst,* he may distract himself from what he should be doing.

▲ *As a public person,* he may retire to write or promulgate his viewpoint, or attain a position of moral or intellectual leadership. *As a businessperson,* he may succeed by working through others. *As an ordinary person,* he may withdraw from worldly matters, or study important spiritual materials.

18.ALL   *All lines changing derives from Hexagram 17 Hunting*

He no longer needs to deal with problems within himself.
Rather, now he needs to look outside of himself
and search for things in the world to pursue.

■ After he has nursed his problems, and he has properly resolved them, he turns his attention to matters outside of himself. This will begin a new phase of externally focused activities from which he hopes to gain.

● *At his best,* he may understand his own strengths and weaknesses, and using this he will find things in the external world to successfully gain and attain. *At his worst,* he may become enamored of external goals and lose the voice of internal wisdom that guides successful endeavors.

▲ *As a public person,* he may champion a major cause that represents a new direction for him. *As a businessperson,* he may become elevated to a higher position that has a completely different business orientation for him. *As an ordinary person,* he may lose touch with what was his reality before, or he may become a counselor or advisor.

19. Leading Others

| TRIGRAMS HE | LINES 110 000 | COMPLEMENTARY HEXAGRAM 33 COMPLYING |

He is leading others. Although this is beneficial,
errors in leadership can easily bring trouble.

■ *The traditional title* for this hexagram is "Approach," although this is somewhat misleading. Whincup uses "Leadership" and the Huangs use "Prevailing." Here the hexagram is titled "Leading Others." This hexagram indicates that he is leading others by supervising, directing, or in some way guiding them. Although authority such as this is beneficial, his control should not be taken for granted or exercised without regard to the situation, because then it will bring trouble. *The complementary hexagram* is Hexagram 33 Complying, which illustrates how even leadership needs to comply with the demands of even greater leaders as well as the requirements of the situation.

● *At his best,* he may be respected for his leadership qualities because he truly knows what to do. *At his worst,* he may be a leader who makes mistakes that, although troublesome, are not disastrous.

▲ *As a public person,* he may be a well-known leader. *As a businessperson,* he may have a reputation for success in business leadership. *As an ordinary person,* he may have personal qualities that make it easy for him to lead others and to help groups achieve their goals.

19.1   *Yang 9 changing line derives from Hexagram 7 Serving as an Officer*

He leads others through his position.
This is the easiest form of leadership to attain as well as to use.

■ He is guiding others by his status, title, rank, or position within an organization. He thus is using his titular authority rather than his authority as an expert or moral leader. This leadership has limitations as to what it expects and what it can accomplish, which both the leader and those he leads understand. This form of leadership is the weakest, but it is also the easiest to come by.

● *At his best,* he may be a leader or teacher who will be respected not only for his position, but also for his character and ability. *At his worst,* he may not be liked or even respected by those he leads, and he may be more an impediment to getting things done than a real contributor.

▲ *As a public person,* he may have a position with the legal authority to direct the operations of an organization. *As a businessperson,* he may direct a company or one of its units. *As an ordinary person,* he may serve others as a good example, or help train others.

19.2 *Yang 9 changing line derives from Hexagram 24 Beginning a Relationship*

He leads others by reaffirming the basis of their relationship.
This is very successful, and he benefits.

■ His leadership is based on the strength of commitments to the relationship. He reaffirms shared commitments and goals. With this as a basis, he is able to gain cooperation from others. This could apply to his superiors or to those who are even stronger than he is.

● *At his best,* he may be respected for his skill as well as for his leadership, and he gains a reputation for being able to get things done. *At his worst,* he may have less ability to manage his subordinates, but he will still manage to help them achieve most goals.

▲ *As a public person,* he may root out corruption or inefficiencies in his group or organization. *As a businessperson,* he may lead a reorganization or implement new procedures. *As an ordinary person,* he may know how to help his friends and associates, and is appreciated for his generous nature.

19.3 *Yin 6 changing line derives from Hexagram 11 Easily Progressing*

Forcefully imposing himself on others is an easy mistake to make,
but it harms his ability to lead them.
To be a truly successful leader, they must choose to follow him.

■ Leadership easily has the potential for conflict and serious mistakes, and here he falls into that trap. True leadership is a partnership between the leader and his followers. He must not forget this and try to impose himself on them when it is not needed.

● *At his best,* he may realize his errors in being too forceful and seek to regain his support. *At his worst,* he may be blind to their alienation, lose the support he needs, and thereby suffer.

▲ *As a public person,* he may assume a prominent position espousing his opinions as though they were facts. *As a businessperson,* he may use manipulation and threats pursuing his goals. *As an ordinary person,* he may find that matters do not go as he expects, and he could suffer until he stops trying to force matters and carefully rethinks his plans.

| 19.4 | *Yin 6 changing line derives from Hexagram 54 Entering a Marriage* |

He gains a position of leadership through a marriage or partnership. His orders now are proper.

■ He has reached a position where by right he can assume leadership of others. Note that this was granted to him through a marriage or partnership. Now his orders are accepted as proper, and good can come from his leadership.

● *At his best,* he may have sought a leadership role as much for what he can bring to others as what he gains himself, so he appreciates his success from both perspectives. *At his worst,* he may be selfishly motivated, and he ends up using his position to manipulate others.

▲ *As a public person,* he may have been appointed to a higher office by a great leader, and he gains the respect and backing of those around him. *As a businessperson,* he may take a strong role in bringing success to his business. *As an ordinary person,* he may get a promotion, become stronger in his relationships with his mate or others, or gain some local fame.

| 19.5 | *Yin 6 changing line derives from Hexagram 60 Having Limited Resources* |

He recognizes the limits to his power, so he is both a wise and effective leader. This is very beneficial for everyone.

■ He has reached a point where he has gained true wisdom as a leader because he understands in what ways his leadership is limited. He can extend his leadership through selecting the proper subordinates or through persuasion. Through these and other means, his leadership brings benefits to everyone.

● *At his best,* he may be a notable person and widely respected for his wisdom and humanity. *At his worst,* he may possess similar qualities, but not be as notable or as famous.

▲ *As a public person,* he may be an especially respected and effective official. *As a businessperson,* he may have gained wide respect in the business world, and be able to assist the entire business community. *As an ordinary person,* he may be able to get what he wants from those around him, and yet he will not desire excess.

19.6   *Yin 6 changing line derives from Hexagram 41 Declining Influence*

He has little influence to persuade others to follow him, so now he uses force. It is very beneficial that no harm comes from this.

■ The most effective leadership is where the subordinates willingly obey the leader. Here, however, he is a leader who has lost the power to persuade others to follow him. Nevertheless, he is so powerful that he can use force to bend others to his will. Normally, such actions would always bring trouble later. Yet, this is not so now. If he does use force, those around him understand that it was done for the highest reasons, and that normally he would not do this.

● *At his best,* he may have a legacy of respect that supports his reputation even though his actions are not popular. *At his worst,* he may be manipulative and coercive, and others will resent his actions.

▲ *As a public person,* he may be given a very powerful position, possibly in control of a police or military unit. *As a businessperson,* he may be able to pry out secrets in the business world, or threaten sanctions to force compliance. *As an ordinary person,* he may be able to get what he wants, even though it may be done through harsh means.

19.ALL   *All lines changing derives from Hexagram 33 Complying*

To achieve his goals as a leader, he has learned to comply with the requirements of the situation, including the demands of his own ruler.

■ Although he is a leader, leaders also need to submit to their rulers and comply with the demands of their situations. Leaders do not become independent from powers greater than theirs; rather, they are even more deeply compliant.

● *At his best,* he may fully understand that to lead is also truly to serve. *At his worst,* he may cynically view his rulers and his career as a way to gain wealth and power, rather than as a deep commitment to a cause and to worthy people.

▲ *As a public person,* he may wholly commit himself to the public good or to a particular party. *As a businessperson,* he may be slavishly committed to maintaining profits over everything else. *As an ordinary person,* he may find that he is involved in a cause that has taken over his life, or he has learned to completely comply with his mate's demands.

20. Preparing Himself

TRIGRAMS EF   LINES 000 011   COMPLEMENTARY HEXAGRAM 34 FORCING MATTERS

He studies and prepares himself because he is not yet ready to act.
His preparations will be beneficial later.

■ *The traditional titles* for this hexagram are "Contemplation" and "View" although these are somewhat misleading. Here the hexagram is titled "Preparing Himself." This signifies he is going through preparations for a major task, but he is not yet ready to act. In the traditional text, the preparation shown is engaging in a religious ritual. There are three different viewpoints shown in the six lines, that of a child, a woman, and a leader. Whatever his status, proper preparation is essential to successfully achieving a task. *The complementary hexagram* is Hexagram 34 Forcing Matters, which illustrates how after proper preparations have been completed, he is able to forcefully apply himself in achieving his goals.

● *At his best,* he may thoroughly prepare himself for his goal. *At his worst,* he may take some preparatory actions, but they may not be proper or adequate for what he wants to do.

▲ *As a public person,* he may be a religious leader, educator, or spokesperson for a new viewpoint. *As a businessperson,* he may be engaged in serious study of new products, markets, or other business matters. *As an ordinary person,* he may be engaged in studies or other preparatory programs to better his life.

20.1   *Yin 6 changing line derives from Hexagram 42 Gaining Benefits*

He is too young or it is too early for him to gain much from
preparing himself now. If he is a follower, this is all right; however,
if he is a leader, this is troublesome.

■ For some reason, such as youth, immaturity, or being too new to his situation, he is not able to prepare himself properly and benefit from gaining knowledge, skills, or enhanced position. His inability here is not a problem if he is going to be following another's lead; however, if he is a leader of others, his inability brings problems. Leaders need to have more advanced abilities even at the beginning.

● *At his best,* he may be young and still learning about life, and others will not depend on him for abilities he does not yet have. *At his worst,* he may have pretensions to power he cannot justify, and he will not have the tools he needs to be an effective leader.

▲ *As a public person,* he may be placed in an assistant's position from which he can assist and learn from those with more ability. *As a businessperson,* he may lack sufficient knowledge of his business to operate it successfully. *As an ordinary person,* he may be immature or too enthusiastic to take the proper steps, and as a result, he could easily get into trouble by attempting to lead or by trusting those who would take advantage of him.

20.2   Yin 6 changing line derives from Hexagram 59 Things Are Swept Clear

Suddenly, things are swept clear around him; all he can do now
is prepare himself by careful observation and inner alignment.

■ The world can be a frightening place, and here he finds that things around him are suddenly changing. To prepare himself while being swept along, all he should do is objectively observe the changes and align himself emotionally or spiritually with the new order.

● *At his best,* he may learn much from the events now affecting him, and he may be motivated to prepare himself in such a way as to better his position in the future. *At his worst,* he may not understand the changes around him or how he will fit into this new world.

▲ *As a public person,* he may have to moderate or back off from his public position rather than take a firm stance in a time of rapid flux. *As a businessperson,* he may have his market suddenly change, and he has to think how his business can adapt. *As an ordinary person,* he may be confused or frightened by events out of his control, yet he needs to take stock of how to prepare himself for the future, and doing this he will succeed later.

20.3   *Yin 6 changing line derives from Hexagram 53 Sharing Commitment*

Preparing himself to share a commitment is not easy. First he
agrees, then he changes his mind. Others can see his doubts;
however, if they also see he has strong desires,
they know he will commit himself eventually.

■ Commitment is not always easy, and it is not always a straight course. Here his task of preparing himself for commitment is going slowly. First he agrees, then he pulls back. Others can see this. However, what is most important is his desire. With strong desires, he will commit himself in time. Others can also see that he will succeed eventually in committing himself when his desires are strong enough. Without such depth of desire, he will only appear weak and likely to fail.

● *At his best,* he may be committed to his future, and others will respect his persistence. *At his worst,* he may be unrealistic in his expectations, excuse his vacillating course, and ultimately fail to properly prepare himself.

▲ *As a public person,* he may advocate contradictory positions before he makes up his mind. *As a businessperson,* he may retreat in response to competitors' advances. *As an ordinary person,* he may find a course of study to be difficult, fall prey to someone who may be deceiving him, or struggle to commit himself to a major goal in life.

20.4 *Yin 6 changing line derives from Hexagram 12 Being Blocked*

His preparations are blocked by someone greater,
and he realizes it would benefit him now to work with that person
rather than to fight with him.

■ He can see that no matter how much he struggles to prepare himself, he will still face the blockage of someone greater than he. Thus, he decides that he would be better off if he joined with him.

● *At his best,* he may gain a good position and benefit from a strong leader or powerful enterprise. *At his worst,* he may realize the weakness of his position, but be unable to win the position he desires.

▲ *As a public person,* he may gain an important position representing a powerful leader. *As a businessperson,* he may become involved in an important project. *As an ordinary person,* he may dedicate himself to an important cause (political, religious, or otherwise), or he may get married.

20.5 *Yang 9 changing line derives from Hexagram 23 Being in a Collapsing Situation*

He is in a collapsing situation; however, if he has prepared himself
to be strong (as a leader should be), he will not be harmed.

■ He sees danger coming, but he can do nothing to halt it. Only having strength counts, for with strength comes the ability to weather negative consequences without harm. If his earlier preparation has made him strong, he will be all right.

● *At his best,* he will have courage and strength to wait out and overcome the difficulties. *At his worst,* he may be weak or not understand the dangers he will be encountering, and thereby he ends up harmed.

▲ *As a public person,* he may be involved in a major scandal. *As a businessperson,* he may have an impending bankruptcy, loss of market share, or legal complication. *As an ordinary person,* he may be in the public spotlight in some negative way, have situations collapse, or find that events all around him cause problems.

20.6   *Yang 9 changing line derives from Hexagram 8 Entering an Alliance*

Because of his preparations, he can now ally himself with others
and assist them in their preparations. By using leadership,
he benefits and comes to no harm.

■ His goal of preparing himself has succeeded. He is now able to marshal his skills and strength, and he seeks an alliance and joins with others. He now is able to assist them in turn in preparing themselves. Using leadership is beneficial for them all, and he comes to no harm.

● *At his best,* he may be a wise and gifted leader who benefits those around him. *At his worst,* he may be capable and strong but somewhat inclined to use others for his own benefit.

▲ *As a public person,* he may have created his own public campaign or agency. *As a businessperson,* he may be involved in a product or market innovation, or a business startup. *As an ordinary person,* he may gain much from wider participation in business and social life, or he may benefit from a career for which he has trained.

20.ALL   *All lines changing derives from Hexagram 34 Forcing Matters*

His time of preparation is over, and now he is ready to
force matters around him. Such a goal is natural
for someone who has newly gained his strength.

■ While he was preparing himself, he was aware of his needs and goals. However, he was in many ways powerless to achieve them. Now that he has discovered strength and know-how within himself, he is anxious to strive for his goals in the world around him. This is something he should do, even though both success and failure will come from it.

● *At his best,* he may be both strong and wise, and realize that "doing" is what is most important for him now. *At his worst,* he may be wholly engaged by achieving all manner of desires and goals, and not realize that he should temper his actions with the perspective of wisdom.

▲ *As a public person,* he may attempt to gain a public office. *As a businessperson,* he may attempt to start a new business or seek a patent for his invention. *As an ordinary person,* he may seek a marriage, business partner, new career, or recover from a long illness.

21. Working on a Problem

TRIGRAMS BG   LINES 100 101   COMPLEMENTARY HEXAGRAM 48 BEING RENEWED

He is working on a problem.
Doing a good job is necessary to get a good result.

■ *The traditional title* for this hexagram is "Biting Through," although this is somewhat misleading. Here the hexagram is titled, "Working on a Problem." The traditional text uses the image of chewing (or biting) through tough, dried meat to symbolize the intent of this hexagram. It is only by conscientiously working on a problem and doing a good job that a successful resolution to the problem can be obtained. *The complementary hexagram* is Hexagram 48 Being Renewed, which illustrates that work must be followed by renewal.

● *At his best,* he may be working hard on what needs his effort. *At his worst,* he may not be working hard enough, or not working on exactly the right thing to get the problem solved.

▲ *As a public person,* he may have a reputation for not shirking what needs to be said and for doing what needs to be done. *As a businessperson,* he may be devoted to making a success out of each and every task he has. *As an ordinary person,* he may clearly understand what he needs to do, and have the strength and energy to do it.

21.1   *Yang 9 changing line derives from Hexagram 35 Advancing Due to Favor*

At the very start, someone is keeping him from acting and perhaps
making a mistake. Since he does not experience any harm,
he should look at the good coming from this.

■ He may feel unhappy about being constrained, but actually, someone is doing him some good by keeping him from harm. This may not be easy to accept, but he can learn something from this if he desires to.

● *At his best,* he may learn something beneficial from the restrictions that have halted him. *At his worst,* he may be spiteful and angry at being restrained; however, even this will not cause him any real harm.

▲ *As a public person,* he may be put on probation or censured before he gets into worse trouble. *As a businessperson,* he may find a competitor has beat him to the market. *As an ordinary person,* he may suffer a medical problem with his feet, be incarcerated, or be under someone's tutelage.

21.2   *Yin 6 changing line derives from Hexagram 38 Looking for a Leader*

He is distracted or deterred from his original goal.
Although this could be harmful, no harm comes; however,
he doesn't progress in his initial endeavor.

■ He becomes engrossed in, distracted by, or deterred by another situation or leader. Thus, he does not deal with the initial issue. Although this could be harmful, he is lucky that no harm comes from this. Note also, however, that he cannot progress in his initial endeavor.

● *At his best,* he may be a bit too curious and engaged in the world and, therefore, too easily distracted from what he should be doing. *At his worst,* he may not be able to define his goals in life or be able to commit himself in order to progress in life.

▲ *As a public person,* he may be given another assignment, which takes away his time and energy from his primary task. *As a businessperson,* he may become deeply committed to an endeavor that has yet to be profitable. *As an ordinary person,* he may become involved in family or work problems, or may suffer a serious illness or medical problem.

21.3   *Yin 6 changing line derives from Hexagram 30 Gaining Enlightenment*

He is working on a problem from which he gains important
knowledge. He experiences troubles, but no real harm.

■ The most important knowledge comes through effort and struggle. That is what he is experiencing here. He does not easily overcome the problem. In fact, he may not eliminate it at all. Yet, he gains by his knowledge, and while he may experience troubles, the problem does not truly harm him.

● *At his best,* he may learn valuable lessons and wisdom, which help him with the problem. *At his worst,* he may learn some good skills, but not be able to positively affect the problem.

▲ *As a public person,* he may be criticized for his handling of his work or his qualifications. *As a businessperson,* he may find hidden problems that hinder his business. *As an ordinary person,* he may find matters more complex and difficult than he realized, and it may be a very troublesome period.

21.4   *Yang 9 changing line derives from Hexagram 27 Desiring*

He is working on a problem and finds his desires motivate him.
Continuing now benefits him.

■ Even when benefits are not expected, they are possible. Here he has been working on a problem when he gets a benefit of some sort through the work. He likes the work and the benefit, and he wants more. His desire thus helps spur him on.

● *At his best,* he may be observant and capable of benefiting from opportunities for advancement that he happens across. *At his worst,* he may fall into a way of extracting some benefit from his situation to the detriment of others.

▲ *As a public person,* he may unexpectedly gain public prominence for his endeavors. *As a businessperson,* he may get a bonus or some other benefit. *As an ordinary person,* he may struggle with some difficulties and obtain a benefit, or unexpected benefits may come through marriage.

21.5   *Yin 6 changing line derives from Hexagram 25 Having No Expectations*

He works on a problem and finds that many benefits come to him.
No harm can come to him as long as he continues to have no
expectations regarding these benefits.

■ The wealth or other benefits he received could simply be a one-time good fortune. While he is pleased with these benefits, he should have no thought that they will continue. Having no expectation, he will not make any assumptions that could harm him in the future. By doing this, he will continue to be receptive to trends and events around him, and he will be capable of responding appropriately.

● *At his best,* he may be appreciative of his benefit, but realistic about his prospects. *At his worst,* he may long for additional rewards or find himself harmed by his expectations.

▲ *As a public person,* he may briefly gain public praise or fame. *As a businessperson,* he may have a windfall profit. *As an ordinary person,* he may have a difficulty unexpectedly turn to his advantage, or he may receive an inheritance from an employer.

21.6   *Yang 9 changing line derives from Hexagram 51 At Fortune's Mercy*

Fate's hand sits uncomfortably hard on him no matter how hard
he works on his problem. There is little he can do to overcome it,
so this is an unfortunate period for him.

■ He has worked as hard as he could on the problem, yet now finds himself powerless to affect matters because fate's hand is now upon him. The only thing he can do is suffer through an unfortunate period.

● *At his best,* he may feel preyed upon by others and helpless to improve matters. *At his worst,* he may feel isolated, abused, or victimized, or may even be incarcerated.

▲ *As a public person,* he may suffer demotion or go through an investigation and trial. *As a businessperson,* he may find his sources of information taken away from him, threatening his ability to conduct his business. *As an ordinary person,* he may refuse to believe what others tell him, eventually to his misfortune; instigate many disputes; or suffer a head injury or hearing loss.

21.ALL   *All lines changing derives from Hexagram 48 Being Renewed*

> He has worked hard on the problems besetting him,
> and this has stressed him.
> Now he needs a period of rest, repair, and renewal.

■ After the period of hard work he has come through, he now needs to recover and repair himself through rest and renewal. Renewal in this sense includes the physical, emotional, and spiritual dimensions of personality through the processes of support, growth, and rebirth.

● *At his best,* he may be open and receptive to being renewed and to changing his life. *At his worst,* he may be exhausted, upset, and find it hard to recuperate.

▲ *As a public person,* he may be put on leave for rest. *As a businessperson,* he may have his career deteriorate, and he needs to prepare for a change. *As an ordinary person,* he may need to recover from stress or illness.

22. Advancing By His Image

TRIGRAMS GD   LINES 101 001   COMPLEMENTARY HEXAGRAM 47 ADVANCING BY HARD WORK

He is advancing by his image, so only small benefits are possible now.

■ *The traditional titles* of this hexagram are "Grace" and "Ornamentation." Whincup titles this "Adorned," and the Huangs use "Decoration." Here the hexagram is titled "Advancing by His Image," in line with the idea that he is trying to make himself appear more desirable in order to succeed. The lines in the traditional text illustrate preparing for a betrothal. *The complementary hexagram* is Hexagram 47 Advancing by Hard Work, which illustrates how superficial images are not able to succeed at all times, and that the ability to work hard is at times required.

● *At his best,* he may carefully prepare an appropriate image and use it to advance himself into a suitable situation. *At his worst,* he may deceive others by his image and end up in an inappropriate situation that causes problems.

▲ *As a public person,* he may gain a great deal of publicity through his image. *As a businessperson,* he may best succeed by being a spokesperson. *As an ordinary person,* he may win approval through his dress or manners, or by "looking the part" in some other way.

22.1   *Yang 9 changing line derives from Hexagram 52 Holding Back*

He acts unpretentiously. He learns by observing quietly.
He assists by gladly doing even the humblest things.
Presenting this image, he advances modestly.

■ By being humble, observant, and unpretentious, he is able to gather useful information and skills. Nothing is beneath his notice or unworthy of learning about. He cooperates whenever and wherever he can. With such an attitude, he will learn a great deal and favorably impress others. In this way modest advance will come.

● *At his best,* he may gain a true understanding of the world around him as well as gain the respect of those around him. *At his worst,* he may become devoted to minor details and lose his perspective on his larger goals and more important worldly issues.

▲ *As a public person,* he may work as an intern in a large organization. *As a businessperson,* he may begin to study everything about how a company works. *As an ordinary person,* he may improve his feet or footwear, or begin a course of study.

22.2   *Yin 6 changing line derives from Hexagram 26 External Restraint*

> He shows his willingness to submit to guidance by superiors
> and the restraint of "the rules." Thus, he is promoted.

■ He is learning how to get along in a large organization or under a headstrong supervisor. It may not be easy at times learning how to submit to restraint, but he does well with it and is rewarded by promotion.

● *At his best,* he may learn how to get along with others who are difficult, or live with the imposition of rules. *At his worst,* he may begrudgingly cooperate and resent it continuously.

▲ *As a public person,* he may be promoted through his obedience or be given a position in public relations. *As a businessperson,* he may gain through connections with a supervisor, or through writing, advertising, or selling. *As an ordinary person,* he may benefit by sprucing up his physical appearance and improving his self-image, or gain through the assistance of others who like him.

22.3   *Yang 9 changing line derives from Hexagram 27 Desiring*

> His desires become visible and bring him problems. However,
> being steadfast in his original goals will be beneficial eventually.

■ He has perhaps gotten a bit cocky, and now he is thinking of other things such as what he desires to have and pleasures he'd like to enjoy. These bring problems to him in perhaps more than one way. In this time of stress and even potential conflict, it is especially beneficial for him to refocus on the goals he set at the beginning, and to rededicate himself to them.

● *At his best,* he may learn to balance his desires, his capabilities, and the potentials of his current situation. *At his worst,* he may lose his perspective, devote too much effort to satisfying his desires, and suffer in the rest of his life.

▲ *As a public person,* he may violate rules and try to keep his actions hidden. *As a businessperson,* he may have too grandiose a view of his position, which interferes with his work. *As an ordinary person,* he may become involved in morally questionable activities, spend too much money, or get into conflicts with those around him.

22.4   *Yin 6 changing line derives from Hexagram 30 Gaining Enlightenment*

He has become enlightened, and now seeks to contribute
and join in a more significant way.

■ He has gained valuable skills and knowledge, and he now has a very concrete goal in mind. He wishes to join in a true partnership with a leader (or organization). Contributions made in this spirit of enlightened cooperation are valuable to him as well as to those around him.

● *At his best,* he may have found a richly rewarding goal and be wholly satisfied committing himself to it. *At his worst,* he may choose a direction more out of opportunism than sincere desire to aid and support.

▲ *As a public person,* he may seek to join an important organization. *As a businessperson,* he may offer buyouts to partners or merger offers to competitors. *As an ordinary person,* he may make offers of marriage or partnership.

22.5   *Yin 6 changing line derives from Hexagram 37 Serving in a Household*

It is as if he were a servant. He finds this somewhat humiliating
but does get some benefits from it.

■ He is in a situation where he is treated as a servant or a personal retainer. That is, he is in a position of low status and meager benefit. He finds this somewhat humiliating, but he gains in other important ways, and eventually will benefit. Other people can see his value and will not be deterred by his lack of wealth or status.

● *At his best,* he may exercise restraint and yet not lose hope for his aspirations. *At his worst,* he may harbor deep resentments that will harm him for a long time.

▲ *As a public person,* he may serve as a personal aide to a powerful person. *As a businessperson,* he may work in the personal services industry. *As an ordinary person,* he may gain profits even though prospects seemed meager, or marry when he can offer his mate nothing.

22.6   *Yang 9 changing line derives from Hexagram 36 Serving as an Assistant*

He is wholly committed to serving his leader.
This avoids trouble and brings him significant benefits.

■ He has gone beyond trying to advance himself. Here he has wholly committed himself to serving his leader or organization. Such wholehearted commitment is desirable since his unselfish service is bound to bring good. He is now recognized as an especially valuable assistant (not merely appearing to be one), and he is rewarded appropriately.

● *At his best,* he is energetic and faithful, and he has earned full respect for his contributions. *At his worst,* he may meet his obligations, but he views his position only as a steppingstone to greater things, and this could later cause him problems.

▲ *As a public person,* he may lead many others in an important cause. *As a businessperson,* he may have a reputation for honesty and integrity in business, which rewards him with profits. *As an ordinary person,* he may find that clear, simple, and honest living avoids problems and brings the greatest rewards, or he may be very happily married and committed to his mate.

22.ALL   *All lines changing derives from Hexagram 47 Advancing by Hard Work*

His time of advancing through his self-image is over,
and now he is anxious to engage himself in the work
around him using his skills and strength.

■ While he was enhancing his image, he was focused on his preparation and his goals. He was in many ways powerless to achieve things outside of himself. Now that he has discovered within himself strength and knowledge, he is anxious to strive for his goals in the world around him. This is something he should do, even though both success and failure will come from it.

● *At his best,* he may be both strong and wise, and realize that "doing" is what is most important for him now. *At his worst,* he may be wholly engaged by achieving all manner of desires and goals, and not realize that he should temper his goals with the perspective of what he should do.

▲ *As a public person,* he may attempt to gain a major public office. *As a businessperson,* he may attempt to start a new business or seek a patent for his invention. *As an ordinary person,* he may seek a marriage, business partner, new career, or recover from a long illness.

23. Being in a Collapsing Situation

TRIGRAMS ED   LINES 000 001   COMPLEMENTARY HEXAGRAM 43 ESCAPING HARM

*Things are collapsing around him, and if he advanced,
he would get into worse trouble.*

■ *The traditional titles* for this hexagram are "Splitting," "Falling," and "Cleavage." Whincup uses "Destruction," and the Huangs use "Loss." According to Whincup, however, the closest literal translation is felling a tree. The title used here is "Being in a Collapsing Situation," and it describes a situation in which his supports are failing, causing him harm. In the traditional text, the lines generally describe a bed being chopped apart. Another related meaning for this hexagram is the world turning upside down. In a period when collapse is occurring around him, it is not wise to attempt any movement, since anything other than holding tight would be making things worse. *The complementary hexagram* is Hexagram 43 Escaping Harm, which illustrates how rather than sitting still for the effects of collapse to affect him, he should strive to escape from his situation.

● *At his best,* he may realize the nature of the problems around him that affect him and do as little as possible to make things worse. *At his worst,* he may be ignorant of the dangers facing him or foolhardy enough to risk advances that are neither secure nor supported.

▲ *As a public person,* he may suffer from loss of reputation, very visible losses of support, or having his cause discredited. *As a businessperson,* he may face bankruptcy. *As an ordinary person,* he may have many difficulties in his life from which he cannot escape, and he can only endure.

23.1   *Yin 6 changing line derives from Hexagram 27 Desiring*

*He has strong desires, but knows that giving into them
would only bring him further misfortune. So, he remains as he is.*

■ He desires something, but knows he does not have the support necessary to achieve it. Attempting to advance on his own would bring even more misfortune now. Staying as he is, however, brings him only some unhappiness.

● *At his best,* he may wisely concentrate on enduring rather than on being swayed by his desires. *At his worst,* he may let his unhappiness and strong desires goad him into unwise actions.

▲ *As a public person,* he may believe firmly in an unpopular cause. *As a businessperson,* he may be gradually losing his position in the workplace or the market. *As an ordinary person,* he may suffer harm through trying to change his life in an important way, or be unhappy living in a difficult situation he is afraid to change.

23.2   *Yin 6 changing line derives from Hexagram 4 Acting Impetuously*

He is acting impetuously in a collapsing situation.
His rash actions threaten him with greater harm.

■ He does not have the wisdom or maturity to deal correctly with the collapsing situation he is in. Rather, he is acting impetuously or immaturely. These actions threaten to bring even greater harm on to him.

● *At his best,* he may come to accept the inevitability of some harm, and think seriously before doing something potentially dangerous. *At his worst,* he may believe in himself and not fully consider the consequences of his failure, and then by failing in some unanticipated way, suffer some serious consequences.

▲ *As a public person,* he may be castigated in public and respond in such a way as to lose his support. *As a businessperson,* he may lose substantial portions of his wealth or business position by not making backup plans and diversifying his business. *As an ordinary person,* he may lose by gambling, deeply offend his boss or mate, or experience a catastrophe during a risky sport.

23.3   *Yin 6 changing line derives from Hexagram 52 Holding Back*

He is knocked back or held down by his collapsing situation,
but he observes what happened and learns from it. He may suffer
some slight harm, but he is now better prepared for the future.

■ Being in a collapsing situation now brings him some potential benefit. While he suffered some setback, he was not seriously harmed by it. He was also able to observe what happened to him, and he learns from it so he is better prepared for the future.

● *At his best,* he may experience a revelation about danger and how to deal with it that will benefit him in the future. *At his worst,* he may suffer some significant harm, and yet not learn much from this.

▲ *As a public person,* he may be demoted. *As a businessperson,* he may experience a series of minor setbacks and not one significant success. *As an ordinary person,* he may suffer a physical injury, or a variety of setbacks, yet he will manage to get through these with only slight difficulty.

23.4   *Yin 6 changing line derives from Hexagram 35 Advancing Due to Favor*

He desires to get out of his collapsing situation,
but does not have the favor of someone powerful to assist him.
Thus, he cannot keep from being harmed.

■ He needs the support of someone powerful to help him in his time of trouble. Unfortunately, he does not have this, so he is stopped where he is, and he is unable to escape some harm.

● *At his best,* he may just be unfortunate in not yet attracting the sponsor he needs despite having desirable qualities. *At his worst,* he may not be able to attract the sponsor he needs at all because of his negative qualities.

▲ *As a public person,* he may wait on the sidelines as an able assistant, or even as an applicant. *As a businessperson,* he may lose substantial wealth or control over his business without the right counsel. *As an ordinary person,* he may lack important things because he doesn't have the friends and helpers he needs.

23.5   *Yin 6 changing line derives from Hexagram 20 Preparing Himself*

The collapsing situation around him threatens him with harm,
so he prepares himself. He is successful because he doesn't
suffer serious harm, and he may even benefit in other ways.

■ Although he is trapped by the collapsing situation, he is not completely helpless. While he may not have sufficient power to change the situation around him, he does have the power to prepare himself by gaining skills, allies, or wisdom. Through this, he will be able to mitigate the harm of the collapsing situation, and perhaps even gain other benefits.

● *At his best,* he may understand what he needs to do to prepare himself. *At his worst,* he may turn first one way then another as he struggles to prepare himself, and may end up not doing much good.

▲ *As a public person,* he may work in an organization being closed down. *As a businessperson,* he may be forced to give up control of his enterprise to others. *As an ordinary person,* he may be forced to marry, be indebted to his mate's family, or dependent on a job offered with heavy strings attached.

23.6 *Yang 9 changing line derives from Hexagram 2 Going with the Flow*

> He knows the collapse in which he finds himself is changing,
> and so he goes with the flow. If he wants to become a leader,
> he should strive to strengthen himself and gain followers.
> If not, he should begin to heal himself and stabilize his life.

■ Even though he has suffered a collapse, he can see that matters are beginning to change again. More to the point, there is much to be done to prepare for the future. Those who want to be leaders should turn to preparation and to trying to gain followers. Those who don't want to be leaders should try to stabilize their lives and build stable homes. Going with the flow now means taking some positive steps to help him in the future.

● *At his best,* he may be confident in himself and in his future, and so can adapt to the stresses in his life. *At his worst,* he may float through this difficult period without believing in himself or his future, and although he survives, he is unclear about his goals.

▲ *As a public person,* he may fall from leadership yet keep ties with key followers and allies for the future. *As a businessperson,* he may lay plans for new business out of serious troubles or natural disasters. *As an ordinary person,* he may suffer a calamity but then be able to get his life back together again through hard, steady work.

23.ALL *All lines changing derives from Hexagram 43 Escaping Harm*

> He surmounts collapse when he realizes that rather
> than directly fighting it, he can escape from it.
> With escape comes complete liberation from collapse.

■ It is only after collapse has hemmed him in that he realizes there is another alternative. Rather than trying to fight it, he can escape and flee from it. This at last brings him true liberation from harm.

● *At his best,* he may have a rebirth in his spirit and yet remain committed to important things in his life. *At his worst,* he may flee what he cannot tolerate and lose important parts of his life in the process.

▲ *As a public person,* he may resign his public life and find a new direction. *As a businessperson,* he may change businesses or careers. *As an ordinary person,* he may leave his job or home, or radically change his commitments in life in some other way.

24. Beginning a Relationship

TRIGRAMS BE   LINES 100 000   COMPLEMENTARY HEXAGRAM 44 MAINTAINING HIS INDEPENDENCE

He is beginning a relationship with a friend
who can be beneficial for him in many ways.

■ *The traditional titles* for this hexagram are "Return" and "The Turning Point," which are misleading. The traditional interpretation is that he is starting something over again. Here it is titled "Starting a Relationship" to more precisely describe the kind of activity being initiated. *The complementary hexagram* is Hexagram 44 Maintaining His Independence, which illustrates how at times it is best to maintain his independence by not getting involved with another person.

● *At his best,* he may begin a relationship with someone who is supportive and complements his own character. *At his worst,* he may begin a relationship for the wrong reasons, which ultimately cause him unhappiness.

▲ *As a public person,* he may pursue a relationship for reasons of publicity or image. *As a businessperson,* he may seek out someone thinking of financial benefits. *As an ordinary person,* he may be attracted to good looks or other superficial characteristics more than he should.

24.1   *Yang 9 changing line derives from Hexagram 2 Going with the Flow*

He finds it is easy to begin a new relationship: he is just going with
the flow. He has no regrets, and benefits flow to him naturally.

■ He starts this relationship with realistic, minimal expectations. Each step thereafter comes easily and naturally. Therefore, benefits also come to him easily and naturally.

● *At his best,* he may be sure of himself, appealing and pleasant to others, and very happy being with those he especially likes. *At his worst,* he may not benefit as much, and he could somewhat overreach the potential of the situation and want more from it than it can deliver.

▲ *As a public person,* he may find a mentor or ally with one of his causes. *As a businessperson,* he may find a new partner. *As an ordinary person,* he may benefit from a new activity or meet new people.

24.2   *Yin 6 changing line derives from Hexagram 19 Leading Others*

He is guiding someone into a relationship, and he benefits from this.

■ His ability, status, or powerful position helps him in guiding someone into a relationship. He uses it appropriately for his benefit.

● *At his best,* he may have a position as a respected leader, and although he uses his status for his benefit, he does not compromise others. *At his worst,* he may have similar rank, yet he manipulates others and loses his principles in attempting to be successful.

▲ *As a public person,* he may be very attractive as a respected official or public figure. *As a businessperson,* he may be wealthy or a high-ranking company officer. *As an ordinary person,* he may have a respected position in his community or church, or be attractive as an older man.

24.3   *Yin 6 changing line derives from Hexagram 36 Serving as an Assistant*

He places himself in a low position, trying to win someone's favor by assisting him. This makes for a difficult beginning to their relationship. However, although he may suffer minor trouble, he is not truly harmed.

■ He is trying to win someone's favor by lowering himself and, in effect, serving him. This is generally a poor way of creating a relationship, and it causes continual problems. Usually this is a difficult situation, but although there may be some stress, there is generally little real harm.

● *At his best,* he may be honest and sincere to others as well as to himself, and have enough character to know which lines not to cross to maintain his self-worth. *At his worst,* he may be hopelessly overcommitted and unable to restrain himself, and end up hurting himself more than the situation warrants.

▲ *As a public person,* he may curry favor from an important figure. *As a businessperson,* he may seek to impress someone with his wealth and service. *As an ordinary person,* he may slavishly serve someone or try to win an internship.

24.4   *Yin 6 changing line derives from Hexagram 51 At Fortune's Mercy*

He is trying to start a new relationship but feels overwhelmed by fate. He feels alone, although there are others around him to whom he could reach out.

■ He is feeling alone, and that he is a victim of fate. To a large extent he is exaggerating, because there are others around him he could get help from if he chose to. He needs to make the effort to look beyond himself and to reach out to others.

● *At his best,* he may overcome his negative feelings and come to terms with the world around him as it is. *At his worst,* he may be first immobilized by his negative feelings, and then emotionally overwhelmed.

▲ *As a public person,* he may lose support for an unpopular position and feel very isolated. *As a businessperson,* he may lose important allies in a time of stress. *As an ordinary person,* he may feel abandoned by someone he loves.

24.5 *Yin 6 changing line derives from Hexagram 3 Gathering Support*

The relationship he is beginning needs to provide him with support,
so he demands it.

■ He sees that for a relationship to be beneficial for him, it must provide him with support. He asks this of the relationship to make sure he gets it.

● *At his best,* he may be clear-headed and emotionally mature, and thus easily able to act in his best interest. *At his worst,* he may not be as capable or emotionally secure, so he does not benefit as much.

▲ *As a public person,* he may launch a campaign of winning friends or gaining a better public reputation. *As a businessperson,* he may seek to gather backers or partners. *As an ordinary person,* he may start new projects, get married, or raise a family.

24.6 *Yin 6 changing line derives from Hexagram 27 Desiring*

His desires conflict with his partner's desires,
and he asks more of the relationship than it can provide.
His conflict with his partner brings harm
that might take a long time to heal.

■ He had been successful in developing the relationship. Now, however, his own desires are conflicting with those of his partner. A serious conflict, which may not heal for a long time, is likely.

● *At his best,* he may gain true understanding of his goals and learn self-control before he does too much damage. *At his worst,* he may lose control and harm himself and those close to him, and need a long time to recover.

▲ *As a public person,* he may not be able to balance his private and personal life, and end up harming both. *As a businessperson,* he may suffer serious losses from lack of attention to business. *As an ordinary person,* he may have a very poor period with losses and conflicts with his mate or employer.

24.ALL   *All lines changing derives from Hexagram 44 Maintaining His Independence*

He understands now that a relationship
may not satisfy his deepest personal needs.
To gain these, he needs to find the way to them
within himself by maintaining his independence.

■ He is pulling back from the seductive power of relationships. He has learned their shortcomings. Most important is the fallacy that he could look to them to fulfill all the deep needs within him. He now knows that he must first be able to look within himself and find the answers there.

● *At his best,* he may have gained great wisdom and learned how to understand and satisfy his deepest needs. *At his worst,* he may realize that something is wrong but not be able to find the answers that he needs.

▲ *As a public person,* he may rededicate himself to fundamental principles or causes. *As a businessperson,* he may go on a retreat or long vacation from business stresses. *As an ordinary person,* he may withdraw from a relationship, seek spiritual guidance or counseling, or study meditation.

25. Having No Expectations

TRIGRAMS BA   LINES 100 111   COMPLEMENTARY HEXAGRAM 46 PROMOTING HIMSELF

He has no expectations, so being open to new things is beneficial.
Since he doesn't know what's best for him,
he shouldn't set major goals.

■ *The traditional titles* for this hexagram are "Innocence" or "The Unexpected," although they are somewhat misleading. Here the hexagram is titled "Having No Expectations." Having no expectations about himself and his future is a curiously ambivalent situation. On one hand, having no expectations is beneficial, since it may allow him to see what is happening around him more clearly and thus respond more naturally and possibly more effectively. On the other hand, most advances come from a forceful will directing changes in a chosen direction; however, at this time he can't provide that. So, if he did try to actively progress, it is likely that it would bring him problems. Staying where he is and doing nothing offers no progress either. *The complementary hexagram* is Hexagram 46 Promoting Himself, which illustrates how after his doubts are resolved he is able to begin promoting himself.

● *At his best,* he may be genuinely open to the world and its experiences. *At his worst,* he may be terribly confused and unable to understand what is happening around him.

▲ *As a public person,* he may appear confused or somewhat foolish. *As a businessperson,* he may find business matters are muddled, or he may lose important information. *As an ordinary person,* he may be lost or find himself in a strange and new environment.

25.1   *Yang 9 changing line derives from Hexagram 12 Being Blocked*

He has no expectations of progress because he is blocked.

■ He sees quite clearly that someone or some situation is blocking him. Since he can do nothing directly about it, he should bide his time. Eventually the situation will change and he can take some action.

● *At his best,* he may have a strong understanding of the realities of his situation and the patience to let matters move at their own speed. *At his worst,* he may feel hopeless about being so helpless, and possibly even frustrated and angry, all of which harm him.

▲ *As a public person,* he may have to abide in his current position and not appear upset at being blocked. *As a businessperson,* he may fret at lost opportunity or lost money. *As an ordinary person,* he may feel that a rival is besting him, or a goal he truly desires is closed to him, and he has no way to redeem himself.

25.2   *Yin 6 changing line derives from Hexagram 10 Taking Risky Action*

Unexpected rewards come to him from risky actions that he took before.

■ In a time of no expectations, even beneficial things can happen. Here he is surprised when actions taken earlier (which might even have appeared quite risky at the time) now pay off. He can now enjoy the benefits of that.

● *At his best,* he may realize that many things have contributed to his rewards, and he will be appropriately grateful to those around him. *At his worst,* he may benefit and respond in a selfish and blind manner, both disappointing those around him and harming his future.

▲ *As a public person,* he may become the protégé of a powerful leader. *As a businessperson,* he may have a long-shot business plan suddenly succeed. *As an ordinary person,* he may benefit from the efforts of others who look upon him favorably, or he may inherit wealth or win a lottery.

25.3   *Yin 6 changing line derives from Hexagram 13 Serving on a Team*

Unexpectedly others have benefited instead of him.

■ He could have lost a possession that was his, and others gain from it; he might have to share a reward that should have been his; or he might get nothing and see others getting what had been destined for him. In all of these types of loss, he sees that others (especially those close to him) are benefiting instead of him.

● *At his best,* he may not be too unhappy or jealous, reflecting on the nature of fate and the cycles of gain and loss. *At his worst,* he may be bitter and deeply unhappy, burdening himself to no good purpose.

▲ *As a public person,* he may have the credit for his efforts taken by another. *As a businessperson,* he may have sudden losses, possibly through his overconfidence. *As an ordinary person,* he may receive unexpected bad news concerning family or friends, or experience sudden losses (particularly due to theft, the fluctuations of the market, or the vagaries of the weather).

25.4   *Yang 9 changing line derives from Hexagram 42 Gaining Benefits*

He gains unexpected benefits,
most likely through his partner or his position.

■ He is fortunate in his choice of partner (or position) because now through it he is gaining benefits. He did not expect this to happen.

● *At his best,* he may benefit through the wisdom of an earlier choice he made, and he responds appropriately. *At his worst,* he may not know how to respond and so acts inadequately or inappropriately, and so he leaves a poor impression.

▲ *As a public person,* he may be benefiting from an alliance with an increasingly successful or powerful partner. *As a businessperson,* he may be getting needed financial backing from a partner. *As an ordinary person,* he may benefit in a number of ways from his mate or from his position at work.

25.5   *Yang 9 changing line derives from Hexagram 21 Working on a Problem*

An unexpected problem appears that may be resolved
if dealt with properly.

■ A problem comes up unexpectedly. If he deals with it properly (that is, doing the right thing in the right way), it will be resolved. Note that in the traditional text it gives the example of an illness that cures itself, so it is possible that leaving a situation alone could be the proper cure for it.

● *At his best,* he may have clear understanding of what is wrong and what he should do to correct it. *At his worst,* he may not truly understand what is happening, and even if he did, he doesn't have the means to resolve it properly.

▲ *As a public person,* he may have a serious problem appear, and he will seek out the advice of others. *As a businessperson,* he may suffer unexpected losses or breakdowns in his business. *As an ordinary person,* he may suffer serious problems or become physically ill.

25.6   *Yang 9 changing line derives from Hexagram 17 Hunting*

His hunt unexpectedly encounters problems. Because he does not
think things through before acting strongly, he makes mistakes,
and the resulting situation is not easily corrected.

■ He takes some strong action, but he does not properly prepare for it. Unexpected problems then overwhelm him. It is not easy to deal with these problems.

● *At his best,* he may learn from his mistakes, and he bears with his difficulties until he can help matters improve. *At his worst,* he may be fierce in his attachment to his ideas regardless if they work or not.

▲ *As a public person,* he may be demoted for an impetuous error or even charged with a crime. *As a businessperson,* he may have his business harmed from a rash decision. *As an ordinary person,* he may lose things important to him, or suffer through unthinking or careless actions.

25.ALL   *All lines changing derives from Hexagram 46 Promoting Himself*

He now has expectations for himself, and he wants
to advance in life. He understands now he must
promote himself properly in order to succeed.

■ The time of having no expectations ends when he makes an internal commitment to himself to have expectations for himself. He also realizes that in order to have expectations he must create an image for himself and promote it out in the world. In this way, he will be able to succeed.

● *At his best,* he can rise to the challenge of creating the "idea" of who he wants to be and how he wants to act. *At his worst,* he may feel the hunger of wanting without being able to understand how to promote himself.

▲ *As a public person,* he may turn his activities toward public endeavors, publicity, or gaining fame. *As a businessperson,* he may seek business opportunities in a variety of ways. *As an ordinary person,* he may become more focused on personal success, communication, and generally being able to succeed in life.

26. External Restraint

TRIGRAMS AD	LINES 111 001	COMPLEMENTARY HEXAGRAM 45 SERVING A LEADER

He is being restrained by external forces,
yet he will benefit from this.

■ *The traditional title* for this hexagram is "The Taming Power of the Great," although this is somewhat misleading. Here the hexagram is titled "External Restraint." It signifies that he is being restrained by strong external forces. However, due to this interference, he actually benefits. He should pay attention and learn from this situation, as well as be grateful for the benefits he gets. *The complementary hexagram* is Hexagram 45 Serving a Leader, which illustrates how serving a leader is a form of restraint which is also a more beneficial situation for him.

● *At his best,* he may gracefully accept this restraint and learn what he can from the situation. *At his worst,* he may be deeply unhappy and upset about being restrained and not learn anything of value from the situation.

▲ *As a public person,* he may find himself restrained by a superior or a policy. *As a businessperson,* he may be restrained by a superior or practical business consideration. *As an ordinary person,* he may be restrained by someone older, stronger, or who knows more, or who has a particularly strong emotional connection, or by the circumstances of life around him.

26.1   *Yang 9 changing line derives from Hexagram 18 Nursing an Illness*

He is only touched by danger, but it is enough for him
to halt his advance and nurse his hurts.

■ He encounters a dangerous, strong external restraint that only just briefly touches him, yet it stops his advance. He realizes that things could have been worse for him. Now he turns to nursing himself, and ends up protecting himself and healing his hurts.

● *At his best,* he may deal realistically with the threats he sees around him and benefit from his restraint. *At his worst,* he may be frightened into passivity and not gain respite from his worries.

▲ *As a public person,* he may be threatened and bow to the pressure by backing down. *As a businessperson,* he may wait for matters to improve before proceeding with his business plans. *As an ordinary person,* he may avoid troubles by withdrawing from activity.

26.2 *Yang 9 changing line derives from Hexagram 22 Advancing by His Image*

Things fall apart, and he can gain nothing from this situation
no matter how he presents matters.

■ Some things work because they have parts that work together. The traditional text uses the example of an axle and axle pin. If it comes apart, it cannot serve its purpose and nothing can be gained. This situation is like that, since the part he needs to work with has separated from him. There is no way he can maintain matters so he can gain from them.

● *At his best,* he may primarily gain understanding from this situation, or experience it in unanticipated ways. *At his worst,* he may suffer deeply from separations in his career or life.

▲ *As a public person,* he may find that alliances or agreements fall apart. *As a businessperson,* he may lose partners, investors, or a business deal. *As an ordinary person,* he may be divorced, lose his job, or suffer a physical injury (particularly to his legs).

26.3 *Yang 9 changing line derives from Hexagram 41 Declining Influence*

He has declining influence, and experiences strong external
restraint. He faces serious conflicts, so he should try to
protect himself and what is important to him.

■ Someone else affects him, but he has decreasing ability to control the situation. They have serious conflicts and he is in some danger in this situation, so he needs to protect himself. It is also good for him to have a clear understanding of what is important to him and to persevere in trying to maintain that.

● *At his best,* he may understand the requirements of the situation, minimize his hurt, and maintain what is important to him. *At his worst,* he may suffer heavy losses, both material and emotional, through the actions of another.

▲ *As a public person,* he may have his career become increasingly subject to the dictates of his boss. *As a businessperson,* he may be increasingly financially dependent upon a partner. *As an ordinary person,* he may be involved in family disputes, separations, or divorce.

26.4 *Yin 6 changing line derives from Hexagram 14 Relying on His Allies*

His allies restrain and guide him, so he benefits through them.

■ Having a wealth of friendships and alliances is both a source of support and a limitation. He benefits greatly through them in many ways, and yet he now must be sensitive to them as well. He feels their influence and guidance on him. Sometimes he sees their contributions enhance him, other times, however, he might just feel restrained by them even though he benefits through them.

● *At his best,* he may learn from others and yet be able to show who he is to himself and his close associates. *At his worst,* he may feel indebted to his associates, and even trapped by the choices he has made in his career and alliances.

▲ *As a public person,* he may be promoted to a position that gives him some freedom to act; yet, he is not entirely independent. *As a businessperson,* he may be sensitive to his business associates' influence on his business. *As an ordinary person,* he may enjoy many friends, but he is aware he cannot satisfy everyone all the time although he wishes it were so.

26.5 *Yin 6 changing line derives from Hexagram 9 Restraining Himself*

While external forces restrain him, he is also restraining himself.
Thus, he is easily kept out of trouble, and he benefits.

■ Powerful people or strong restraints around him keep him from harm. Their task is made easier, however, because he is also restraining himself. He benefits from this double restraint.

● *At his best,* he may work with those stronger, learn what he can, and prove his worth in his limited situation. *At his worst,* he may resent being so weak and helpless, end up not learning anything, and even hate those who are helping protect him.

▲ *As a public person,* he may be given a figurehead position or one where the real power is held by another. *As a businessperson,* he may do a marketing or advertising campaign that is subtle and restrained in style. *As an ordinary person,* he may find work and family matters are without great difficulty or effort, or he is easily tamed by those close to him.

26.6 *Yang 9 changing line derives from Hexagram 11 Easily Progressing*

He is easily restrained because he follows his Tao.
This is extremely successful.

■ The restraints he feels bless him by guiding him into acting properly (being in accord with his Tao). That is, he works with the time, place, and destiny of everything and everyone to achieve what can be achieved. If he can advance, he does so easily because none of his energies is wasted and all their results are optimal. If this is a time of withdrawal, he does not worry about losing ground because he knows he will advance again. If this is a time of recuperation, he can relax knowing he gains the restoration he needs. Truly knowing his Tao, however, is more than an intellectual understanding; it is actually to flow along his proper path of destiny. It seems that he can make no error, and for a time this may be true.

● *At his best,* he may have an intuitive connection with the universe that greatly benefits him. *At his worst,* he may succeed, but he will not make his success contribute to the welfare of those around him, and thus will not be universally respected and admired.

▲ *As a public person,* he may advance through widespread appreciation of his abilities and character. *As a businessperson,* he may profit greatly by a deep understanding of his market and business. *As an ordinary person,* he may find everything comes to him easily, and he will be happy for profits, good friendships, and increased social standing.

26.ALL   *All lines changing derives from Hexagram 45 Serving a Leader*

He sees his path is to serve a leader.
While his service will restrain him in some ways,
it also opens up new possibilities for advancement.

■ The other types of restraint pictured in this hexagram are largely external to him. Here, however, the restraint is one he is imposing on himself. Self-restraint is a critical factor, since it indicates selection of a goal and marshalling the internal force necessary to achieve it. Such a combination is essential to success in the world.

● *At his best,* he may have reached a self-awareness that will allow him to succeed well in life. *At his worst,* he may realize that to escape his current situation, he must serve someone stronger, and view this as a necessary evil.

▲ *As a public person,* he may dedicate himself to a great leader or cause. *As a businessperson,* he may have an invention or "business champion" to follow. *As an ordinary person,* he may get married, join a startup business enterprise, or dedicate himself spiritually.

27. Desiring

TRIGRAMS BD   LINES 100 001   COMPLEMENTARY HEXAGRAM 28 WORKING TOWARD A GOAL

He has desires but sees no way they can be fulfilled;
therefore, he shouldn't covet the possessions of others
when he can't earn them himself.

■ *The traditional titles* for this hexagram are "The Corners of the Mouth" and "Providing Nourishment," although they are somewhat misleading. The Huangs use "The Cheeks" and Whincup uses "Bulging Cheeks." Here the hexagram is titled "Desiring" to better fit the meaning of the hexagram. It signifies he has desires that he is unable to satisfy. If he got too close to others' wealth, he would be very jealous and covet it, and this would lead him into trouble. *The complementary hexagram* is Hexagram 28 Working Toward a Goal, which illustrates how working toward a goal is the best way to satisfy his desires.

● *At his best,* he may have desires that will motivate him and help him to earn them. *At his worst,* he may be overwhelmed by greed for what others possess, and he may be motivated to use underhanded means to gain them.

▲ *As a public person,* he may be an inspiring motivational speaker or a hate-filled rabble-rouser. *As a businessperson,* he may seek ways to copy others' products or enter their market niche. *As an ordinary person,* he may lust after others' good or positions, or strive to copy those he adulates.

27.1   *Yang 9 changing line derives from Hexagram 23 Being in a Collapsing Situation*

Desiring someone else's wealth when he has so much less
puts him in a collapsing situation.

■ He doesn't have the potential to even begin to fulfill his desires, and he sees others with wealth or things that he desires. He has so much less by comparison he is very unhappy. In this situation, his judgment is likely to be poor and he could get into serious trouble.

● *At his best,* he may find himself very limited in what he can do, and this will minimize the harm that he can do. *At his worst,* he may doggedly pursue things that he can't have, and end up being seriously harmed.

▲ *As a public person,* he may be charged with corruption or connive to get something that belongs to another. *As a businessperson,* he may struggle to take over another's business or use improper means to enrich himself. *As an ordinary person,* he may divorce his mate, leave his job, alienate his patron, or find some way of harming himself through his desires.

27.2   *Yin 6 changing line derives from Hexagram 41 Declining Influence*

He has declining ability to get what he desires,
so he takes what he can, however he can.
Continuing to do this will cause serious harm.

■ He is doing something very improper. His needs have not decreased, but his ability to fulfill his desires honorably (and perhaps legally) has. Thus, he now uses any way he can to succeed. While he might profit from this for a short while, it will not work in the long run.

● *At his best,* he may come to his senses and try to moderate his risky actions. *At his worst,* he may let his greed run out of control, and in the end, he could alienate friends and family or even risk prison and lawsuits.

▲ *As a public person,* he may attempt to deceive and manipulate the system for gain. *As a businessperson,* he may attempt stealing or deceiving others for financial gain. *As an ordinary person,* he may use underhanded means to advance, steal, or cheat those around him, or possibly suffer disgrace or jail.

27.3   *Yin 6 changing line derives from Hexagram 22 Advancing by His Image*

He is learning the hard way that having his greediness
made visible will bring him misfortune. His image suffers
and it will take a long time for him to recover.

■ He is caught through his visible greed and deceit, and he is punished severely. This is an important life lesson he is learning, and it is a hard one. It will mark him deeply (externally, internally, or both) and also take a long time to fully recover from.

● *At his best,* he may learn his lesson well relatively quickly and not suffer unduly. *At his worst,* he is severely punished; he is marked so others see his shame, and it will take years for him to recover.

▲ *As a public person,* he may suffer public contempt or formal punishment for trying to gain too much. *As a businessperson,* he may steal from his company and be punished. *As an ordinary person,* he may suffer by civil punishment or incarceration, or through loss of respect by others.

27.4   *Yin 6 changing line derives from Hexagram 21 Working on a Problem*

> He is working hard and very productively
> toward satisfying his desires.
> This is a good approach, and will bring him benefits.

■ Having desires is not wrong *per se.* What is most important is how they are fulfilled. Here he is working hard toward gratifying them in the proper ways, and he will benefit from this.

● *At his best,* he may understand how to balance his needs with what is achievable, and he is conscientious in working toward fulfilling them. *At his worst,* he may be overzealous and overcommitted, so although he does achieve his goals, he also creates problems for himself and others.

▲ *As a public person,* he may earn a reputation for his dedication and achievements. *As a businessperson,* he may gain wealth through hard work and being focused on the bottom line. *As an ordinary person,* he may pursue advanced studies, or work hard to gain wealth, or identify himself with a cause or crusade.

27.5   *Yin 6 changing line derives from Hexagram 12 Gaining Benefits*

> His desires exceed what he can gain. He should not push hard
> because that would make matters worse.

■ Here his desires and those of his leader, associates, or family are in conflict. He is not strong enough to win this contest, so he should not force this struggle. He should appreciate that this relationship is important to him and provides benefits in other ways, although this time he will be unhappy through it.

● *At his best,* he may accept the limitations in his situation and balance them with the good that comes through it. *At his worst,* he may not easily accept being limited in his desires, and his struggles to satisfy himself will only make him more miserable.

▲ *As a public person,* he may secretly be in contention with his mentor or leader, and be unable to force through the issue. *As a businessperson,* he may find his business plans restrained by his financial backer. *As an ordinary person,* he may find his desires conflict with those of his mate, his mentor, or his supervisor.

27.6   *Yang 9 changing line derives from Hexagram 24 Beginning a Relationship*

He desires to begin a special new relationship,
and it is good for him to do so.

■ He desires to reach out to others, and this could be very beneficial because it could benefit them as well as him. This exemplifies the best of what a relationship brings to people. Everyone contributes something of value, and everyone receives something in return. His desire here is not just a selfish wish, but helps create something real and beneficial. This also illustrates that personal relationships are in general more important and valuable than material goods.

● *At his best,* he may share what is important within him and in doing so create a valuable connection to other people. *At his worst,* he may gain respect in his new relationships but not win true devotion.

▲ *As a public person,* he may become respected as a statesman, or join a new enterprise. *As a businessperson,* he may become famous for his negotiation skills. *As an ordinary person,* he may become a teacher or guide, or begin important new personal relationships.

27.ALL   *All lines changing derives from Hexagram 28 Working Toward a Goal*

He realizes that working toward a goal is highly desirable
for its own sake, and not just for the desires it can satisfy.
Effort for its own sake is something he will come to appreciate.

■ Here he has overcome the limitation of desire alone by realizing that the act of attaining is also something beneficial. With this awareness, he can finally free himself of the burden of greed. Furthermore, this also enables him to be more effective in attaining his desires, since now goals, plans, and effort can be utilized more effectively.

● *At his best,* he may have mastered his own desires and compulsions, and he could become a craftsman who truly values his work. *At his worst,* he may feel compelled to work hard, and he may lose the balance that rest, recuperation, reflection, and enjoying life's idle pleasures contribute to a happy and successful life.

▲ *As a public person,* he may become rededicated to public service. *As a businessperson,* he may work hard for enhancing his reputation or gaining recognition for his invention. *As an ordinary person,* he may become motivated to succeed in life and work, or become engrossed in an invention or creation.

28. Working Toward a Goal

TRIGRAMS FH   LINES 011 110   COMPLEMENTARY HEXAGRAM 27 DESIRING

He is working toward a goal that may not be easy to achieve,
yet this will bring him progress.

■ *The traditional title* for this hexagram is "The Preponderance of the Great," although this is somewhat misleading. The Huangs use "Great Excess," and Whincup uses "Big Gets By," both of which are also misleading. Here the hexagram is titled "Working Toward a Goal." The hexagram uses as its symbolic representation a heavily burdened, and therefore bent, ridge beam. This symbol demonstrates the great forces involved. However, it also shows that like the bent beam, he is bearing up under the burden, and he is accomplishing what he set out to do. *The complementary hexagram* is Hexagram 27 Desiring, which illustrates how work must have desires behind it to be highly motivating and successful.

● *At his best,* he may be firmly committed to working toward his goal, and doing this is both productive and emotionally beneficial. *At his worst,* he may he locked into a routine of hard work without good recompense or emotional reward.

▲ *As a public person,* he may be a role model of the work ethic to others. *As a businessperson,* he may have a business plan that he is wholly engaged in pursuing. *As an ordinary person,* he may need to put a lot of time and energy into his plans to succeed, or have a very demanding job.

28.1   *Yin 6 changing line derives from Hexagram 43 Escaping Harm*

He escapes his past by making a new beginning.
Because he is sincere, he comes to no harm;
however, he can't gain much benefit now either.

■ He escapes from his past to begin something new. He makes a good beginning, but he still can't do much to really improve things. This is just a first step, so there is only a little benefit here.

● *At his best,* he may truly have a spiritual rebirth that will help guide him in a new and better direction. *At his worst,* he may make a new beginning, but it may prove not to be the best direction for him, or he may not have enough of a true commitment to keep on his new course.

▲ *As a public person,* he may obtain an entry-level or stepping-stone position in a new field. *As a businessperson,* he may prepare for a new venture thoroughly or enter into it in a very small way. *As an ordinary person,* he may begin a new relationship, begin a new career, or go in a new direction in life.

28.2   *Yang 9 changing line derives from Hexagram 31 Ability to Change Matters*

Due to his hard work, he can change matters and gain important benefits. This is possible even if he is old or weak or in decline.

■ A goal coupled with hard work often can be achieved. Here his effort pays off. Even if he is old, weak, or in some other way in decline, with concentrated effort directed toward his goal, he can obtain benefits. He does need to try hard enough, however.

● *At his best,* he may be able to tap into his deep-seated awareness of himself, and from this derive the determination which will bring him success. *At his worst,* he may see what he desires and see how to get it, but just not quite be able to bring everything together to get what he wants.

▲ *As a public person,* he may gain an important position or an opportunity to really achieve something significant. *As a businessperson,* he may make good profits through exceptional or unconventional efforts. *As an ordinary person,* he may obtain a good job if unemployed, begin a new family, marry a younger woman, or feel rejuvenated.

28.3   *Yang 9 changing line derives from Hexagram 47 Advancing by Hard Work*

He has been advancing through hard work,
but now finds himself dangerously stressed.
Now even trying harder cannot prevent some harm from coming.

■ He comes to realize that hard work by itself is not always sufficient or appropriate to his needs. Here he finds himself heavily stressed and overburdened, and mistakes and errors are likely. Trying harder is not going to resolve these problems; therefore, some misfortune will come.

● *At his best,* he may awaken to the realization that life demands more from people than they can provide, and this is why friends, allies, and even paid supporters are essential to his success. *At his worst,* he may rely too much on himself and his sense of personal power, and then suffer when he cannot mitigate things beyond his control.

▲ *As a public person,* he may take risks he perhaps shouldn't. *As a businessperson,* he may suffer business losses or an erosion of his position despite how hard he works. *As an ordinary person,* he may have many problems at work, home, or elsewhere, including possibly health problems, especially with his feet, hands, or eyes.

28.4   *Yang 9 changing line derives from Hexagram 48 Being Renewed*

He finds the means to deal with the stresses of his work
and thereby renews himself.

■ Work is hard. Sometimes it becomes a great burden that needs to be relieved, if only for a little while. Here he has found the relief he needs. It could be a hidden strength he has, or it could be someone special to him, or it could be a diversion or a holiday. All of these allow him to put his burden aside and renew himself.

● *At his best,* he may realize how much he means to others, and how he, in turn, can rely on them for his own renewal. *At his worst,* he may lose himself in superficial diversions (such as wine, women, and song, or even worse) to renew his spirit, and he could end up harming himself.

▲ *As a public person,* he may enter the spotlight through a highly public romance. *As a businessperson,* he may participate in a new sport with colleagues. *As an ordinary person,* he may begin a regular exercise routine, find a new hobby, or develop a special friendship or romance.

28.5   *Yang 9 changing line derives from Hexagram 32 Committing Himself*

Striving only to meet his commitments will not achieve great things.
Although he does get benefits from this, they won't last long.

■ He is working hard but for only what he is committed to. Thus, while he does succeed, the benefit he gets will not be great. To achieve great things, he must attempt great things. The traditional text illustrates this with images of an old woman getting a young husband, and an old willow that briefly flowers. The gains he makes now will quickly fade.

● *At his best,* he may gain awareness of what will succeed and what will fail, and then wisely allocate his energies to what will be best for him. *At his worst,* he may throw his energies away on futile efforts and on remembrance of his successes.

▲ *As a public person,* he may enjoy his position for a while longer, but soon he will be retired or replaced. *As a businessperson,* he may experience a decline in his business even though it appears fine at present. *As an ordinary person,* he may experience some slight improvement in his life, although decline is inevitable; he may suffer by having a domineering wife or mother; or he may marry a woman who will not make a family with him.

28.6   *Yin 6 changing line derives from Hexagram 44 Maintaining His Independence*

> Although he gets in a difficult work situation,
> he keeps his head, so no real harm comes.

■ He encounters serious problems in his work. However, by keeping an independent viewpoint, he understands what is going wrong and what he should do. Through this, he manages to avoid being harmed.

● *At his best,* he may have critical insights into what to do and how to do them, and doing these, he easily escapes harm. *At his worst,* he may largely understand what is occurring, but lack everything he needs to completely deal with it, so some minor problems will hinder him.

▲ *As a public person,* he may overcommit himself to a cause and need to back out. *As a businessperson,* he may go into a risky venture and need to spread the risk. *As an ordinary person,* he may attempt something new or unknown, or have difficulties with a mate or supervisor, and need to gain help from friends.

28.ALL   *All lines changing derives from Hexagram 27 Desiring*

> He realizes hard work cannot achieve all his goals.
> Some desires will always remain unreachable.

■ Working hard and striving for his goals has been important to him, yet here he understands and accepts the limitations to that approach. He must accept that some desires will always remain just desires without hope of fulfillment. Living with desires that cannot be fulfilled will weigh on him, but this burden has become a part of him.

● *At his best,* he may allow a desire that cannot be fulfilled to have a role in his life, but he will restrict it to a small corner where it will not harm him. *At his worst,* he may accept the inevitability of unrealized dreams and ambitions in his life and not be able to limit the harm it brings him.

▲ *As a public person,* he may feel disappointed with lack of promotion or public recognition. *As a businessperson,* he may be very envious of the financial success of others in his business. *As an ordinary person,* he may have an unrequited love or lifelong feelings of having made the wrong career choice, or he may have goals or ideas that he will never be able to deal with as he desires.

29. Being Trapped

TRIGRAMS CC	LINES 010 010	COMPLEMENTARY HEXAGRAM 30 GAINING ENLIGHTENMENT

DOUBLED TRIGRAMS MEANING: *K'AN*, TRIGRAM C, SIGNIFIES PITFALLS, TROUBLES, AND DIFFICULT TASKS.
(SEE PAGE 46 FOR MORE ABOUT THIS TRIGRAM.)

He is surrounded by traps, so he should believe in himself
because that is essential for finding a way out.

■ *The traditional title* for this hexagram is "The Abysmal," although this is somewhat misleading. Whincup uses "Pits," and the Huangs use "Water." Here the hexagram is titled "Being Trapped." This hexagram illustrates the presence of pits surrounding him into which he could easily fall, and if he takes almost any action, he is liable to fall into one. His situation is not easy to get out of, yet there is a way he can do so. *The complementary hexagram* is Hexagram 30 Gaining Enlightenment, which illustrates how awareness and enlightenment are the first steps out of any trap.

● *At his best,* he may quickly come to realize the nature of the trap he is in, then look and find a way out. *At his worst,* he may blunder about blindly seeking a way out.

▲ *As a public person,* he may represent a "hopeless" cause, or he may be caught in some impropriety that threatens his position. *As a businessperson,* he may have a business problem that appears intractable at first. *As an ordinary person,* he may suffer the consequences of a bad decision he made, or harm himself by a bad fall.

29.1   *Yin 6 changing line derives from Hexagram 60 Having Limited Resources*

He is trapped by having limited resources.

■ He has limited resources available to him. Being limited like this makes it very difficult, if not impossible, for him to progress. At times even survival may be difficult. He will have to wait until he has more resources before he can try to advance as he wishes.

● *At his best,* he may bide his time and work to strengthen himself. *At his worst,* he may feel angry at being poor, which only makes the time he must wait seem even longer and more miserable.

▲ *As a public person,* he may be politically outmaneuvered by someone and not have the contacts he needs to resolve the situation beneficially for him. *As a businessperson,* he may suffer losses through the manipulations of others. *As an ordinary person,* he may be tricked by someone, be in unfortunate financial circumstances, have poor health, or experience a serious fall.

29.2 *Yang 9 changing line derives from Hexagram 8 Entering an Alliance*

> He is trapped by his alliances and commitments to others.
> He cannot do entirely what he wants,
> although he can attain some small goals.

■ His alliances and relationships with others are beneficial in many ways; however, they can also be traps that limit what he can do. Clearly, he is better off having them, but he pays a price for this security. Even in this situation, though, he is able to attain small goals without a problem.

● *At his best,* he may see clearly what he can and cannot accomplish, and he is satisfied with his arrangements. *At his worst,* he may strive for goals that upset his allies and threaten his stable existence.

▲ *As a public person,* he may feel hedged in by compromises he has made and by strong opponents. *As a businessperson,* he may have contracts and business arrangements that inhibit his scope of action. *As an ordinary person,* he may have options open to him that are fraught with danger, and he may feel driven to take action even if he knows it may not be in his best interest.

29.3 *Yin 6 changing line derives from Hexagram 48 Being Renewed*

> Gaining too much renewal is a trap into which it is easy to fall.
> A little is beneficial, but too much can bring him harm.

■ Can he resist the seductions of success, satisfaction, and pleasure? It is hard to run from it, and it is hardly seen as a trap at first since success, satisfaction, and pleasure are good things that help renew him. Thus, this trap cannot be run from, it must be overcome from within.

● *At his best,* he may taste, but not gorge on or become habituated to, pleasures. *At his worst,* he may lose control of himself, especially if he has been deprived, and end up seeking pleasure above more important things.

▲ *As a public person,* he may become a publicity-seeker or manipulator of people who can give him what he desires. *As a businessperson,* he may have overspent and even taken company funds. *As an ordinary person,* he may be manipulated by superiors (boss, mate, or his family), or manipulate those around him for his pleasure.

29.4 *Yin 6 changing line derives from Hexagram 47 Advancing by Hard Work*

He is trapped in the endless toil of his work.
This trap does not harm him, but it barely provides for his survival.
He should look to others to help him get out.

■ Hard work is important in the world because it is the main means by which wealth is produced. It is also important in that it can bring people a sense of value and self-worth. However, hard work that is not properly rewarded or recognized is a trap into which people can fall. He is in such a trap now, and all his effort seems only to barely keep him going. The way out of this trap is not by striving to work harder, but by looking to find another way out for himself. His best chance is through the help of someone outside. Even just a little bit of help might be all he needs, perhaps even just pointing out a new direction.

● *At his best,* he may have a strong and courageous heart, and a spirit to help him surmount his daily grind and recognize the truth when he sees it. *At his worst,* he may resign himself to his powerlessness, content himself to enduring, and sacrifice himself to what he thinks is his fate.

▲ *As a public person,* he may be made an assistant to someone he dislikes and who takes public credit for his work. *As a businessperson,* he may be overworked and not able to alter his business workload. *As an ordinary person,* he may find himself locked into a hard and deadening routine at work or home, or he may marry or flee out of desperation.

29.5 *Yang 9 changing line derives from Hexagram 7 Serving as an Officer*

Becoming a leader gets him out of the trap he was in,
and he comes to no harm.

■ Traps usually seem to affect the weak or the unwilling. By becoming a leader, he is showing both strength and determination. Both of these qualities are necessary to get out of his trap, and by using them, he does so.

● *At his best,* he may have a commitment to succeed and the ability to make it so. *At his worst,* he may exacerbate his negative qualities in triumphing over his adversity, and these may only grow worse even after he finds there is no need to use them.

▲ *As a public person,* he may favorably advance his position when others thought he couldn't. *As a businessperson,* he may help turn around a deteriorating situation through his suggestions or leadership. *As an ordinary person,* he may find that problems with a boss or mate resolve themselves favorably when he honestly clears the air.

29.6   *Yin 6 changing line derives from Hexagram 59 Things Are Swept Clear*

He is trapped in a flood of events that sweeps away everything he
relies on. The misfortune he experiences lasts for a long time.

■ Here an out of control situation is shown, since everything he relies on no longer
can help him. The consequences of this "flood" cannot be known in advance, and
neither can its duration. Eventually the flood will pass and he will regain control of
his life. However, in the meantime, he will suffer some serious misfortune.

● *At his best,* he may be able to provide some stability in his life and prepare for
when times improve. *At his worst,* he may have serious losses, be hurt, and be very
disturbed for a long time.

▲ *As a public person,* he may be punished or demoted in a wave of changes. *As a
businessperson,* he may be forced to accept another's leadership or takeover of the
company. *As an ordinary person,* he may be sued, jailed, or held in thrall by someone stronger than he.

29.ALL   *All lines changing derives from Hexagram 30 Gaining Enlightenment*

To get free of the traps around him, he first must free his mind
and spirit by gaining awareness of the truth. Truth can dissolve
the walls in his mind and make his heavy burdens light.
With this, he can now see his proper path.

■ The only way out of any trap is to first understand that it is a trap. Enlightenment
can free us of the traps that are within us. He now wishes to free himself from the
traps he sees, so he seeks enlightenment. Seeking enlightenment may not truly
bring it, but it will help free him of the traps holding him now.

● *At his best,* he may gain a pure and true understanding of his soul and his role in
life, and this will serve him as both a comfort and a guide. *At his worst,* he may
struggle with the intangibles in his life, and while failing to truly understand the Tao,
he will succeed in finding a new positive direction to travel.

▲ *As a public person,* he may gain a new understanding of people's needs, which
will help guide him in his public career. *As a businessperson,* he may learn how to
place his business activities in balance with his home and personal life. *As an ordinary person,* he may seek a marriage, new career, recuperate from a long illness, or
become engaged in a search for truth through new disciplines.

30. Gaining Enlightenment

TRIGRAMS GG   LINES 101 101   COMPLEMENTARY HEXAGRAM 29 BEING TRAPPED

DOUBLED TRIGRAMS MEANING: *LI*, TRIGRAM G, SIGNIFIES KNOWLEDGE, BRILLIANCE, TRUTH, AND WISDOM. *(SEE PAGE 47 FOR MORE ABOUT THIS TRIGRAM.)*

He is gaining enlightenment, and this is beneficial.
It is also better for him to have a companion in this.

■ *The traditional titles* for this hexagram are "The Clinging" and "Fire," although Whincup points out the more ancient ideogram used was "Shining Light." Here it is titled "Gaining Enlightenment" because this better describes the actual meaning of the hexagram. It signifies that he gains, uses, and passes along truth, knowledge, and understanding. Understanding is the best way for him to get out of the pitfalls in life and to succeed in his endeavors. Having a partner in gaining enlightenment will also aid him in a number of ways. *The complementary hexagram* is Hexagram 29 Being Trapped, which illustrates how seeking enlightenment only for itself can be a trap, since action and achievement need to be enlightenment's culmination.

● *At his best,* he may gain a deep understanding of his situation and the alternatives facing him. *At his worst,* he may strive for enlightenment, but not gain all that he should in order to make the best choices.

▲ *As a public person,* he may study public trends and opinions. *As a businessperson,* he may be studying marketing or production technology. *As an ordinary person,* he may be a teacher or student, or simply be an intelligent observer of life around him.

30.1   *Yang 9 changing line derives from Hexagram 56 Wandering*

He is searching for knowledge. Those around him
respect his quest and do him no harm.

■ He goes through life now as a seeker after knowledge and truth. Others see this, and they respect his dedication and study. His commitment and striving for knowledge make it easy for others to see that his intentions are good, and they do not harm him.

● *At his best,* he may truly be a truth-seeker whose soul thrives on knowledge and understanding, and he will not mind the meager lifestyle he has adopted. *At his worst,* he may be struggling to gain knowledge for his career while others who are envious of his opportunities attempt to interfere with his life.

▲ *As a public person,* he may be on a public inspection trip or may be studying to master an important policy question. *As a businessperson,* he may be investigating new markets or production techniques. *As an ordinary person,* he may be asked to join a club or association, devote himself to serious study, or travel to open his eyes to the world.

30.2   *Yin 6 changing line derives from Hexagram 14 Relying on His Allies*

He has friends and allies whose understanding and brilliance illuminates things for him, so he benefits.

■ He is extremely fortunate to have people around him whose ability and knowledge are greater than his, and they share their knowledge with him. He is thus enriched with valuable insights and information, and he benefits greatly.

● *At his best,* he may be an avid student who has brilliant teachers and friends, and he will gain a richly rewarding education. *At his worst,* he may learn about the less desirable side of life from ne'er-do-wells around him.

▲ *As a public person,* he may have a group of powerful mentors. *As a businessperson,* he may recruit experts who help him to succeed. *As an ordinary person,* he may be taught a great deal by family and friends, or be able to learn how to succeed by watching those around him.

30.3   *Yang 9 changing line derives from Hexagram 21 Working on a Problem*

He is working on a difficult problem. He comes to understand that it does not have a good solution. Some misfortune is inevitable.

■ He comes to see that some things do not have good solutions. Whatever he does, however hard he works at it, the situation cannot be resolved well. He might want to get whatever benefit he can from this situation, because harm in some form will come.

● *At his best,* he may be keen and dedicated, yet after he understands his failure, he does not take it to heart. *At his worst,* he may become angry and upset, and will let this poison his mind and heart for a long time.

▲ *As a public person,* he may see the coming end of his career. *As a businessperson,* he may have a declining business that has no opportunity for rescue. *As an ordinary person,* he may have a serious illness, gradually lose a loved one, or face a declining work or family situation.

30.4   *Yang 9 changing line derives from Hexagram 22 Advancing by His Image*

He is seeking enlightenment by relying on himself,
although he needs the assistance of others. Without their assistance,
he will face complications and problems for which he has
no solution, and thus he will suffer some harm.

■ The traditional text shows him suffering from a number of sudden catastrophes. His solitary pursuit of enlightenment may not be the cause of this, but being alone makes it harder for him to gain the wisdom and knowledge he needs. Having a companion or partner is important in many respects, and here the lack of one is a serious detriment.

● *At his best,* he may quickly learn it is beneficial to have a companion or partner. *At his worst,* he may arrogantly believe his character, his work, or his studies place him beyond the need for others' assistance, and he will suffer repeatedly because of this.

▲ *As a public person,* he may have offended powerful interests through his actions, or he may have overstepped his authority. *As a businessperson,* he may see or experience disasters that seem to present opportunities for windfall profits, except they will likely not be reached. *As an ordinary person,* he may experience sudden disasters at work, at home, or his life in general may be difficult.

30.5   *Yin 6 changing line derives from Hexagram 13 Serving on a Team*

He had joined with others in accepting certain knowledge,
but he comes to realize that this knowledge has shortcomings.
Now he grieves for the truth he did not attain,
although he should try to gain benefit from what he can.

■ True enlightenment, or full and true knowledge of anything, is only an ideal that cannot be reached. Thus, he realizes that he is like everyone else in failing, and he laments this. However, he also awakens to the fact that some things *can* be known, and it is beneficial for him to focus on these. Doing this properly will bring him some benefit.

● *At his best,* he may accept the limitations to knowledge that are revealed to him, and he will pursue the knowledge that will bring him success. *At his worst,* he may redouble his efforts to learn what he cannot know, and in doing this waste his time and effort.

▲ *As a public person,* he may work in public relations. *As a businessperson,* he may join a committee representing business complaints, or be an engineer or scientist working on a team. *As an ordinary person,* he may realize his education was inadequate or that what he was taught is not the whole truth.

30.6   *Yang 9 changing line derives from Hexagram 55 Serving Greatness*

He has enlisted himself in a great cause
or in a campaign for a great leader.
Trying to educate and convert others is beneficial now.

■ His search for enlightenment has brought him to the realization that he should help enlighten others with the same enlightenment he himself found. Therefore, he devotes himself to reaching out to others and to trying to gain converts to his way of thinking.

● *At his best,* he may have deep compassion for others and genuinely try to help them with something that will help them instead of trying to persuade them for his own benefit. *At his worst,* he may become a true believer who is fanatical in his certainty that he has the answers for everyone else.

▲ *As a public person,* he may strive to become a leader of men in a great cause. *As a businessperson,* he may join a great business enterprise or a public campaign for an economic goal. *As an ordinary person,* he may join the military, enter a clan or community, or enlist in someone's cause.

30.ALL   *All lines changing derives from Hexagram 29 Being Trapped*

He has failed to attain the benefits he thought he would get
through enlightenment. He believed this would be his salvation,
but now he sees only the mundane path of a foolish man before him.
He now feels disheartened and trapped.

■ He began his quest for enlightenment with the desire and expectation that it would solve the problems he sees in life. Now, however, he realizes that he cannot reach the goal of true enlightenment. His attempt to escape the humdrum aspects of life has failed, and he still needs to come to grips with the daily troubles that still haunt him. Realizing all this he now feels trapped.

● *At his best,* he may awaken to the warmth and succor from the good things which life has to offer even in the most meager settings. *At his worst,* he may fall into deep despair and depression from his perceived failures and inability to understand the Tao.

▲ *As a public person,* he may not show his distress over failing to attain the goal he set for himself. *As a businessperson,* he may turn his attention to mundane business activities or focus on older markets. *As an ordinary person,* he may become very depressed from the failure of his plans.

31. Ability to Change Matters

TRIGRAMS DH   LINES 001 110   COMPLEMENTARY HEXAGRAM 41 DECLINING INFLUENCE

He has the ability to change matters, and he benefits by doing so.
Doing this with a partner is even better.

■ *The traditional titles* for this hexagram are "Influence," "Stimulation," and "Compelling." The Huangs use "Cutting," and Whincup uses "Movement." Whincup also notes that it means moving something as well as exerting influence. Here the hexagram is titled "Ability to Change Matters" because it signifies that he has the ability to change matters. Having a partner in attempting change is highly desirable. Taking a partner in the traditional text is literally taking a wife, but a broader meaning applies. A partner allows him to make better choices as well as to extend his influence. *The complementary hexagram* is Hexagram 41 Declining Influence, which illustrates how when ability to change matters fades, a period of declining influence results.

● *At his best,* he may have the strength and wisdom to produce the results he desires. *At his worst,* he may have the strength to change things, but may not have the wisdom to get the right results.

▲ *As a public person,* he may have a powerful position. *As a businessperson,* he may be a leader either in public or behind the scenes. *As an ordinary person,* he may know how to "work within the system" to get things done, or he may inspire those around him to assist him in his goals.

31.1   *Yin 6 changing line derives from Hexagram 49 Being Revolutionary*

His revolutionary viewpoint is not very able to bring about change.

■ Revolutionary ideas are usually not able to succeed without extensive preparation beforehand. Since he is at the beginning, he has not done this. Therefore, his ideas and abilities will not be viewed very seriously at this point.

● *At his best,* he may have very worthwhile ideas and abilities, and he will learn from this to bide his time and to properly prepare others to receive his ideas. *At his worst,* he may make grandiose plans that fail, and he will feel embittered and angry thereafter.

▲ *As a public person,* he may be a spokesperson for unpopular, new ideas. *As a businessperson,* he may realize he is unable to significantly improve matters. *As an ordinary person,* he may be generally powerless at work or at home, so he may profit most by being accommodating, or he may shift his endeavors to a slightly different arena.

31.2   *Yin 6 changing line derives from Hexagram 28 Working Toward a Goal*

He is working to change matters,
but it will take more time and effort to succeed.

■ It takes a certain amount of preparation and work to change matters, and he has not yet reached the point where he can succeed. However, if he keeps on working hard toward his goal, eventually he will succeed.

● *At his best,* he may rise to the challenge of achieving his goal, rededicate himself to the task, and eventually succeed. *At his worst,* he may lose heart, not see his way, and fail at his goal.

▲ *As a public person,* he may perform well if supervised, but otherwise not be able to succeed easily. *As a businessperson,* he may not be able to positively affect matters due to too few resources or inadequate supporters. *As an ordinary person,* he may find that no matter how hard he tries few benefits will come to him.

31.3   *Yang 9 changing line derives from Hexagram 45 Serving a Leader*

He attempts to change matters, but he is stopped by his leader.
A confrontation would be unfortunate, so he should halt his efforts.

■ He is attempting to change matters when his leader (his superior at work, his mate, or a similar figure) stops him. If he tried to force the issue, it would bring an unfortunate confrontation, which would damage him and his relationship. Therefore, he should stop and save what is more important to him.

● *At his best,* he may be aware of what is most important to him so he can easily pull back when there is a conflict between one of his goals and the needs of others who are important to him. *At his worst,* he may not understand the impact of his actions on others and cause a deep rift between him and others who are important to him.

▲ *As a public person,* he may offend a superior or run afoul of policies or procedures. *As a businessperson,* he may find himself subject to the control of another. *As an ordinary person,* he may find that someone has a great deal of influence over him, unless he wishes to harm or destroy that relationship.

31.4   *Yang 9 changing line derives from Hexagram 39 Bumbling by Himself*

He needs the assistance of others to be able to change matters.
Without their help, he would bumble and fail.

■ He can act by himself, but if he did so he could easily make mistakes and fail. Others are willing to assist him, though, and when he avails himself of their help he can succeed.

● *At his best,* he may honestly be able to understand his own strengths and weaknesses, and turn to others to help with his shortcomings. *At his worst,* he may be headstrong or prideful, and not ask others for the assistance he needs to succeed.

▲ *As a public person,* he may work with others in order to be promoted to a powerful position. *As a businessperson,* he may hire consultants or obtain the advice of experts to expand his business or profits. *As an ordinary person,* he may find that small goals can be accomplished by himself, but that he needs the assistance of others for greater ones.

31.5   *Yang 9 changing line derives from Hexagram 62 Independently Getting By*

He uses all of his strength and succeeds in changing matters.
Afterward he may be weak, but he will be satisfied.

■ Even someone of limited strength can attain significant results when they concentrate all of their strength on their goal. Expending so much energy may leave him feeling enervated, but he has no regrets because of his accomplishments.

● *At his best,* he may know how to direct all of his energy to attain noble and difficult achievements. *At his worst,* he may strive very hard toward his aims, and when he doesn't achieve all that he hoped for, he finds some gratification in limited success despite his disappointment.

▲ *As a public person,* he may serve as a minor functionary in an organization and acts outside his normal area of responsibility. *As a businessperson,* he may surprise others by bringing together different elements and producing a business success. *As an ordinary person,* he may commit himself to a course of action and strive greatly to achieve it, which he generally will do.

31.6   *Yin 6 changing line derives from Hexagram 33 Complying*

He is complying with the limitations of his situation. Since he cannot
act directly, he uses persuasion to get others to change matters for him.

■ He has a very limited capability in the situation, and he is not able to affect matters directly. What he can do, however, is to communicate with and persuade others to change things. Doing this, he is successful in improving matters even in a situation that he could not otherwise affect.

● *At his best,* he may recognize the subtleties in the situation and understand how to help others to help everyone. *At his worst,* he may be selfish and manipulative, and be able to persuade others to do what he wishes.

▲ *As a public person,* he may find his advice is sought out and heeded. *As a businessperson,* he may have to defend his policies. *As an ordinary person,* he may be especially effective in personal appeals to bosses, friends, and family, or he may become committed to a cause, or become involved in a lawsuit.

31.ALL   *All lines changing derives from Hexagram 41 Declining Influence*

He is losing the ability to change matters.
Now he must accept his decreasing power and declining influence.

■ The time of being able to change matters is ending for him. Now he realizes that he is entering a period in which he will have less influence and be less effective in changing matters. While this is not good news, some progress may still be possible.

● *At his best,* he will gracefully accept the cyclic nature of life, and that "downs" are as much a part of his life as "ups" are. *At his worst,* he may angrily resent the failures and disappointments that come to him, and he will not be able to deal gracefully with what he sees as continual bad luck.

▲ *As a public person,* he may be eclipsed by another public figure. *As a businessperson,* he may have a business that is somewhat obsolete or passé. *As an ordinary person,* he may have a debilitating illness or old age, suffer from being laid off, or be in the process of a divorce.

32. Committing Himself

TRIGRAMS FB   LINES 011 100   COMPLEMENTARY HEXAGRAM 42 GAINING BENEFITS

He is committing himself, and this is good because even
weak commitments can avert trouble and improve his situation.

■ *The traditional titles* for this hexagram are "Duration" and "Enduring," although these are somewhat misleading. The Huangs title this "Steadfastness," and Whincup uses "Constancy." Here this hexagram is titled "Committing Himself." In general, making commitments to someone or something strengthens relationships. If he commits himself to a goal, he is also more likely to benefit as well. The most important thing about making a commitment is that he truly be able to keep it. *The complementary hexagram* is Hexagram 42 Gaining Benefits, which illustrates how strong and effective commitments tend to bring benefits.

● *At his best,* he may make a commitment out of a deep awareness that it is true for him. *At his worst,* he may make a commitment out of a desire for gain or for a quick and easy solution, and thus may not be truly committed at all.

▲ *As a public person,* he may make a promise in a public ceremony. *As a businessperson,* he may agree to a partnership. *As an ordinary person,* he may make a promise to someone important to him, or to himself.

32.1   *Yin 6 changing line derives from Hexagram 34 Forcing Matters*

He has forced matters by committing himself too soon.
This brings minor trouble but doesn't affect the outcome.

■ He has tried to force matters and made a commitment too early. This will bring him some trouble, but it is likely to be minor as well as short-term. It also doesn't change the result.

● *At his best,* he may learn and mature from his mistake, and he could go on to achieve his goal. *At his worst,* he may be impetuous, unable to control himself, and make his situation worse by repeated errors.

▲ *As a public person,* he may have tried to seek public support from publicity and failed to make his case. *As a businessperson,* he may have brought a product or project out too early. *As an ordinary person,* he may be immature or impetuous, and he may suffer from bad decisions, such as a job change, investment, or marriage.

32.2   *Yang 9 changing line derives from Hexagram 62 Independently Getting By*

Being independent delays his making a commitment
but does not stop it. Eventually his doubts and regrets
about his choices fade away.

■ His independence will delay the commitment he is considering making, but he will be able to make this commitment. After he does that he will get benefits from it, and his earlier doubts and regrets will be forgotten.

● *At his best,* he may appreciate his gains and moderate his expectations as he gains more perspective. *At his worst,* he may continue to want more than he can possibly get, and thus delay his commitment.

▲ *As a public person,* he may understand that he is responsible for something that helps people, and he can take some pride in this. *As a businessperson,* he may have apprehensions concerning an alliance or business endeavor, which eventually fade. *As an ordinary person,* he may find that happiness gradually enters his life and that he is content.

32.3   *Yang 9 changing line derives from Hexagram 40 Getting Free*

He gets free from his commitments, but this brings him some trouble.

■ He escapes from his commitments one way or another. These commitments could be to himself, to his associations, or to others close to him. He might put on a false front, be deceitful, forget his promises, or loose his ability to keep his commitments despite his best intention. Perhaps he thought he could take this commitment for granted, but this is not so. Commitments should be reinforced from time to time. Escaping from his commitments like this will only bring him trouble.

● *At his best,* he may be swayed by his desires and be brought back to his senses after a while. *At his worst,* he may feel trapped by his lies and manipulations and so tries escaping from his commitments, yet he still experiences harm.

▲ *As a public person,* he may abuse his position for his personal gain. *As a businessperson,* he may be found to be dishonest or responsible for unethical manipulations. *As an ordinary person,* he may abandon his mate, cheat his business or family, make a major change in his lifestyle, or experience many difficulties including lawsuits.

32.4 *Yang 9 changing line derives from Hexagram 46 Promoting Himself*

He is promoting himself rather than keeping his commitments.
Further attempts to gain will fail.

■ He is hunting for ways to gain, especially through other people, rather than keeping his commitments. However, this fails because now his reliability is suspect. He should have been paying attention to his commitments, because now he is open to other harm as well. This could bring more misfortune.

● *At his best,* he may be jolted out of his dreams and quickly learn to take care of his responsibilities. *At his worst,* he may strive compulsively for gain, and his failures will not teach him anything, so he could suffer serious harm.

▲ *As a public person,* he may strive for a position, a promotion, or an honor instead of taking care of his responsibilities, and may fail. *As a businessperson,* he may have a business sideline fail, and he could suffer even more in his main business. *As an ordinary person,* he may strive for advancement and fail despite his best efforts.

32.5 *Yin 6 changing line derives from Hexagram 28 Working Toward a Goal*

He unswervingly keeps working toward his goals. Such zealous
commitment is good for a follower, but not always for a leader.

■ He feels duty bound to keep working toward his goals. Although this sounds good, it is not entirely so. A leader needs to have flexibility to forge new alliances and change his commitments as necessary. Too great a commitment lessens his options, and ultimately it could be harmful. Followers, however, should have the primary aim of being fully yet honorably committed to their leaders. Understanding which role he has at this moment will tell him how to understand this situation. In the traditional text, this is referred to as being beneficial for a woman but not for a man.

● *At his best,* he may gain from the options presented to him without causing difficulties for those who depend on him, and without losing the support of his own leader. *At his worst,* he may be unable to adjust his commitments, and he will cause problems for those around him and will suffer himself.

▲ *As a public person,* he may get into trouble through inflexibly following rules or by backing a declining leader. *As a businessperson,* he may suffer losses by following through with a contract he could have declined. *As an ordinary person,* he may be blamed for matters not entirely his fault (though wives could suffer less than husbands), or force his opinions and rules on those near him.

He is committed to governing matters, but destiny cannot be so easily controlled. His fate may not be what he desires or thinks.

■ Commitments and desires are not the same as reality. Yet, he wishes that he could control matters and make them so. Since destiny has an awkward way of intruding and upsetting his plans, he suffers through being stressed, and his capabilities are affected, adding to his misfortune. He may strive for shortcuts or seek out fortunetellers to avoid problems. Unfortunately, his destiny cannot be avoided.

● *At his best,* he may control his anxiety and recklessness to some extent to minimize his misfortunes, but he will still feel thwarted. *At his worst,* he may be mostly out of control, and he will be able to do little effectively and, therefore, suffer much.

▲ *As a public person,* he may be in charge of a failing program and find it very hard to improve. *As a businessperson,* he may worry excessively about business problems, or study business-forecasting techniques. *As an ordinary person,* he may have a difficult marriage or work situation, he may have serious health problems, or he may consult an astrologer.

When commitments are well and truly made,
a time of gaining benefits is coming.

■ Commitments are an important route for being able to bring benefits into one's life. The more firm the commitment, the more likely it is that over time it will provide increasing benefit (although this is certainly not guaranteed). This is one reason why marriage is used as an example in this hexagram. Successful marriages require long-term commitments, and generally, long-lasting ones provide the best benefits. This also illustrates that the most benefit comes from those commitments that are truly proper for him.

● *At his best,* he may be able to choose good commitments to benefit from. *At his worst,* he may go from goal to goal, always changing in midstream, and thereby minimizing his benefit from his commitments.

▲ *As a public person,* he may put his entire reputation and all his energies behind a program, and as it succeeds, his reputation will rise. *As a businessperson,* he may not succeed until he has risked much of his wealth. *As an ordinary person,* he may make major personal commitments, such as marriage, family, or career.

33. Complying

TRIGRAMS DA   LINES 001 111   COMPLEMENTARY HEXAGRAM 19 LEADING OTHERS

Complying with his present situation is the proper thing to do.
Now, only minor goals should be pursued.

■ *The traditional titles* of this hexagram are "Retreat," "Withdrawal," and "Retiring." Both Whincup and the Huangs use "Piglet" as the proper word, based on a probable error in transcription in ancient times. "Complying" is the title used here, since submission and acceptance are indicated in the traditional text's lines. The image of the domesticated piglet illustrates being able to prosper in captivity. Compliance does not mean cowardice, but rather the wisdom to know that no good can come from trying to press ahead when the situation is not right. However, minor matters can be effectively attended to, and more important matters will slowly progress of their own accord. *The complementary hexagram* is Hexagram 19 Leading Others, which illustrates that to overcome the limitations of his situation, the best way is to take a strong role and lead others in a cooperative effort to change things.

● *At his best,* he may understand his situation and still manage to be happy and productive in it. *At his worst,* he may understand his situation and feel a sense of hopelessness about it, or not understand it and thus not be able to make even small gains to make himself happier.

▲ *As a public person,* he may be a spokesperson for what he does not believe in. *As a businessperson,* he may accept working in a business in which he would prefer not to work. *As an ordinary person,* he may feel compelled to follow the dictates of someone else or accept life's constraints on him.

33.1   *Yin 6 changing line derives from Hexagram 13 Serving on a Team*

He is joined with others in a situation of some danger.
Even together they cannot overcome it,
nor can they escape from it. They can only endure it.

■ He is not alone in a dangerous situation; however, being with others does not help him much because all together they cannot overcome it or escape from it. He also cannot forge ahead or withdraw by himself. He must curb any tendency toward recklessness or impatience, particularly with regard to his superiors. He must deal with it as best he can, work well with his fellows, and bide his time.

● *At his best,* he may serve as an example and help those near him understand that they must wait for matters to improve. *At his worst,* he may be unable to deal with this difficult situation, and he may end up making matters far worse than they are.

▲ *As a public person,* he may be one of a group under investigation. *As a businessperson,* he may face a significant business dilemma. *As an ordinary person,* he may minimize trouble through quiet living or looking to others for leadership.

33.2 *Yin 6 changing line derives from Hexagram 44 Maintaining His Independence*

He cannot maintain his independence as he wishes;
yet, even so, he prospers.

■ Firm rules or restraints take his independence from him. However, in a way they also support him, guide his actions, and protect him from harm. He may also receive other benefits from this situation. He may find this situation, even if it is not ideal, is acceptable.

● *At his best,* he may understand the tradeoffs in his life and accept what he has as a tolerable situation at this time. *At his worst,* he may be afraid to seriously look at alternatives in his life and not take responsibility for his future.

▲ *As a public person,* he may be guided by rules or even establish good policies based on them. *As a businessperson,* he may work well within limitations and succeed. *As an ordinary person,* he may have some material progress and be content to be guided by someone stronger or, if has a physical disability, make use of physical-supporting devices or restraints.

33.3 *Yang 9 changing line derives from Hexagram 12 Being Blocked*

His options are blocked, and danger is all around him.
For help, he should look to others also in restricted situations
and try to benefit from them.

■ He has few choices and feels very threatened. However, some good may come from reaching out to others who are also in restricted situations. From them, he may learn useful things or get other forms of help.

● *At his best,* he may be able to learn how to weather his situation from others. *At his worst,* he may be trapped and suffer despite his best efforts.

▲ *As a public person,* he may realize that all public activities are fraught with danger, so he should try to make his most important actions private. *As a businessperson,* he may benefit by listening to others in the marketplace or in his industry. *As an ordinary person,* he may have a serious illness or problem that inhibits him, and he may need to rely on his mate or family.

33.4 *Yang 9 changing line derives from Hexagram 53 Sharing Commitment*

He can benefit from a shared commitment with his leader,
but not with anyone else.

■ Having a leader he can make a shared commitment with could be very beneficial for him. However, he should not try to make commitments with anyone else because he will not benefit. Properly complying with this situation requires that he make and keep connections with the right people.

● *At his best,* he is a committed and compliant partner and can thus truly share in the benefits of the relationship. *At his worst,* he is simply complying with the demands of someone stronger because he is weak, and thus he will not gain much in benefits.

▲ *As a public person,* he may place his trust in someone who secretly provides him with guidance. *As a businessperson,* he may follow the business plans of his partner. *As an ordinary person,* he may find that his mate provides guidance in the marriage, or that he is dependent on help he receives from someone else.

33.5 *Yang 9 changing line derives from Hexagram 56 Wandering*

He would like to but cannot leave the situation he is in,
although remaining in it allows him to gain some benefit.

■ Although leaving his restricted situation is on his mind, he understands and accepts that it is not possible for him at this time. However, he can get some benefits from remaining by fully complying with the requirements of the situation.

● *At his best,* he gracefully accepts his constraints, and he graciously accepts the benefits he receives, although neither is truly what he wants. *At his worst,* he resents being tied down, and even though he should show some gratitude for the benefits he receives, he offends others.

▲ *As a public person,* he may want to make his own path to prominence, although he knows he would do best by following the accepted path. *As a businessperson,* he may gain considerably if he goes along with others' plans. *As an ordinary person,* he may find a generally good period by accepting restrictions and matters as they are.

33.6 *Yang 9 changing line derives from Hexagram 31 Ability to Change Matters*

Events change and bring him benefits,
more than he could have expected in his situation.

■ External conditions have changed, but he hasn't changed them. Factors in the past that were restrictions now bring him benefits, or perhaps other people now help him to escape from his restrictions. He may now even be free to help himself to some extent. Overall, he is very fortunate that he can surmount his situation.

● *At his best,* he may benefit from the wisdom of others, his own understanding, and simple luck. *At his worst,* he may be blind to others' contributions to his good fortune, not contribute to his own well-being, and not appreciate how transitive his luck will be.

▲ *As a public person,* he may retire after a distinguished career. *As a businessperson,* he may improve matters by waiting for his opportunities then acting appropriately. *As an ordinary person,* he may find a generally good period comes by fully cooperating with those matters controlling his life, and not pushing himself or his wishes on others.

33.ALL *All lines changing derives from Hexagram 19 Leading Others*

He understands and accepts that he should
now reach out to others and lead them.

■ His lessons have been learned well, and now he understands the role he can play in guiding others. So, he reaches out to others to lead them. In doing this, he benefits both himself and them.

● *At his best,* he may pass along important lessons in life to those who need them and gain the recognition of those he helps. *At his worst,* he may be too egocentric to truly understand the needs of others, and the force of his personality will intrude excessively into their lives.

▲ *As a public person,* he may start a crusade or outreach organization, or write a book to enlighten others. *As a businessperson,* he may develop a product that is for many people. *As an ordinary person,* he may seek to become a teacher or minister, or generally like to help people.

34. Forcing Matters

TRIGRAMS AB   LINES 111 100   COMPLEMENTARY HEXAGRAM 20 PREPARING HIMSELF

He is able to force matters, and it is beneficial to do so.

■ *The traditional title* for this hexagram is "The Power of the Great," although this is somewhat misleading. Whincup uses "Big Uses Force," and the Huangs use "Great Injury." Here the hexagram is titled "Forcing Matters." The traditional text uses a ram as the symbol of being able to force matters. However, it should be remembered that strength by itself does not bring about being right (which depends more upon understanding the laws of heaven and earth) or being a success (which depends more upon the approval and rewards of fellow men). Thus, strength needs to be coupled with wisdom and even the right situations for a truly successful outcome. *The complementary hexagram* is Hexagram 20 Preparing Himself, which illustrates that before he can gain the ability to force matters, he must first prepare himself by gaining the appropriate skills, knowledge, resources, and personal characteristics necessary to be forceful.

● *At his best,* he may have the requisite strength and understanding to produce highly effective and beneficial results. *At his worst,* he may have the strength to create a result, but not the wisdom to determine how to get the result he desires, and so he ends up being unhappy.

▲ *As a public person,* he may launch a public campaign or a highly publicized lawsuit. *As a businessperson,* he may launch a takeover or corporate raid, or gamble on a bold marketing plan. *As an ordinary person,* he may deliver an ultimatum or force his will on those around him.

34.1   *Yang 9 changing line derives from Hexagram 32 Committing Himself*

He is committing himself to being forceful, but his position is
too low (or he is too weak or inexperienced) to succeed.
He might suffer slight harm from trying.

■ His strength was inadequate, although his commitment may have been sufficient. Not being forceful in the right way could cause some harm. If so, he probably didn't adequately prepare himself, perhaps through being arrogant, reckless, or impetuous.

● *At his best,* he may learn from his experience so that he can succeed next time. *At his worst,* he may suffer from his mistakes yet not learn anything from his experience.

▲ *As a public person,* he may attempt to achieve goals outside his field of activities. *As a businessperson,* he may rely on luck rather than on his careful preparation. *As an ordinary person,* he may be involved in minor disputes due to his personality or experience injuries (especially of the foot).

34.2   *Yang 9 changing line derives from Hexagram 55 Serving Greatness*

> He acts forcefully in the cause of greatness,
> and when he succeeds, he prospers.

■ He is acting strongly for a great cause or leader. He has enough force and whatever else he needs to be successful, and his success brings him benefits.

● *At his best,* he may take proper account of everything around him and thus make good decisions. *At his worst,* he may attain power but create poor solutions that bring meager results to him.

▲ *As a public person,* he may use a position of prominence or public trust to advance a cause or leader. *As a businessperson,* he may find that strong business action helps his cause. *As an ordinary person,* he may find that his desire to play an important part in his cause is met, and he is rewarded.

34.3   *Yang 9 changing line derives from Hexagram 54 Entering a Marriage*

> He is trying to force a marriage, but the situation is not proper for it.
> It is dangerous to continue this effort.

■ One of the unhappiest things in life is trying to force a relationship to work when it simply cannot. That is his situation here. Success is not possible, and continuing to try will only cause ongoing problems.

● *At his best,* he may be hurt from a hopeless situation despite his best efforts. *At his worst,* he may let the inferior qualities of his nature predominate, and he could lose family, position, money, and friends.

▲ *As a public person,* he may have to accept a publicly visible failure of his plans and efforts. *As a businessperson,* he may find that a merger is doomed to failure.

As an ordinary person, he may experience a difficult relationship or have serious disputes with those close to him.

34.4   *Yang 9 changing line derives from Hexagram 11 Easily Progressing*

Forcing matters will easily help him attain his goals,
and his concerns about doing so will fade away.

■ He has mastered the ability to use force to affect matters, and doing so is now easy for him. Benefits come to him, and his concerns with using this tactic fade away with his successes.

● *At his best,* he may be self-possessed and capable, and his success will be an appropriate reward for his hard work. *At his worst,* he may have no particular aims and no special skills, yet even so, his affairs will flourish modestly. However, this is an opportunity wasted.

▲ *As a public person,* he may find forcing a promotion or success in an important task comes easily. *As a businessperson,* he may find profits and progress at hand through strong action. *As an ordinary person,* he may find this a favorable period for new endeavors, although he may have to start things at first.

34.5   *Yin 6 changing line derives from Hexagram 43 Escaping Harm*

Not everything can be controlled, but what can't is too minor
for him to be concerned about it. He escapes any real harm.

■ Even the most successful and most well-controlled situations will not be perfect. It is quite likely that some minor thing will go awry, escape attention, or be mishandled. That is the case here. There is no point in worrying about such trivial matters. This also shows how strong and successful his control is otherwise: even when something goes wrong, he escapes harm.

● *At his best,* he may be effective and properly able to balance the big picture with the myriad details, and so be able to let minor faults go. *At his worst,* he may not be able to easily cope with unexpected difficulties, even trivialities, because of his doubts or fears.

▲ *As a public person,* he may have to accept losses that were his responsibility. *As a businessperson,* he may experience a decline in his status or reputation stemming from very minor matters. *As an ordinary person,* he may experience many minor problems or losses that fundamentally aren't as serious as he believes them to be.

34.6   *Yin 6 changing line derives from Hexagram 14 Relying on His Allies*

His allies interfere with him, so he cannot force matters now as he
wishes. Eventually, though, he may gain some benefit from this.

■ Here, he finds that his allies have interfered with him, and now he cannot act as
he intended to achieve his aims. He should remember that they are still his allies,
and there was some reason that they did what they did. He may not understand or
agree with it now, but eventually he might benefit from their actions.

● *At his best,* he may be wise enough to know when to act and when to hold back,
and from this he benefits later. *At his worst,* he may have unrealistic goals and insufficient skills to attain them, and he could offend others close to him by his actions.

▲ *As a public person,* he may face dismissal or forced early retirement. *As a businessperson,* he may need to halt activities and restructure his business enterprises
before they can succeed. *As an ordinary person,* he may force matters and obtain
unexpected opposition and undesirable results.

34.ALL   *All lines changing derives from Hexagram 20 Preparing Himself*

He has been attempting to force matters,
but now he needs to recuperate, reevaluate his goals,
and prepare himself for new circumstances.

■ He has expended his energy in attempting to force matters, and that path
appears closed to him now. Now he must give pause, reexamine his goals and his
path in life, and set new goals, develop new tools, and, in general, prepare himself
for a future advance. Thus, this preparation is an important part of his ability to succeed in the future.

● *At his best,* he may view this as a time of nourishment and enrichment as well as
a time of achievement in a different way. *At his worst,* he may be exhausted physically or spiritually, and yet be resentful in having his plans interrupted.

▲ *As a public person,* he may experience a stress breakdown from overwork. *As a
businessperson,* he may make mistakes from trying to do too much, which force
others to sideline him. *As an ordinary person,* he may experience health problems
from unhappiness or stress.

35. Advancing Due to Favor

TRIGRAMS EG	LINES 000 101	COMPLEMENTARY HEXAGRAM 5 ACTING PREMATURELY

He advances due to his leader's favor,
and he receives rewards and privileges.

■ *The traditional title* for this hexagram is "Progress," although this is somewhat misleading. Here the hexagram is titled "Advancing Due to Favor." The traditional hexagram text speaks specifically of the advancement of a younger brother of one of the Chou kings. Although an important and able person in his own right, his advancement came through the beneficence of his ruler in recognition of his loyalty and capable support. He did not seek to gain advancement only through his own individual effort. This hexagram illustrates that in human society rewards generally come from the beneficence of superiors rewarding their subordinates. *The complementary hexagram* is Hexagram 5 Acting Prematurely, which illustrates the problems of trying to advance when things are not yet in place to support it. In this hexagram, things are in place to support him, and it is because of support from above that things go so easily for him.

● *At his best,* he may sincerely believe in his leader, and be recognized and rewarded by him in return. *At his worst,* he may be putting on a deceitful show for the purpose of gain, and this will serve only to cheapen his sense of values even if he does get some benefits from it now.

▲ *As a public person,* he may be publicly praised. *As a businessperson,* he may be given an important promotion. *As an ordinary person,* he may become a close confidant of someone important to him, or rise in status through the assistance of a superior.

35.1	*Yin 6 changing line derives from Hexagram 21 Working on a Problem*

He is working on a problem, but his effort is rejected.
He should remain loyal to his leader to avert harm.

■ He is working on a problem, preparing his own solution. However, his leader rejects it, so he should wait and continue to show his loyalty. He must let his leader decide how the problem is to be solved.

● *At his best,* he may be loyal despite this setback, and thereby gain his leader's respect. *At his worst,* he may be frustrated or angry, and he could even harm himself through foolish actions.

▲ *As a public person,* he may find his goals thwarted by superiors. *As a businessperson,* he may need to rethink his situation because of factors he doesn't yet understand. *As an ordinary person,* he may find his goals unattainable, yet his loyalty will count for more in the end.

35.2	*Yin 6 changing line derives from Hexagram 64 Continuing a Task*

He should let someone else guide him to success,
especially his closest connections.

■ Here, he should not press ahead on his own. Rather, he should look to others to help guide him to success. Their direct help and support will be his best routes to advancement. In particular, family or other close connections could be especially significant. In this way, his path could even become part of others' plans.

● *At his best,* he may be thankful and pleased with the guidance and assistance he gets. *At his worst,* he may be too headstrong to accept others' help, and he could offend them.

▲ *As a public person,* he may get a powerful mentor. *As a businessperson,* he may obtain good advice from a consultant, or develop connections with important families. *As an ordinary person,* he may find his desires fulfilled through his family or his mate's family.

35.3	*Yin 6 changing line derives from Hexagram 56 Wandering*

He can gain from many people,
so he should look more widely around him for assistance.

■ He is free to do as he wishes. He is not tied down or burdened with commitments to just one leader. So, he can deal with a number of them at the same time and gain benefits.

● *At his best,* he may have a personality that will be able to blossom in his own time and space, and he can relate well to many people for his benefit. *At his worst,* he may waste his time and energy, and not truly achieve anything or benefit greatly.

▲ *As a public person,* he may be given a "position without portfolio." *As a businessperson,* he may be placed on an extended leave or sabbatical. *As an ordinary person,* he may be able to travel, dabble in whatever he chooses, or live on the largesse of the public.

35.4   *Yang 9 changing line derives from Hexagram 23 Being in a Collapsing Situation*

He relies on his own abilities, but without the assistance of others,
he could experience disaster.

■ He is overconfident, perhaps too greedy, and he relies too much on himself alone. This is dangerous, because it is generally best to work with others in achieving goals in human society. In addition, they could provide a safety net, which he lacks.

● *At his best,* he may see the dangers before he causes a calamity, and establish the relationships he needs with others. *At his worst,* he may be blind to his weaknesses (and the pitfalls around him) until disaster befalls him.

▲ *As a public person,* he may unwisely believe too much in the written rules rather than understanding the unwritten rules that also affect events. *As a businessperson,* he may find his perfect plans go awry despite his best efforts. *As an ordinary person,* he may find himself embroiled in petty disputes, and he may feel a lack of friends in his life.

35.5   *Yin 6 changing line derives from Hexagram 12 Being Blocked*

He is no longer being blocked, and he knows he will progress.
Rewards will easily come now.

■ He now has great confidence that he will succeed. Others look upon him favorably, and even he does not believe he can fail. Rewards will come to him easily.

● *At his best,* he may understand the requirements of the situation and fully succeed, pleasing both him and his supporters. *At his worst,* he may succeed to some extent, but end up disappointing those he needed not to disappoint.

▲ *As a public person,* he may easily gain public attention with his successes. *As a businessperson,* he may be able to put his program into effect without opposition. *As an ordinary person,* he may experience a generally favorable period with no money worries.

35.6   *Yang 9 changing line derives from Hexagram 16 Standstill*

He can only benefit by actions he takes within his own domain,
so no great gain is possible.
Attempts to gain elsewhere would bring trouble.

■ Unable to achieve anything elsewhere, he can gain only from actions he takes within the domain that he controls. Of course, no major gain or loss can come from this. Note that if he tried to advance himself anywhere else, he would get into trouble, so it is better that he not try.

● *At his best,* he may experience minor improvements within his own domain even though he may feel frustrated by not being able to do more. *At his worst,* he may foolishly try to advance himself on others and end up rebuffed and harmed.

▲ *As a public person,* he may launch a publicity campaign aimed at enhancing his own position rather than doing anything really worthwhile. *As a businessperson,* he may try to enhance efficiency or cut corners to reduce costs rather than solve more fundamental business problems. *As an ordinary person,* he may improve his home, enhance his resume, or try to make his life better in small ways.

35.ALL *All lines changing derives from Hexagram 5 Acting Prematurely*

He believes he can gain by advancing himself. He is so anxious to press ahead that he does not care if he is ready or not.

■ While success depends to some extent on the favor of others, he understands that he also needs to act on his own behalf to help himself succeed. Even if he does not have the favor of others now, he still wants to press ahead and try to succeed on his own. Unfortunately, he is so anxious that he may not pay proper attention to timing, the requirements of the situation, or even if he has gained the right skills and knowledge.

● *At his best,* he may be deeply committed to his success, and with the proper attention to the requirements of his situations, he will be able to do so. *At his worst,* he may be uncompromising in his desires and blind in his actions, and thus be unable to progress.

▲ *As a public person,* he may attempt to rally public opinion rather than get the backing of powerful insiders. *As a businessperson,* he may find himself removed from where the real decisions are made. *As an ordinary person,* he may have lost important friends.

36. Serving as an Assistant

TRIGRAMS GE   LINES 101 000   COMPLEMENTARY HEXAGRAM 6 HAVING A COMPLAINT

He is serving as an assistant,
and he benefits by facing his difficulties.

■ *The traditional title* for this hexagram is "Darkening of the Light," which is very confusing and misleading. According to Whincup, the ideograms used today literally mean "the light is wounded." Both Whincup and the Huangs follow suggestion that this problem arose because of an ancient error in transcribing the word "wounded" for the word "pheasant." The Huangs thus title this "The Crying Pheasant," and Whincup uses "The Bright Pheasant." Here, however, the title used is "Serving as an Assistant." The bright pheasant represents a brilliant but powerless assistant to a more powerful person. Like the brightly colored pheasant that has difficulty flying, the brilliant assistant has difficulty achieving his own success under his leader. During such a period, he must persevere and rely on his inner strength when positive results are lacking in other areas. Although he can get some benefits now, real progress can come only from being in a different situation. *The complementary hexagram* is Hexagram 6 Having a Complaint, which illustrates how the problems facing the brilliant assistant can grow so serious that he must question his ability to continue to serve.

● *At his best,* he may recognize the limitations of his situation, work within its constraints, and obtain some rewards for his efforts. *At his worst,* he may make errors in judgment, and suffer many complications from his leader.

▲ *As a public person,* he may be a press secretary or aide to an important person. *As a businessperson,* he may be an intern or assistant. *As an ordinary person,* he may have a supporting role with a supervisor, mate, or community leader.

36.1   *Yang 9 changing line derives from Hexagram 15 Acting With Propriety*

He has disagreements with his leader, so he discusses them
with him. He is acting properly even though he
might suffer slight harm doing so.

■ Here, he has some serious disagreements with his leader, and he could choose one of several paths: He could simply disregard his concerns and be obedient. He could walk away from the situation and seek another position elsewhere. Alternatively, he could go to his leader and forthrightly discuss his concerns hoping that this will improve the situation in some way. He chooses the latter path. This is the proper thing to do, since his concerns might be important in improving the situation and benefit his leader as well. However, it is also possible that he could be punished or criticized for doing this, so there is some potential risk.

● *At his best,* he may be committed to doing the right thing and be able to withstand the consequences. *At his worst,* he may try to do the right thing, but due to weakness or confusion, not achieve the good he had hoped for, and he could possibly suffer from this.

▲ *As a public person,* he may know that now he should use private persuasion rather than public communication to achieve his goals. *As a businessperson,* he may find himself in a conflict that he tries to wriggle out of. *As an ordinary person,* he may have problems with his mate or boss that he will work hard to resolve.

36.2   *Yin 6 changing line derives from Hexagram 11 Easily Progressing*

He does not expect the attack he suffers from his leader,
yet he is easily able to overcome it.

■ He suffers an attack from his leader or a friend who he thought was protective. For example, this could be through an ally of his leader's, through a way his leader should have been protecting him and wasn't, or through an avenue where he didn't think he would be attacked by his leader. Whatever the attack, however, he is easily able to overcome it.

● *At his best,* he may be able to overcome this setback and build stronger ties with those who help him. *At his worst,* he may marshal resources and recover from the damage, but end up alienating those who help him.

▲ *As a public person,* he may be attacked by someone he trusted. *As a businessperson,* he may suddenly have new competitors or obstacles to his business. *As an ordinary person,* he may suffer a betrayal or a physical injury.

36.3   *Yang 9 changing line derives from Hexagram 24 Beginning a Relationship*

He is beginning a relationship with another leader.
Improving his situation by switching to a superior leader is wise.

■ Either he has been actively looking for a new leader or a new leader has come to his attention during the course of his normal affairs. He can improve his situation by finding a better leader to follow. Advancing this way is always good.

● *At his best,* he may recognize a powerful leader and begin a new career with him in a better position. *At his worst,* he may fawningly attach himself to someone else hoping that his situation will improve.

▲ *As a public person,* he may very visibly switch causes or parties for its publicity effect. *As a businessperson,* he may switch to a new business enterprise or career, or even to a new competitor. *As an ordinary person,* he may change his allegiance to someone new.

36.4   *Yin 6 changing line derives from Hexagram 55 Serving Greatness*

> He is granted a taste of greatness by his leader
> just as he was about to renounce him.

■ His leader surprises him by allowing him to gain something of great value. This could be a financial reward, special honor, public favor, or some honor that could come only from his leader. This could also mean his leader agrees to follow his plans rather than to reject them. Now his thoughts about renouncing his leader have been pushed aside, and he rededicates himself to his leader.

● *At his best,* he may come to understand how he can work with his leader and yet still attain his goals. *At his worst,* he may be satisfied but for the moment, and later more problems will arise that poison their relationship.

▲ *As a public person,* he may be given an important role. *As a businessperson,* he may find that one of his pet projects is given the go-ahead. *As an ordinary person,* he may have strongly positive feelings for his leader as well as confidence in the future.

36.5   *Yin 6 changing line derives from Hexagram 63 Beginning a New Task*

> He is beginning a new and different kind of service to his leader.
> His old path is done, and he can gain more on the new one.

■ What he did before has been finished. Now his leader assigns him to something new that promises to be even better for him. This could also possibly mean beginning new tasks with a new leader.

● *At his best,* he may be able to advance and gain greatly from his new assignment. *At his worst,* he may not be fully up to the demands of his new situation, and so he does not benefit as much as he hoped.

▲ *As a public person,* he may begin a new public campaign, or he may seek out someone he respects to offer his services to. *As a businessperson,* he may be assigned to a new product or business situation. *As an ordinary person,* he may experience family difficulties, a marriage or longstanding contract may end, or he may take a radically different direction.

36.6   *Yin 6 changing line derives from Hexagram 22 Advancing by His Image*

> However much he enhances his image,
> it is not enough for what he tries to do.
> Thus, he fails and grieves.

■ Enhancing his image can't help him enough in preparing for the problems he faces now with his leader (or perhaps with the real world). Here, despite his best efforts at preparing himself, he fails to accomplish his goal when challenged. This shows he still needs the guidance and support of his leader.

● *At his best,* he may gain something of value through his failure that will benefit him next time. *At his worst,* he may harm both himself and others through his anger or shame, and even worse, not grow positively through the experience.

▲ *As a public person,* he may make a serious mistake that affects both others and his career. *As a businessperson,* he may find that preventable setbacks harm business. *As an ordinary person,* he may find matters becoming increasingly difficult, or his health may deteriorate.

36.ALL   *All lines changing derives from Hexagram 6 Having a Complaint*

> His difficulties with his leader have gone beyond what he can
> accept easily. Now he has a complaint against his leader,
> and he must pursue it to get it resolved favorably.

■ The difficulties and problems that he had can no longer be ignored. Now they have become a complaint that won't go away, and so need to be resolved in a more serious fashion.

● *At his best,* he may put this complaint into proportion with the rest of his relationship with his leader, and thus seek a balanced and workable solution. *At his worst,* he may angrily demand something that cannot be obtained.

▲ *As a public person,* he may seek a legal hearing. *As a businessperson,* he may seek to negotiate a settlement. *As an ordinary person,* he may have difficult discussions with his mate or boss.

37. Serving in a Household

TRIGRAMS GF   LINES 101 011   COMPLEMENTARY HEXAGRAM 40 GETTING FREE

He is serving in a household,
so he should be obedient and supportive now.

■ *The traditional titles* for this hexagram are "The Family" or "The Clan," although these are a little misleading. Whincup notes the words literally mean "house people," and refers to the family and retainers in an extended household. The household portrayed here is the ancient Chinese household. Thus, it is neither an extended family nor a nuclear family in Western terms, since it includes an extended family as well as their servants all living and working cooperatively together. Here the hexagram is titled "Serving in a Household," and illustrates someone working (or serving) in the household. In this household, some are leaders, and some are followers, but all should be guided by a spirit of cooperation and shared goals. Above all, good relationships between members should be preserved through observance of proper behavior and temperance. In these ways, the household as a whole prospers and so does each of its members. *The complementary hexagram* is Hexagram 40 Getting Free, which illustrates how one grows and gains freedom from the household and advances into the outside world.

● *At his best,* he may know his place in the household and benefit through his proper relations with those around him. *At his worst,* he may feel hemmed in by his responsibilities and restrictions, and believe his rewards are insufficient.

▲ *As a public person,* he may represent his family to outsiders. *As a businessperson,* he may have a subordinate role behind the scenes that helps the business succeed. *As an ordinary person,* he may have strong emotional ties with others in a family or clan, and they all benefit through shared efforts together.

37.1   *Yang 9 changing line derives from Hexagram 53 Sharing Commitment*

As part of a household, he develops a shared commitment with it,
and his regrets about being there will pass.

■ He now has a place in a household. He could view this either as a trap or as a refuge. Over time, he develops a commitment to the household and to those within it. His regrets and doubts about being there will pass.

● *At his best,* he may learn toleration and patience while he strengthens himself. *At his worst,* he may resent his restrictions, even though he sees that good comes from them.

▲ *As a public person,* he may work in a secretive or tightly regulated agency. *As a businessperson,* he may deal with secret business plans. *As an ordinary person,* he may find many restrictions at home and learn to put up with them.

37.2   *Yin 6 changing line derives from Hexagram 9 Restraining Himself*

He can serve effectively within the household because it is easy
for him to restrain himself. He benefits by doing this.

■ If he were strong, he could do whatever he wanted out in the world. However, because he is weak, others can easily get him to serve within the confines of the household. He understands this. So, by restraining himself and attending to his duties there, he is able to benefit.

● *At his best,* he may grow in strength and wisdom while he is protected. *At his worst,* he may waste time or energy and not gain fully from his opportunities.

▲ *As a public person,* he may have a position in a subsidiary or supporting agency. *As a businessperson,* he may work in a supporting role, such as billing or maintenance. *As an ordinary person,* he may work around the home, or serve as a caretaker or companion.

37.3   *Yang 9 changing line derives from Hexagram 42 Gaining Benefits*

There are conflicts, yet he is able to gain benefits
if he deals with the most significant problems.

■ Living under rules can be difficult, and these will at times cause conflicts. By focusing on what is most important and what needs to be done (rather than what he would like to have or what is pleasurable), he is able to gain increased benefits for himself.

● *At his best,* he may be judicious in his actions, so the conflict will be minimized and his benefits maximized. *At his worst,* he may complain bitterly and offend many; so, although he gains, he also leaves poisoned relationships behind.

▲ *As a public person,* he may deal successfully with bureaucratic complications. *As a businessperson,* he may fight extra restrictions on his activities. *As an ordinary person,* he may experience both good and ill coming from the same situation.

37.4   *Yin 6 changing line derives from Hexagram 13 Serving on a Team*

He has truly joined himself with the household,
so now he fully shares in its prosperity.

■ The household shares its bounty with every member. By truly joining himself to the household, he is now able to share fully in its riches.

● *At his best,* he may benefit spiritually as well as materially through his contributions to the household. *At his worst,* he may consume without contributing much of anything, and this weighs on his spirit.

▲ *As a public person,* he may obtain a good position by joining an organization. *As a businessperson,* he may be given a bonus. *As an ordinary person,* he may enjoy a period of benefit coming from his family.

37.5   *Yang 9 changing line derives from Hexagram 22 Advancing by His Image*

He has enhanced himself, so now both he and the household benefit.

■ Now, his enhancement of his image benefits the household. This is a very beneficial step for everyone as well as for himself. While he has the hefty support of the household behind him, he is now like the sharp point at the tip of the spear and gives the household something especially effective through his service.

● *At his best,* he may have prepared himself and may be rewarded by improvements to his status and wealth. *At his worst,* he may not have fully prepared himself, or prepared himself in a way that offends others, and so does not gain much.

▲ *As a public person,* he may be working toward a position in a different agency. *As a businessperson,* he may be studying areas of knowledge outside his business. *As an ordinary person,* he may obtain the help of an elder in his family or a mentor to aid him, or he prepares himself for a new school.

37.6   *Yang 9 changing line derives from Hexagram 63 Beginning a New Task*

He is not a servant of the household; he can set his own tasks.

■ He has succeeded in his role in the household. He has gained in strength and wisdom, and has won the household's respect. Now he can begin doing what is important to him and not only what is important to others.

● *At his best,* he may have stayed in the household long enough to truly gain in character and strength, so the lessons he learned will benefit him in the future. *At his worst,* he may have not have gained much in character and wisdom, so his freedom to do new things won't be very productive.

▲ *As a public person,* he may go on to a more publicly visible position. *As a businessperson,* he may change firms and gain in stature. *As an ordinary person,* he may leave home or change his circumstances, going from a secure position to a more risky one.

37.ALL   *All lines changing derives from Hexagram 40 Getting Free*

He is free of the household, so can do whatever he wants
and go wherever he wants.

■ He has grown in maturity so much that the household is no longer his home. He no longer needs its security, and staying there to him is more of a hindrance than a benefit. Home is now wherever he is. Now he is free to go wherever he chooses and do whatever he wants.

● *At his best,* he may treasure positive feelings and memories of home, which will enrich his life in the future. *At his worst,* he may flee a terrible home life, and carry it as a burden throughout his life.

▲ *As a public person,* he may break his allegiance with his former leader or organization. *As a businessperson,* he may seek opportunities in other businesses or fields. *As an ordinary person,* he may leave home or begin a long endeavor that leads him away from home.

38. Looking for a Leader

TRIGRAMS HG   LINES 110 101   COMPLEMENTARY HEXAGRAM 39 BUMBLING BY HIMSELF

He is looking for a leader,
so only minor tasks should be done on his own.

■ *The traditional title* for this hexagram is "Opposition," although this is somewhat misleading. Whincup titles this "Estrangement," and the Huangs use "Abandoned." Whincup notes that originally the title meant having eyes that look in different directions. Here the hexagram is titled "Looking for a Leader." It signifies he is looking around him and evaluating potential leaders to guide him. Without having a strong leader to rely on, he should attempt to do only small things on his own. If he attempted a major task without assistance, he would likely make errors. The lower lines refer to how he can return to his existing leader after looking elsewhere; the upper lines refer to his going on to a new one. *The complementary hexagram* is Hexagram 39 Bumbling by Himself, which illustrates how without proper leadership it is easy to get into trouble.

● *At his best,* he may strive for stability in his life by doing as little as possible while he evaluates potential leaders. *At his worst,* he may forget his tenuous position and make mistakes, or not even do a good job in evaluating other leaders.

▲ *As a public person,* he may lead a group of people seeking a leader for them all to follow. *As a businessperson,* he may be investigating new business opportunities. *As an ordinary person,* he may be searching for a new wife, a new friend, a new mentor, or even a new job.

38.1   *Yang 9 changing line derives from Hexagram 64 Continuing a Task*

He should continue with his old leader. It is not too late
for him to go back, and no harm comes from doing this.

■ He is at the very start of his effort to look elsewhere, and if he chose, he could go back and resume his former situation. It is beneficial having a way out like this that does not harm him. He should only look elsewhere if he is sure remaining is impossible.

● *At his best,* he may carefully evaluate his options and make a decision he is pleased with. *At his worst,* he may make a decision based on fear or anger or thoughtless haste, and he will rue this for long in the future.

▲ *As a public person,* he may have different career options beckoning him. *As a businessperson,* he may find a new endeavor is not what he thought it would be, and he may return to his earlier situation. *As an ordinary person,* he may leave one mate or job for another and later reconsider.

38.2   *Yang 9 changing line derives from Hexagram 21 Working on a Problem*

Working on his problems with his leader can eliminate difficulties, so he won't have to look for a new leader.

■ He should discuss his problems with his leader in order to reduce or eliminate them. Rather than needing to look elsewhere, now because his problems have been resolved, his ties with his leader can be reinforced.

● *At his best,* he may truly come to understand both himself and his leader, and from this develop a relationship that works for them both. *At his worst,* he may pick up some hints that can better his situation.

▲ *As a public person,* he may find that his leader recognizes his abilities and promotes him after he pleads his cause with him. *As a businessperson,* he may discuss organizational problems with his leader that lead to workplace changes. *As an ordinary person,* he may be able to fulfill his desires with the aid of a close friend or associate.

38.3   *Yin 6 changing line derives from Hexagram 14 Relying on His Allies*

He sees that his friends and allies who have similar situations to his own also have difficulties. This example shows him that his situation with his leader is not so bad.

■ He sees others in comparable situations also struggling and suffering. He learns from this that perhaps he wanted too much, and that his situation is not so bad. With this understanding, he can now more easily remain.

● *At his best,* he may understand that although nothing is completely secure, he should balance independence and dependence as well as develop ties with those who can help him. *At his worst,* he may not take this lesson to heart, so sometime he will be overly dependent and then harmed when the support he needs is withdrawn.

▲ *As a public person,* he may avoid being caught in turbulent times by minimizing his obligations to others. *As a businessperson,* he may find he is initially considered a second choice, but later may be chosen. *As an ordinary person,* he may have initial difficulties with family and friends that can ease later if he pays attention to their difficulties.

38.4   *Yang 9 changing line derives from Hexagram 41 Declining Influence*

> While he has declining influence with his leader,
> he finds a new one who can help him.
> He relies on them and so danger passes.

■ He finds a new leader he can look to for help. With their assistance, he can deal successfully with the problems he faces, and so he relies on them.

● *At his best,* he may find a trusted advisor and true friend. *At his worst,* he may find someone who can help, but he could end up paying a high price later.

▲ *As a public person,* he may find an ally who can do him some good. *As a businessperson,* he may develop a mentorship or find a consultant who makes a success of a business endeavor. *As an ordinary person,* he may find an end to his problems, enter into a marriage, or go on a trip to visit a great person.

38.5   *Yin 6 changing line derives from Hexagram 10 Taking Risky Action*

> He takes a risky action, which serves a leader's cause,
> and it succeeds. With this, he wins a place
> with the leader and his regrets pass.

■ Either he takes a gamble on his own or he is given an invitation to try. His risky action, which furthers a leader's cause, succeeds. Because of this, he wins a place with the leader and his regrets pass.

● *At his best,* he may prove he has courage and wisdom to someone who needs him. *At his worst,* he may simply be lucky, and next time, he could fail and be rewarded only for trying.

▲ *As a public person,* he may prove he is worthy of an important appointment. *As a businessperson,* he may be innovative and successful. *As an ordinary person,* he may obtain help from his family or his mate's family, or he could marry.

38.6   *Yang 9 changing line derives from Hexagram 54 Entering a Marriage*

He seeks a marriage but feels threatened doing so.
However, if he tries, he can win a place and benefit.

■ Here he is acting as a leader, seeking a follower or a mate. He is aware of some danger around him or suspicion of him; however, he needn't fight because he has the ability to win others over to his cause. In this way, he succeeds as a leader.

● *At his best,* he may learn to overcome his own fears and inhibitions, and thereby find friends and allies. *At his worst,* he may struggle to make friends, only to fail and feel embittered and isolated.

▲ *As a public person,* he may have a backwater position and need to find an ally or mentor to help advance him. *As a businessperson,* he may find matters difficult initially, but partnerships and working relationships will eliminate the problems. *As an ordinary person,* he may initially have problems, or be falsely accused by someone close to him and have the truth emerge later.

38.ALL   *All lines changing derives from Hexagram 39 Bumbling by Himself*

Relying too much on himself, he begins to bumble.

■ He now begins to make mistakes, bumbling in his attempt to progress, because he is relying too much on his own efforts and understandings.

● *At his best,* he may make sincere efforts to progress, but be either unable or unlucky to get the results he needs. *At his worst,* he may begin to suffer serious harm being without guidance in his efforts to progress.

▲ *As a public person,* he may enter into a series of mistakes that harm his career. *As a businessperson,* he may make mistakes that lose money. *As an ordinary person,* he may make mistakes that affect his life in many ways, and his relationships are particularly susceptible.

39. Bumbling by Himself

TRIGRAMS DC   LINES 001 010   COMPLEMENTARY HEXAGRAM 38 LOOKING FOR A LEADER

He is bumbling by himself, so he should hold back
or even retreat rather than advance alone.
He would benefit by having a leader to follow.

■ *The traditional title* for this hexagram is "Obstruction," although this is somewhat misleading. The Huangs title it "Admonishment," and Whincup uses "Stumbling." Here this is titled "Bumbling by Himself." It signifies he bumbles by trying to advance relying only on himself. He would be better off by holding back or even retreating if he is alone. However, if he had a leader to follow, he could progress. Without that support, however, trying too much by himself will bring problems. *The complementary hexagram* is Hexagram 38 Looking for a Leader, which illustrates that gaining a leader to rely on will bring him benefits.

● *At his best,* he may have the modest goal of keeping things stable, and he is able to do this without too much difficulty. *At his worst,* he may not realize his vulnerability, he may have unattainable goals, he may make rash decisions, and he may suffer serious consequences.

▲ *As a public person,* he may not have the support of others, and so he is publicly vulnerable and liable to make mistakes. *As a businessperson,* he may need the support of business experts who have skills he does not. *As an ordinary person,* he may feel particularly friendless, be single, or be prone to alienate others through his actions.

| 39.1 | *Yin 6 changing line derives from Hexagram 63 Beginning a New Task* |

He bumbles at the beginning of a new task,
but stopping right away mitigates his problems.

■ Although he bumbled in beginning a new task, he immediately stopped his efforts. This has mitigated (or even eliminated) the problems he encountered. This is when it is easiest to rectify the errors.

● *At his best,* he may be able to quickly understand his errors and thus mitigate his mistakes. *At his worst,* he may have stopped not because he knew better, but because he was forced to.

▲ *As a public person,* he may be praised for avoiding or resolving problems. *As a businessperson,* he may decide it is best to halt a business project. *As an ordinary person,* he may find that reviewing commonsense principles helps him make good decisions.

39.2   *Yin 6 changing line derives from Hexagram 48 Being Renewed*

He bumbles but benefits by being renewed.

■ He is fortunate that after he bumbles he is renewed. His spirit, body, or other resources are rested and repaired. It is almost as if his bumble didn't harm him at all. In the traditional text, it indicates he was doing this for the benefit of someone else; thus, that other person may be renewing him.

● *At his best,* he may benefit from this circumstance and use it to progress. *At his worst,* he may receive a badly needed but short respite.

▲ *As a public person,* he may make a mistake and yet receive favorable attention from an important official. *As a businessperson,* he may encounter barriers to a new enterprise, which money can eradicate. *As an ordinary person,* he may find his difficulties will later be overcome or compensated, or possibly an important connection made.

39.3   *Yang 9 changing line derives from Hexagram 8 Entering an Alliance*

He bumbles trying to progress alone,
so he searches out allies who can help him.

■ The reason he bumbled was because he did not have the proper support, and he knows this. This understanding is beneficial, but it may not be easy trying to find the proper allies for him, although he may succeed in doing so.

● *At his best,* he may understand his needs and the qualities of those around him, and thus be able to find the appropriate allies. *At his worst,* he may be forced to find a partner and select one who harms him in the end.

▲ *As a public person,* he may need to build alliances in new organizations. *As a businessperson,* he may seek new backers. *As an ordinary person,* he may marry or begin a family, he may be unexpectedly injured, or he may decide to obtain assistance in pursuing his goals.

Yin 6 changing line derives from Hexagram 31 Ability to Change Matters

He bumbles because any changes he makes will bring trouble,
so he needs to strengthen himself.

■ He is at a difficult point. He can neither advance nor retreat without causing problems. He might try to understand the nature of the problems around him and reach out to others for aid, or he might develop strong psychological, managerial, or organizational skills. However, generally external solutions won't be effective, so he must develop his character to deal with his troubles.

● *At his best,* he may control his worst tendencies and prepare himself to face challenges. *At his worst,* he may struggle to affect events the way he wants and end up being harmed from unanticipated consequences.

▲ *As a public person,* he may find that he is trapped in an awkward position that harms his reputation. *As a businessperson,* he may find himself in a serious bind that will cost him. *As an ordinary person,* he may be very unhappy being in a situation that has no good solutions.

39.5 *Yang 9 changing line derives from Hexagram 15 Acting with Propriety*

He bumbles, but acting with propriety brings him assistance.

■ He bumbles but he knows what to do: he needs to use tried and true solutions and not experiments, reach out to his friends and allies, and combine his efforts with others' contributions. Doing all of these, he can overcome his problems.

● *At his best,* he may have good friends who can advise and assist him. *At his worst,* he may use friends to assist him but at a price to be reckoned later.

▲ *As a public person,* he may obtain a position with the aid of friends. *As a businessperson,* he may find an alliance to take over an endangered enterprise. *As an ordinary person,* he may find a serious health problem is mitigated by the aid and support of many good friends.

39.6 *Yin 6 changing line derives from Hexagram 53 Sharing Commitment*

He bumbles but decides that sharing commitments
with a leader would bring him benefits.

■ He has decided that finding a leader with whom he shares the same values and commitments will allow him to join with the leader. From this commitment, he could obtain continuing benefits, and so this is very desirable to him.

● *At his best,* he may recognize someone he would be happy to ally himself with for a long time. *At his worst,* he may join a cause or organization out of opportunism and later be unhappy being there.

▲ *As a public person,* he may find promotion comes easily when he is loyal to his superior and follows procedures. *As a businessperson,* he may discover that connections to famous figures or philanthropic endeavors bring recognition or profit. *As an ordinary person,* he may enjoy associations (marriage, vocation, or avocation) that are valuable and worthwhile.

39.ALL   *All lines changing derives from Hexagram 38 Looking for a Leader*

> Bumbling by himself has taught him that he needs to change his situation, so he begins to look for a leader to assist him.

■ Bumbling is a sign of having self-inflicted problems. Now he has realized the solution is to find someone to assist him, so he now actively begins to look for a leader who can help guide him.

● *At his best,* he may be able to transcend the limitations that have affected him in the past and thus glimpse a new future for himself. *At his worst,* he may have run out of options in his current area and may therefore be forced to look elsewhere.

▲ *As a public person,* he may look for positions or opportunities. *As a businessperson,* he may look at different businesses for keys to success. *As an ordinary person,* he may break with the past, take a big gamble, or explore new areas.

40. Getting Free

TRIGRAMS CB   LINES 010 100   COMPLEMENTARY HEXAGRAM 37 SERVING IN A HOUSEHOLD

Getting free is beneficial when others are holding him back.

■ *The traditional title* for this hexagram is "Deliverance," and is somewhat misleading. The Huangs use "Letting Loose," and Whincup uses "Getting Free," which is also the title used here. It signifies that he decides to extricate himself from the restrictions around him to open up his future possibilities. *The complementary hexagram* is Hexagram 37 Serving in a Household, which illustrates the supportive yet also restrictive situation from which he is seeking his release. The pair of these can also be viewed in terms of psychological development, as a young person leaves the family home to strike out on his own as a mature adult.

● *At his best,* he may realize that he has matured beyond the need for the restrictions he feels, so his freedom is necessary for his continuing growth. *At his worst,* he may be getting free out of premature youthful rebelliousness, so he is not yet really able to take advantage of the new possibilities he has.

▲ *As a public person,* he may lead a new movement or splinter group. *As a businessperson,* he may start his own business or successfully sell himself to his boss's boss. *As an ordinary person,* he may grow up and leave home, or break free of the social conventions of a group he is in.

40.1   *Yin 6 changing line derives from Hexagram 54 Entering a Marriage*

Freeing himself through entering a marriage is
usually successful and is easily done.

■ Freeing himself by entering a marriage (or partnership) is usually the easiest way of succeeding in getting free. This is likely because it does not require any conflict with his prior situation, but rather is seen as the natural path that he will be taking eventually. This is also the typical way in which a young adult of today frees himself from his family; that is, by starting his own family.

● *At his best,* he may understand the possibilities facing him, and he will create a marriage that suits him. *At his worst,* he may be driven by necessity, and end up with a marriage of convenience which does not suit him.

▲ *As a public person,* he may work for a joint taskforce or develop a power-sharing agreement. *As a businessperson,* he may develop proposals and solicitations for mergers or joint operations. *As an ordinary person,* he may get married or find that, in general, new endeavors should be advanced early for their later success.

40.2   *Yang 9 changing line derives from Hexagram 16 Standstill*

He overcomes his standstill and succeeds in getting free
by trying hard. He can gain many benefits by doing this.

■ Getting free sometimes requires great or ongoing effort. Although he was at a standstill, he is able to overcome it through hard work. Doing this, he might find that he now gets a number of benefits.

● *At his best,* he may find his efforts bring him many benefits, including very important ones. *At his worst,* he may struggle very hard to get free, and although he succeeds, he gets only marginal benefits.

▲ *As a public person,* he may win a promotion to a prominent position or achieve some fame. *As a businessperson,* he may find his business efforts successful, and his reputation may also rise. *As an ordinary person,* he may make important gains through hard work, particularly in assets, but they could be in other life areas as well.

40.3   *Yin 6 changing line derives from Hexagram 32 Committing Himself*

He doesn't want to get free of his situation
because he has committed himself to it, but he now finds
himself attacked and driven away despite his desires.

■ Here he is getting free, albeit involuntarily. He is truly committed to his situation, but outside events could conspire to make this impossible to maintain. In some way, he will be attacked (or possibly some other aspect of the situation will be damaged) so that he simply cannot remain in the situation he desires.

● *At his best,* he may have courage enough to stand against the forces arrayed against him. *At his worst,* he may be blind to what has really happened or may be too weak to do anything.

▲ *As a public person,* he may face demotion or a reprimand unless he exercises caution. *As a businessperson,* he may encounter attempts to undermine his position or his markets. *As an ordinary person,* he may have losses or other problems that are caused by others.

He gains a position that offers a little bit of freedom; then,
with the help of others, he increases it.

■ Here, he proves his ability first by freeing himself, even if it is just a tiny bit, and then by leading others who come to him. Everyone benefits from his leadership, and he attains his goals.

● *At his best,* he may gain a place of independence and power that benefits him. *At his worst,* he may be lucky in freeing himself a little bit and having his friends help him to minimize his problems.

▲ *As a public person,* he may extricate himself from some difficulty and in the process gain good supporters. *As a businessperson,* he may start a new venture and be aided by friends. *As an ordinary person,* he may experience troubles, ask for help, and have friends help him.

He works hard to free himself,
and others see this so they trust him.

■ He is working hard on his own behalf, and this inspires others to place their confidence in him. Both his work and the trust of others are valuable assets that will benefit him in his effort.

● *At his best,* he may be sincere and capable, and this inspires others to ally themselves with him. *At his worst,* he may be used to some extent by others, but this does him no harm.

▲ *As a public person,* he may be engaged on a big project, which will promote him. *As a businessperson,* he may be working on a new moneymaking venture. *As an ordinary person,* he may work through the problems facing him, and he could establish important ties with others.

He is so strong that he doesn't need to get free to succeed.
It is possible for him to get almost anything he desires
even in his present circumstance.

■ Here, he has gained so much strength that he can succeed in his goals despite not having his freedom. Almost anything that he wants to have he will succeed in getting. This also means that he will be maintaining the relationship he previously considered so restrictive.

● *At his best,* he may be powerful yet respectful of others and his ties with them. *At his worst,* he may abuse or manipulate the situation around him to further his position.

▲ *As a public person,* he may be satisfied in his present position. *As a businessperson,* he may find ways of getting more money without leaving his current situation. *As an ordinary person,* he may get extra money or achieve a notable task.

40.ALL   *All lines changing derives from Hexagram 37 Serving in a Household*

He doesn't want to be free.
He wants a secure household in which he can thrive.

■ Here, he realizes that he doesn't need freedom. Rather, having a secure position means working in a protected environment, such as inside his family's enterprise or household. With this kind of security, he will be able to nurture himself, grow in important ways, and still achieve his goals.

● *At his best,* he may be responding to a real need to nurture, heal, and prepare himself for the future. *At his worst,* he may be driven by difficulties in the real world, which he can't begin to deal with.

▲ *As a public person,* he may resist overtures for a promotion to another unit. *As a businessperson,* he may want to keep on doing business the way he's always done it. *As an ordinary person,* he may try to remain home, or he may seek a comfortable mate to marry.

41. Declining Influence

TRIGRAMS HD LINES 110 001 COMPLEMENTARY HEXAGRAM 31 ABILITY TO CHANGE MATTERS

He has declining influence now; however, it doesn't harm him to remain faithful to his goals and it may even be beneficial later. He should prepare himself for the future, and a small but appropriate gift to his leader will show his commitment.

■ *The traditional title* for this hexagram is "Decrease," although Whincup titles it "Reduction." Here the hexagram is titled "Declining Influence." It signifies that in a time of his declining influence, he should not give up his principles or his goals, but rather keep to them. He should also prepare himself for the future, and this includes giving his leader (who may be partly responsible for his decline) a small gift to show that he is still committed to him. A freely given token of his commitment is a powerful statement that will strengthen his position. (This is still done in contemporary Chinese society.) Thus, he should focus on his commitments to others, his responsibilities, and his preparations for the future. In these ways, he may mitigate his negative tendencies and the decline in his status, and thereby prepare for the future. *The complementary hexagram* is Hexagram 31 Ability to Change Matters, which illustrates that after his decline has stopped, he will gain increasing ability to change matters.

● *At his best,* he may realize his decline is only temporary, and he will suitably prepare himself for the future and wait. *At his worst,* he may feel his decline more intensely, not handle daily affairs as well, not try to prepare for the future, and not be as optimistic as he could otherwise be in general.

▲ *As a public person,* he may fall out of favor or he may be forgotten. *As a businessperson,* he may lose the ear of his superior. *As an ordinary person,* he may lose influence over those around him, experience a decrease in his status at work or in an organization, or dedicate himself to a plan to reestablish himself.

41.1 *Yang 9 changing line derives from Hexagram 4 Acting Impetuously*

He has declining influence but comes to no harm because, although he was acting impetuously, it was with sincerity.

■ His decline is due to acting rashly, immaturely, or inappropriately. Impetuous or otherwise immature actions are easy to fall into, especially at the beginning. Here, he makes that mistake and suffers some decline; however, it is not serious because it is offset by his sincerity.

● *At his best,* he may be making youthful mistakes that can be easily forgiven because they know he will learn better. *At his worst,* he may be making mistakes he knows he shouldn't, but his commitment will still help mitigate harm.

▲ *As a public person,* he may make a bad policy decision because he is swayed by personal reasons. *As a businessperson,* he may be overly pushy in a sales transaction. *As an ordinary person,* he may earn the respect of those around him despite his foolish action.

41.2   *Yang 9 changing line derives from Hexagram 27 Desiring*

He has declining influence because he desires too much for himself. When his actions help those around him, he will gain success.

■ He sees opportunities for action, but he should approach them carefully. If he is selfish in his aims, he will not get what he wants. He is most likely to succeed when he tries to do something that will help other people. He can then get some benefit from the success of his effort, but that should not be his prime motivation.

● *At his best,* he may be caring of others and sincere in his efforts to do some good, and he will benefit from his commitment and the successful result. *At his worst,* he may not be able to uncouple his efforts from his desires, and thus his efforts will be inadequate and unsuccessful.

▲ *As a public person,* he will be most successful with modest proposals rather than grandiose ones. *As a businessperson,* he makes real progress by knowing the needs of his market. *As an ordinary person,* he may expect that helping others will be the best way to help himself, or that the less radical his ideas the more easily accepted they will be.

41.3   *Yin 6 changing line derives from Hexagram 26 External Restraint*

He has declining influence because he is restrained either by someone close to him or by the lack of support he needs. In adversity, he needs to rely on his core supporters.

■ Here, he is in a situation of adversity, and finds he is being restrained by others. This could take two different forms: either restraint by someone close to him (perhaps an assistant, associate, or his leader), or restraint because he needs assistance from someone (in which case he has to find and/or persuade them to assist). In a time of adversity such as this, he needs to find his core supporters and rely on them. In the traditional text, it specifically says that if he has two supporters, he will lose one, but if he is alone, he will find one.

● *At his best,* he may find a true friend who will help him spiritually and materially. *At his worst,* he may lose a number of friends or family and feel the loss deeply.

▲ *As a public person,* he may develop a close relationship with an equal or superior. *As a businessperson,* he may enter into a joint business enterprise with a partner. *As an ordinary person,* he may lose friends or family, or he may marry from a position of weakness.

41.4   *Yin 6 changing line derives from Hexagram 38 Looking for a Leader*

With his declining influence, he does what he can to find a leader to join. If he gets the leader's help, he can avert further harm.

■ He desires a leader to guide and assist him. If he can get the leader's assistance, it will help save him from further harm. However, the more he can reduce his problems himself, the easier it will be for him to persuade a leader of his worthiness.

● *At his best,* he may have established important new relationships that will benefit him when he needs assistance. *At his worst,* he may have squandered an important connection in pursuit of a dream or illusion.

▲ *As a public person,* he may be engaged in establishing ties with other groups. *As a businessperson,* he may be developing new business connections for changing his career. *As an ordinary person,* he may be looking for a mate or partner while he still has his health, youth, or reputation.

41.5   *Yin 6 changing line derives from Hexagram 61 Having Limited Allegiance*

He is able to establish limited allegiance with a leader in spite of his declining influence. Although he will get some benefit now, he could benefit even more later.

■ He gains a potentially important ally, someone with whom he could establish an important relationship. This is just the first step, however, and even though he gets some benefit out of it now, eventually he could benefit even more.

● *At his best,* he may gain important benefits and insights that will greatly benefit his life through another. *At his worst,* he may be disappointed with the help he gets and not know how to capitalize on it in the future.

▲ *As a public person,* he may be able to establish a public alliance. *As a businessperson,* he may profit from having inside information. *As an ordinary person,* he may experience revolutionary insights or have new opportunities revealed to him through a new ally.

41.6   *Yang 9 changing line derives from Hexagram 19 Leading Others*

His influence grows because he guides others and they all benefit. Now new endeavors are favored, and he even gains an assistant.

■ Because his guiding of others is so successful, his influence grows. This is a good time for him to initiate new endeavors. He even gains someone to assist him.

● *At his best,* he may bring benefits to many and profit greatly from this, even finding a mate or partner. *At his worst,* he may find some benefit but not to a great extent.

▲ *As a public person,* he may bring acclaim to his organization, and it grows as a result. *As a businessperson,* he may be very successful in training, launching new programs, or consulting. *As an ordinary person,* he may have his reputation grow in his community because of his efforts to help others, or he may gain a collaborator or he may get married.

41.ALL   *All lines changing derives from Hexagram 31 Ability to Change Matters*

His declining influence has ended, and he now has the ability to change matters and achieve his goals.

■ He has overcome his limitations and his inability to affect situations. Now he can directly change matters by himself; he needs only to choose when and where he will do so.

● *At his best,* he may be able to do much good as well as benefit from his getting involved. *At his worst,* he may interfere in others' affairs excessively, or try to manipulate others for his own benefit.

▲ *As a public person,* he may have an important opportunity to exercise his position's power or authority. *As a businessperson,* he may be promoted to a line position, or take charge of a business unit. *As an ordinary person,* he may become more involved in his family's activities, or he takes control of a community project.

42. Gaining Benefits

TRIGRAMS BF   LINES 100 011   COMPLEMENTARY HEXAGRAM 32 COMMITTING HIMSELF

He is gaining benefits now, so this is a good time
for him to advance important endeavors.

■ *The traditional title* for this hexagram is "Increase." Here the hexagram is titled "Gaining Benefits." It signifies he is now experiencing increasing benefits coming to him. Thus, this is an especially good time for him to advance his more important endeavors. However, purely selfish or petty endeavors are not as likely to bring him benefits. *The complementary hexagram* is Hexagram 32 Committing Himself, which illustrates that benefits tend to come through firm commitments that he makes both to other people as well as to the pursuit of his own goals.

● *At his best,* he may be gaining benefits from his earlier commitments and efforts. *At his worst,* he may not benefit as much or he may receive largely undeserved benefits.

▲ *As a public person,* he may be in the spotlight with his successes. *As a businessperson,* he may reap rewards from investments or plans put into effect long before. *As an ordinary person,* he may benefit from family connections, education, or plans made long before.

42.1   *Yang 9 changing line derives from Hexagram 20 Preparing Himself*

He is now able to benefit from his earlier preparations.
Also, continuing to prepare for future advances
will allow him to gain more benefits in the future.

■ This illustrates several important principles: One is that his earlier preparations are bringing him benefits now. Another is that preparations begun now will be able to bring him benefits in the future. Finally, when benefits do come to him, it is wise to view it as an opportunity to begin to prepare for his next advance. Just sitting on his laurels and enjoying benefits coming from past work without thinking about investing in the future is not wise.

● *At his best,* he may prepare not only for what he expects, but also for what he does not expect, and thus he can succeed despite any obstacle. *At his worst,* he may be optimistic and lucky, so even though his preparation was limited, it was adequate to allow some success.

▲ *As a public person,* he may initiate new programs successfully and gain in status. *As a businessperson,* he may start new ventures, which will be profitable. *As an ordinary person,* he may find his most important desires can come true with hard work.

42.2   *Yin 6 changing line derives from Hexagram 61 Having Limited Allegiance*

He gains because he has given only limited allegiance
to his leader, so now his leader strives to win him over.
Maintaining this policy will bring him further benefits.

■ One way of gaining benefits is through being courted. Here his leader, to whom he has only given "limited allegiance," is striving to win him over. This could be done through gifts, praise, and different forms of assistance. As long as he maintains his limited allegiance, he may expect more of these benefits from his leader.

● *At his best,* he may use his position wisely and to great benefit without destroying the trust the leader has in him. *At his worst,* he may eventually be perceived as an untrustworthy opportunist and be disgraced.

▲ *As a public person,* he may forbear making a policy decision pending the outcome of negotiations. *As a businessperson,* he may negotiate for a better contract. *As an ordinary person,* he may find he benefits through his spouse, his in-laws , or his associates.

42.3   *Yin 6 changing line derives from Hexagram 37 Serving in a Household*

He is serving in a household and is able to benefit
despite having some problems there. Maintaining his
commitments gives him the opportunity to lead others.

■ He may not benefit greatly serving in a household, but benefits do exist, and he should use them. Here, by maintaining his commitments to the household, he is given the chance to lead others. This benefits him in several ways, and it is a good opportunity for growth.

● *At his best,* he may take this opportunity, grow from the experience, and increase his status in the household. *At his worst,* he may make terrible mistakes and end up harming himself and his status in the household.

▲ *As a public person,* he may serve as an emissary for dealing with difficult situations. *As a businessperson,* he may profit in several ways through disturbances. *As an ordinary person,* he may come through a troublesome period financially stable, or strengthen his marriage through marital difficulties.

42.4 *Yin 6 changing line derives from Hexagram 25 Having No Expectations*

Everyone benefits when he leads unselfishly,
especially in performing a major task.

■ Having no expectations of benefit enables him to bring benefits to those around him simply by his trying to do the best he can. Thus, when a major task is performed, it could be very beneficial to them all, including to him.

● *At his best,* he may devote himself to doing what is proper and what is necessary, and thereby bring great benefits to many. *At his worst,* he may have selfish motives and find that others benefit more from his activities than he does.

▲ *As a public person,* he may achieve success through service-oriented activities. *As a businessperson,* he may provide leadership, which produces good profits and earns the respect of his comrades. *As an ordinary person,* he may improve his home or lead his family in new endeavors.

42.5 *Yang 9 changing line derives from Hexagram 27 Desiring*

He benefits when his desires are honestly expressed.

■ When his true desires are expressed, he benefits. This allows others to see what he wants, so they are better able to respond to him. He might gain benefits from them, or he might benefit only internally through understanding himself and what his true goals are. Even without external rewards, what he gains internally could be as significant to him.

● *At his best,* he may live his desires through his heart, mind, and body, and to him, it is his calling and his art. *At his worst,* his desires may not be as clear to others as they are to him, and thus he is only able to gain small benefits.

▲ *As a public person,* he may be able to achieve much in his position, and thus gain even more favorable attention. *As a businessperson,* he may find that success comes when his business reflects his interests and abilities. *As an ordinary person,* he may find greater enjoyment in life by coming to terms with what is most important to him.

42.6   *Yang 9 changing line derives from Hexagram 3 Gathering Support*

He is attacked by those who previously supported him.
It is difficult for him to keep true supporters now.

■ He has succeeded so well that others attack him to gain wealth or erode his position. The more set in his ways or predictable he is, the more easily he will experience some misfortune. The more committed he is to those who helped him in the past, the more vulnerable he is through them. Being too "fat and happy" brings misfortune.

● *At his best,* he may be sensitive to how others regard him and flexible in his viewpoint and actions, and thus minimize others' jealousy and his vulnerability. *At his worst,* he may be unpleasantly surprised and suffer serious losses from his insensitivity and rigidity.

▲ *As a public person,* he may be charged with improprieties by jealous rivals. *As a businessperson,* he may find associates are uniting against him, those he trusted are stealing his business secrets, or his prior backers are cutting him off or suing him. *As an ordinary person,* he may experience theft of his property, and perceptions that he is greedy and unappreciative.

42.ALL   *All lines changing derives from Hexagram 32 Committing Himself*

In seeking how to increase his benefits, he needs to begin by
committing himself. Having firm commitments will enable him to
build a strong base and eventually gain wealth and other benefits.

■ The normal path to gaining benefits is by building something up, and this begins by first making a commitment to do so. Here, he is taking that first essential step.

● *At his best,* he may realize what he should do, and he has the ability to do it, to achieve his goals. *At his worst,* he may be too much of a dreamer or a fraud, and thus his commitments are weak and not very able to produce benefit.

▲ *As a public person,* he may be seeking a position as an aide to a powerful leader. *As a businessperson,* he may be studying to find new business opportunities. *As an ordinary person,* he may be committed to finding a new home, new career, or a mate.

43. Escaping Harm

TRIGRAMS AH   LINES 111 110   COMPLEMENTARY HEXAGRAM 23 BEING IN A COLLAPSING SITUATION

*He escapes harm, but hears the distress of others who
could not escape. When he is threatened by great danger,
he knows it is better for him to flee than to resist.*

■ *The traditional titles* of this hexagram are "Breakthrough," "Removal," and "Resoluteness," although these are misleading. The Huangs use "Stride." Whincup uses "Flight," and says that the title literally means to run quickly. Here the hexagram is titled "Escaping Harm." This signifies that his best course is to flee and escape the dangers he sees around him, rather than to try to resist. Through escape, he can first attain safety and later strengthen himself. *The complementary hexagram* is Hexagram 23 Being in a Collapsing Situation, which illustrates what will happen if he does not flee a seriously harmful situation.

● *At his best,* he may be astute enough to save himself and those close to him before they suffer any harm. *At his worst,* he may escape some harm, but not as much as he would like.

▲ *As a public person,* he may be very visible in his flight from danger. *As a businessperson,* he may convert his assets before a market decline. *As an ordinary person,* he may escape harm at work, at home, or in his other life activities through timely action on his part.

43.1 *Yang 9 changing line derives from Hexagram 28 Working Toward a Goal*

*Just as he begins working toward his goal, he is hurt.
Therefore, he stops his effort, surveys the damage, and reviews his
options before proceeding. In this way, he escapes further harm.*

■ At the very beginning of his effort, he is harmed. A poor beginning is easy to overcome, yet if he continues, he will make matters worse and perhaps not even succeed. Therefore, he should halt before he compounds his mistakes, take stock of the situation, and change things so he can proceed. This is not only the safe thing for him to do, it is the best way of achieving his goals.

● *At his best,* he may be weak in his execution, but have understanding that will save him from further trouble. *At his worst,* he may suffer serious harm and press ahead through stubbornness or ignorance and suffer even more grievous harm.

▲ *As a public person,* he may suffer a reprimand for a poor decision. *As a businessperson,* he may be threatened or removed to another assignment. *As an ordinary person,* he may be rash and impetuous and suffer through his mistakes, or suffer foot problems.

43.2   *Yang 9 changing line derives from Hexagram 49 Being Revolutionary*

By having a revolutionary outlook, he remains alert to danger;
therefore, he cannot be harmed by surprise.

■ Due to his being a revolutionary, he has already emotionally separated himself, and even perhaps physically removed himself as well, from his earlier situation. However, he is still alert to the dangers around him. This perspective keeps him from getting hurt by unexpected problems.

● *At his best,* he may normally take good precautions to protect himself. *At his worst,* he may be warned of possible problems and act to minimize their effect.

▲ *As a public person,* he may be given a position in charge of security. *As a businessperson,* he may gain through his written efforts. *As an ordinary person,* he may experience worries or shocks, such as attempted burglaries or other losses, and he may be helped by his friends and allies.

43.3   *Yang 9 changing line derives from Hexagram 58 Sharing Himself*

He shares his concerns about the dangers around him.
However, despite whatever he does,
instead of finding praise, he finds shame.
He may be angry, but he suffers no real harm.

■ His expectations of gaining praise for his alertness are denied, and he becomes angry. He may even now try to escape on his own. However, if he does he will be dissatisfied even then. Despite all of this, he does not suffer any real harm.

● *At his best,* he may be unable to do the right thing to bring himself satisfaction, although he escapes any real harm. *At his worst,* he may be too prideful or too angry to properly consider his alternatives, and thus end up hurting himself somewhat.

▲ *As a public person,* he may resign his position and seek out another that is no better. *As a businessperson,* he may find his salary or reputation do not improve despite his best efforts. *As an ordinary person,* he may experience many minor troubles, including separation or divorce, or critical rumors about him.

43.4   *Yang 9 changing line derives from Hexagram 5 Acting Prematurely*

Although he heard warnings, he did not escape early enough, so now he accepts his fate. His regrets will pass.

■ He avoided making a decision to escape while he was able, so now he must accept what happens to him. Although this is distasteful to him, his regrets will pass in time. He escapes harm because he finds the results are not as bad as he thought they would be.

● *At his best,* he may learn from his mistakes and be willing to take appropriate measures to save himself in the future. *At his worst,* he may obstinately refuse to see the truth until it is forced upon him by difficult circumstances.

▲ *As a public person,* he may be in a position in which he has no real power or in which he cannot perform adequately, and thus he reluctantly yields his authority to others. *As a businessperson,* he may find himself powerless to lead, and so he follows the lead of another. *As an ordinary person,* he may suffer physical injuries to his legs or ears, or be unable to escape from the changes in his life that threaten him.

43.5   *Yang 9 changing line derives from Hexagram 34 Forcing Matters*

He forces matters and nimbly escapes danger.

■ He forces a way to escape danger. Not only does he escape danger, he might even benefit from the result.

● *At his best,* he may be able to use vision and ability to reveal the true situation, and with courageous action, he can escape it without harm. *At his worst,* he may be foolhardy and lucky in escaping a danger that he created.

▲ *As a public person,* he may escape from political intrigues through his public statements. *As a businessperson,* he may escape from bad business by making good business deals. *As an ordinary person,* he may avoid serious pitfalls, both personally and financially.

43.6 *Yin 6 changing line derives from Hexagram 1 Acting Fiercely*

He does not see danger coming, and so can't escape from it.
Now, even fighting fiercely in his defense, he cannot escape harm.

■ He is not alerted to imminent danger and is therefore harmed. He arrived at his position through his own efforts, and now he could find himself with few allies or helpers. However strong he is, he is not strong enough to avoid harm whatever he does.

● *At his best,* he may have others who will later aid and comfort him, even if now he suffers some harm. *At his worst,* he may be foolish and disliked, so he can gain nothing from others to help him.

▲ *As a public person,* he may need to resign from his position under fire. *As a businessperson,* he may suffer some financial losses. *As an ordinary person,* he may be attacked from an unexpected quarter, find his plans have gone awry, or suffer through an older relative.

43.ALL *All lines changing derives from Hexagram 23 Being in a Collapsing Situation*

When he is being harmed and can no longer escape
even more harm, he has arrived at a collapsing situation.

■ Some harm can be sustained in the normal course of events. Some can be sustained while in advancing or retreating. However, unremitting harm without end is indicative of being in a collapsing situation. At this point, his options to escape are gone, and his defense has also failed. He has reached a collapsing situation.

● *At his best,* he may be wise enough to realize the truth, but too weak to change matters on his own, so he will have to bide his time until matters improve on their own. *At his worst,* he may not understand the vagaries of fate, and thus not be able to sustain his inner spirit during a time of great stress and unhappiness.

▲ *As a public person,* he may be forced out of office or imprisoned. *As a businessperson,* he may be bankrupted or imprisoned. *As an ordinary person,* he may be bankrupt, suffer serious health problems, or other very serious problems.

44. Maintaining His Independence

TRIGRAMS FA   LINES 011 111   COMPLEMENTARY HEXAGRAM 24 BEGINNING A RELATIONSHIP

He is trying to maintain his independence
because the leader who wants him is overwhelming.

■ *The traditional title* for this hexagram is "Coming to Meet," which is misleading. The Huangs use "Rendezvous," and Whincup uses "Subjugated." Here the hexagram is titled "Maintaining His Independence." In this hexagram, he is admonished not to wed a woman because she is too strong, but the concept of giving up his independence applies equally well to any leader who is very strong and seeks a relationship with him. In a situation where the other person is disproportionately powerful, maintaining his independence is best. In the first half of the lines, he is able to maintain his independence, but in the second half, he loses it. *The complementary hexagram* is Hexagram 24 Beginning a Relationship, which illustrates that at times it is best to give up independence and enter into a relationship.

● *At his best,* he may be comfortable and sure that maintaining his independence is the best thing for him to do, and all his needs are being met in his current situation. *At his worst,* he may maintain his independence out of irrational fear and with his needs unmet.

▲ *As a public person,* he may maintain his own position rather than support someone else. *As a businessperson,* he may not sell his company, or not give in to the seductive flattery of someone else in the firm. *As an ordinary person,* he may remain single because of doubts about the other, not accept a position or job offer from someone he is suspicious about, or not go into debt.

44.1   *Yin 6 changing line derives from Hexagram 1 Acting Fiercely*

He fiercely maintains his independence.
Remaining as he is averts potential harm.

■ He is expressing who he is very strongly. Such strength provides a sound foundation that is also keeping him firmly anchored in the present realities. This prevents him from too easily getting into harmful situations. Thus, while he may not be progressing as much as he might like, he is also safe and sound.

● *At his best,* he may be firmly committed to fundamental principles that will keep him from getting into trouble. *At his worst,* he may be restrained more by his obstinacy than by understandings that could help him avert harm.

▲ As *a public person,* he may be passed over for promotion because he is too strongly identified with his current position. As *a businessperson,* he may not be able to engage in new enterprises due to prior commitments. As *an ordinary person,* he may be limited by what he knows, or be cautious of being guided and helped by someone with a more elevated position.

44.2   *Yang 9 changing line derives from Hexagram 33 Complying*

He maintains his independence through
using factors in the situation for his benefit.

■ Here, he has some resources to use to aid him in maintaining his independence. They may not be a lot, but they are enough to sustain him in his struggle. He needs to understand what these resources are to be able to use them. Having these, he should not surrender, but rather should fight for his position.

● *At his best,* he may have friends and allies who will be invaluable in helping him achieve his goals. *At his worst,* he may be able to get assistance from others through less than good means, and their service may be marginal but enough so that he does not suffer much harm.

▲ As *a public person,* he may rely on his connections to assist him in seeking a promotion. As *a businessperson,* he may use his friends and resources in pursuit of new enterprise. As *an ordinary person,* he may gain profits or other benefits from those around him, or a woman may become pregnant.

44.3   *Yang 9 changing line derives from Hexagram 6 Having a Complaint*

He has a complaint against his leader. This maintains
his independence and keeps him from greater harm.

■ His complaint is actually a blessing, since it prevents him from becoming too vulnerable or dependent. If he had no complaint, he would be more easily enticed into something that he would later regret far more. Some minor harm might come to him now, but it is far better to suffer a minor harm than a larger one.

● *At his best,* he may realize that his complaint is just a sign of fundamental problems, and he takes this lesson to heart. *At his worst,* he may simply be angry and focus on his complaint rather than see the danger that really exists.

▲ *As a public person,* he may satisfy his public rather than abandon them for a momentary advantage. *As a businessperson,* he may discover a problem that he cannot overlook despite the inducements of a superior. *As an ordinary person,* he may deal with various business or other problems, and thereby keep out of other troubles.

44.4	*Yang 9 changing line derives from Hexagram 57 At His Leader's Mercy*

Without resources, he is at his leader's mercy.
Now he cannot maintain his independence, nor should he try to,
because it would only bring misfortune.

■ With no resources, he is entirely at his leader's mercy. How can he hope to keep his independence? Trying to do so only makes him appear disloyal or dishonest, and this would bring harm to him.

● *At his best,* he may have proven his value and commitment in the past, so even in his present circumstances, he will be treated with some care by his leader. *At his worst,* he may be seen to be an opportunist; with nothing to redeem himself, he could suffer much harm.

▲ *As a public person,* he may be dismissed or suffer demotion. *As a business-person,* he may go through serious financial straits or bankruptcy. *As an ordinary person,* he may suffer through various financial troubles or lawsuits, or suffer through ill health.

44.5	*Yang 9 changing line derives from Hexagram 50 Governing Matters*

His potential to govern matters is now clear,
yet this is not enough to keep him independent.
He can still benefit somewhat from this situation.

■ Here his true potential is visible, and his ability allows him to flourish despite other constraints on him. While independence may not be possible for him in this situation, he could have a limited degree of autonomy as long as he is working for his leader.

● *At his best,* he may appropriately rise to whatever situation he faces, and he will gain in self-knowledge and position. *At his worst,* he may gain power in a situation, but gain an uncertain reputation as a result.

▲ *As a public person,* he may find that people are listening to him because of a sudden twist of fate. *As a businessperson,* he may find a sudden increase in his wealth or status due to a change in the market or due to discovery of a hidden fact. *As an ordinary person,* he may assume a more powerful role in his relationships, although he is still dependent upon another.

44.6   *Yang 9 changing line derives from Hexagram 28 Working Toward a Goal*

He struggles with someone who tries to keep him from his goals.
This is troublesome, but no real harm comes even if
he can't maintain his independence.

■ He wants to go toward his goals, but someone else wants to keep him from them. Even though he cannot resist their influence, he is not really harmed.

● *At his best,* he may not suffer even though he can't progress toward his goals. *At his worst,* he may lose sight of his goals and be completely distracted by someone else.

▲ *As a public person,* he may become locked in a power struggle with an opponent. *As a businessperson,* he may be sued by a competitor. *As an ordinary person,* he may engage in wasteful struggles with others or experience a serious accident.

44.ALL   *All lines changing derives from Hexagram 24 Beginning a Relationship*

He chooses to give up some of his independence
and begin a relationship.

■ While relationships pose problems, they also bring very powerful possibilities to benefit. He had been resisting being overpowered in a relationship, but now he seeks to enter one in order to gain its benefits.

● *At his best,* he may understand that he will benefit by facing and overcoming obstacles in the proper way. *At his worst,* he may be seduced or driven by need, and thus not be fully able to make the best decisions.

▲ *As a public person,* he may accept public acclaim. *As a businessperson,* he may accept a position he previously refused. *As an ordinary person,* he may seek a partnership, or accept a marriage proposal.

45. Serving a Leader

TRIGRAMS EH   LINES 000 110   COMPLEMENTARY HEXAGRAM 26 EXTERNAL RESTRAINT

He is serving a leader and benefits from it.
A great leader and a great cause can bring people together
to make a major change in the world.

■ *The traditional titles* for this hexagram are "Gathering Together" and "Massing." The Huangs title this "Illness," and Whincup uses "Gathering Around." Here the hexagram is titled "Serving a Leader." It illustrates the gathering together of many individuals around a leader. Benefits come to those who serve this leader. If this leader is also serving a great cause, then many more individuals will contribute their efforts. However, only a great leader committed to a great cause can truly unite people together to bring about profound changes in the world. *The complementary hexagram* is Hexagram 26 External Restraint, which illustrates the limitations that external reality imposes, as opposed to the limitations that come through devotion to a cause.

● *At his best,* he may join a cause as well as a leader, and the intangible benefits he gets as a result of his service are as important as the material rewards. *At his worst,* he may serve a leader strictly seeking material reward, and this is sufficient for him.

▲ *As a public person,* he may become a public advocate of a leader or a cause. *As a businessperson,* he may seek a position close to an important business figure. *As an ordinary person,* he may join a movement, seek a marriage with a powerful person, or join a community organization having a charismatic leader and committed following.

45.1   *Yin 6 changing line derives from Hexagram 17 Hunting*

He is still hunting, and so has not yet joined a leader.
He may be held back by doubts and fears,
although he would overcome them if he did join.

■ Although he is hunting for a leader to serve, he has not yet made up his mind. He might be experiencing doubts and fears that are holding him back. However, he should be reassured that he would be pleased if he did join and that no harm would come to him. He is showing weakness now, but the strength he desires must first come through deciding to make a choice.

● *At his best,* he may truly feel a calling inside him, and he only needs a little time to reach it. *At his worst,* he may be weak and fickle, and fundamentally unable to make a decision that is not forced on him by outside circumstance.

▲ *As a public person,* he may remain neutral and not establish any alliances, and thus weaken his position. *As a businessperson,* he may oppose new means of doing business or new products, and thus not prosper. *As an ordinary person,* he may have a proposal of marriage or a career opportunity to consider and may be unable to decide.

45.2　　*Yin 6 changing line derives from Hexagram 47 Advancing by Hard Work*

He is working hard to gain a place with a leader.
However, in addition to his abilities,
he should show his commitment by a meaningful gift.

■ He is working hard to achieve a committed relationship with his leader. However, in addition to proving himself by his abilities, he should also consider giving a small but appropriate offering of some sort. Its true value will be seen as an expression of sincerity rather than its monetary cost. Good can come from this.

● *At his best,* he may be effective in whatever he does, and his thoughtful actions and sincerity will impress his leader. *At his worst,* he may be unceasing in his effort to achieve his aims, whether their effect is good or bad on those around him, so he may manage to achieve some limited success despite the damage he does.

▲ *As a public person,* he may prepare a proposal to present to advance his reputation. *As a businessperson,* he may plan a business endeavor, or he may need to contribute extra funds to ensure success in a business venture. *As an ordinary person,* he may work hard to win acceptance of his marriage proposal, or he may strive to form a partnership.

45.3　　*Yin 6 changing line derives from Hexagram 31 Ability to Change Matters*

Serving a leader changes things for him, and with it
comes some minor trouble and even possibly some regrets.
However, he experiences no real harm.

■ He could not have anticipated all the changes that have taken place in his life with joining a leader, and with some of these he feels regret. He might also experience some minor conflicts that he did not anticipate. However, despite these minor complications, he is not really harmed.

● *At his best,* he may understand these minor difficulties were bound to occur, and he won't be bothered. *At his worst,* he may nettled by these small bothersome disturbances, and they will make his life unsettled.

▲ *As a public person,* he may be given an assignment that involves dealing with many complaints or minor problems. *As a businessperson,* he may experience business stagnation but some personal growth. *As an ordinary person,* he may enter into a difficult marriage or alliance, or experience the loss of a family member.

45.4   *Yang 9 changing line derives from Hexagram 8 Entering an Alliance*

He gets closer to his leader
by entering a more meaningful alliance with him.

■ This position indicates both closeness of spirit and intimate communications between him and his leader. This comradeship brings about a more meaningful alliance with his leader and is very beneficial in some ways.

● *At his best,* he may be sincere, honest, discrete, and not abuse the trust placed in him, and thereby he benefits. *At his worst,* he may lose his integrity or discretion, or abuse the trust shown him in some way, and from this, reduce the benefits of his position.

▲ *As a public person,* he may accomplish much as long as he is identified with his leader. *As a businessperson,* he may profit greatly, although he shouldn't assume everything will go the way he wants. *As an ordinary person,* he may enjoy a very beneficial period as long as he attempts to understand his leader's needs.

45.5   *Yang 9 changing line derives from Hexagram 16 Standstill*

If he serves a leader who reaps rewards while he remains
at a standstill, he shouldn't continue to serve that leader.

■ He may be serving a leader who is benefiting, while he finds that he gets very little materially out of the situation. He sees he will continue to remain at a virtual standstill in this situation, so he should consider leaving to find a better place.

● *At his best,* he may watch and learn from great people, waiting for his opportunity and, when he is ready, easily depart without harsh feelings. *At his worst,* he may desire recognition he hasn't earned and may resent not getting what he feels he deserves, and this anger gradually poisons him.

▲ As *a public person,* he may serve as a minor functionary under a great leader. *As a businessperson,* he may be unable to profit while his employer grows wealthier. *As an ordinary person,* he may experience doubt and unhappiness in his personal relationship with someone who he holds in awe.

45.6   *Yin 6 changing line derives from Hexagram 12 Being Blocked*

His leader blocks his service. He complains and has regrets,
but is being restrained more than he is being harmed.

■ He finds that his leader is blocking his efforts. He complains, cries, and has regrets; however, he is not truly being harmed. He has very little chance to progress, however.

● At *his best,* he may come to accept limitations he cannot change. At *his worst,* he may bitterly resent what he believes to be unwarranted intrusion in his affairs.

▲ As *a public person,* he may find promotion or privileges being withheld. *As a businessperson,* he may find that new business is being given to someone else. *As an ordinary person,* he may have his mate, his family, or his boss restricting and controlling what he does.

45.ALL   *All lines changing derives from Hexagram 26 External Restraint*

He sees that he is being restrained
by forces stronger than he is.

■ He had joined a leader hoping for the chance to progress, but he recognizes that he is being restrained by external forces that he cannot resist. He realizes they are likely to continue, although this too will end.

● At *his best,* he may be attuned to the cycles of progress and retreat that comprise life, so he is able to tide over this period. At *his worst,* he may feel despair when all he sees is restriction and failure.

▲ As *a public person,* he may have unsympathetic political bosses, so he waits for a change in administrations. *As a businessperson,* he may scale his business activities to the economic cycle. *As an ordinary person,* he may have problems due to incarceration, or illness, and he must wait for whatever influences are disturbing his life to depart.

46. Promoting Himself

TRIGRAMS FE   LINES 011 000   COMPLEMENTARY HEXAGRAM 25 HAVING NO EXPECTATIONS

He is promoting himself and thereby benefits.
He should not fear to seek a leader or to pursue a great endeavor.

■ *The traditional title* for this hexagram is "Pushing Upward." The Huangs title this "Ascendance," and Whincup uses "Rising." Here the hexagram is titled "Promoting Himself." It signifies that he is promoting himself, and through this, he succeeds in increasing his status. He should not fear or doubt his abilities to persuade a leader of his worth. Also, engaging in a great endeavor is beneficial, because if he did not try he could never succeed. Self-promotion is likely to require a great deal of effort over a period of time to succeed, so it calls for confidence and fortitude as well as the skills he will need to employ. *The complementary hexagram* is Hexagram 25 Having No Expectations, which illustrates a situation without direction or hope of advancement.

● *At his best,* he may have true confidence in his abilities, which allows him to recognize the nature of the situation he is dealing with and thus appropriately promote himself. *At his worst,* he may have too high an opinion of himself or inappropriate goals in mind, and while some success is possible, he will not be satisfied with the result.

▲ *As a public person,* he may be able to advance himself to a more visible public position. *As a businessperson,* he may be a highly effective salesperson who can reach many, or an assistant able to lobby successfully for his advancement. *As an ordinary person,* he may know how to convince those around him of his ability or desirability at work, in his community, or in his personal relationships.

46.1   *Yin 6 changing line derives from Hexagram 11 Easily Progressing*

He can easily progress when he promotes himself.

■ His self-promotion goes very easily, and he benefits from it. This implies that others will be very receptive to him; however, he should always strive to do his best and not slack off on his efforts. Half-hearted efforts usually don't succeed well.

● *At his best,* he may have his best qualities easily recognized, and be rewarded appropriately. *At his worst,* he may misrepresent himself to advance, and although this may not cause problems now, it almost certainly will cause problems in the future.

▲ *As a public person,* he may seek a promotion and easily succeed. *As a businessperson,* he may establish trusted business relationships and gain profits through them. *As an ordinary person,* he may find it easy to improve his reputation and increase his status.

46.2   *Yang 9 changing line derives from Hexagram 15 Acting with Propriety*

In promoting himself, acting properly is more important than the abilities he offers.

■ Here, he is showing that he knows salesmanship is the key to advancement. What advantage is there in having abilities if he cannot first show his worth as a person? Thus, he understands the requirements of the situation and acts appropriately.

● *At his best,* he may truly touch the heart of his leader with his sincerity and understanding, and he benefits from a gracious response. *At his worst,* he may be crass and scheming in his self-promotion, and although benefiting, he doesn't benefit as much.

▲ *As a public person,* he may win the favor of his superior. *As a businessperson,* he may pass along good business information to a more powerful businessman as an inducement. *As an ordinary person,* he may find that his problems are eased by proper actions.

46.3   *Yang 9 changing line derives from Hexagram 7 Serving as an Officer*

Although he can act like a leader, it brings him neither benefit nor loss. Others need to recognize his leadership first.

■ Here his effort at self-promotion fails because he is not fully able to lead others regardless of his abilities. Thus, his efforts did not produce the expected benefits that he desired. To get to this point, he may have had a temporary opportunity he could not capitalize on.

● *At his best,* he may be an effective leader, even though he doesn't significantly benefit. *At his worst,* he may not learn from his experience at leadership, and so he wastes even this opportunity to benefit.

▲ *As a public person,* he may be in a position that has more status than real power or real benefits. *As a businessperson,* he may succeed to some degree but gain little profit. *As an ordinary person,* he may be popular but later realize it did not truly benefit him.

46.4   *Yin 6 changing line derives from Hexagram 32 Committing Himself*

He is promoting himself by making a strong and close
commitment to his leader, and thus is able to benefit.

■ He promotes himself by getting close to his leader, sharing confidences and personal activities. He does this not only because he wants to promote himself, but also because he is committed to his leader. In addition, he sees it as a desirable sign of favor from his leader that he is allowed to do so.

● *At his best,* he may honestly serve his leader and enjoy his commitments. *At his worst,* he may be very calculating in his efforts to get close, and he may demean himself by sacrificing who he is for what he thinks he should be.

▲ *As a public person,* he may take a strong public position close to the heart of his leader, and be given greater access to him as a consequence. *As a businessperson,* he may profit personally or financially through important cultural or religious ties. *As an ordinary person,* he may participate in his mate's family activities.

46.5   *Yin 6 changing line derives from Hexagram 48 Being Renewed*

He promotes himself correctly, one step at a time,
and is renewed as he progresses.

■ One important aspect of promoting himself correctly is that the effort is sustainable. That is, he advances one step at a time, sometimes pausing and resting for renewal, and sometimes being renewed by seeking and receiving benefits. Here, he knows the correct way to promote himself, so his self-promotion is highly successful.

● *At his best,* he may be diligent in caring for his needs as well as in promoting his goals. *At his worst,* he may not be as effective or as conscientious as he should be in his promotion, and so he suffers some problems as a consequence. He does benefit, however.

▲ *As a public person,* he may progress properly through the rungs of advancement without jealousies or rancor from his associates. *As a businessperson,* he may develop a profitable new market or enterprise through a series of correct actions. *As an ordinary person,* he may proceed with confidence one step at a time.

46.6 *Yin 6 changing line derives from Hexagram 18 Nursing an Illness*

He is trying to promote himself but has a problem that needs to be nursed. Although the best approach may be unclear, treating the problem properly will bring success.

■ He must take care of a problem that he has in order for his self-promotion to be successful. The fact that he does not understand it is daunting; however, if he maintains a positive attitude and unrelentingly works on it, he may find the proper treatment to succeed.

● *At his best,* he may develop a deep understanding of his strengths and weaknesses that will prove very beneficial. *At his worst,* he may fail to deal with a major weakness that hinders developing his situation.

▲ *As a public person,* he may be in charge of a program that has some major problems. *As a businessperson,* he may consider a risky venture. *As an ordinary person,* he may engage in a risky enterprise, or he may have a serious illness that requires proper treatment.

46.ALL *All lines changing derives from Hexagram 25 Having No Expectations*

After he has explored all avenues of self-promotion, he no longer has any expectations for success. He realizes he must just wait and see what comes.

■ Here, he has explored every avenue of self-promotion, and nothing has changed for him. Now he is left with a period of having no expectations and waiting to see how fate will move him.

● *At his best,* he may graciously accept an inevitable change in his fortunes. *At his worst,* he may become angry, depressed, or otherwise unstable from changes that he cannot control.

▲ *As a public person,* he may be placed in a background position or at the bottom of a long list. *As a businessperson,* he may be unable to promote himself or his products. *As an ordinary person,* he may face retirement or declining health.

47. Advancing by Hard Work

TRIGRAMS CH   LINES 010 110   COMPLEMENTARY HEXAGRAM 22 ADVANCING BY HIS IMAGE

He is advancing by hard work, and his actions bring him benefits.
Spoken words are not believed; only visible results count.

■ *The traditional titles* for this hexagram are "Oppression" and "Exhaustion," which are misleading. Whincup uses "Burdened," and the Huangs use "Trapped." Here the hexagram is titled "Advancing by Hard Work." It signifies that he is burdened but advances through hard work. The hexagram lines illustrate the many burdens he must endure. To be effective with his heavy burdens, he must take strong actions. What he says is not believed; only his actions are persuasive. *The complementary hexagram* is Hexagram 22 Advancing by His Image, which illustrates that his appearance in other's eyes is all that is necessary for advancing his position.

● *At his best,* he may have the strength of his convictions as well as strength in other ways to deal with the burdens he has. *At his worst,* he may feel burdened by hopelessness as well as by external problems, so his strength to deal with them and his ability to advance are reduced.

▲ *As a public person,* he may be seen as a hard worker, tirelessly engaged in advancing his cause. *As a businessperson,* he may have a hard-working support role in the company. *As an ordinary person,* he may have many responsibilities and yet still work hard to advance himself.

47.1   *Yin 6 changing line derives from Hexagram 58 Sharing Himself*

He is working hard and sharing heavy burdens. This will continue.

■ He is working hard to help bear the burdens of others. It does not matter if he voluntarily assumed them or if he was required to, because now these burdens to him are truly his. He will give them up only when they naturally end or when he can no longer bear them.

● *At his best,* he may be true to his commitments in spirit and deed, and his sacrifices in turn nurture his spirit. *At his worst,* he may resent his commitments, but find he has no option, and so he begrudges what he should willingly give.

▲ *As a public person,* he may share a responsibility with another official. *As a businessperson,* he may be a general partner in an enterprise. *As an ordinary person,* he may share parenting or community responsibilities.

47.2   *Yang 9 changing line derives from Hexagram 45 Serving a Leader*

He is working hard because the leader he serves has given him
heavy responsibilities. With these, he also gets benefits,
so thankfulness is proper while complaints are not.

■ He is blessed with a position that has responsibilities as well as benefits. As much as he might dislike the burden of the responsibilities (and the hard work they entail), he is pleased with the benefits he gets. It is proper for him to show his thankfulness and minimize his complaints.

● *At his best,* he may be conscientious in his service and be properly grateful for his opportunities and benefits. *At his worst,* he may resent what he is required to give and belittle the benefits he receives in return.

▲ *As a public person,* he may have a very responsible, busy position. *As a businessperson,* he may have to work so hard that it takes a toll on his personal life. *As an ordinary person,* he may marry someone with many young children or become involved in a very active community organization.

47.3   *Yin 6 changing line derives from Hexagram 28 Working Toward a Goal*

He is working hard toward a goal,
but he experiences so many adversities he cannot succeed.

■ This line shows the burden of difficulties that even hard work cannot entirely overcome. Sometimes all he can do is keep on working hard, despite the ills that befall him, until things change on their own for the better. He may be able to attain his goal later. Examples in the traditional text of the adversities include being weighed down (by stones), experiencing bothersome distractions (by thorns and thistles), and not having necessary support (his wife is not home).

● *At his best,* he may keep his courage and hope alive despite his adversities. *At his worst,* he may become very unhappy and ineffectual due to his many adversities.

▲ *As a public person,* he may suffer problems, demotion or dismissal, and the end of his alliances. *As a businessperson,* he may find unexpected difficulties coming from close associates, market downturns, lawsuits, and so on. *As an ordinary person,* he may have family problems or disputes, accidents may harm his reputation, or he may suffer ill health or other burdensome setbacks.

47.4　　*Yang 9 changing line derives from Hexagram 29 Being Trapped*

> He is trapped by circumstances around him and has to
> work through these difficulties to reach a good end.

■ In some way, he agreed to or created these difficulties for himself, but now he feels trapped. He cannot just walk away, but neither is his situation hopeless. He can work through his difficulties and make the best of them. In the end he can gain some benefit.

● *At his best,* he may learn to live with the choices he has made in life, and if he wants to change, he will apply himself appropriately toward those goals as well. *At his worst,* he may feel bitter or resentful that he doesn't have what he wants, and he finds it hard to work to change his life the way he wishes.

▲ *As a public person,* he may experience problems due to regulations, protocol, and other limitations of his situation. *As a businessperson,* he may encounter restriction in his activities due to how he has structured his business. *As an ordinary person,* he may find many small problems coming from his mate's friends, social commitments, or family, or he may experience problems or a lack of recognition at work.

47.5　　*Yang 9 changing line derives from Hexagram 40 Getting Free*

> He works hard to free himself of his burdens and responsibilities.
> It goes slowly because it requires time.
> Thankfulness at the end is appropriate.

■ He will gain his freedom through hard work. The ultimate reward of work is freedom from hard work in the future. However, this is normally not easily or quickly attained. Usually it takes a long time and seems to go very slowly. However, it is proper to be reflective and appreciative at the end of his labors when he can rest.

● *At his best,* he may understand the meaning of hard work and attainment, so his efforts are illuminated by wisdom as he toils. *At his worst,* he may struggle inside as he works, and he seeks only to loose awareness of himself with distractions when he isn't toiling.

▲ *As a public person,* he may work and prepare his replacement for when he retires. *As a businessperson,* he may work and prepare investments for his retirement. *As an ordinary person,* he may suffer health problems and need to take life easier, or he may put his affairs in order.

47.6   *Yin 6 changing line derives from Hexagram 6 Having a Complaint*

He has so many complaints that he doesn't know what to do.
By taking any number of actions, he can break free
of his confusion and begin anew. For him,
choosing a course is harder than doing the work.

■ He is now confounded and confused because there are so many things wrong, and there are so many possibilities for action. His ability is not at question; rather, it is just his difficulty in deciding what to do. To be able to succeed, he just must select a direction and then apply himself. Clearly, moving forward in almost any direction is better than remaining and doing nothing.

● *At his best,* he may be able to rise over the confusion of petty matters and view the heart of his situation. *At his worst,* he may remain confused, worry incessantly about making the proper choice, and generally feel powerless because he lacks clear motivation.

▲ *As a public person,* he may find himself entrapped in contradictory alliances or by contradictory rules. *As a businessperson,* he may be tied up through legal documents or suffer a series of declining investments. *As an ordinary person,* he may find himself surrounded by a complicated situation that has no easy exit, but from which he can work to free himself if he chose.

47.ALL   *All lines changing derives from Hexagram 22 Advancing by His Image*

His hard work and his burdens have tired him. Now he desires
the easy path of relying on his image or reputation to benefit.

■ Hard work is tiring, and his burdens have exhausted him. He now primarily wishes to not work hard, so now he will rely on his image for whatever benefits he can get.

● *At his best,* he may have learned that he can gain respite and benefits from the image of himself that he has built through much hard work. *At his worst,* he may long to take it easy, but find that he has not built as good an image as he would like, thus relying on it will not produce the benefits he really needs.

▲ *As a public person,* he may be trying to gain a new position, perhaps as a figurehead. *As a businessperson,* he may be looking to new business opportunities, perhaps on the board or as an advisor. *As an ordinary person,* he may be rehearsing proposals or reviewing interview skills for gaining a promotion.

48. Being Renewed

TRIGRAMS FC   LINES 011 010   COMPLEMENTARY HEXAGRAM 21 WORKING ON A PROBLEM

He is being renewed after his struggles. After sufficient renewal,
he will resume them. It is important that he have a good source
of renewal, since inadequate renewal brings some harm.

■ *The traditional title* for this hexagram is "The Well." This is one of two hexagrams
that focuses on a physical object rather than on the central character. (The other is
Hexagram 50 Governing Matters.) The actual object referred to in the traditional
text is a well that nourishes, or renews, the town around it. The title used here is
"Being Renewed," since it gives a better description of the meaning of the hexagram. A working well must be in good repair, contain clean water, and have a sufficient quantity for the needs of those who depend on it. Failing these, the town itself
must fail. The need for water can refer not only to a physical need, but also to emotional and spiritual needs. With regard to people, not only must they obtain renewal periodically, they should also provide renewal in turn to others by being a source
of learning, inspiration, love, and support. *The complementary hexagram* is Hexagram 21 Working on a Problem, which illustrates that work depends upon renewal.
Both work and renewal are essential for endeavors to succeed.

● *At his best,* he may find people and a place that renew his spirit as well as sustain
his body. *At his worst,* he may not obtain as complete a renewal as he needs, and
this reduces his ability to work and to achieve what he desires.

▲ *As a public person,* he may take a highly visible rest. *As a businessperson,* he may
gain a bonus or reward, which stimulates him to better performance. *As an ordinary person,* he may benefit from a vacation, emotional support from friends and
family, or a loving relationship with someone dear to him.

48.1   *Yin 6 changing line derives from Hexagram 5 Acting Prematurely*

Renewal now is premature because the source
of renewal is not yet ready.

■ In seeking rest, repair, or relaxation, as in everything else, timing is critical. If the source of renewal is not yet available to him, then he just will not be renewed. He either can wait, seek alternatives, or seek ways of assisting the source to be prepared.

● *At his best,* he may learn when the right time is, and until then, he makes do. *At his worst,* he may suffer harm because he truly cannot wait.

▲ *As a public person,* he may find that a source of support he expected has not been won over yet. *As a businessperson,* he may find that money alone cannot get him the support he needs. *As an ordinary person,* he may find that he needs to cultivate people more or develop his patience.

48.2   *Yang 9 changing line derives from Hexagram 39 Bumbling by Himself*

He tries to be renewed but bumbles,
and so he receives inadequate renewal.

■ His abilities and skills are important even in seeking renewal. Here, he makes mistakes and thus suffers from faulty or inadequate renewal.

● *At his best,* he may learn from his errors, and be able to quickly recover so as to receive what he needs. *At his worst,* he may be blind to his mistakes, and in addition, be harmed by his inadequate renewal.

▲ *As a public person,* he may have struggled and won only severe budgetary limitations, or inadequate political support. *As a businessperson,* he may find he has returned or damaged goods, or a partnership deal falls through. *As an ordinary person,* he may find his resources are barely sufficient or were obtained in an undesirable way, or he has offended people he respects.

48.3   *Yang 9 changing line derives from Hexagram 29 Being Trapped*

He finds himself trapped and so cannot be renewed.
He needs renewal, but without help, he cannot get it.

■ He feels he is trapped, and is unable to get renewal by himself. He must either break out of his trap (perhaps by first changing his perspective), or else he must get assistance from someone else. He runs a real risk of not being renewed, and succeeding will be a struggle.

● *At his best,* he may be able to reach out and win friends who will come to his aid. *At his worst,* he may be locked into a trap of his own devising and not be able to see it.

▲ *As a public person,* he may find himself harassed and overworked in a backwater position. *As a businessperson,* he may have a product or enterprise that has potential, but he does not understand how to successfully market it. *As an ordinary person,* he may not succeed in what he attempts despite having good potential, or he may succeed through a partnership or a marriage.

48.4　　*Yin 6 changing line derives from Hexagram 28 Working Toward a Goal*

His renewal comes through working toward it.
It is good that he can get what he needs this way.

■ He is fortunate that he has such a clear and meaningful goal, since his goal also serves to help renew him. Being able to visualize the results of his work is a powerful renewal tool. Being able to take his work into his heart and soul is another powerful renewal. Being able to do both of these can almost make his work itself a renewal, but being able to finally bring his goal to fruition is even better.

● *At his best,* he may have a dream that drives his ambition. *At his worst,* he may be obsessed by his goal, so that it gives him no respite and blinds him to the other important things in life.

▲ *As a public person,* he may have a public cause that motivates him. *As a businessperson,* he may be an inventor trying to get his invention to market. *As an ordinary person,* he may be studying a new career, or striving for an important personal goal.

48.5　　*Yang 9 changing line derives from Hexagram 46 Promoting Himself*

His ability to promote himself brings him renewal.
He also brings renewal to those around him.

■ He succeeds abundantly in renewing himself. Then he becomes like the well itself, a bountiful source of refreshment benefiting those around him. This illustrates that not only is his renewal highly successful, but also that renewal has social aspects, spreading out in society, through family, friends, compatriots, coworkers, and even strangers.

● *At his best,* he may be able to bring those around him to see his dreams and his abilities, and be able to show others how to share with him. *At his worst,* he may be able to deceive others and manipulate them with lies and false images.

▲ *As a public person,* he may gain a prominent and important public relations position. *As a businessperson,* he may have a product that everyone uses, or a position of leadership in the business community. *As an ordinary person,* he may have a beneficial and optimistic period, and he shares his rich emotional bounty with those around him.

48.6 *Yin 6 changing line derives from Hexagram 57 At His Leader's Mercy*

Renewal ultimately depends on his leader's mercy, yet that mercy always comes, and everyone who looks to his leader also benefits.

■ His leader's willingness to bring renewal benefits everyone. Here, obtaining renewal is not a struggle; rather it is more like a blessing graciously bestowed on those who seek it.

● *At his best,* he may receive life's blessings with an appreciation of both failure and reward that strengthens his power. *At his worst,* either he may be blind and unappreciative of the blessings he receives or he may be fearful of being denied what he needs.

▲ *As a public person,* he may always be dependent upon the favor of a powerful leader. *As a businessperson,* he may fear that the business cycle won't pick up enough. *As an ordinary person,* he may enjoy the benefits of a loving and supportive mate, and his friends and family share in the couple's positive feelings.

48.ALL *All lines changing derives from Hexagram 21 Working on a Problem*

His time of renewal is over, and now he can turn again to working on a problem. Serious intentions require serious labor.

■ After his body is rested, his mind relaxed, and his soul lightened, then he is able to turn again to the task that he has set himself. He is now able to work on a problem and bring optimal effort to bear to resolve it. The more he is committed to achieving his goal, the more intense his work effort will become, and the more likely his success will be.

● *At his best,* he may be able to rededicate himself fervently and effectively to his goal. *At his worst,* he may have been forced into this prematurely so now his performance suffers from unmet needs as well as from unhappy feelings.

▲ *As a public person,* he may return to an active position after a period spent in study. *As a businessperson,* he may need to redesign a product to make it successful once again in the marketplace. *As an ordinary person,* he may return from a long vacation and resume his job, or his honeymoon ends and now the marriage begins.

49. Being Revolutionary

TRIGRAMS GH   LINES 101 110   COMPLEMENTARY HEXAGRAM 4 ACTING IMPETUOUSLY

The time of revolutionary or radical change has come,
and now others can believe in its cause. It is beneficial for him
to promote change. By doing this, his regrets will disappear.

■ *The traditional title* for this hexagram is "Revolution." Here the hexagram is titled "Being Revolutionary." It signifies that he has revolutionary ideas or goals, and the time has come for him to espouse his ideas or take more concrete actions. He can even lead others if he chooses. When he continues to work for change, his regrets will disappear. *The complementary hexagram* is Hexagram 4 Acting Impetuously, which illustrates that simple impetuosity does not have the maturity that being truly revolutionary does.

● *At his best,* he may be inspiring and correct in his assessment of the situation and, therefore, easily be able to help bring about the changes he desires. *At his worst,* he may be foolhardy or grossly wrong in his assessment of the situation, and thus whatever he achieves will be seriously flawed.

▲ *As a public person,* he may be an inspiring spokesperson for a cause. *As a businessperson,* he may be involved in a take over or a radical change in the business. *As an ordinary person,* he may lead others to major changes in their lives, radically change his own life, or become committed to a radical new cause.

49.1   *Yang 9 changing line derives from Hexagram 31 Ability to Change Matters*

His ability to change matters is so minimal
that he is even restricted by ordinary affairs.

■ His revolutionary power is only beginning. He may have the desire to effect change, but he does not have the ability as yet. Even ordinary, domestic, or mundane matters are able to restrain him now.

● *At his best,* he may be content with doing his duty and receiving simple rewards because he does not believe the time for revolution has come. *At his worst,* he may be bound by meager resources, and he feels too powerless or too inept to alleviate his suffering.

▲ *As a public person,* he may be closely regulated by rules and procedures. *As a businessperson,* he may not be able to promote improvements or new enterprises, especially when he is caught up in the daily routine of simply keeping things going. *As an ordinary person,* he may find himself wholly engaged in domestic, work, or community affairs.

49.2   *Yin 6 changing line derives from Hexagram 43 Escaping Harm*

The time for revolutionary action has arrived,
and taking actions now will be beneficial and not harm him.

■ He is now able to act to further his revolutionary goals, and he will not suffer for this. Note that revolution does not require violent or damaging actions, but merely bringing about a radical change.

● *At his best,* he may see that the time for change has come, and he will help initiate it in a significant way. *At his worst,* he may be involved only with small changes around him rather than important ones affecting many.

▲ *As a public person,* he may be part of a public relations effort to radically alter conditions. *As a businessperson,* he may profit from radical changes occurring in his business or in the society around it. *As an ordinary person,* he may suddenly have opportunities to advance himself or his family, or he may help change things around him.

49.3   *Yang 9 changing line derives from Hexagram 17 Hunting*

He is hunting for the proper course in a time of revolution.
Both highly aggressive action and taking no action lead to harm,
but reinforcing the radical changes already underway
can help complete the revolution.

■ If he is too aggressive in promoting revolutionary ideas, it brings disaster. However, being known as a revolutionary and doing nothing also puts him in danger. A successful revolution requires more than just one attempt to instill the new concepts; it requires repetition and reinforcement. Thus, the proper course of action now is to pursue revolutionary goals persistently and steadily where the revolution needs reinforcement. Some difficulties might appear, but with appropriate reinforcement, revolutionary ideas can succeed.

● *At his best,* he may be able to promote his cause by becoming a renown and respected moral leader. *At his worst,* he may be so fervent and unable to restrain his enthusiasm or his aggression that he offends many people and hinders his goals.

▲ *As a public person,* he may learn how to convince others to listen with an open mind to what he says. *As a businessperson,* he may need to pay close attention to what is happening around him to avoid mistakes and losses, rather than being too committed to his plans. *As an ordinary person,* he may feel a great deal of stress and need to restrain himself from taking severe action that would ultimately prove harmful; instead, slow and steady improvement should be attempted.

49.4   *Yang 9 changing line derives from Hexagram 63 Beginning a New Task*

The revolution is completed. Now is the time to consolidate
its leadership and achieve consensus. The last doubts
and regrets will disappear after consensus is achieved.

■ The revolution has succeeded. Choosing new leadership is necessary after such a radical change, since the old one identified too closely with the old values. Thus, changing the leadership further promotes the effectiveness of the revolution. Consolidation is now necessary, and after it is achieved, regrets will disappear as unity is achieved. This begins a new period of stability.

● *At his best,* he may be a champion of promoting everyone's benefit rather than that of a few. *At his worst,* he may be involved in consolidating power and benefits for only a few, especially himself.

▲ *As a public person,* he may join a new leadership group. *As a businessperson,* he may work closely with others to consolidate new markets or gain control over new business regulations. *As an ordinary person,* he may make some significant changes in his professional, personal, and social life, including making new friends, finding new employers, and divorcing or remarrying.

49.5   *Yang 9 changing line derives from Hexagram 55 Serving Greatness*

He attains greatness through revolution.
Now others look to him and believe in him.

■ He has reached a position of greatness. Indeed, he is so great that he does not fear the future because he is strong enough to face whatever comes. He has many followers who believe in him and who look to him for guidance. This can also mean that the revolution brings benefits to those closest to it.

● *At his best,* he may be a leader who inspires others with his strength, courage, and capabilities. *At his worst,* he may inspire fear, hatred, and helplessness in his enemies, although he could also bully and intimidate his allies and followers.

▲ *As a public person,* he may gain a position of prominence due to his vast following. *As a businessperson,* he may earn great profits and be widely sought for his business leadership. *As an ordinary person,* he may become well respected in his local circle and enjoy their trust.

49.6   *Yin 6 changing line derives from Hexagram 13 Serving on a Team*

The time of revolutionary change has ended.
Continuing to advance it would bring misfortune. It is best for
him to join himself with others in the society that now exists.

■ The period of revolutionary ideas has run its course; no revolution can last indefinitely. If he continued to act as a strong advocate of continuing revolution, he would suffer some misfortune. Now he should simply join himself with his fellow man in the society that exists.

● *At his best,* he may open himself to the important things in life, such as love, nurturing, and enjoyment, because he understands his place. *At his worst,* he may not be able to accept that the realities of existence limit how much good can be done in any revolution, and he will push his revolutionary goals too far, and bring misfortune on himself.

▲ *As a public person,* he must decide to effectively govern or idealistically govern. *As a businessperson,* he may enjoy good profits and reputation as long as he relies on the fundamental values of those around him. *As an ordinary person,* he may enjoy a good period by developing close ties with those around him in the community and at work.

49.ALL   *All lines changing derives from Hexagram 4 Acting Impetuously*

Forcing a revolution without achievable goals, that is,
without the likelihood of practical or reasonable results,
is only acting impetuously.

■ Revolution should be a tactic based on need. Once the objectives have been met, then the revolution has succeeded. Permanent revolution cannot sustain itself. Pushing a revolution past the point where it can do any good is also foolish. Revolution attempted without achievable goals or pushed beyond the point where it does any good is simply foolishly impetuous.

● *At his best,* he may be so idealistic and sincere that he exemplifies unrealistic and unattainable goals. *At his worst,* he may try to force his unattainable ideals on those around him and possibly do great harm.

▲ *As a public person,* he may be a spokesperson who plays to his large following with his writings or speeches. *As a businessperson,* he may have the dream of business success so much in his eyes that he cannot realize his ideal is failing until he suffers great losses. *As an ordinary person,* he may not listen to the advice of family and friends, and pursue his ideals regardless of their consequences, thus often resulting in harm to him.

50. Governing Matters

TRIGRAMS FG	LINES 011 101	COMPLEMENTARY HEXAGRAM 3 GATHERING SUPPORT

His governance of matters is very capable,
and he can benefit through it.

■ *The traditional title* for this hexagram is "The Cauldron." Here the hexagram is titled "Governing Matters." This is a somewhat obscure hexagram and is one of the two that directly refer to physical objects (the other is Hexagram 48 Being Renewed). The cauldron referred to is a bronze ceremonial pot known as a *ding*, which was used in ancient China. It was the center of rites on formal state occasions and in sacred rituals of the king. The connection between the state and the ancestor gods was very close and strong. The ding thus represents the symbol of governmental authority and legitimacy. *The complementary hexagram* is Hexagram 3 Gathering Support, which illustrates that the most important step in being able to govern matters is building a strong base of support.

● *At his best,* he may be a capable and legitimate leader who provides good decisions that benefit those around him. *At his worst,* he may be strong in leadership, but flawed in either his legitimacy or the quality of his decisions.

▲ *As a public person,* he may be a powerful leader of a cause or philosophy, and others look to him for guidance. *As a businessperson,* he may be a company executive or have critical knowledge, which gives him control of the situation. *As an ordinary person,* he may be looked to by those around him for guidance, be a powerful head of a family or community group, or be able to persuade and control those around him.

50.1	*Yin 6 changing line derives from Hexagram 14 Relying on His Allies*

Governance of matters begins by relying on
his friends and allies for assistance.

■ In a time of new beginnings such as this, it is important to have the right tools to do the job. When he is weak, he has little margin for error. Here, he can call on his friends and allies to help him. With their help, he can succeed in his goals.

● *At his best,* he may understand that his power depends on his ability to motivate people, and he has the ability to do so. *At his worst,* he may try to use others without a proper regard for them, and thus weaken the bond between them.

▲ *As a public person,* he may be able to reestablish his damaged reputation by turning to public leaders. *As a businessperson,* he may save his enterprise with the help of friends. *As an ordinary person,* he may need to rely on those around him to straighten out the problems he is in.

50.2 *Yang 9 changing line derives from Hexagram 56 Wandering*

His enemies are helplessly wandering so they can't harm him, and thus his governance of matters succeeds.

■ His enemies are unable to effectively oppose him. It is as though they are lost and cannot see how to attack him, or perhaps he can easily sidestep whatever they do. Thus, his governance succeeds more due to their weakness than his own strength. He still benefits, however.

● *At his best,* he may understand the situation he is in and act appropriately both to win friends and to advance his causes. *At his worst,* he may achieve his goals but at the same time fan jealousy and hatred in others, and later this will harm him.

▲ *As a public person,* he may act with more impunity than normally. *As a businessperson,* he may be able to advance his interests very easily and profit because his competitors have difficulties. *As an ordinary person,* he may enjoy a very favorable position, have little or no criticism from others, and have no one standing in his way.

50.3 *Yang 9 changing line derives from Hexagram 64 Continuing a Task*

He loses strength and supporters. However, by keeping on his course, his governance of matters eventually will improve.

■ There are ups and downs on any course. Here matters are deteriorating for him. He is losing strength as well as supporters, so he might also lose heart. However, if he keeps his course long enough, matters will once again improve for him.

● *At his best,* he may understand the trends of the time, and so he rides out current difficulties and believes in his later success. *At his worst,* he may rigidly keep on his course, blind to the fact that some modifications could make a real difference in the result.

▲ *As a public person,* he may encounter opposition from an opponent, hindrance from poor regulations, or physical deterioration in the system. *As a businessperson,* he may not be able to effect changes or policies he can show are desirable. *As an ordinary person,* he may loose allies, friends, or a mate, and in time, he can gain new ones.

50.4   *Yang 9 changing line derives from Hexagram 18 Nursing an Illness*

His governance of matters has been harmed,
his allies are dishonored, and he loses respect.
Now he must nurse matters back to health.

■ He is facing dishonor and disrepute, and his allies cannot help him in this time of trial. He must nurse matters back to health himself. Helping his allies and attending to the needs of those around him will also help him repair the damage.

● *At his best,* he may care deeply and strive with all his heart to rebuild what he has worked so hard for, and his caring makes a critical difference in this task. *At his worst,* he may be deeply dispirited by a rejection that he feels all too personally, and this hinders his ability to rebuild public trust and the loyalty of his team.

▲ *As a public person,* he may be demoted, dismissed, or investigated. *As a businessperson,* he may have business opportunities ruined through corruption. *As an ordinary person,* he may be cheated or be implicated in illegal or immoral activities.

50.5   *Yin 6 changing line derives from Hexagram 44 Maintaining His Independence*

He maintains his independence,
thus his governance of matters remains strong.

■ By keeping himself from submitting to the demands of those who wish to influence or control him, he preserves his own power. His ability to do this shows his own personal strength and commitment to his governance, and also helps maintain his power over his adherents.

● *At his best,* he may be respected for strong leadership, honorable goals, and capable decision-making by his followers as well as others. *At his worst,* he may fiercely and bullishly oppose others, and this will make him less flexible as well as poison his reputation in dealing with others.

▲ *As a public person,* he may remain in his position despite manipulations or threats. *As a businessperson,* he may pursue actions against competitors that bring profits as well as earn respect. *As an ordinary person,* he may be his own person, neither oppressing those near him who are weaker nor being slavishly obedient to those who are stronger, and this earns him respect from all those around him.

50.6   *Yang 9 changing line derives from Hexagram 32 Committing Himself*

His commitment to governance is a powerful ideal
that may entice him to attempt almost any goal.

■ His governance is based on the ideals of governance. Thus, he is not subject to manipulation, bribery, or selfishly using his position. Rather, he strives to do the best things to promote his continuing governance. This generally means benefiting those around him in the best way possible. Having such an attitude makes it possible to achieve many things because he easily wins others' cooperation. He should be wary, however, of setting goals that are too idealistic, since success is far less certain.

● *At his best,* he may combine idealism with practicality so that he can achieve exceptional results. *At his worst,* he may not be very ambitious, so he is respected and appreciated but only in a small venue.

▲ *As a public person,* he may inspire himself through his pronouncements. *As a businessperson,* he may convince others to support efforts that benefit important goals, or to develop products that are inherently of great public benefit. *As an ordinary person,* he may be the recipient of some special philanthropy that inspires him in a great goal.

50.ALL   *All lines changing derives from Hexagram 3 Gathering Support*

Governing means ultimately having the support of those he
governs. Without support, he will certainly fail.
So, he strives to gain supporters.

■ Governance is based on his ability to attract those adherents who will support his cause. With no adherents, he has nothing to govern, although much to strive for. With adherents, he is able to formulate plans and obtain help in having them carried out. Winning (and keeping) support is thus essential to his plans. Periodically, he must prove to his followers that their trust in him is not misplaced, and this is little different from winning their trust in the first place.

● *At his best,* he may know how to reach out to others by linking their hopes and their dreams with his role. *At his worst,* he may strive to manipulate others for his benefit.

▲ *As a public person,* he may start a campaign to advance his popularity. *As a businessperson,* he may seek backers for his ideas or goals. *As an ordinary person,* he may strive to become a leader in his local circle.

51. At Fortune's Mercy

TRIGRAMS BB   LINES 100 100   COMPLEMENTARY HEXAGRAM 57 AT HIS LEADER'S MERCY

DOUBLED TRIGRAMS MEANING: *CHEN*, TRIGRAM B, SIGNIFIES AGITATION, MOVEMENT, THREATS, SHOCKING EVENTS, AND THUNDEROUS CHANGE.   *(SEE PAGE 45 FOR MORE ABOUT THIS TRIGRAM.)*

He is at fortune's mercy, and it brings upset and fear.
After it passes, he is relieved that worse did not occur. Its effects
may spread far, but they don't harm what is important to him.

■ *The traditional titles* for this hexagram are "The Arousing," "Shock," and "Thunder," although these do not give a clear meaning of the hexagram. Here the hexagram is titled "At Fortune's Mercy." It signifies he is helplessly buffeted by fate, and both surprised and changed by matters beyond his control. The traditional text uses the example of thunderbolts to illustrate the fearful power of outrageous fortune. Thunderbolts can be terrifying, but after they pass by, their magnificence, excitement, and power can be appreciated. Relief is also a common reaction, since even though things were threatened and some may have changed, no great harm occurred. *The complementary hexagram* is Hexagram 57 At His Leader's Mercy, which illustrates the tendency to seek shelter with those who are stronger and can provide some protection.

● *At his best,* he may be somewhat upset by fortune's influence, but he quickly realizes the benefits in his life. *At his worst,* he may be seriously agitated by fortune's influence, and it will require some time until he has adapted successfully to various new difficulties he faces.

▲ *As a public person,* he may suddenly have his position undermined or discredited before the public. *As a businessperson,* he may suddenly face lawsuits, a takeover, or collapse of some aspect of the business. *As an ordinary person,* he may have sudden problems or radical changes that he did not want to appear in his life.

51.1   *Yang 9 changing line derives from Hexagram 16 Standstill*

He is at such a standstill that outrageous fortune hardly
touches him. Being brought to a state of alert is better than
not being alert at all, so this actually helps him somewhat.

■ If he is stagnant, outrageous fortune actually helps wake him up. At least if he is alert, he can now see what is happening around him so he can think about moving forward again. The result here is positive, even if it may be slightly disconcerting.

● *At his best,* he may have some awareness of what is happening around him, and thus he can minimize its effects on him. *At his worst,* he may be unaware of what is developing, and thus he is unable to help himself from even slight harm.

▲ *As a public person,* he may be so lulled by routine that he is unable to face an unexpected problem. *As a businessperson,* he may experience an unexpected and sudden financial jolt or other business problem. *As an ordinary person,* he may have an unexpected problem or unpleasant surprise that will work out well in the end, or at least not harm him very much.

51.2   *Yin 6 changing line derives from Hexagram 54 Entering a Marriage*

He seeks a marriage for safety in weathering outrageous fortune.
Although some harm may come from this initially,
eventually he will recover.

■ He seeks a position of safety through a partnership or marriage to weather the effects of outrageous fortune. Doing this, however, he still suffers some slight harm, but he will have time to recover from his losses later.

● *At his best,* he may carefully plan and succeed at establishing an important alliance, even though it places him at some slight disadvantage initially. *At his worst,* he may be driven by fear of loss to be manipulative and deceitful, and although he achieves his goal, it poisons the important relationship he tried to create, so it will take time to recover.

▲ *As a public person,* he may outmaneuver enemies by forming critical alliances. *As a businessperson,* he may try to move his business or assets out of harm's way. *As an ordinary person,* he may have serious fears and try to find a refuge with friends or family.

51.3   *Yin 6 changing line derives from Hexagram 55 Serving Greatness*

If he strives for greatness, he will escape harm even though the
effects of outrageous fortune hit all around him.

■ He understands that the only safety lies in becoming so strong that he can't be harmed by outrageous fortune. Thus, he tries to attain greatness to overcome the dangers. This may not be easy but he can succeed if he is sufficiently motivated, and this tactic keeps him from harm.

● *At his best,* he may feel challenged to achieve his best, and he succeeds wonderfully. *At his worst,* he may suffer some harm from having the desire to be greater than he is, but fails because of lack of faith in himself, motivation, or ability to do what he wants to do.

▲ *As a public person,* he may strive to achieve public approval or wide respect for his ability. *As a businessperson,* he may experience very unsettled markets and only innovative, aggressive action will protect his business. *As an ordinary person,* he may experience many problems at work, at home, or in the community, and only vigorous self-interest will maintain his position.

51.4   *Yang 9 changing line derives from Hexagram 24 Beginning a Relationship*

Outrageous fortune hits him through a friend
when their relationship suddenly comes apart.
Now it will take time to recover and to rebuild the relationship.

■ Here outrageous fortune comes through a valued relationship, such as with a lover, a friend, or an ally. Whatever happens, it virtually destroys the relationship, and now he finds himself needing to rebuild that relationship afresh. This outrageous fortune could also affect his finances, his social or business position, his health, or his life in other ways.

● *At his best,* he may suffer an important loss, but the loss is one that he desires to rebuild properly. *At his worst,* he may have an important relationship destroyed, and he finds it impossible to reconstruct it positively; therefore, he is left with painful feelings and memories.

▲ *As a public person,* he may experience deterioration of his relationship with his mentor. *As a businessperson,* he and an ally or partner may lose confidence in each other. *As an ordinary person,* he may suddenly lose emotional support or suffer damage to his reputation.

51.5   *Yin 6 changing line derives from Hexagram 17 Hunting*

Outrageous fortune hits all around him; yet,
if he continues seeking, he can escape harm.

■ He keeps his presence of mind and continues to engage in whatever he was doing before outrageous fortune appeared. Hunting is the task implied, but it could be almost any form of activity or advancement. Even in this time of danger, he is not harmed by doing this.

● *At his best,* he may balance caution with courageous action, find what he desires, and thus succeed in his goals. *At his worst,* he may be too rash or too inept to do what he attempts to do, and thus suffers some harm.

▲ *As a public person,* he may see dangerous conflicts around him, which he can avoid with care. *As a businessperson,* he may have to search carefully for solutions to business problems. *As an ordinary person,* he may find a job in a period of economic trouble.

51.6   *Yin 6 changing line derives from Hexagram 21 Working on a Problem*

Outrageous fortune strikes those around him,
but he works on a way to assure his safety and so escapes harm.

■ He sees those around him being overcome or devastated by outrageous fortune. He works on a way to escape harm and he succeeds, not by using force, but finding something or someone to protect himself.

● *At his best,* he may prepare himself in the best way he knows how and saves himself from harm. *At his worst,* he may prepare himself but in a faulty way, so he suffers somewhat.

▲ *As a public person,* he may try to fortify his position by following procedures, or by strengthening his outside alliances, or by other ways. *As a businessperson,* he may work even harder to make sure his business or business position is secure. *As an ordinary person,* he may get an education or job training to enhance his position, or strive to establish a relationship with someone who can benefit him.

51.ALL   *All lines changing derives from Hexagram 57 At His Leader's Mercy*

He places himself at his leader's mercy
to escape the threat of outrageous fortune.

■ He realizes that the only way to escape being at fortune's mercy is to find someone so strong that he will serve as a bulwark against capricious, outrageous fortune. Being at his leader's mercy—that is, having ties that bind him to his leader and yet help limit his exposure to risk—will give him more safety than he has now. Therefore, he is happy to enter this relationship.

● *At his best,* he may find a leader who he respects and to whom he is pleased to offer his allegiance. *At his worst,* he may seek security at any cost and not realize at the time how great that cost will be later.

▲ *As a public person,* he may seek a position with a powerful public leader. *As a businessperson,* he may seek a merger with a larger and more successful company. *As an ordinary person,* he may seek a marriage or mentor in the hopes of greatly improving his life.

52. Holding Back

| TRIGRAMS DD | LINES 001 001 | COMPLEMENTARY HEXAGRAM 58 SHARING HIMSELF |

DOUBLED TRIGRAMS MEANING: *KEN*, TRIGRAM D, SIGNIFIES RESTRAINT, INDECISION, HIDDEN THINGS, AND SECRETS.
(SEE PAGE 46 FOR MORE ABOUT THIS TRIGRAM.)

*He is holding back by being passive and inconspicuous,
and by doing this escapes harm.*

■ *The traditional titles* for this hexagram are "Keeping Still" and "Mountain," although these are somewhat misleading. Here the hexagram is titled "Holding Back." It signifies that he is held back by his doubts and indecisive nature. By being passive and inconspicuous, he withdraws from interaction with others. This gives him a form of safety. *The complementary hexagram* is Hexagram 58 Sharing Himself, which illustrates that the opposite of holding himself back is sharing himself with others.

● *At his best,* he may hold back and remain hidden for good reasons while he bides his time and observes the situation unfolding around him. *At his worst,* he may be overwhelmed by indecision or fear and lock himself up by holding himself back or remaining hidden.

▲ *As a public person,* he may retire from the spotlight or remain silent on a controversial or important issue. *As a businessperson,* he may withhold an investment, a product, or an expansion. *As an ordinary person,* he may withdraw from the world or strive not to be noticed by those around him, be deeply indecisive, or have secrets that he does not wish to reveal to those near him.

52.1   *Yin 6 changing line derives from Hexagram 22 Advancing by His Image*

*He is easily able to be inconspicuous
or appear so insignificant that it averts trouble for him.*

■ By not drawing attention to himself or appearing to be not worth bothering with, he escapes those who would harm him. He finds that putting on a successfully deceitful front is very easy to do.

● *At his best,* he may understand how to disguise himself perfectly for his environment, like a chameleon, and thereby escape harm without compromising his true nature. *At his worst,* he may be frightened into passivity and cowardice, and this will demean or haunt him in the future.

▲ *As a public person,* he may strive to become a faceless bureaucrat to escape notoriety. *As a businessperson,* he may dissemble to discourage investigation into his business affairs. *As an ordinary person,* he may hold back from acting, or disguise himself from others, in response to his fears.

52.2 *Yin 6 changing line derives from Hexagram 18 Nursing an Illness*

He holds back while he nurses himself. It is better if he does not take actions yet, even though he might want to.

■ By nursing himself, he is healing something. Clearly, this indicates that he is not fully himself and therefore weak or more vulnerable than if he were fully healed. Therefore, he is wise to complete healing before taking action that might otherwise attract those who would harm him. He might not want to do this, but he should.

● *At his best,* he may understand his strengths and weaknesses, and he will conserve his strength until he knows it is a good time to use it. *At his worst,* he may be terribly sick or weak, and he knows if he did not keep hidden, he would be dragged into a situation that would harm him.

▲ *As a public person,* he may know he is not strong enough to set rules or exceptions to rules, so he passes difficult situations on to higher authorities. *As a businessperson,* he may not have the backing to initiate new endeavors or expansions. *As an ordinary person,* he may feel unable to overcome the circumstances around him now; however, with more time and preparation, he believes he may.

52.3 *Yang 9 changing line derives from Hexagram 23 Being in a Collapsing Situation*

He is in a collapsing situation and cannot escape harm although he tries to protect himself by holding back.

■ In a really bad situation, just trying to hide isn't good enough. Thus, his efforts to escape by holding back fail, and he will likely experience some harm.

● *At his best,* he may understand that sometimes it is impossible to escape harm by holding himself back no matter how hard he tries; therefore, he prepares for negative consequences as well. *At his worst,* he may be harmed and may not have allowed for this possibility, and thus suffers even more harm.

▲ *As a public person,* he may serve in a post that is now responsible to someone hostile to him. *As a businessperson,* he may be a subordinate who is being manipulated by a superior, or an author whose written material exposes him to danger. *As an ordinary person,* he may experience many problems, which only serves to toughen his resolve, to lower his respect for others, and to make him less sympathetic.

52.4   *Yin 6 changing line derives from Hexagram 56 Wandering*

> He holds himself back so well that he cannot be harmed.
> His enemies just pass him by.

■ Here, he has achieved such a high level of passivity and inconspicuousness that he is nearly invisible. Those who want to harm him cannot see him, find him, or touch him. Rather, they helplessly wander around and their actions do not harm him. This line is similar to the first line, but it shows a higher level of control and a more effective result.

● *At his best,* he may have attained a high level of security that gives him great peace. *At his worst,* he may lose touch with the reality around him, and this will make it more difficult for him to reintroduce himself into society.

▲ *As a public person,* he may have perfected the art of being a bureaucrat who is known to serve only the rules. *As a businessperson,* he may hide his investments or controls so that his role is invisible. *As an ordinary person,* he may follow rules and meet people's expectations to avoid problems, or he may suffer an illness that requires inactivity.

52.5   *Yin 6 changing line derives from Hexagram 53 Sharing Commitment*

> He secretly holds back even though he is making commitments.
> Yet, over time, matters will improve and his doubts will pass.

■ Here, he is affirming his commitment to a leader, and yet he has some serious doubts that he is not expressing. By not expressing them, he is protecting himself, and he may question whether this alliance is best for him. However, with time he will find that his situation will improve and his doubts will fade. Remaining silent about his doubts and having a wait-and-see attitude works out best.

● *At his best,* he may see great potential in an alliance and know that too much criticism at the beginning could stifle its realization. *At his worst,* he may go along with someone else's plan for an alliance because he is too weak to do anything else.

▲ *As a public person,* he may join a difficult leader or one he does not entirely agree with. *As a businessperson,* he may promote publications or media in a field he is not entirely happy with. *As an ordinary person,* he may have good relationships with those around him, marry or join an organization despite having doubts, or have a job where his image is being marketed.

52.6   *Yang 9 changing line derives from Hexagram 15 Acting With Propriety*

> Holding himself back is the proper thing to do now.
> There are important or hidden factors at work here,
> and holding back will protect him.

■ He should hold back because there are things that are not presently visible which will harm him. By holding back, he can protect himself. Other things he could do would also harm him, so holding back is actually the best thing he can do.

● *At his best,* he may have a valuable (although passive) role to play in an important relationship, and he will gain greatly from it. *At his worst,* he may have only a minor role to play, and he will not gain much from it.

▲ *As a public person,* he may be appointed to a confidential advisory post or to do secret work. *As a businessperson,* he may find success comes from working quietly behind the scenes. *As an ordinary person,* he may have to take a backseat to family or mate, build up his boss's image with his own hard work, or recover from a serious illness through bed rest.

52.ALL   *All lines changing derives from Hexagram 58 Sharing Himself*

> He comes to realize that he can protect himself and even gain
> benefits by sharing himself with others rather than holding back.

■ Being passive and inconspicuous is a way to escape harm, but that also means foregoing many of the social interactions that enrich us. He has learned that withdrawal has its limitations, and so now he desires to gain through sharing and interacting with others.

● *At his best,* he may be inspired to form happy relationships that share things of value. *At his worst,* he may be driven by loneliness or despair to share, and he is never free enough from guilt, fear, or pain to get the most out his relationships.

▲ *As a public person,* he may launch a campaign to win friends and influence people. *As a businessperson,* he may seek to make his dreams a reality by getting the support of others. *As an ordinary person,* he may become involved in social activities, or seek a mate or partner.

53. Sharing Commitment

TRIGRAMS DF   LINES 001 011   COMPLEMENTARY HEXAGRAM 54 ENTERING MARRIAGE

He is sharing a commitment, and both leaders and followers
can gain by doing this.

■ *The traditional titles* for this hexagram are "Development" and "Gradual Progress." Here the hexagram is titled "Sharing Commitment." It signifies that benefits can come to anyone through a shared commitment. *The complementary hexagram* is Hexagram 54 Entering a Marriage, which represents taking a shared commitment to its logical conclusion by entering a formal close partnership.

● *At his best,* he may make a shared commitment that brings him benefits he could not gain on his own. *At his worst,* he may not commit himself as much as he should to have it give him many benefits.

▲ *As a public person,* he may advocate or ally himself with someone else's cause. *As a businessperson,* he may seek a mutually profitable partnership with another company or an association with another individual in his office. *As an ordinary person,* he may find a true friend or a powerful romantic interest.

53.1   *Yin 6 changing line derives from Hexagram 37 Serving in a Household*

He is sharing a commitment with a household.
Although he could have some difficulties due to inexperience,
he will not be harmed even if others speak against him.

■ He is entering a new situation through joining with others in a household. If he is inexperienced, this could cause him some problems; yet others speaking against him cannot harm him since he had made a commitment to their shared household. In a new situation, he should act carefully, but he will also be given a chance to prove himself because of his commitment.

● *At his best,* he may realize that to others he appears as an intruder, so he moderates his actions and makes friends all around. *At his worst,* he may make terrible blunders and alienate many around him, so that it will take much time to undo the harm he has helped cause.

▲ *As a public person,* he may be given an assignment in a task force or group. *As a businessperson,* he may expand into new markets or join a new company. *As an ordinary person,* he may attempt new endeavors that those around him may criticize, although he will do well if he is committed to doing a good job and listens to them.

53.2   *Yin 6 changing line derives from Hexagram 57 At His Leader's Mercy*

Even when he finds himself at his leader's mercy,
things go well for him because of their shared commitment.

■ Even when he is powerless to stop his leader from harming him, if that is the intention, he will find that matters go well for him because they share a commitment. This means that mistakes and errors on his part aren't as likely to be punished as they might be otherwise.

● *At his best,* he may have won a special place in his leader's heart, and he is pleased and gratified that he responds equally. *At his worst,* he may take advantage of the special favors granted him, and he strives as much as he can to manipulate matters for his benefit.

▲ *As a public person,* he may be pleased that his leader grants him public recognition or a more advanced position. *As a businessperson,* he may expect tough competition from an industry leader, yet finds it not as bad as he thought. *As an ordinary person,* he may expect severe criticism from his mate, and instead find appreciation and forgiveness.

53.3   *Yang 9 changing line derives from Hexagram 20 Preparing Himself*

When harm threatens his safety, it is better for him
to rely on those with whom he's made commitments
rather than just on himself.

■ His preparations now put him in good standing. When potential harm threatens him, he can turn to the shared commitments he has nurtured with others. Through them, he can find safety. Relying only on himself would not help him successfully avert harm.

● *At his best,* he may easily be able to gain assistance to resolve an unanticipated problem. *At his worst,* he may be foolishly committed to what he thinks is right. Not relying on the assistance he could get from others could end up harming him.

▲ *As a public person,* he may reaffirm his commitments when they are made with others, or withdraw from an endeavor if he is alone. *As a businessperson,* he may have prepared a plan but give it up to avoid a big struggle. *As an ordinary person,* he may plan something new, and have to decide whether he wants to really push ahead with this, or instead protect what he has already gained.

53.4   *Yin 6 changing line derives from Hexagram 33 Complying*

He complies with the demands of his situation
and seeks a commitment that will bring him security.

■ He is facing some problems. However, in recognition of the dangers and necessities in the situation, he seeks to make a commitment that will bring him security.

● *At his best,* he may recognize the path to safety lies in listening to those who know more, and complying with their ideas could save him. *At his worst,* he may be cowardly, so he slavishly submits to the orders of those stronger, and hides in their shadows.

▲ *As a public person,* he may be a successful go-between and negotiator. *As a businessperson,* he may engage in a risky venture but have an escape plan fully developed. *As an ordinary person,* he may enter into some difficult and risky endeavors, and he needs to rely on his friends and family to see him through the dangers.

53.5   *Yang 9 changing line derives from Hexagram 52 Holding Back*

He is carried along by his shared commitments
and, therefore, gains benefits.

■ The time is now ripe for his advance, so he does not even have to strive for it to happen. He is passive, and yet he advances.

● *At his best,* he may be recognized for his good qualities and how he helps those around him, so his advance is naturally positive and completely unforced. *At his worst,* he may be recognized for his negative qualities and how he uses those around him, so his notoriety grows like a shadow that follows him even though he is benefiting now.

▲ *As a public person,* he may be given a highly visible position. *As a businessperson,* he may become an author or spokesperson of a public service organization. *As an ordinary person,* he may become attuned to mental or spiritual matters, or be promoted by acclaim to a leadership position among his fellows.

He bumbles but finds that it doesn't matter. Because of his shared commitments, he attains benefits beyond what he could imagine.

■ His bumbling doesn't interfere with the successes he enjoys now. His shared commitment has blossomed and brought him unimagined benefits.

● *At his best,* he may grow tremendously in his perspectives and attitudes. *At his worst,* he may become embroiled in things that, although good at the moment, could become problems for him later.

▲ *As a public person,* he may become a spokesperson for a cause he didn't know about before. *As a businessperson,* he may achieve success through written, artistic, or philanthropic endeavors. *As an ordinary person,* he may become involved in spiritual or artistic matters and receive widespread recognition.

He desires to maintain his shared commitments
by entering into a marriage.

■ The benefits he has found coming from his shared commitments have been considerable, and he desires to secure them. The natural way to do this is to enter into a marriage or an especially close partnership.

● *At his best,* he may find his soul mate. *At his worst,* he may desire to establish his own family so much that he risks entering too quickly into an unworkable match.

▲ *As a public person,* he may advertise for possible mates. *As a businessperson,* he may attempt to attract a mate using his wealth or status. *As an ordinary person,* he may try to find a mate through family, friends, work, community organizations, or his ordinary activities.

54. Entering a Marriage

TRIGRAMS HB   LINES 110 100   COMPLEMENTARY HEXAGRAM 53 SHARING COMMITMENT

He is entering a marriage, but being aggressive at the beginning
is harmful, and even trying to pursue a plan is not favorable.

■ *The traditional title* for this hexagram is "The Marrying Maiden." Here the hexagram is titled "Entering a Marriage." It warns that being too aggressive in entering a marriage or trying to develop it like a planned campaign will be unfortunate. A marriage is not something that can be planned. Marriage depends on the natural interaction of the two partners and shared growth over time, so it cannot be fully anticipated, planned, or forced. *The complementary hexagram* is Hexagram 53 Sharing Commitment, which represents the foundation that a marriage or partnership needs to have in order to work well.

● *At his best,* he may enter into a marriage or partnership with his eyes open, listen with his heart, and have an adaptable frame of mind. *At his worst,* he may be rigidly forceful and not pay attention to the real needs of his partner and the relationship.

▲ *As a public person,* he may experience celebrity in his courtship and marriage. *As a businessperson,* he may enter into a marriage for financial gain. *As an ordinary person,* he may enter into a marriage or partnership with varying degrees of success or failure.

54.1   *Yang 9 changing line derives from Hexagram 40 Getting Free*

He is freest to pursue and succeed in his goals
at the beginning of a marriage.

■ The start of the marriage is when he has the most freedom to initiate new actions, persuade his partner, build shared objectives, and set precedents. Thus, in some ways, this is the time when he can make the most rapid progress toward his goals within the marriage. This is also a time when he will feel very free because the marriage freed him from other restrictions and generally brought him the things that he wants.

● *At his best,* he may come to see what is most important in his mate, and gain satisfaction by discovering this. *At his worst,* he may be confused by the new things in his life that he discovers, and he may be unable to properly readjust his thinking to make this relationship work well.

▲ *As a public person,* he may discover he has a behind-the-scenes role in partnership. *As a businessperson,* he may have his business overshadowed by his partner, yet his long-term prospects remain good. *As an ordinary person,* he may find a new position at work or in the community, or he may become newly wed.

54.2 *Yang 9 changing line derives from Hexagram 51 At Fortune's Mercy*

Fate has a way of intruding and upsetting things.
When it does, it is best to take no strong actions,
to minimize harm, and to stabilize his marriage.

■ When things change unexpectedly, especially in a major way, it is best to just hold tight and repair the damage to his marriage. Staying out of more trouble, which he could easily cause through inappropriate actions, is the key idea here.

● *At his best,* he may realize his vulnerability and wisely remain in the background. *At his worst,* he may press himself forward and then be shamed or attacked in some other demeaning way.

▲ *As a public person,* he may face a very complex situation in which his mate takes a lead, which he should allow. *As a businessperson,* he may need to let experts act for him. *As an ordinary person,* he may suffer unfortunate circumstances caused by relatives or old acquaintances.

54.3 *Yin 6 changing line derives from Hexagram 34 Forcing Matters*

By forcing matters, he damages his marriage.

■ Pushing matters too far or too fast could easily result in harm. Thus, he should try not to force matters. Regrettably, however, he may not be able to help himself from getting into some trouble through impatience or excessive desire.

● *At his best,* he may believe he needs to stand up for an important principle, whether or not he comes to some harm from doing so. *At his worst,* he may be foolish or stupid in pursuit of an unworthy goal and may even be resentful for being hurt in the end.

▲ *As a public person,* he may be harmed when he makes a principled stand to his boss. *As a businessperson,* he may suffer some losses, as well as criticism, because he tried something without the approval of his partner. *As an ordinary person,* he may be fired, get divorced, or suffer a public scandal.

54.4   *Yang 9 changing line derives from Hexagram 19 Leading Others*

He is guiding his marriage, although it will take longer
than he expects to succeed.

■ Doing things right often takes more time and effort, but the results are worth it. Here, he is guiding his partner toward an important goal. However, it may take longer than he wants for this to succeed.

● *At his best,* he may help others to advance themselves or their relationships. *At his worst,* he may have an ulterior motive in manipulating people for reasons they do not know, and he could eventually be discovered and suffer some harm for it even when he gains that which he desires.

▲ *As a public person,* he may experience a delay in an alliance. *As a businessperson,* he may have a merger or acquisition delayed or in doubt. *As an ordinary person,* he may suffer a delay in a project that he is trying to accomplish.

54.5   *Yin 6 changing line derives from Hexagram 58 Sharing Himself*

He is truly sharing himself in his marriage.
This brings out the best in him and makes him especially desirable.

■ Outward appearances can be important, but the things that really win sincere admiration and alliance come from within. Here, he is truly sharing himself, and his sincerity deepens the bonds in the marriage.

● *At his best,* he may develop especially close emotional ties with others. *At his worst,* he may hide some important secrets from others, and this will inhibit those relationships from blossoming as they should.

▲ *As a public person,* he may gain a loyal following through his personality and character. *As a businessperson,* he may obtain a reputation for success and even outshine "experts." *As an ordinary person,* he may enjoy local fame, especially through contests or media events, or he may develop especially close ties with his mate or friends.

54.6   *Yin 6 changing line derives from Hexagram 38 Looking for a Leader*

Both he and his mate are looking for ties to others. Without a real
commitment to each other, a successful marriage is not possible.

■ Marriage partners need to act in accord with each other. They need to care about each other. They need to understand each other. Here both are looking somewhere else, rather than to each other, so the partnership could be faltering. Whatever they do should strengthen the relationship rather than weaken it.

● *At his best,* he may realize that his marriage is now in a period where both he and his mate are looking outside of it to meet their needs, but it can be saved if they both wish it. *At his worst,* he may not understand why he and his partner are alienated, and he may not even care about the marriage; therefore, its collapse is inevitable.

▲ *As a public person,* he may have a role that is a pretense. *As a businessperson,* he may be looking for a way out of his business situation. *As an ordinary person,* he may be in a suffering marriage or partnership.

54.A1.1.   *All lines changing derives from Hexagram 53 Sharing Commitment*

A marriage by itself does not automatically bring great benefits. It is necessary to have shared commitments for a successful result.

■ A marriage is only the start of a process of struggle and effort to make life satisfying for both partners. For many marriages, it also means the start of a family and ties to other individuals. Great benefits can come from a marriage, but these need to be built, step-by-step, through shared commitments.

● *At his best,* he may be firmly committed to the marriage so he is able to put his heart and soul into building it. *At his worst,* he may not care as deeply as he could. Although the marriage does progress to some extent, its results disappoint him, and yet he is largely responsible.

▲ *As a public person,* he may devote himself to a long-term program. *As a businessperson,* he may strive to break down barriers between the partners, or enhance operation of the business, so their enterprise will succeed. *As an ordinary person,* he may rededicate himself to his marriage or partnership.

55. Serving Greatness

| TRIGRAMS GB | LINES 101 100 | COMPLEMENTARY HEXAGRAM 59 THINGS ARE SWEPT CLEAR |

*He is serving greatness. A great leader or cause
can bring many blessings, and he should reap the
benefits of this now and put his worries aside.*

■ *The traditional title* for this hexagram is "Abundance," although this is somewhat misleading. Here the hexagram is titled "Serving Greatness." This signifies that serving a great unifier is a wonderful thing. A great leader or a great cause can have a widespread effect and bring many benefits to those involved. Such greatness, however, does not last forever; therefore, he should enjoy the benefits he can get now, because they, too, will not last forever. *The complementary hexagram* is Hexagram 59 Things Are Swept Clear, which illustrates that a great movement brings true changes, sweeping away old causes and leaders and setting the stage for new ones to emerge.

● *At his best,* he may be happy, productive, and well rewarded in the great cause he is serving. *At his worst,* he may be involved in a great cause but be burdened by doubts and fears.

▲ *As a public person,* he may be a major participant or spokesperson for a leader or cause. *As a businessperson,* he may have a supporting role involving operations. *As an ordinary person,* he may be an adherent, participant, or supporter to one degree or another in a great cause or for a great leader.

| 55.1 | *Yang 9 changing line derives from Hexagram 62 Independently Getting By* |

*He is independent when he meets the great leader,
yet he still finds it easy to benefit.*

■ When he first joins the great leader (or cause), he does not suffer because he is somewhat independent and only weakly allied. Rather, he finds it easy to gain benefits. He gets even more than he expected.

● *At his best,* he may recognize the bond he and his leader share, so he views it as an honor to offer his services, and his leader in turn sees the compliment. *At his worst,* he may take advantage of the situation and strive to get as much as he can, not realizing that his greed is being noted and will weigh against him later.

▲ *As a public person,* he may be publicly praised by a powerful leader. *As a businessperson,* he may develop a connection with an important businessman. *As an ordinary person,* he may profit by getting to know a new boss or someone who will become his mate.

55.2   *Yin 6 changing line derives from Hexagram 34 Forcing Matters*

He acts too forcefully, so now he needs to renew his allegiance
to the great leader in order to maintain his position.

■ When he acts too forcefully, he upsets things and raises doubts about his commitment or his competence. Thus, renewing his allegiance to the great leader (or cause) is important for maintaining his position.

● *At his best,* he may apply himself for the benefit of his leader, even to the extent of doing difficult and unpopular things that may get him into trouble. *At his worst,* he may abuse the authority and position he has for his own benefit.

▲ *As a public person,* he may be under a cloud of suspicion, even if he is doing the right thing. *As a businessperson,* he may not be able to advance his causes until he assuages the doubts of his leaders or partners. *As an ordinary person,* he may find life difficult due to the suspicions of his boss or mate until he is able to reassure them.

55.3   *Yang 9 changing line derives from Hexagram 51 At Fortune's Mercy*

Although he suffers some harm from outrageous fortune,
his place with the great leader is secure.

■ Even serving a great leader does not exempt him from the effects of outrageous fortune. Here, he suffers one such effect, yet even though he must experience some harm, he can rest assured that his place with the great leader (or cause) is secure.

● *At his best,* he may accept the blows of fate, but he will appreciate what he has which is secure. *At his worst,* he may exacerbate his losses and harm, not quite realizing that his leader cannot help him.

▲ *As a public person,* he may, as one of a number of subordinates, act beyond his means and suffer as a result. *As a businessperson,* he may strive to implement progressive plans but not have the leadership's backing to do so. *As an ordinary person,* he may feel jealousy for his mate, be envious of others at work, or be injured through foolish actions.

55.4   *Yang 9 changing line derives from Hexagram 36 Serving as an Assistant*

He is closely assisting the great leader, so what he does
can be readily seen. This could easily benefit him.

■ He is working very closely with the great leader (or cause), serving as an assistant. Such intimate access to a power center is very desirable and can bring him good fortune.

● *At his best,* he may be pleased to be close to his leader regardless of his role or reward, and for this he is doubly rewarded. *At his worst,* he may use closeness as a tool to increase his power or wealth, but doing this invites the suspicion and envy of others who do not view him as a friend.

▲ *As a public person,* he may work directly with a great leader as his secretary or assistant. *As a businessperson,* he may be responsible for putting a superior's ideas into action. *As an ordinary person,* he may be intimate with his boss, or closely watched by his mate.

55.5   *Yin 6 changing line derives from Hexagram 49 Being Revolutionary*

His abilities and his revolutionary ideas earn him praise
and promotion. He is no longer just an assistant;
he now gains some greatness himself.

■ Here, he gains great honor. His inherent worth comes to the fore with his abilities and revolutionary ideas being recognized. He is promoted so he is no longer just an assistant to the great leader (or cause), but now he has gained a position of his own with some real power.

● *At his best,* he may become a powerful and effective leader in his own right. *At his worst,* he may be promoted, yet he may harbor jealousy or feel that he has not been rewarded sufficiently.

▲ *As a public person,* he may be promoted to a high position or earn a prestigious award. *As a businessperson,* he may be awarded or become famous for his accomplishments or writings. *As an ordinary person,* he may obtain community recognition or the special blessings of his boss or mate.

55.6   *Yin 6 changing line derives from Hexagram 30 Gaining Enlightenment*

He realizes that greatness is only an illusion. Eventually the truth
will be found out and he will lose status and wealth.

■ The truth is that he is flawed and makes mistakes. He cannot live up to the image of his greatness that has been perpetuated. Eventually these and other shortcomings will be revealed, and the illusion of his greatness will be shown. Then he will lose wealth and status. Also, all of this could apply to him indirectly through the great leader or cause having its own inadequacies and flaws revealed.

● *At his best,* he may realize that all great men have feet of clay, and he takes his loss of status in stride. *At his worst,* he may be deeply shocked and hurt by his reversal of fortune, and may not be able to cope with it well at all.

▲ *As a public person,* he may have been deceived by a superior and suffer some misfortune from it. *As a businessperson,* he may find his wealth and position are based on fraud or misrepresentation. *As an ordinary person,* he may suffer from misrepresentations by his boss, his mate, or his mate's family, and have to come to a new understanding in order to progress.

55.ALL   *All lines changing derives from Hexagram 59 Things Are Swept Clear*

When the truth about the great leader is at last revealed,
things are swept clear. A new beginning will be coming.

■ The greatness or beneficence of the leader (or cause) was overrated. Now it is revealed to be seriously flawed, and the truth will spread. When all deceits and illusions are swept clear, new beginnings are truly possible.

● *At his best,* he may open his head and heart to the truth, and this serves as a powerful stimulant for growth. *At his worst,* he may find it difficult to accept the truth, and difficult to reorganize his life in order to begin again.

▲ *As a public person,* he may be acquitted or exonerated of charges against him. *As a businessperson,* he may have come through a bankruptcy. *As an ordinary person,* he may get to the bottom of secrets, and from this make new beginnings.

56. Wandering

TRIGRAMS DG   LINES 001 101   COMPLEMENTARY HEXAGRAM 60 HAVING LIMITED RESOURCES

He is wandering and so can only accomplish small things.

■ *The traditional title* for this hexagram is "The Wanderer." Here the hexagram is titled "Wandering." This hexagram shows someone who wanders, hoping to better himself by finding a place that promises enough benefits for him to stay. In the absence of finding something positive, it is best for him to continue wandering. A time of wandering is also a time of little productive accomplishment, although personal growth can, of course, occur. *The complementary hexagram* is Hexagram 60 Having Limited Resources, which illustrates that meager resources are both the cause of and the requirement for wandering.

● *At his best,* his character may be benefiting from his wandering. *At his worst,* he may find that meager rewards and little personal growth come from wandering.

▲ *As a public person,* he may be publicly involved with travel. *As a businessperson,* he may be a travel agent, he may be searching for a business enterprise, or he may be trying to find his career. *As an ordinary person,* he may need to find a new career, business, or home, or he may need to take a trip.

56.1	*Yin 6 changing line derives from Hexagram 30 Gaining Enlightenment*

He is wandering and in need of knowledge.
Since he doesn't have the knowledge he needs, slight harm comes.

■ He could be wandering or searching for knowledge, or he could need knowledge to assist him in his wandering. Whichever it is, he doesn't have the knowledge he needs, and this void brings him some slight harm.

● *At his best,* he may be lacking in knowledge, but be strong in his desire to learn and able to learn quickly, so his harm is minimal. *At his worst,* he may not understand how critical his weakness is, so he will suffer more seriously from his ignorance.

▲ *As a public person,* he may have responsibilities but insufficient knowledge to do the job. *As a businessperson,* he may lack assistants with ability, and so his business suffers. *As an ordinary person,* his lack of certain necessary skills may hamper him and deny him success.

56.2   *Yin 6 changing line derives from Hexagram 50 Governing Matters*

In his wanderings, he has reached a refuge where he can control matters, preserve his possessions, and even gain a loyal helper.

■ He reaches a safe place in his wandering. He can now rest and do repairs, and he can benefit for himself. He is even able to find someone who will be loyal and helpful to him. This could be a very beneficial and productive time for him.

● *At his best,* he may blossom, given the right circumstances. *At his worst,* he may luck into a situation where others overvalue him and make his life easy.

▲ *As a public person,* he may obtain a secure position with a loyal following. *As a businessperson,* he may put himself into an especially safe business in which he has an active role. *As an ordinary person,* he may obtain a home, rebuild his fortunes, enter into a close and loyal relationship, or get married.

56.3   *Yang 9 changing line derives from Hexagram 35 Advancing Due to Favor*

Without the support of someone strong, he cannot maintain his situation. Since he is vulnerable, he now resumes wandering.

■ He had been dependent on someone else for support, but then he loses that support. Now he cannot safely remain in his situation, so he must move on and seek something better.

● *At his best,* he may have lost a good friend, and he resigns himself to a new and different start in his life. *At his worst,* he may resent the turn in his fortunes, and his anger and hurt make it harder for him to adapt to his changed circumstances.

▲ *As a public person,* he may lose his position and his staff. *As a businessperson,* he may lose much of his investment as well as his closest advisor. *As an ordinary person,* he may lose his home, a close friend, or his mate.

56.4   *Yang 9 changing line derives from Hexagram 52 Holding Back*

Although he has gained a place with some security, he still holds himself back, neither fully trusting it nor being truly content.

■ His wandering has ended, but he remains suspicious and doubtful. He holds himself back, waiting to see how matters will work out.

● *At his best,* he may understand that the benefits he now enjoys may be temporary, and so he allows himself to rest and renew himself without becoming dependent on future expectations. *At his worst,* he may feel he is being deceived by the promises made, so the reality he experiences is deeply disturbing even though he gets some benefit.

▲ *As a public person,* he may be promoted to a figurehead position. *As a businessperson,* he may have sold his enterprise and remain on in a powerless advisory position. *As an ordinary person,* he may get a new job, gain profits and status, or establish a new marital relationship; however, he will not be content because he feels weak or not fully appreciated.

56.5   *Yin 6 changing line derives from Hexagram 33 Complying*

> He tries repeatedly to succeed, but not until he complies with the demands of the situation will he gain rewards.

■ There are two important elements to this. First, he does not give up. He keeps on trying until eventually he succeeds. Second, he does not force his will on an unbending reality. Rather, success comes only when he succeeds in understanding the nature of the situation around him, and by working with this reality, he is finally able to succeed. Success brings him rewards and a desirable position.

● *At his best,* he may know how to force himself to overcome difficult obstacles through persistence and wisdom in understanding his situation. *At his worst,* he may be persistent, but also lucky, so that he succeeds as much by chance as by his own merit.

▲ *As a public person,* he may reveal the wrongdoings or incompetence of a high official and be rewarded. *As a businessperson,* he may eventually start a new business, or he may show he deserves a promotion. *As an ordinary person,* he may attempt a goal now beyond his reach at work, in the community, or in his personal life, and succeed by skill as well as by hard work.

56.6   *Yang 9 changing line derives from Hexagram 62 Independently Getting By*

> He loses his position and valuables through his independence, so he grieves.

■ He suffers losses, and he grieves for them. However, he caused this loss himself by his decreasing commitment in his situation, or through becoming independent from it in some way. In doing this, eventually he could not protect or keep what he had.

● *At his best,* he may realize that this is just another phase for him, and he can accept the easy times as well as the hard. *At his worst,* he may fervently mourn the loss of the wealth and status he had.

▲ *As a public person,* he may find unexpected prominence causes his earlier position to be lost. *As a businessperson,* he may lose investments or business activities through negligence or arrogance. *As an ordinary person,* he may lose his home through fire, lose valuables through carelessness, or lose a job through arrogance or insensitivity.

56.ALL   *All lines changing derives from Hexagram 60 Having Limited Resources*

> Having little wealth and no position,
> he truly has limited resources.

■ Those who have limited resources need to conserve and protect what they have. Those who have little would suffer if any of their resources were taken from them.

● *At his best,* he may have much courage because he realizes that courage is the best defense against adversity. *At his worst,* he may be cravenly fearful, and he feels any loss as though it were a loss of his own blood.

▲ *As a public person,* he may be a civil servant retired on a small pension. *As a businessperson,* he may be a struggling inventor. *As an ordinary person,* he may live on a meager budget, have few friends, or be in poor health.

57. At His Leader's Mercy

TRIGRAMS FF	LINES 011 011	COMPLEMENTARY HEXAGRAM 51 AT FORTUNE'S MERCY

DOUBLED TRIGRAMS MEANING: *SUN,* TRIGRAM F, SIGNIFIES SUBMISSION, COMMITMENT, AND JOINING HIMSELF TO STRENGTH.   *(SEE PAGE 46 FOR MORE ABOUT THIS TRIGRAM.)*

He is at his leader's mercy; however,
he is not harmed and may even gain small benefits.

■ *The traditional titles* for this hexagram are "The Gentle," "The Penetrating," and "The Wind," although these are misleading. Whincup uses "Kneeling in Submission." Here the hexagram is titled "At His Leader's Mercy." It signifies that being at his leader's mercy shows both his commitment to his leader and his vulnerability and weakness. He joins himself with someone stronger for protection and guidance, and sincerely accepts their control, trusting in them to honor his service to them. *The complementary hexagram* is Hexagram 51 Being at Fortune's Mercy, which illustrates a situation where he has no one to intervene to protect him.

● *At his best,* he may be satisfied with the leader he has chosen and may be comfortable and safe in his situation. *At his worst,* he may be in an inadequate or capricious situation, and consequently unhappy with his choice but not able to get out of it.

▲ *As a public person,* he may be in service to a leader and be in the public eye for a moment. *As a businessperson,* he may be deeply dependent upon his superior or his company. *As an ordinary person,* he may have a mate who is stronger than he is or a friend who is dominating.

57.1	*Yin 6 changing line derives from Hexagram 9 Restraining Himself*

He always follows his leader to be safe,
and he is thus easily restrained.

■ He is so easily restrained that his leader only has to tell him what to do, and he does it without thinking twice. He always follows his leader, primarily to assure his safety.

● *At his best,* he may realize the nature of his weakness, so he seeks out a leader who complements it. *At his worst,* he may submit to a leader inappropriately or with intentions at odds with what he should do.

▲ *As a public person,* he may be low on an appointment list in an organization. *As a businessperson,* he may be a minor hireling in the enterprise. *As an ordinary person,* he may be an "ordinary person" without any distinguishing aspects, so he always does the conventional thing.

57.2 *Yang 9 changing line derives from Hexagram 53 Sharing Commitment*

> He establishes a sincere commitment with his leader,
> so serving his leader brings him benefits.

■ By making a true and meaningful commitment to his leader's service, he now gains a position as well as other benefits.

● *At his best,* he may learn his role and perform it well, and be suitably rewarded for it. *At his worst,* he may progress on an expected path of advancement without any special effort on his part or without any special rewards.

▲ *As a public person,* he may be appointed to a highly visible position based on his beliefs. *As a businessperson,* he may advance to a decision-making position. *As an ordinary person,* he may become a confidant of his boss, respected and admired by his peers, or loved by his desired mate.

57.3 *Yang 9 changing line derives from Hexagram 59 Things Are Swept Clear*

> His faults and mistakes are revealed, so things are swept clear.
> Being disgraced, he may suffer some harm. To counteract
> these problems, he must fully submit to his leader now.

■ Things he did not want revealed have been revealed. When he is forced to admit his failures, his disgrace is visible. He cannot escape some misfortune, so a meaningful submission to his leader is now essential.

● *At his best,* he may be punished for attempting certain things that are beyond the scope of his position, but this may be mitigated by his sincere repentance. *At his worst,* he may be terribly disgraced and punished for his faults, and may find his pride now stands in the way of getting help.

▲ *As a public person,* he may be publicly demoted, reprimanded, or penalized. *As a businessperson,* he may be demoted, fined, or suffer a large loss. *As an ordinary person,* he may suffer disgrace in dealings with those at work, at home, or in his community.

57.4 *Yin 6 changing line derives from Hexagram 44 Maintaining His Independence*

He has some success in maintaining his independence
because he gains some benefits, so now his concerns fade.

■ His situation improves, and he gets over his difficulties. He is now able to resist humiliating submission to his leader and may even gain some benefits by not doing so.

● *At his best,* he may apply his abilities and resources wisely and gain in power and status. *At his worst,* he may become so successful that he now stands out too much from others, thus making him more vulnerable.

▲ *As a public person,* he may gain in status and position. *As a businessperson,* he may learn how to deal with adversity and to profit in a variety of situations. *As an ordinary person,* he may first become reconciled to his situation and then find he can rise above it.

57.5 *Yang 9 changing line derives from Hexagram 18 Nursing an Illness*

He nurses his situation, and as matters improve, he is able to gain
more benefits. New endeavors may even be attempted and end well.

■ This line indicates a number of good things in this position. Simply continuing will bring him good fortune; however, he may also benefit by beginning new ventures. He also finds benefits come through his position serving his leader or cause. Things work out well at the end because he is making the effort to nurse them to success, and he has multiple ways of doing so.

● *At his best,* he may have learned how to truly succeed in his situation and he profits greatly. *At his worst,* he may work on improving his situation, and it does improve to some extent, even though it may not be as much as he would wish.

▲ *As a public person,* he may very successfully execute his leader's policies and maintain his position. *As a businessperson,* he may make profits and maintain his position under a great leader. *As an ordinary person,* he may find matters going well in many ways, and can easily smooth problems over with bosses or his mate.

57.6 *Yang 9 changing line derives from Hexagram 48 Being Renewed*

He is threatened and may even suffer harm; therefore, he renews
his loyalty to his leader. Freedom for him now is not possible.

■ By reaffirming his submission, he is foregoing the chance to gain his freedom. He does this, however, because he realizes his vulnerability, and he needs to reaffirm his ties and loyalties for his safety.

● *At his best,* he may sincerely renew his pledges. *At his worst,* he may feel forced by circumstance to pledge what is not truly in his heart.

▲ *As a public person,* he may be demoted or dismissed and lose his leader's favor. *As a businessperson,* he may lose much wealth despite entreaties to those who might assist him. *As an ordinary person,* he may throw himself on the mercy of his boss, community leader, or spouse.

57.ALL   *All lines changing derives from Hexagram 51 At Fortune's Mercy*

> In the end, he must admit that he is at fortune's mercy.
> Nothing he or his leader can do can prevent
> outrageous fortune from affecting him.

■ He originally sought to overcome his weakness and protect himself by submitting to a leader. Now, however, he realizes the ultimate futility of that. He is going to be vulnerable in life regardless of whatever he does. Perhaps his leader can help him in some ways, but outrageous fortune will always be able to affect him.

● *At his best,* he may come to accept the limitations to his options in life without feeling hopeless or unhappy. *At his worst,* he may recognize his fundamental powerlessness, and feel terribly vulnerable and unhappy with his life.

▲ *As a public person,* he may gain in stature from his equanimity in the face of trouble. *As a businessperson,* he may gain respect by mapping out a variety of contingencies to minimize loss, while knowing that complete safety is impossible. *As an ordinary person,* he may come to accept religion or other understandings to help him with the role of fortune and fate in his life.

58. Sharing Himself

TRIGRAMS HH	LINES 110 110	COMPLEMENTARY HEXAGRAM 52 HOLDING BACK

DOUBLED TRIGRAMS MEANING: *TUI*, TRIGRAM H, SIGNIFIES FREE EXPRESSION, HAPPINESS, AND COMMUNION.
(SEE PAGE 47 FOR MORE ABOUT THIS TRIGRAM.)

He is sharing himself with others, and this is beneficial for everyone.

■ *The traditional titles* for this hexagram are "Joyous" and "Lake," although these are somewhat misleading. The traditional text interprets this hexagram to mean pleasure. Whincup notes that another noted commentator interprets it to mean speak, and the Huangs say it can mean talking. Whincup also says it literally means straight, connecting, or exchange, so he titles this "Stand Straight." Here the hexagram is titled "Sharing Himself." It signifies that he joyfully and willingly shares himself, communicating and communing with others. Sharing like this is beneficial, and ultimately brings satisfaction to everyone involved. This is not always easily or safely done, so the upper lines show the dangers and difficulties with sharing. *The complementary hexagram* is Hexagram 52 Holding Back, which illustrates that sometimes it is best to hold oneself back and not share.

● *At his best,* he may be strong through his honesty and openness as he shares what is important to him with others. *At his worst,* he may be a compulsive talker and weaken himself through indiscriminate sharing of everything in his life.

▲ *As a public person,* he may attain renown as a communicator or psychologist. *As a businessperson,* he may be involved with communications, entertainment, or public relations. *As an ordinary person,* he may open himself to others important to him.

58.1	*Yang 9 changing line derives from Hexagram 47 Advancing by Hard Work*

At the beginning, sharing himself requires hard work,
but even then, it brings benefits.

■ This could apply two ways: It might take hard work to get him to want to share, or it might take hard work for him to actually share meaningfully. Sharing is so powerful, however, that even at the beginning it can produce benefits for him as well as for others.

● *At his best,* he may be worthy of his leader's confidence and trust. Through his sharing, he may benefit significantly. He will find it easy to begin an endeavor, and success will not be as difficult to obtain as he fears. *At his worst,* he may not pursue the opportunity that is given, and he may even feel resentful. He may be lazy, not have a sense of direction, or not know what to do. Thus, he does as little as possible, responding rather than fully contributing, and thus does not benefit as he might otherwise.

▲ *As a public person,* he may become someone's protégé. *As a businessperson,* he may establish a subsidiary or sideline for himself through the assistance of another. *As an ordinary person,* he may leave home, begin a new career, or begin an important intimate relationship.

58.2   *Yang 9 changing line derives from Hexagram 17 Hunting*

He is sought out by his leader to share himself, and he loyally agrees. After doing this, his doubts and regrets will pass, and he will benefit.

■ Although he could refuse to share, he has ties of loyalty that bind him to his leader. His leader now asks for his commitment and cooperation, so he places his trust in his leader and agrees to share. Later, he finds that following his leader's request does bring benefits to him, and his doubts and regrets fade.

● *At his best,* he may gain recognition or fame as well as profit through his contributions. He will always be respectful and thankful to his leader. *At his worst,* he may not attain much status or wealth, but he will be content in his leader's regard. He will gain some benefit through his association with his leader, perhaps by being his intermediary or representative. He might still wonder if he made the right decision, however.

▲ *As a public person,* he may be called upon to make a public demonstration of his support for a leader (or cause). *As a businessperson,* he may be asked to commit to his superiors' plan. *As an ordinary person,* he may be asked to do something he wouldn't otherwise do, but he agrees anyway, hoping for the best.

58.3   *Yin 6 changing line derives from Hexagram 43 Escaping Harm*

Sharing himself goes badly, so the benefits of doing it escape him. He could even experience some harm.

■ He seeks to share without paying attention to the requirements of the situation. He may not have the proper assistance of others, or he may do something ineptly or excessively, in a poor place, or at a bad time. He may try to rope someone else into his plans but find he is unable to do so. Whatever he sets out to do yields the wrong result, and he suffers unanticipated problems. Even fate could step in and turn what was a marginal situation into one wholly outside his control. Benefits he hoped for just don't come.

● *At his best,* he may be able to properly launch his ventures; however, he will encounter problems in sustaining them. He might put too much attention into one area, and not enough into where it is really needed. Unable to free himself of his difficulties, it seems whatever he does will make him unhappy. *At his worst,* he may not have the trust and cooperation of those he needs, and he may be easily harmed by others. He may be seen as fawning, manipulative, or simply undesirable. He might fail repeatedly. This could be a very unhappy period.

▲ *As a public person,* he may make a public confession. *As a businessperson,* he may have to seek outside assistance for his business. *As an ordinary person,* he may suffer ongoing problems from his failed attempts to gain in his relations with others, particularly with the opposite sex or his boss.

58.4   *Yang 9 changing line derives from Hexagram 60 Having Limited Resources*

He does not share himself because what he can offer is not needed.
He experiences neither benefit nor loss.

■ He is not needed. Perhaps what he offers isn't what was really wanted, or perhaps the need was already filled by someone else. No benefits come from this, but neither does any harm.

● *At his best,* his willingness to share is seen as something positive, and others will think better of him in the future. He might also be satisfied with what actually occurred even though he did not gain from it. *At his worst,* he may feel deprived of the chance to share. He may feel unappreciated and not be satisfied.

▲ *As a public person,* he may be relieved that he does not have to take action, but he will make the most of his willingness to share anyway. *As a businessperson,* he may find his business efforts do not get a positive response. *As an ordinary person,* he may have family or work problems resolved unexpectedly without gain or loss, or a health problem may quietly fade away.

58.5   *Yang 9 changing line derives from Hexagram 54 Entering a Marriage*

His trust in another is destroyed, and the close alliance
he wanted with him is no longer desirable.
Now he pulls back and relies only on himself.

■ He had a goal in mind with his sharing: he wanted a marriage or a partnership.

However, his trust in the other has been seriously harmed or destroyed, so such a close relationship is no longer possible. Now he pulls back into himself.

● *At his best,* he may be very honorable and be shocked to discover secretive or nefarious purposes in those with whom he associates. He will not be happy as long as he continues in this association, so he may resign his position or look elsewhere, withdraw his support, or even try to find some way of rectifying matters. *At his worst,* he may be a weak individual, and he will want more from others than they can give him. He could resent their failure to give him the help he thinks he needs. He will also be unhappy as long as he remains in this situation; however, he may not have the strength he needs to truly become independent on his own.

▲ *As a public person,* he may discover misrepresentations or corruption, and divorce himself from this to develop his own public image. *As a businessperson,* he may be deliberately given incorrect information that leads to losses, or he may be manipulated for a competitor's benefit. *As an ordinary person,* he may be very unhappy with people he trusted, so now he believes he shouldn't trust them at all.

58.6   *Yin 6 changing line derives from Hexagram 10 Taking Risky Action*

He is forced to take the risky action of honestly sharing himself
and speaking dangerous things.

■ Circumstances beyond his control have forced matters. Now his sharing is honest, but sudden and forced. This is a mixture of both favorable and unfortunate elements. The result will depend as much upon those around him and what they want as upon him.

● *At his best,* he may be a very capable and mature person. He will be able to be honest and profit from the sudden change in the situation. *At his worst,* he may be shown in a bad light, and not be able to undo the negative consequences of the situation. He may also be victimized as a result.

▲ *As a public person,* he may experience unexpected publicity, perhaps an exposé. *As a businessperson,* he may lose some business and compensate by starting another. *As an ordinary person,* he may suffer some losses and take a new direction, he may get divorced, or he may suffer from eye or throat problems.

58.ALL   *All lines changing derives from Hexagram 52 Holding Back*

He has learned that sharing himself and even the truth itself
are not without their dangers. Sometimes it is better to hold back,
to keep secrets, or even to stay hidden.

■ Being open and truthful can be wonderful at times. However, these can also be dangerous. Openness implies some vulnerability and thus the potential to be harmed. The truth is also something that in many times and places should not be said aloud. One of the important practical issues in life is how much to hide and from whom. To do these, he needs to learn how to hold himself back.

● *At his best,* he may understand that holding back leads to security as well as to pleasure when truths are judiciously concealed. *At his worst,* he may fear the pain of discovery and compulsively hide things that he fears, even when doing so harms himself.

▲ *As a public person,* he may maintain a public image and hide a radically different private life behind it. *As a businessperson,* he may hide assets, or he may be secretive about business plans. *As an ordinary person,* he may seek a life of quietness and disdain public displays.

59. Things Are Swept Clear

TRIGRAMS CF   LINES 010 011   COMPLEMENTARY HEXAGRAM 55 SERVING GREATNESS

Things are swept clear by a powerful force,
and this brings extensive change.

■ *The traditional titles* for this hexagram are "Dispersion" and "Dissolution," although these are somewhat misleading. Whincup notes the name of this hexagram translated literally is flood, swept apart, or dispersed, and he uses "The Flood" as the title. The Huangs use "Flowing." The title used here is "Things Are Swept Clear" to encapsulate these concepts. In the traditional text, the lines portray the action of a great flood that sweeps everything before it. Such a force causes some damage, but also brings some benefits as well. For example, it fertilizes the ground and allows new things to begin growing. Thus, significant new changes will be coming even though there may be initial difficulties as part of the process. The powerful force that drives these changes could be a great cause, a great leader, or the combination of both. *The complementary hexagram* is Hexagram 55 Serving Greatness, which illustrates that serving a great movement is to facilitate sweeping changes throughout his life.

● *At his best,* he may find everything around him changed; yet, surprisingly, he and his situation are not harmed. *At his worst,* he may be carried along by powerful forces that he does not agree with or understand, and he ends up confused and somewhat debilitated.

▲ *As a public person,* he may find his position and public persona altered by major changes and outside events. *As a businessperson,* he may find that business is radically changed by new market forces or new technologies, or a business takeover radically reshapes his company. *As an ordinary person,* he may find himself swept along by a popular movement either as a voluntary participant or as a subject of its action.

59.1   *Yin 6 changing line derives from Hexagram 61 Establishing Limited Allegiance*

When things are swept clear,
he can find an ally to help keep him from harm.

■ Having a clear arrangement with an ally or an associate means that he has access to their assistance in his time of need. With this assistance, he can easily weather the effects of the changes occurring.

● *At his best,* he may have an effective and reliable associate who can assist him. *At his worst,* he may call for assistance, but not get as much as he needs or when he needs it to wholly protect himself.

▲ *As a public person,* he may be rescued from a serious problem by an "informal ally." *As a businessperson,* he may benefit from the example or suggestions of a successful business ally. *As an ordinary person,* he may receive important help from family, friends, boss, or mate.

59.2   *Yang 9 changing line derives from Hexagram 20 Preparing Himself*

> When things are swept clear, he will find he has been
> properly prepared, so his concerns and fears will pass.

■ After radical changes occur, he discovers that his earlier preparations have benefited him. Instead of facing harm, as he perhaps feared, he discovers that he has potential opportunities for growth and benefits. He gains confidence by this turn of events, and this also benefits him.

● *At his best,* he may gain insight into what he should do with his skills, and he can see his potential for advancement. *At his worst,* he may become smugly secure in his situation, not realizing that he still needs to do his best and respond appropriately to changed circumstances.

▲ *As a public person,* he may find himself prominent in a business or public reorganization. *As a businessperson,* he may benefit from others' misfortunes or through his successful writings. *As an ordinary person,* he may escape from danger, become committed to a religion, or find a new home.

59.3   *Yin 6 changing line derives from Hexagram 57 At His Leader's Mercy*

> When things are swept clear, he finds himself at his
> leader's mercy. Although he may be frightened at first,
> he knows his leader will protect him.

■ When radical changes come, he fears for himself, yet he need not. He comes to realize his leader (or cause) will protect him. So, he will be safe in the end, despite the dangers that may still come.

● *At his best,* he may have taken foolish chances but not done anything fundamentally wrong, so he does not fear punishment. *At his worst,* he may have done serious wrong, but he realizes he can play on his leader's feelings to escape harm, except that even this has its price.

▲ *As a public person,* he may have transferred to another position because of some mistakes he made. *As a businessperson,* he may find himself being closely scrutinized now because he is under suspicion. *As an ordinary person,* he may experience a great crisis in his family or at work, and he relies on his mate or boss for guidance.

| **59.4** | *Yin 6 changing line derives from Hexagram 6 Having a Complaint* |

When things are swept clear, having specific complaints can bring him benefits.

■ There are two slightly different ways to view this: Either his complaint has led to his being swept into a hearing where his complaint will be judged fairly, or the onset of a period where things are swept clear causes his complaints, which he then presents to his leader for reparation. However, regardless of how his complaint arose, he is given a chance to tell his story or to explain his ideas. Now his contributions or his worth are recognized, and he can benefit.

● *At his best,* he may at last be able to contribute the changes he has longed to see, and he is pleased with being rewarded. *At his worst,* he may not have any concrete improvements to make, but he wins recompense for harm he has suffered.

▲ *As a public person,* he may receive recognition, perhaps a prize or a promotion for his ideas. *As a businessperson,* he may succeed in attracting supporters for a new enterprise. *As an ordinary person,* he may receive an unexpected increase in his status in the community, at work, or at home; or he benefits from a complaint or lawsuit.

| **59.5** | *Yang 9 changing line derives from Hexagram 4 Acting Impetuously* |

He impetuously joins a great leader or cause, and he greatly benefits.

■ Here his enthusiasm and impetuosity lead him to join a leader or cause, and he is swept along by the major changes it brings. He may even become the leader's assistant or a specially placed helper and, in this way, gain many benefits.

● *At his best,* he may be enthusiastic and willing to learn, so he benefits greatly in his role. *At his worst,* he may be deceitful and avaricious, trying to gain too much too quickly, so he may gain enemies, who for the moment cannot touch him.

▲ *As a public person,* he may have a temporary appointment at a high level, or work closely as an intern with a great leader. *As a businessperson,* he may be an intern from a school, learning about the workplace and the business world. *As an ordinary person,* he may be very youthful or immature in a relationship with a mate or in the workplace.

59.6 *Yang 9 changing line derives from Hexagram 29 Being Trapped*

After things are swept clear, he sees that he
is trapped in his situation. He does not suffer harm,
except perhaps for the loss of his illusions.

■ If he thought he was doing entirely the right thing serving his leader or cause, he finds out that he was wrong. There are things he does not agree with but cannot change. In fact, he now realizes he is in a trap. Continuing to serve does not mean that he is actually suffering harm, but having the truth revealed does hurt.

● *At his best,* he may realize there is more to life than meets the eye, and often there are burdens that must be graciously accepted, so he does not fear for himself. *At his worst,* he may resent being trapped, and this poisons his attitude.

▲ *As a public person,* he may have his actions questioned by his boss when he thought there was no doubt he was doing the right thing. *As a businessperson,* he may have his business forcibly restructured against his desires. *As an ordinary person,* he may have some difficulties revealed, such as marital problems, lawsuits, or career problems.

59.ALL *All lines changing derives from Hexagram 55 Serving Greatness*

Sweeping everything clear allows him to reaffirm his commitments
to a great leader or cause. Doing this gives him a new beginning,
and he can gain greatly from this.

■ The act of sweeping everything clear reveals all secrets, exposes all corruption, and highlights the values that are so worth having and propagating. A new beginning is always inherently good, and a new beginning is, at times, always required. Here, a new beginning allows him to rebuild his relationship with his leader and reaffirm his commitment to his cause.

● *At his best,* he may welcome truth and the chance to rethink his life's choices. *At his worst,* he may not respect the truth for what it is, but rather he uses it for his own advantage, twisting it for his own purposes if need be.

▲ *As a public person,* he may welcome participation in a therapeutic retreat. *As a businessperson,* he may go through an audit. *As an ordinary person,* he may undergo therapy with a mate to repair and reaffirm their marital ties.

60. Having Limited Resources

TRIGRAMS HC	LINES 110 010	COMPLEMENTARY HEXAGRAM 56 WANDERING

*He has limited resources. If used wisely, he may have enough
to get by. However, if he doesn't use them wisely,
he will need to take corrective action.*

■ *The traditional title* for this hexagram is "Limitation." The Huangs use "Frugality" and Whincup uses "Restraint." Here the hexagram is titled "Having Limited Resources." It signifies that while having resources is essential for a productive and happy life, now he does not have an abundance of resources. Some limitation is good because it requires him to set priorities, define a clear course of action, and husband resources for their efficient use. *The complementary hexagram* is Hexagram 56 Wandering, which illustrates that when his resources are too meager, he will need to look for more elsewhere.

● *At his best,* although he may have limited resources, they will be sufficient for his needs if he is wise in using them. *At his worst,* he may suffer from insufficient resources, or he may have sufficient resources but use them wastefully.

▲ *As a public person,* he may make appeals for the poor or the disadvantaged. *As a businessperson,* he may struggle with insufficient capital, human resources, or raw materials. *As an ordinary person,* he may live on a tight budget or have few resources for his needs.

60.1 *Yang 9 changing line derives from Hexagram 29 Being Trapped*

His limited resources keep him from getting into trouble.

■ When he has few resources, he should be wary about how he uses them, since he cannot afford to waste them. Here, he doesn't even have enough to waste by beginning something that might not work out. Such severe limitations are not pleasant, but they can be tolerated.

● *At his best,* he may utilize his resources to the best extent possible to meet his needs; however, he does not have enough to begin something new. *At his worst,* he may be unable to do what he hopes to, and he becomes very disturbed, which only makes matters worse.

▲ *As a public person,* he may be halted from doing what he said he would do by lack of resources. *As a businessperson,* he may decide to wait and see, because there are currently no good opportunities. *As an ordinary person,* he may be confused as to what to do, and thus not do anything except survive.

60.2   *Yang 9 changing line derives from Hexagram 3 Gathering Support*

He tries to gather support, but does not succeed in gaining much.
His resources are so limited that they cannot
keep him from some harm.

■ Resources from other people can take the form of physical assets or the form of their active support. Here, he has gone to people to gather what support he can, but he finds he does not gain as much as he needs. His resources are thus too limited to keep him from some harm.

● *At his best,* he may be too ambitious in his goals of gaining support from others; however, he is somewhat successful, so he knows he is progressing and will do better in the future. *At his worst,* he may be angry and upset by his failure to gain the supporters he was counting on.

▲ *As a public person,* he may feel weighed down by constraints and be unsuccessful in overturning them; thus, he cannot protect himself. *As a businessperson,* he may not be able to gain support for his plans. *As an ordinary person,* he may take some steps toward a desired goal, but his doubts or suspicions hinder him and he alienates others; therefore, he doesn't succeed as he needed to.

60.3   *Yin 6 changing line derives from Hexagram 5 Acting Prematurely*

He has initiated action too soon, so he cannot
bring all of his resources to bear as he needs.
Although this is troublesome, no real harm results.

■ Acting too early can cause problems. Here, he acts before he has properly marshaled his resources, so he finds that his effective actions are limited. It does not matter how much he has on paper if he needs it right now and cannot access it. He might not lose much in this situation, but neither can he gain much.

● *At his best,* he may have been forced by matters of timing to act prematurely, even though he knew there would be problems if he did. *At his worst,* he may be too immature or unwise to time his actions well, and he may not learn from this experience either.

▲ *As a public person,* he may launch a campaign at the wrong time. *As a businessperson,* he may not follow proper procedures and thus suffer some unpleasantness. *As an ordinary person,* he may not have a boss or parent to supervise him when supervision is needed, or he may lack self-control and easily get into trouble.

60.4   *Yin 6 changing line derives from Hexagram 58 Sharing Himself*

> He pools his resources with those of others,
> so all together they have enough to succeed.

■ Pooling of resources to achieve goals has been an essential requirement of human progress from the very beginning. That he can do this is very good, because it means he has a greater chance to succeed. In this way, he is imposing some limits on himself, but he gains greatly in other ways.

● *At his best,* he may be able to work with others cooperatively toward a common goal. *At his worst,* he may be persuaded by someone else to share in a cooperative project, even though there are doubts that he will truly benefit.

▲ *As a public person,* he may be known as someone who works well within a bureaucracy or organization. *As a businessperson,* he may obtain good profits working in a business cooperative. *As an ordinary person,* he may experience limitations and yet not feel burdened because he shares with others, or he may have a good reputation of being a community activist.

60.5   *Yang 9 changing line derives from Hexagram 19 Leading Others*

> His leadership has limited capabilities,
> yet he succeeds as far as it goes.

■ His capabilities for leading others are limited. This does not stop him from succeeding, although the degree of his success may also be limited.

● *At his best,* he may be judicious in his use and accumulation of power to accomplish limited goals. *At his worst,* he may be too judicious for fear of risking too much, and so reduces his chances of success.

▲ *As a public person,* he may have policies that he enforces with sensitivity and some discretion. *As a businessperson,* he may have limited dealings with others that are successful. *As an ordinary person,* he may desire a stronger role than he is able to pursue with those around him, and yet still succeeds to some degree.

60.6 *Yin 6 changing line derives from Hexagram 61 Having Limited Allegiance*

He is unwilling to fully commit himself to a goal.
Although this brings some trouble, his regrets will pass,
and his actions will protect what is important to him.

■ He is exercising cautious judgment here. He knows that it is foolish to risk everything on any single situation when there are ways of diversifying his risk. Here, he is limiting his risk, and his reserve protects him. He understands that he should protect some of his resources. This causes some trouble, but he can survive because this is the price he pays for his security.

● *At his best,* he may clearly understand his priorities, and he does not feel bad about how he apportions them. *At his worst,* he may be conflicted, confused, and attacked because he cannot deal well with competing claims for his commitments and his resources.

▲ *As a public person,* he may be publicly on probation or under restraint. *As a businessperson,* he may have suspicious and difficult dealings with associates. *As an ordinary person,* he may experience many demands for his service and support.

60.ALL *All lines changing derives from Hexagram 56 Wandering*

He wants a better life for himself,
so he wanders seeking better opportunities.
Because he has nothing to tie him down,
he can do this easily.

■ Wandering is a good way to search out a place in which to settle and build a life to better himself. However, wandering is only possible when he has few possessions and no strong commitments to tie him down. If he is at that point, wandering is easily accomplished and is a potentially productive step.

● *At his best,* he may search out a better place in the world, since he is strongly motivated to find it. *At his worst,* he may simply wander aimlessly around and not know what he is truly looking for.

▲ *As a public person,* he may go from cause to cause, or campaign to campaign, without being able to fully commit to one. *As a businessperson,* he may try his hand at one business or occupation after another. *As an ordinary person,* he may move around for a while, trying different localities and different occupations, until he finds a place to settle down.

61. Having Limited Allegiance

TRIGRAMS HF   LINES 110 011   COMPLEMENTARY HEXAGRAM 62 INDEPENDENTLY GETTING BY

He has limited allegiance with an ally.
Undertaking tasks with him is beneficial.

■ *The traditional title* for this hexagram is "Inner Truth." Whincup uses "Wholehearted Allegiance," and the Huangs use "Sincerity." All of these are somewhat misleading. Here it is titled "Having Limited Allegiance" because, as Whincup notes, the word that he translates as "wholehearted" was also used in ancient times to mean "middle." In the traditional text, it shows piglets and fish as religious offerings. These are halfway between the magnificent sheep and oxen given by the rich, and the flowers and baskets given by the poor. Likewise, limited allegiance lies midway between being strong, independent, and without allegiance to a leader, and being weak and wholly committed to a leader (and thus having his actions dictated by him). Limited allegiance can mean an explicit contractual agreement or an informal arrangement between him and someone else (usually referred to below as his ally). Limited allegiance could thus be beneficial for him in a variety of ways. *The complementary hexagram* is Hexagram 62 Independently Getting By, which illustrates that without commitments to others he would be independent and only just getting by, since great rewards require stronger connections and the assistance of others.

● *At his best,* he may have a beneficial arrangement with someone that is appropriate to his abilities and needs. *At his worst,* he may have an arrangement with someone that does not benefit him as much as he would like, or that demands more of him than he feels he ought to give.

▲ *As a public person,* he may publicly demonstrate loyalty or be an advocate for a cause or person. *As a businessperson,* he may have informal business alliances with supporters or competitors. *As an ordinary person,* he may have informal arrangements that benefit him.

61.1   *Yang 9 changing line derives from Hexagram 59 Things Are Swept Clear*

When things are swept clear,
he can rely on his ally to help him.

■ He knows he can rely on his ally for assistance when a time of trouble comes, so he is prepared.

● *At his best,* he may believe in his allies, so he works well with them in troublesome times. *At his worst,* he may not be sure how far he can rely on his allies, so his doubts limit his own effectiveness.

▲ *As a public person,* he may be concerned with complications from his personal life or conflicts of interest with his position. *As a businessperson,* he may worry about betrayal by his partners in a business deal, and turn to his closest friends for help. *As an ordinary person,* he may see problems coming and be glad that he has allies and friends to turn to; however, he may have some doubts about whether their help will be enough.

61.2   *Yang 9 changing line derives from Hexagram 42 Gaining Benefits*

A leader offers benefits to join with him,
so he and the leader come to an agreement.

■ Here, he is induced to offer his allegiance by the promise of money or some other reward. He believes the benefits he gets will make it all worthwhile. Such purchased allegiance by its very nature is limited.

● *At his best,* he may see good gains for him materially as well as in nontangible ways. *At his worst,* he may simply be persuaded by promises of wealth that might not come to pass.

▲ *As a public person,* he may be given a more important position if he joins a cause or a leader. *As a businessperson,* he may be given offers to sell or merge his business with another. *As an ordinary person,* he may benefit by an alliance with a respected friend, older family member, his mate's family, or his mate.

61.3   *Yin 6 changing line derives from Hexagram 9 Restraining Himself*

He is so weak that he is more a captive than an ally,
but he does have some choices. He might resist; he might
do nothing but bemoan his fate; he might fawn over his leader;
or he might give in and go along as best as he can.
None of these is beneficial, but he can choose what he will do.

■ Here his options are spelled out very clearly. None of these is pleasant, but he can choose. Giving in and going along at least might make his life easier, but what is the real cost to him of doing this? Toadying is to completely lose his self-respect by currying favor from his new boss, but could he ever really be trusted or respected after this? Bemoaning his fate is to make himself whinny and hopelessly useless, and afterward he becomes an object of scorn and ridicule. Trying to resist only flaunts his pride and foolishness, and could ultimately break him, too. These are his options.

● *At his best,* he may understand the trap he is in, and carefully choose the solution that appears best to him. *At his worst,* he may make a choice swayed by intense emotion and without regard to the consequences.

▲ *As a public person,* he may be forced by a superior to choose sides. *As a businessperson,* he may find his business taken over and himself turned into a puppet. *As an ordinary person,* he may be forced to choose between unpleasant alternatives because someone stronger than he is can harm him with impunity.

61.4   *Yin 6 changing line derives from Hexagram 10 Taking Risky Action*

> He takes the risky action of running away from his ally,
> but later he returns. In the end, he comes to no harm.

■ The two images given in the traditional text in this line are a horse running away and the moon coming full. In time, the horse will get hungry and return. Over time, the moon wanes, then waxes again. His ally understands this cyclic pattern of events, and so he is not harmed upon his return because it was expected. What could have been fraught with danger ended all right for him.

● *At his best,* he may have learned much from his time on his own, and he comes back wiser and more thankful for what he has. *At his worst,* he may come back feeling defeated and willing to be slavishly obedient in order to recoup the security he had before.

▲ *As a public person,* he may temporarily leave his position to try something new. *As a businessperson,* he may resign to start his own business, but then come back after it fails. *As an ordinary person,* he may run away from family or a mate, but find he is better off if he returns.

61.5   *Yang 9 changing line derives from Hexagram 41 Declining Influence*

> He is truly committed to his ally, and so now doesn't
> have as much influence with him as before.
> Despite this, he can still reap some benefits.

■ He sees the value of his ally's leadership, so now he honestly offers his commitment and becomes more of a subordinate than an ally. By doing this, he loses much of his independence, as well as his leverage. His decline in influence does not bother him, however, since he still gets some benefits.

● *At his best,* he may have come to truly honor his leader, so his service is also a gift to him, and his leader also returns an appropriate regard for him. *At his worst,* he may not be truly appreciated, but he still believes that giving his service is what he should do.

▲ *As a public person,* he may be assigned a highly trusted but powerless position close to a leader. *As a businessperson,* he may become a figurehead or spokesperson for a firm or product. *As an ordinary person,* he may establish stronger ties to someone, such as a mate or boss, or join a cause.

61.6 *Yang 9 changing line derives from Hexagram 60 Having Limited Resources*

He would like to surpass his ally, but because he has limited resources, he cannot. Trying to do this would bring trouble.

■ Now he wants to go beyond his ally and become great himself. To do this, however, requires significant resources, which he does not have. Note that these resources could include personal qualities as well as skills and material assets. Without these, he is not capable and would suffer serious problems.

● *At his best,* he may realize the impossibility of his ambition, so he keeps himself out of trouble. *At his worst,* he may lose his head and try to achieve his ambitions, and he will suffer as long as he tries.

▲ *As a public person,* he may try for an elective office, or he may have to content himself with a subsidiary role in the organization. *As a businessperson,* he may have to back down on a promotional campaign or business venture he was developing. *As an ordinary person,* he may find himself losing a silent "status struggle" with his mate, partner, or boss.

61.ALL *All lines changing derives from Hexagram 62 Independently Getting By*

He accepts that he cannot surpass his ally;
he can only establish his own independence and manage to get by.

■ His limitations conflict with his own desires, and the only compromise that works is for him to establish his own independence. He may not have as much or be able to do as much without the assistance of others, but he will have his independence, and this is important enough for him.

● *At his best,* he may understand himself well, and happily accept his role in life. *At his worst,* he may have had dreams of glory that were hard to give up, and so he views his situation as one of defeat, which deeply disturbs him.

▲ *As a public person,* he may retire from a high-pressure, high-profile position in the public eye. *As a businessperson,* he may switch his career to one more pleasing to him. *As an ordinary person,* he may change his life to make it more personally satisfying, less demanding, and more healthful for him.

62. Independently Getting By

TRIGRAMS DB   LINES 001 100   COMPLEMENTARY HEXAGRAM 61 HAVING LIMITED ALLEGIANCE

He is independently getting by, and can accomplish small tasks when he keeps within his abilities.

■ *The traditional title* of this hexagram is "Preponderance of the Small," although this is somewhat misleading. The Huangs use "Small Excess," and Whincup uses "Small Gets By." The title used here is "Independently Getting By." This signifies that he is weak but independent, and yet he can still prosper to some extent if he follows the right course of action. What is essential is his understanding of his abilities and limitations, and selecting goals and taking actions that are appropriate to them. In such situations, small profits or limited gains are all that can be reasonably expected, and gaining some benefit is better than gaining none. Note there is an unstated assumption that great endeavors require the cooperation or assistance of other individuals to be achieved. Being independent in this manner also means that great rewards are not attainable, although some people prefer independence to material benefits. *The complementary hexagram* is Hexagram 61 Having Limited Allegiance, which illustrates that additional benefits, including greater security, can be obtained by having limited allegiance with someone with more resources than he has.

● *At his best,* he may understand himself and his situation so well that his independent life still brings him benefits. *At his worst,* he may not be able to gain as much as he would like due to not properly linking his actions with his resources.

▲ *As a public person,* he may not be powerful, yet he still maintains an independent position in the public eye. *As a businessperson,* he may lack connections or resources considered important for success. *As an ordinary person,* he may have physical or learning disabilities, or lack education or a high position in his community, or he may choose to live by himself, yet he still prospers.

62.1   *Yin 6 changing line derives from Hexagram 55 Serving Greatness*

Although he might desire to attempt a great task, he knows that for him only small tasks can be accomplished quickly and easily.

■ Here the warning about knowing his limits is made explicit. If the task can be done quickly and easily, he will have success. However, if it is one that will take much time or effort, he will have great trouble.

● *At his best,* he may attend to small things that need to be done. *At his worst,* he may forget his fundamental weakness, become overly ambitious, and end up getting into serious trouble.

▲ *As a public person,* he may launch a program he isn't competent to manage, and then encounter problems. *As a businessperson,* he may successfully make minor adjustments to keep his business running. *As an ordinary person,* he may desire to progress but get into trouble by being too aggressive in taking risks.

62.2   *Yin 6 changing line derives from Hexagram 32 Committing Himself*

> He should find a go-between who has close connections
> to the leader he wishes to meet. This is proper
> when he has no connection at all with the leader.

■ When he wants to meet with a leader with whom he has no connections, he should seek out one of the leader's assistants to serve as a go-between. Showing the assistant he has something to offer the leader will gain him the access he needs.

● *At his best,* he may know how to contact a person behind the great leader. *At his worst,* he may not know how to get the contact he needs, so he could blunder and lessen his opportunity significantly.

▲ *As a public person,* he may have a prominent position and need to seek a quiet way to contact someone else. *As a businessperson,* he may obtain the assistance of experts or technically proficient advisors in preparing a business presentation. *As an ordinary person,* he may be helped by a family elder, his mate's friend, or an assistant to a boss at work.

62.3   *Yang 9 changing line derives from Hexagram 16 Standstill*

> He is at a standstill and even suffers some harm because of his
> independence. He may not have prepared himself properly,
> or he may have been attacked from behind.

■ He is vulnerable now because of his independence and his weakness. He likely made some errors of judgment to get to this place, either by not preparing himself, or by trusting someone he shouldn't have. Now he will pay the price of being too independent by suffering some harm.

● *At his best,* he may realize that he can do nothing now, so he prepares himself and patiently waits. *At his worst,* he may hurt from a feeling of helplessness or weakness as well as the harm he actually suffers.

▲ *As a public person,* he may have enemies unexpectedly attack him. *As a businessperson,* he may have to suddenly come up with cash, his market may be invaded by competitors, or his reputation may be defamed to discredit him. *As an ordinary person,* he may suffer betrayal by someone close, he may not have properly protected or insured his property and so suffers a loss, or he may suffer a serious illness.

62.4   *Yang 9 changing line derives from Hexagram 15 Acting With Propriety*

He deals properly with his situation and so avoids the danger around him. Thus, he manages to maintain his independence.

■ He is not able to overcome the difficulties around him with strength, so he tries to avoid them, minimize them, or prepare to deal with the consequences of potentially harmful things happening. His preparations and the way he responds to the problems that arise are sufficient to escape any serious harm. Thus, he is able to maintain his independence.

● *At his best,* he may understand his situation, and he acts accordingly to succeed. *At his worst,* he may lack full understanding, but he still acts properly to succeed to some extent.

▲ *As a public person,* he may have a number of pitfalls around him, which he will avoid. *As a businessperson,* he may have some success in solving critical, small problems. *As an ordinary person,* he may have many conflicts and problems around him, and he will do best by minimizing them.

62.5   *Yin 6 changing line derives from Hexagram 31 Ability to Change Matters*

He succeeds in changing matters, but because of his independence, he doesn't get all the benefits he wants, although he does get some.

■ He did what he thought necessary to succeed in changing things, but his judgment was at fault because he still did not fully benefit. He gets some rewards, but due to his independence (or weakness), he doesn't get as much as he wanted.

● *At his best,* he may rethink his expectations and resign himself to what is more realistic. *At his worst,* he may be deeply disappointed that his efforts didn't produce the results he expected.

▲ *As a public person,* he may find deceptions and delays are hidden behind agreements. *As a businessperson,* he may not profit much from a "sure fire" business plan. *As an ordinary person,* he may need to take care of fundamentals, such as health, education, or other training for reaching his goals, but it is likely he will still have to wait longer for significant benefits to come.

62.6   *Yin 6 changing line derives from Hexagram 56 Wandering*

He wanders from the proper course for someone who is
independent but weak. Perhaps he overreaches his abilities,
acts inappropriately in the situation, or even surrenders his
independence. He has no easy recourse, and he suffers some harm.

■ He has made serious errors. He may have forgotten his limitations, capabilities, or goals. Perhaps he attempted too much, did not obtain proper support, or lost sight of his original plan. Now he will suffer for his mistakes.

● *At his best,* he may be attracted too much by outside interests or lofty goals, so he does not pay enough attention to the essentials. *At his worst,* he may be arrogant and have too inflated an opinion of his abilities to be modest or attentive to the reality around him.

▲ *As a public person,* he may not have followed necessary guidelines and thus brings problems down on himself. *As a businessperson,* he may find that his marketing strategies or advertising campaigns fail. *As an ordinary person,* he may cause difficulties by losing his self-control or trying to gain too much, or he may even give up what he was trying to protect.

62.ALL   *All lines changing derives from Hexagram 61 Establishing Limited Allegiance*

He looks outside himself for safety, but does not want to give up
his independence entirely. Therefore, he seeks to establish
only a limited allegiance with an ally.

■ When he wants help from someone strong, that person may in turn want a real commitment from him. However, he is not willing to commit himself too much and give up his independence entirely, but he is willing to provide some limited degree of commitment. This may be agreeable to both parties, so a limited or contractual allegiance may be formed.

● *At his best,* he may find someone who could use his support but does not want too much from him. *At his worst,* he may be manipulated by his weakness into making a commitment that is more than he bargained for.

▲ *As a public person,* he may seek an alliance with someone for mutual gain. *As a businessperson,* he may seek a limited marketing arrangement with a middleman. *As an ordinary person,* he may seek an intimate companion but not a marriage.

63. Beginning a New Task

| TRIGRAMS GC | LINES 101 010 | COMPLEMENTARY HEXAGRAM 64 CONTINUING A TASK |

He has completed one task and now looks ahead to the next.
However, if he is weak, he should be careful. Even when new
beginnings appear favorable, trouble generally tends to come;
therefore, a reserve of strength or resources may be needed for success.

■ *The traditional title* for this hexagram is "After Completion." Whincup uses "Already Across," and the Huangs use "Fulfillment." The title used here is "Beginning a New Task." It signifies that he is now progressing on to his next endeavor. The warning about needing more resources is intended to assure that he keeps a measure of reserve strength available in the new endeavor. Unforeseen complications and problems are normal, so he needs to make allowance for them. The best time to avoid problems is at the very beginning, by picking the right goal. *The complementary hexagram* is Hexagram 64 Continuing a Task, which illustrates that after a task is well and truly begun, continuing it will be needed to see it through to completion.

● *At his best,* he may know what his next goal is and how he should reach it. *At his worst,* he may be somewhat uncertain in directing his attention and energies, and so may find that troubles come easily.

▲ *As a public person,* he may begin a new campaign. *As a businessperson,* he may launch a new product or enterprise. *As an ordinary person,* he may make a change in his life or begin working toward a new goal.

63.1 *Yang 9 changing line derives from Hexagram 39 Bumbling by Himself*

He bumbles at the very start of his task,
but no real harm comes to him even if it is a serious mistake.

■ Mistakes he makes at the beginning of a new task are more akin to hindrances. Similar mistakes made later could pose serious problems. Here, however, he can pick himself up, learn from his mistake, and try another approach—or even set a new goal.

● *At his best,* he may quickly learn from his mistakes. *At his worst,* he may simply be lucky to avoid harm.

▲ *As a public person,* he may not be able to attain his goal unless he gets assistance. *As a businessperson,* he may need to reorganize his business because it isn't working well. *As an ordinary person,* he may not seem to be able to get anything done easily, but neither will he be harmed by these problems.

63.2   *Yin 6 changing line derives from Hexagram 5 Acting Prematurely*

It is still early in the development of his task, so matters are not yet securely underway. However, he needn't worry because eventually they will be, and then he will be able to benefit.

■ In his new endeavor, he has taken some actions that either leave him open to harm or leave matters in an uncertain state. He will likely need to obtain the help of someone else to complete what he cannot do himself. He could feel vulnerable and worry about this; however, in time, matters will become more secure. After that happens, he will be able to benefit.

● *At his best,* he may prematurely count on the friendship of others to protect him, and eventually they come through. *At his worst,* he may expect too much, struggle, and worry until he manages to get the assistance he needs.

▲ *As a public person,* he may have spoken out too soon and find himself alone in his position for an uncomfortable period. *As a businessperson,* he may risk a business opportunity that he cannot yet manage successfully. *As an ordinary person,* he may have jeopardized the trust of his mate or family.

63.3   *Yang 9 changing line derives from Hexagram 3 Gathering Support*

He is seeking support, but everything will take more time to succeed, and not be as easy to accomplish as he wishes. So, if he is not strong and committed to his task, he should reconsider before starting it.

■ Here he needs to judge whether or not he should continue on this path. He is attempting to gather support to make achieving his task easier. However, gaining support will not be as easy as he thinks, and even if he does get it, succeeding in the task will not be as easy as he had hoped. If he has doubts about his abilities or his commitment, he should think very carefully. Inadequacies in these could easily mean failure.

● *At his best,* he may be very determined and thus able to succeed in his goal despite some questions. *At his worst,* he may be weak and filled with doubt, and so likely to fail.

▲ *As a public person,* he may need to gather supporters, which taxes his abilities. *As a businessperson,* he may strive to develop backers for his product or business plan. *As an ordinary person,* he may face obstacles that demand his best efforts to overcome; some will be overcome, while others will not.

63.4   *Yin 6 changing line derives from Hexagram 49 Being Revolutionary*

Being too revolutionary brings him difficulties. He suffers
no real harm, but memories of them are not easy to forget.

■ Being too revolutionary gives him a past that seems to haunt him. To erase these memories, he needs to first accept his responsibility, make amends if possible, and then forgive himself for problems he may have caused.

● *At his best,* he may be able to balance his ideals with the realities around him, and express who he is now to those around him. *At his worst,* he may be plagued by memories of the past and criticisms in the present, and he may be locked into negative psychological cycles that harm him.

▲ *As a public person,* he may be involved in discussions about his past as well as his current goals and ideals. *As a businessperson,* he may experience a decline in his reputation or minor losses caused by past actions. *As an ordinary person,* he may suffer personal attacks that he must work hard to overcome, or deal with deep doubts about his past choices.

63.5   *Yang 9 changing line derives from Hexagram 36 Serving as an Assistant*

His task progresses well when he subordinates himself to it.
Now his actions show his intent better than his words.

■ He can gain some real progress toward his goals when he makes achieving them his highest priority. He needs to fully keep his commitments when they advance his goals. He also cannot enhance his position by boasting or putting on a false front. His actions are real and significant, and this is how he proves himself to others as well as how he advances his goals.

● *At his best,* he may be committed to working step-by-step to achieve success, and everyone around him is confident in him because his actions have proven himself to them. *At his worst,* he may be committed to his goal, but somewhat uncertain in his abilities, and so he looks to others to help him succeed.

▲ *As a public person,* he may imaginatively follow procedures to help his organization succeed. *As a businessperson,* he may more profitably focus his attention on small endeavors rather than on large ones. *As an ordinary person,* he may find more success comes from modest, attainable goals rather than larger, more elaborate plans.

63.6   *Yin 6 changing line derives from Hexagram 37 Serving in a Household*

*Through successfully attaining his goals in the past,
he has gradually risen to leadership. Now those around him
wonder if he is the right leader for the current situation.*

■ The fruit of his success is attainment of status and leadership. However, even once obtained, these are not secure from doubt or challenge. Now others are questioning his ability or suitability. Is he out of date? Has he lost his abilities? Is he too committed to someone or something that is no longer appropriate? He needs to be able to answer such questions as well as deal honestly with whether continuing his leadership is best for everyone.

● *At his best,* he may have untouched depths that the current crisis will bring out and mature. *At his worst,* he may be attuned only to his own needs, or just not be able to deal with matters outside his experience.

▲ *As a public person,* he may overreach his abilities and experience, and thus damage his reputation. *As a businessperson,* he may overextend his business enterprise and face some losses extricating himself. *As an ordinary person,* he may have overcommitted himself to a cause or person and not know how to extricate himself without harm.

63.ALL   *All lines changing derives from Hexagram 64 Continuing a Task*

Ongoing success requires continually trying to advance matters.

■ Most things are not easily accomplished, and when they are easily done, they probably are not being done well. True success comes from working to make sure that the endeavor truly does succeed in all the ways that it should. Halfway solutions ultimately are not successes, and ongoing success requires keeping on.

● *At his best,* he may rise to the challenge of trying to bring about ongoing success. *At his worst,* he may hold things as they are, but of course, his endeavor will eventually fail even though matters appear successful now.

▲ *As a public person,* he may lead a progressive movement. *As a businessperson,* he may strive to lock in existing markets as well as develop new technologies. *As an ordinary person,* he may accept the need to gracefully lose the past and to look toward the future.

64. Continuing a Task

TRIGRAMS CG　　　LINES 010 101　　　COMPLEMENTARY HEXAGRAM 63 BEGINNING A NEW TASK

He is continuing a task, although if he is weak,
he may suffer some harm before he finishes.

■ *The traditional title* for this hexagram is "Before Completion." Whincup uses "Not Yet Across," and the Huangs use "Unfulfillment." The title used here is "Continuing a Task." It signifies he is engaged in an ongoing endeavor. The traditional text uses the image of fording a stream to indicate this. If he is too weak or has too few resources, he is likely to suffer some harm before he completes his task. However, even if he is harmed, it may not be so bad. *The complementary hexagram* is Hexagram 63 Beginning a New Task, which illustrates that after the present task is completed, because life is an ongoing, interlocking series of steps, a new task will emerge.

● *At his best,* he may be committed to completing what he set out to do, and he has the strength and resources necessary to get it done. *At his worst,* he may be trying to complete the task, yet he lacking in something, which will delay completion or harm him in some way

▲ *As a public person,* he may be encouraging others, and attempt to help them succeed. *As a businessperson,* he may be involved in allocating resources or solving problems. *As an ordinary person,* he may be working toward a goal, but at the same time have a burden.

64.1　　*Yin 6 changing line derives from Hexagram 38 Looking for a Leader*

He struggles with his task, so he looks for someone to help him.
Without their assistance, he could get into more trouble.

■ Errors make any task harder to complete. Here, he sees trouble, so he looks for someone to help him. Without good assistance, matters could easily deteriorate further.

● *At his best,* he may be distracted by worthwhile and important matters, so even though he suffers some problems, he has gained something of value that will help him later. *At his worst,* he may have problems that waste his opportunity to advance, or he may make a blunder that will set him back.

▲ *As a public person,* he may be pushed into a vulnerable and potentially danger-ous position. *As a businessperson,* he may discover serious hidden pitfalls and need to get good advice. *As an ordinary person,* he may easily get into trouble that also affects those near him, so he should pay attention to what he does and ask for help.

64.2 *Yang 9 changing line derives from Hexagram 35 Advancing Due to Favor*

To continue his task, he needs someone else's favor.
He can succeed only with their support.

■ The obstacles he faces require more than just what he can provide by himself. He will also need the assistance of someone else; with that assistance, he can succeed.

● *At his best,* he may count on his friends and allies to help with a difficult problem. *At his worst,* he may need to beg or connive assistance from someone to help him with what he cannot resolve alone.

▲ *As a public person,* he may need to call in favors, or ask one of a powerful leader, to help him. *As a businessperson,* he may encounter strong opposition but find a way to work around it with business partners. *As an ordinary person,* he may achieve success by relying on those closest to him for support when he runs into trouble.

64.3 *Yin 6 changing line derives from Hexagram 50 Governing Matters*

In continuing his task, he must study the situation to understand
how to affect it, and he must be persistent in his attempts
to control it. Success will not be easy.

■ He is not at the point where he can easily control matters. Rather, he must har-monize himself with the situation by seeking to understand what is needed. Gain-ing a strong understanding, keeping his goals in mind, and maintaining a firm commitment to what is the proper action will produce the best results.

● *At his best,* he may be firmly committed and persistent, but he still takes the time to understand what to do, and takes the long view in how best to do it. *At his worst,* he may be distracted by continual problems, become confused, question his direc-tion or commitment, and generally lose control of the situation.

▲ *As a public person,* he may find himself bothered by continual problems that interfere with his goals. *As a businessperson,* he may need to put a great deal more effort into his business, but he should guard against hasty actions. *As an ordinary person,* he may face a number of complex problems with his life, work, and family, and he should put off acting as long as possible until he is sure what is best to do.

64.4   *Yang 9 changing line derives from Hexagram 4 Acting Impetuously*

Enthusiastic action will help him continue his task.
His doubts and fears will pass, and he can benefit in the end.

■ Enthusiasm is what is most needed now. It will help him overcome his doubts and fears, and to apply himself and succeed. Taking these steps will ease his mind and make success a reality. Enthusiastic commitment eventually will bring him results.

● *At his best,* he may get in touch with the enthusiasm of youth, idealism, or dreams to help him achieve his goals. *At his worst,* he may be overcome by too much youthful enthusiasm and impatience, rush into action, and succeed to some extent even though he made some bad choices.

▲ *As a public person,* he may lead a campaign, launch a new program, or create an alliance. *As a businessperson,* he may spearhead a new business endeavor. *As an ordinary person,* he may enthusiastically dedicate himself to achieving something at work, in his community, or at home.

64.5   *Yin 6 changing line derives from Hexagram 6 Having a Complaint*

He has complaints about continuing his task, so he brings them to his leader. He will be able to benefit when his complaints are dealt with.

■ He is taking his concerns to his leader for resolution. Getting a positive response to his concerns from his leader will then bring him benefits.

● *At his best,* he may understand what is the right thing to do for others as well as for himself, and he has the strength to discuss this, so he succeeds. *At his worst,* he may be driven by selfish concerns and complain strongly, so he succeeds in benefiting himself to some extent, but he also leaves a bad impression that lingers.

▲ *As a public person,* he may have critical discussions with an important leader and be promoted to an important position. *As a businessperson,* he may be praised for his commitment to his work, or for his writings if he is an author. *As an ordinary person,* he may strive to make his personal life more successful, and by confidently bringing up difficult family issues, he succeeds in improving everyone's life.

64.6   *Yang 9 changing line derives from Hexagram 40 Getting Free*

He gets free from his task. Now he can choose a new task,
but if it isn't appropriate, he won't be able to benefit.

■ He is able to free himself from the demands of his old task in some way. Perhaps he completed it, or it was transferred to someone else, or perhaps the need for it has ended. Now he can choose his next task. If he selects appropriately, he will be able to benefit from it.

● *At his best,* he may feel reborn and have the joy of beginning a new phase of his life. *At his worst,* he may feel driven away by unhappiness or anger, remain poisoned by his negative feelings, and thus may be hobbled by his past.

▲ As *a public person,* he may seek a position in a different organization. As *a businessperson,* he may be motivated to start his own business. As *an ordinary person,* he may change the direction of his life and begin anew.

64.ALL   *All lines changing derives from Hexagram 63 Beginning a New Task*

When his task is completed, he begins a new one.

■ Every path through life has a beginning and an end. Here the end is recognized. Of course, an end always signifies that a new beginning is being born, although exactly what the new path is going to be may be unclear.

● *At his best,* he may be satisfied with an ending, knowing that life is full of endings, which signify the coming of new beginnings. *At his worst,* he may find it hard to accept an ending, so it hampers his being able to choose his new beginning well.

▲ As *a public person,* he may retire from his position and select a new path in life. As *a businessperson,* he may fundamentally change his business, or how he conducts it. As *an ordinary person,* he may thoroughly reevaluate his life and do something that works better for him now.

Hexagram Lookups

TRADITIONAL HEXAGRAM LOOKUP

UPPER LOWER	A	B	C	D	E	F	G	H
A	1	34	5	26	11	9	14	43
B	25	51	3	27	24	42	21	17
C	6	40	29	4	7	59	64	47
D	33	62	39	52	15	53	56	31
E	12	16	8	23	2	20	35	45
F	44	32	48	18	46	57	50	28
G	13	55	63	22	36	37	30	49
H	10	54	60	41	19	61	38	58

ALTERNATIVE HEXAGRAM LOOKUPS

STEP 1: Identify the trigram letters by number or graphic representation.

000		E	100		B
001		D	101		G
010		C	110		H
011		F	111		A

STEP 2: Use the pair of trigram letters to identify the hexagram number. The left letter is the lower (first) trigram.

A		B		C		D	
AA	1	BA	25	CA	6	DA	33
AB	34	BB	51	CB	40	DB	62
AC	5	BC	3	CC	29	DC	39
AD	26	BD	27	CD	4	DD	52
AE	11	BE	24	CE	7	DE	15
AF	9	BF	42	CF	59	DF	53
AG	14	BG	21	CG	64	DG	56
AH	43	BH	17	CH	47	DH	31
E		F		G		H	
EA	12	FA	44	GA	13	HA	10
EB	16	FB	32	GB	55	HB	54
EC	8	FC	48	GC	63	HC	60
ED	23	FD	18	GD	22	HD	41
EE	2	FE	46	GE	36	HE	19
EF	20	FF	57	GF	37	HF	61
EG	35	FG	50	GG	30	HG	38
EH	45	FH	28	GH	49	HH	58

HEXAGRAMS IN NUMBER ORDER

The *Trigrams* column displays the two trigrams that make up the hexagram. The eight "doubled trigram" hexagrams are boldfaced, allowing you to quickly find these trigrams by hexagram number.

The "Hexagrams Listed by Number" column lists all the hexagrams in order by number and displays the titles used in this book. The "Complementary Hexagrams" column to the right shows its "thematic opposite," which is created by changing all of a hexagram's lines to their opposites (that is, all yin lines change to yang lines, and vice versa).

All hexagrams are listed twice in the table: once in the left column, and once in the right. *Italicized lines* indicate the second time that a pair of hexagrams is shown in the table. For example, the complementary hexagrams 1 and 2 are in the first two lines, so the second line (the one for Hexagram 2) is in italics. It is also offset to the right slightly for greater ease in use. This format allows you to either look up information by hexagram number or scan through the list skipping the duplicated pairs.

TRIGRAMS	HEXAGRAMS LISTED BY NUMBER	COMPLEMENTARY HEXAGRAMS
AA	1 Acting Fiercely	2 Going with the Flow
EE	*2 Going with the Flow*	*1 Acting Fiercely*
BC	3 Gathering Support	50 Governing Matters
CD	4 Acting Impetuously	49 Being Revolutionary
AC	5 Acting Prematurely	35 Advancing Due to Favor
CA	6 Having a Complaint	36 Serving as an Assistant
CE	7 Serving as an Officer	13 Serving on a Team
EC	8 Entering an Alliance	14 Relying on His Allies
AF	9 Restraining Himself	16 Standstill
HA	10 Taking Risky Action	15 Acting with Propriety
AE	11 Easily Progressing	12 Being Blocked
EA	*12 Being Blocked*	*11 Easily Progressing*

TRIGRAMS	HEXAGRAMS LISTED BY NUMBER	COMPLEMENTARY HEXAGRAMS
GA	*13 Serving on a Team*	*7 Serving as an Officer*
AG	*14 Relying on His Allies*	*8 Entering an Alliance*
DE	*15 Acting with Propriety*	*10 Taking Risky Action*
EB	*16 Standstill*	*9 Restraining Himself*
BH	17 Hunting	18 Nursing an Illness
FD	*18 Nursing an Illness*	*17 Hunting*
HE	19 Leading Others	33 Complying
EF	20 Preparing Himself	34 Forcing Matters
BG	21 Working on a Problem	48 Being Renewed
GD	22 Advancing by His Image	47 Advancing by Hard Work
ED	23 Being in a Collapsing Situation	43 Escaping Harm
BE	24 Beginning a Relationship	44 Maintaining His Independence
BA	25 Having No Expectations	46 Promoting Himself
AD	26 External Restraint	45 Serving a Leader
BD	27 Desiring	28 Working Toward a Goal
FH	*28 Working Toward a Goal*	*27 Desiring*
CC	29 Being Trapped	30 Gaining Enlightenment
GG	*30 Gaining Enlightenment*	*29 Being Trapped*
DH	31 Ability to Change Matters	41 Declining Influence
FB	32 Committing Himself	42 Gaining Benefits
DA	*33 Complying*	*19 Leading Others*
AB	*34 Forcing Matters*	*20 Preparing Himself*
EG	*35 Advancing Due to Favor*	*5 Acting Prematurely*
GE	*36 Serving as an Assistant*	*6 Having a Complaint*
GF	37 Serving in a Household	40 Getting Free
HG	38 Looking for a Leader	39 Bumbling by Himself

TRIGRAMS	HEXAGRAMS LISTED BY NUMBER	COMPLEMENTARY HEXAGRAMS
DC	*39 Bumbling by Himself*	*38 Looking for a Leader*
CB	*40 Getting Free*	*37 Serving in a Household*
HD	*41 Declining Influence*	*31 Ability to Change Matters*
BF	*42 Gaining Benefits*	*32 Committing Himself*
AH	*43 Escaping Harm*	*23 Being in a Collapsing Situation*
FA	*44 Maintaining His Independence*	*24 Beginning a Relationship*
EH	*45 Serving a Leader*	*26 External Restraint*
FE	*46 Promoting Himself*	*25 Having No Expectations*
CH	*47 Advancing by Hard Work*	*22 Advancing by His Image*
FC	*48 Being Renewed*	*21 Working on a Problem*
GH	*49 Being Revolutionary*	*4 Acting Immaturely*
FG	*50 Governing Matters*	*3 Gathering Support*
BB	51 At Fortune's Mercy	57 At His Leader's Mercy
DD	52 Holding Back	58 Sharing Himself
DF	53 Sharing Commitment	54 Entering a Marriage
HB	*54 Entering a Marriage*	*53 Sharing Commitment*
GB	55 Serving Greatness	59 Things are Swept Clear
DG	56 Wandering	60 Having Limited Resources
FF	*57 At His Leader's Mercy*	*51 At Fortune's Mercy*
HH	*58 Sharing Himself*	*52 Holding Back*
CF	*59 Things are Swept Clear*	*55 Serving Greatness*
HC	*60 Having Limited Resources*	*56 Wandering*
HF	61 Having Limited Allegiance	62 Independently Getting By
DB	*62 Independently Getting By*	*61 Having Limited Allegiance*
GC	63 Beginning a New Task	64 Continuing a Task
CG	*64 Continuing a Task*	*63 Beginning a New Task*

HEXAGRAMS IN LINE ORDER

The "Hexagram Lines" column shows the sixty-four hexagram lines in ascending sequence. Lines one to six run left to right. (*yin,* —— = 0; and *yang,* —— = 1)

The "Trigrams" column indicates the two trigrams corresponding to the lines by the letter code used in this book. The lower (first) trigram is on the left; the upper (second) trigram is on the right. The "Hexagram Number and Title" column shows the hexagram number and title.

HEXAGRAM LINES		TRIGRAMS	HEXAGRAM NUMBER AND TITLE	
000		**E**		
000	000	EE	2	Going with the Flow
000	001	ED	23	Being in a Collapsing Situation
000	010	EC	8	Entering an Alliance
000	011	EF	20	Preparing Himself
000	100	EB	16	Standstill
000	101	EG	35	Advancing Due to Favor
000	110	EH	45	Serving a Leader
000	111	EA	12	Being Blocked
001		**D**		
001	000	DE	15	Acting with Propriety
001	001	DD	52	Holding Back
001	010	DC	39	Bumbling by Himself
001	011	DF	53	Sharing Commitment
001	100	DB	62	Independently Getting By
001	101	DG	56	Wandering
001	110	DH	31	Ability to Change Matters
001	111	DA	33	Complying
010		**C**		
010	000	CE	7	Serving as an Officer
010	001	CD	4	Acting Impetuously
010	010	CC	29	Being Trapped
010	011	CF	59	Things are Swept Clear
010	100	CB	40	Getting Free
010	101	CG	64	Continuing a Task
010	110	CH	47	Advancing by Hard Work
010	111	CA	6	Having a Complaint
011		**F**		
011	000	FE	46	Promoting Himself
011	001	FD	18	Nursing an Illness
011	010	FC	48	Being Renewed
011	011	FF	57	At His Leader's Mercy

HEXAGRAM LINES		TRIGRAMS		HEXAGRAM NUMBER AND TITLE
011	100	FB	32	Committing Himself
011	101	FG	50	Governing Matters
011	110	FH	28	Working Toward a Goal
011	111	FA	44	Maintaining His Independence
100		**B**		
100	000	BE	24	Beginning a Relationship
100	001	BD	27	Desiring
100	010	BC	3	Gathering Support
100	011	BF	42	Gaining Benefits
100	100	BB	51	At Fortune's Mercy
100	101	BG	21	Working on a Problem
100	110	BH	17	Hunting
100	111	BA	25	Having No Expectations
101		**G**		
101	000	GE	36	Serving as an Assistant
101	001	GD	22	Advancing by His Image
101	010	GC	63	Beginning a New Task
101	011	GF	37	Serving in a Household
101	100	GB	55	Serving Greatness
101	101	GG	30	Gaining Enlightenment
101	110	GH	49	Being Revolutionary
101	111	GA	13	Serving on a Team
110		**H**		
110	000	HE	19	Leading Others
110	001	HD	41	Declining Influence
110	010	HC	60	Having Limited Resources
110	011	HF	61	Having Limited Allegiance
110	100	HB	54	Entering a Marriage
110	101	HG	38	Looking for a Leader
110	110	HH	58	Sharing Himself
110	111	HA	10	Taking Risky Action
111		**A**		
111	000	AE	11	Easily Progressing
111	001	AD	26	External Restraint
111	010	AC	5	Acting Prematurely
111	011	AF	9	Restraining Himself
111	100	AB	34	Forcing Matters
111	101	AG	14	Relying on His Allies
111	110	AH	43	Escaping Harm
111	111	AA	1	Acting Fiercely

HEXAGRAM INTERCONNECTIONS

The gray *Hex* column shows the *index hexagram* referred to in the other columns of the table.

The *line number* columns show from where each of the six moving lines of the *index hexagram* derive their meaning. Thus, the first line in the table shows the derivation of lines 1.1, 1.2, 1.3 (and so on) as coming from hexagrams 44, 13, 10 (and so on). Note that Hexagram 44-line 1 itself points back to Hexagram 1-line 1 because each hexagram line is conceptually paired with one other line in the table. (*Yang line numbers are italic.* Yin line numbers are roman.)

The *Comp.* column shows the complementary hexagram produced by changing all six lines of the *index hexagram* to their opposites. (In the hexagram text, the word "all" is used in place of a number when all six lines change.) The complement to Hexagram 1 (111 111) is Hexagram 2 (000 000).

The *Inverted* column shows the hexagram produced by reversing the order of the two trigrams of the *index hexagram.* Doubled trigram hexagrams such as Hexagram 1 remain the same, but Hexagram 3 (BC) becomes Hexagram 40 (CB).

The *Mirrored* column shows the hexagram produced by reversing the order of all the hexagram lines of the *index hexagram* in a mirror image. Hexagram 3 (100 011) becomes Hexagram 4 (110 001).

HEX	LINE 1	LINE 2	LINE 3	LINE 4	LINE 5	LINE 6	COMP.	INVERTED	MIRRORED
1	*44.1*	*13.2*	*10.3*	*9.4*	*14.5*	*43.6*	2	1	1
2	24.1	7.2	15.3	16.4	8.5	23.6	1	2	2
3	*8.1*	60.2	63.3	17.4	*24.5*	42.6	50	40	4
4	*41.1*	23.2	18.3	*64.4*	59.5	7.6	49	39	3
5	*48.1*	*63.2*	*60.3*	43.4	*11.5*	9.6	35	6	6
6	10.1	*12.2*	44.3	*59.4*	*64.5*	*47.6*	36	5	5
7	19.1	*2.2*	46.3	40.4	29.5	4.6	13	8	8
8	3.1	29.2	39.3	45.4	*2.5*	20.6	14	7	7
9	*57.1*	*37.2*	*61.3*	1.4	*26.5*	*5.6*	16	44	10
10	*6.1*	25.2	1.3	*61.4*	38.5	*58.6*	15	10	9
11	*46.1*	*36.2*	*19.3*	34.4	5.5	26.6	12	12	12
12	25.1	6.2	33.3	*20.4*	*35.5*	*45.6*	11	11	11
13	*33.1*	1.2	*25.3*	37.4	30.5	49.6	7	14	14
14	*50.1*	*30.2*	38.3	26.4	1.5	*34.6*	8	13	13
15	36.1	46.2	*2.3*	62.4	39.5	52.6	10	23	16

HEX	LINE 1	LINE 2	LINE 3	LINE 4	LINE 5	LINE 6	COMP.	INVERTED	MIRRORED
16	51.1	40.2	62.3	2.4	45.5	35.6	9	24	15
17	45.1	58.2	49.3	3.4	51.5	25.6	18	54	18
18	26.1	52.2	4.3	50.4	57.5	46.6	17	53	17
19	7.1	24.2	11.3	54.4	60.5	41.6	33	45	20
20	42.1	59.2	53.3	12.4	23.5	8.6	34	46	19
21	35.1	38.2	30.3	27.4	25.5	51.6	48	55	22
22	52.1	26.2	27.3	30.4	37.5	36.6	47	56	21
23	27.1	4.2	52.3	35.4	20.5	2.6	43	15	24
24	2.1	19.2	36.3	51.4	3.5	27.6	44	16	23
25	12.1	10.2	13.3	42.4	21.5	17.6	46	34	26
26	18.1	22.2	41.3	14.4	9.5	11.6	45	33	25
27	23.1	41.2	22.3	21.4	42.5	24.6	28	62	27
28	43.1	31.2	47.3	48.4	32.5	44.6	27	61	28
29	60.1	8.2	48.3	47.4	7.5	59.6	30	29	29
30	56.1	14.2	21.3	22.4	13.5	55.6	29	30	30
31	49.1	28.2	45.3	39.4	62.5	33.6	41	41	32
32	34.1	62.2	40.3	46.4	28.5	50.6	42	42	31
33	13.1	44.2	12.3	53.4	56.5	31.6	19	26	34
34	32.1	55.2	54.3	11.4	43.5	14.6	20	25	33
35	21.1	64.2	56.3	23.4	12.5	16.6	5	36	36
36	15.1	11.2	24.3	55.4	63.5	22.6	6	35	35
37	53.1	9.2	42.3	13.4	22.5	63.6	40	50	38
38	64.1	21.2	14.3	41.4	10.5	54.6	39	49	37
39	63.1	48.2	8.3	31.4	15.5	53.6	38	4	40
40	54.1	16.2	32.3	7.4	47.5	64.6	37	3	39
41	4.1	27.2	26.3	38.4	61.5	19.6	31	31	42
42	20.1	61.2	37.3	25.4	27.5	3.6	32	32	41
43	28.1	49.2	58.3	5.4	34.5	1.6	23	10	44
44	1.1	33.2	6.3	57.4	50.5	28.6	24	9	43
45	17.1	47.2	31.3	8.4	16.5	12.6	26	19	46
46	11.1	15.2	7.3	32.4	48.5	18.6	25	20	45
47	58.1	45.2	28.3	29.4	40.5	6.6	22	60	48
48	5.1	39.2	29.3	28.4	46.5	57.6	21	59	47
49	31.1	43.2	17.3	63.4	55.5	13.6	4	38	50
50	14.1	56.2	64.3	18.4	44.5	32.6	3	37	49

HEX	LINE 1	LINE 2	LINE 3	LINE 4	LINE 5	LINE 6	COMP.	INVERTED	MIRRORED
51	*16.1*	54.2	55.3	*24.4*	17.5	21.6	57	51	52
52	22.1	18.2	*23.3*	56.4	53.5	*15.6*	58	52	51
53	37.1	57.2	*20.3*	33.4	*52.5*	*39.6*	54	18	54
54	*40.1*	*51.2*	34.3	*19.4*	58.5	38.6	53	17	53
55	*62.1*	34.2	*51.3*	*36.4*	49.5	30.6	59	21	56
56	30.1	50.2	*35.3*	*52.4*	33.5	*62.6*	60	22	55
57	9.1	*53.2*	*59.3*	44.4	*18.5*	*48.6*	51	57	58
58	*47.1*	*17.2*	43.3	*60.4*	*54.5*	10.6	52	58	57
59	61.1	*20.2*	57.3	6.4	*4.5*	*29.6*	55	48	60
60	*29.1*	*3.2*	5.3	58.4	*19.5*	61.6	56	47	59
61	*59.1*	*42.2*	9.3	10.4	*41.5*	*60.6*	62	28	61
62	55.1	32.2	*16.3*	*15.4*	31.5	56.6	61	27	62
63	*39.1*	5.2	*3.3*	49.4	*36.5*	37.6	64	64	64
64	38.1	*35.2*	50.3	*4.4*	6.5	*40.6*	63	63	63

Notes

Chapter 2: History

1. Greg Whincup. *Rediscovering the I Ching.* Garden City, New York: Doubleday and Co., 1986, pp. 17–18.

2. Kerson Huang and Rosemary Huang. *I Ching.* New York: Workman Publishing, 1987, p. 50.

3. Whincup, p. 23.

4. Iulian K. Shchutskii, trans. by William L. MacDonald and Tsuyoshi Hasegawa with Hellmut Wilhelm, with an Introduction by Gerald W. Swanson, *Researches on the I Ching.* Princeton, New Jersey: Bollingen Series LXII. 2, Princeton University Press, 1979, p. 154.

5. Richard Wilhelm, translated by Cary F. Baynes. *The I Ching, or Book of Changes: The Richard Wilhelm Translation rendered into English by Cary F. Baynes, Forward by C. G. Jung, Preface to the Third Edition by Hellmut Wilhelm.* Princeton, New Jersey: Bollingen Series XIX, Princeton University Press, 1967, p. 4.

6. Huang and Huang, p. 50.

7. John Lagerwey. *Taoist Ritual in Chinese Society and History.* New York: Macmillan Publishing Co., 1987, p. 8. Whincup, p. 16.

8. Whincup, p. 16.

9. Anne D. Birdwhistell. *Transition to Neo–Confucianism: Shao Yung on Knowledge and Symbols of Reality.* Stanford, California: Stanford University Press, 1989, p. 143. Although this was said specifically in reference to understanding Shao Yung's writings, this is referring to the many symbols and concepts from older writings.

10. These are noted in both Whincup, and in Huang and Huang, under their respective hexagrams.

11. Whincup, p. 18.

12. Huang and Huang, p. 50.

13. Whincup, p. 16.

14. Huang and Huang, p. 44.

15. Shchutskii, p. 176.

16. Alan Watts, with Al Chung–Liang Huang. *Tao: The Watercourse Way.* New York: Pantheon Books, 1975, pp. 27–28.

17. Whincup, p. 15.

18. Huang and Huang, pp.51–52.

19. Shchutskii, pp. 191–192.

20. Huang and Huang, pp. 54–55.

21. This process would conclude by producing the following line values: 6 for old yin (a changing line), 7 for young yang, 8 for young yin, and 9 for old yang (a changing line). These values are also noted in this book's hexagram text next to the line number.

22. Kidder Smith, Jr., Peter K. Bol, Joseph A. Adler, and Don J. Wyatt. *Sung Dynasty Uses of the I Ching.* Princeton, New Jersey: Princeton University Press, 1990, p. 100.

23. Birdwhistell, p. 7.

24. In the published English versions of Shao's system, which were described in the following books, the correction noted below needs to be applied:

W. K. Chu, and W. A. Sherrill. *The Astrology of I Ching: Translated from the 'Ho Map Lo Map Rational Number' Manuscript by W. K. Chu, Edited and Commentaries Added by W. A. Sherrill.* York Beach, Maine: Samuel Weiser, 1976, p. 35.

W. A. Sherrill, and W. K. Chu: *An Anthology of I Ching.* London: Routledge and Kegan Paul, 1977, p. 169.

The Earthly Number Trigram Table contains the following errors: earthly number 20 should be trigram G, and earthly number 50 should be trigram H. Without these corrections, the system can generate only trigrams A through F, and so cannot access all the I Ching's hexagrams. These changes were initially developed theoretically by an analysis of the structure of the table, and then tested and confirmed empirically, so they are correct.

Chapter 3: Theory

1. Alan Watts, with Al Chung–Liang Huang. *Tao: The Watercourse Way*. New York: Pantheon Books, 1975, pp. 36–37.

2. Johnson F. Yan. *DNA and the I Ching: The Tao of Life*. Berkeley, California: North Atlantic Books, 1991, p. 1.

3. Yan, p. 1.

4. Anne D. Birdwhistell. *Transition to Neo–Confucianism: Shao Yung on Knowledge and Symbols of Reality*. Stanford, California: Stanford University Press, 1989, p. 102.

5. Watts, p. 36.

6. Birdwhistell, p. 59.

7. For an introduction to the symbolism of ancient numbers, refer to:

   John Lagerwey. *Taoist Ritual in Chinese Society and History*. New York: Macmillan Publishing Co., 1987, pp. 3–17.

   Kidder Smith, Jr., Peter K. Bol, Joseph A. Adler, and Don J. Wyatt. *Sung Dynasty Uses of the I Ching*. Princeton, New Jersey: Princeton University Press, 1990, pp. 110–127

   Birdwhistell, pp. 60–62, 71–76, and many other places in passing in the text.

8. For a brief discussion of how Shao used the Ho Tu in his models, see Smith, et al., p. 120–122. For a more traditional discussion of the trigrams, numerology, and the I Ching, see W. A. Sherrill, and W. K. Chu, *An Anthology of I Ching*. London: Routledge and Kegan Paul, 1977, pp. 8–23.

9. Yan, p. 10.

10. Yan, p. 2.

11. Smith, et al., p. 118.

References

Commentary on references and additional resource citations (for printed publications as well as online resources) is available on the author's website at:
http://www.newagequest.com/iching.

Birdwhistell, Anne D. *Transition to Neo-Confucianism: Shao Yung on Knowledge and Symbols of Reality.* Stanford, California: Stanford University Press, 1989.

Chu, W. K., and Sherrill, W. A.: *The Astrology of I Ching: Translated from the 'Ho Map Lo Map Rational Number' Manuscript by W. K. Chu, Edited and Commentaries Added by W. A. Sherrill.* York Beach, Maine: Samuel Weiser, 1976. (Refer to the correction in Note 24 under Chapter 2 on page 336.)

Huang, Kerson and Huang, Rosemary. *I Ching.* New York: Workman Publishing, 1987.

Jou, Tsung Hwa. *The Tao of I Ching: Way to Divination.* Taiwan. Tai Chi Foundation, 1984.

Lagerwey, John. *Taoist Ritual in Chinese Society and History.* New York: Macmillan Publishing Co., 1987.

Liu, Da. *I Ching Numerology.* San Francisco: Harper and Row, 1979.

Pattee, Rowena: *Moving with Change: A Woman's Re-integration of the I Ching,* Foreword by José Argüelles. New York: Arkana Paperbacks, 1986.

Shchutskii, I. K., trans. by William L. MacDonald and Tsuyoshi Hasegawa with Hellmut Wilhelm, with an Introduction by Gerald W. Swanson: *Researches on the I Ching,* Princeton, New Jersey: Bollingen Series LXII. 2, Princeton University Press, 1979.

Sherrill, W. A., and Chu, W. K.: *An Anthology of I Ching.* London: Routledge and Kegan Paul, 1977. (Refer to the correction in Note 24 under Chapter 2 on page 336.)

Smith, Kidder, Jr., Bol, Peter K., Adler, Joseph A., and Wyatt, Don J. *Sung Dynasty Uses of the I Ching.* Princeton, New Jersey: Princeton University Press, 1990.

Watts, Alan, with Al Chung-Liang Huang: *Tao: The Watercourse Way.* New York: Pantheon Books, 1975.

Whincup, Greg. *Rediscovering the I Ching.* Garden City, New York: Doubleday and Co., 1986.

Wilhelm, Richard, translated by Cary F. Baynes. *The I Ching, or Book of Changes: The Richard Wilhelm Translation rendered into English by Cary F. Baynes, Forward by C. G. Jung, Preface to the Third Edition by Hellmut Wilhelm.* Princeton, New Jersey: Bollingen Series, Princeton University Press, 1967.

Yan, Johnson F. *DNA and the I Ching: The Tao of Life.* Berkeley, California: North Atlantic Books, 1991.

Index

Ad hoc inquiries, 8, 10, 55, 56
  results of, 18–19

Baynes, Cary F., 23, 25
Bead Bag Method, 11, 12–13
Beads-on-a-String Method, 12, 13, 15

Calendar-based oracle, 11, 34, 35
Changing lines, 4, 5, 7–8, 41–42, 48, 50–51
Ch'in Dynasty, 28
Chou Dynasty, 25
  conquest of the Shang by, 27
  connection of founding with the I Ching
    text, 29
  Duke of, 27
  Eastern Chou period, 27
  establishment as dominant power, 27
  Warring States period, 27
  Western Chou period, 27
  See also Wen.
Chou I, 22, 27, 29
Chu Hsi, 34
Chuang-tzu, 30, 37
Chuo Chuan, 30
Classic of Change, 22
Complementary opposite. See Changing lines.
Conceptual map, 16
Confucianism
  and Han Dynasty, 28, 32
  influence of, on the I Ching, 28, 30, 31
  and the Ten Wings, 30
Confucius
  reinterpretation by, of the I Ching, 24–25,
    28, 30

Divination. See Fortunetelling.
Diviners. See Fortunetelling.

Earthly numbers, 51, 52

Feng shui, 34, 35, 53
Five Classics, 28
Flexible list, 18
Fortunetelling, 29, 31–32

Geomancy. See Feng shui.
Gilgamesh, 21
Gui Gang, 29

Han Dynasty, 22, 28, 30, 32
  and coin tosses, 32
Heavenly numbers, 51, 52
Hexagram, 1
  alternative lookup of, 5–6
  and changing lines, 5, 7–8, 41–42, 48,
    50–51
  diagrammatic expression of yin and yang
    in, 43
  doubled-trigram hexagrams, 47
  general meanings of, 47
  lines of, 3–5
  meanings of line positions, 48–50
  selection methods for, 10–14, 15
  traditional lookup of, 5–6
Ho Lo Li Shu (Ho Map Lo Map Rational
    Number), 35
Ho T'u, 51, 52
Hsia Dynasty, 22, 25

TAO TE CHING
The Way of Virtue
Lao Tzu • Translated by Patrick M. Byrne

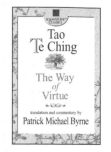

The *Tao Te Ching* has served as a personal road map for millions of people. It is said that its words reveal the underlying principles that govern the world in which we live. Holding to the laws of nature—drawing from the essence of what all things are—it offers both a moral compass and an internal balance. A fundamental book of the Taoist, the *Tao Te Ching* is regarded as a revelation in its own right. For those seeking a better understanding of themselves, it provides a wealth of wisdom and insights.

Through time—from one powerful dynasty to another—many changes have been made to the original Chinese text of the *Tao Te Ching.* Over the last century, translators have added to the mix by incorporating their interpretations. For those readers who are looking for a purer interpretation of the *Tao Te Ching,* researcher Patrick M. Byrne has produced a translation that is extremely accurate, while capturing the pattern and harmony of the original.

$10.95 • 128 pages • 5.5 x 8.5-inch quality paperback • 2-Color • Religion/Chinese • ISBN 0-7570-0029-0

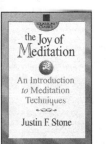

THE JOY OF MEDITATION
An Introduction to Meditation Techniques
by Justin F. Stone

Experienced meditators, knowing the techniques to use, go about their business as directly and purposefully as a skilled carpenter. The fact is that there is nothing vague about the process of meditation. In this classic work, author and teacher Justin F. Stone presents easy-to-follow instructions for many common forms of meditation including Zazen (Zen Meditation), Japa (one of the oldest spiritual practices in India), Satipatthana (Mindfulness), Nei Kung meditation, and Tibetan meditations. In addition, while cultural and religious aspects of certain meditations are covered, readers are free to experience each technique according to their own personal preferences.

Meditation can be a powerful tool to improve health, sharpen concentration, reduce stress, and enhance spirituality. *The Joy of Meditation* was created to be a simple book of instructions for using that tool. By concentrating on the practice itself, and not on the dogma, readers will be able to choose those methods of meditation best suited to meet their individual needs.

$12.95 • 128 pages •5.5 x 8.5-inch quality paperback • 2-Color • Body, Mind & Spirit/Meditation • ISBN 0-7570-0025-8

THE BUDDHA'S GOLDEN PATH
The Classic Introduction to Zen Buddhism
Dwight Goddard

In 1929, when author Dwight Goddard wrote *The Buddha's Golden Path,* he was breaking ground. No American before him had lived the lifestyle of a Zen Buddhist monk, and then set out to share the secrets he had learned with his countrymen. This title was the first American book published to popularize Zen Buddhism. Released in the midst of the Great Depression, in its own way, it offered answers to the questions that millions of disillusioned people were beginning to ask—questions about what was really important in their lives. Questions we still ask ourselves today.

As a book of instruction, *The Buddha's Golden Path* has held up remarkably well. As a true classic, it has touched countless lives, and has opened the door for future generations in this country to study and embrace the principles of Zen.

$14.95 • 208 pages • 5.5 x 8.5-inch quality paperback • 2-Color • Religion/Zen Buddhism • ISBN 0-7570-0023-1

BUSHIDO
The Way of the Samurai
Tsunetomo Yamamoto • Translated by Minoru Tanaka
Edited by Justin F. Stone

In eighteenth-century Japan, Tsunetomo Yamamoto created the *Hagakure,* a document that recorded his thoughts on samurai values and conduct. For the next two hundred years, the *Hagakure* was secretly circulated among the "awakened" samurai—the samurai elite. In 1906, the book was first made available to the general Japanese public, and until 1945, its guiding principles greatly influenced the Japanese ruling class—particularly those individuals in military power. However, the spirit of the *Hagakure* touched a deeper nerve in Japanese society. It was this book that shaped the underlying character of the Japanese psyche, from businessmen to politicians, from students to soldiers.

From its opening line, "I have found the essence of Bushido: to die!" this work provides a powerful message aimed at the spirit, body, and mind of the samurai warrior. It offers beliefs that are difficult for the Western mind to embrace, yet fascinating in their pursuit of absolute service. By reading *Bushido: The Way of the Samurai,* one can better put into perspective the historical path that Japan has taken for the last three hundred years, and gain greater insight into the Japan of today.

$9.95 • 128 pages • 5.5 x 8.5-inch quality paperback • 2-Color • Philosophy/Martial Arts • ISBN 0-7570-0026-6